Bridal

11th edition

BARGAINS

Secrets to throwing
a fantastic wedding
on a realistic
budget

Over 700,000 copies sold!

**The book
the wedding industry
does NOT want you
to read!**

DENISE & ALAN FIELDS

The Copyright Page and Zesty Lo-Cal Recipes

French horn, electric guitar and samples by Denise Fields
Drums, stand-up bass, and spelling mistakes by Alan Fields
Additional percussion and backing vocals by Ben & Jack Fields
Backing vocals on "Bridal Magazines & Night Screams" by Ric Ocasek
Piano solo on "Wedding Cakes" by Robin Thicke

Cover, interior design and cello by Epicenter Creative, Boulder, CO
Actual heartfelt gratitude to our distributor, IPS

This book was written to the music of the Barenaked Ladies,
which probably explains a lot.

Alan Fields appears courtesy of Howard & Patti Fields.
Denise Fields appears courtesy of Max & Helen Coopwood.
Denise & Alan wish to thank their sons, Ben & Jack for their funkiness.
More thanks to Amy's Ice Cream, Hey Cupcake! and Smitty's BBQ.

Published by Windsor Peak Press, 436 Pine Street, Suite 7000, Boulder, CO, 80302. To order this book, check your local bookstore, call (800) 888-0385 or order online at www.WindsorPeak.com. Or send $14.95 plus $3 shipping to Windsor Peak Press, 436 Pine Street, Suite 7000, Boulder, CO, 80302. Quantity discounts are available.

Questions or comments? Feel free to contact the authors at (303) 442-8792; e-mail at authors@BridalBargainsBook.com; or write to them at the above address. Web: BridalBargainsBook.com

Library in Congress Cataloging in Publication Data
Fields, Denise
Fields, Alan
    Bridal Bargains: Secrets to Throwing a Fantastic Wedding on a Realistic Budget/Denise and Alan Fields. 8th Edition. Includes index.
    1. Wedding—United States—Planning.
    2. Consumer education—United States. 3. Shopping—United States.
ISBN 978-1-889392-46-2   93-093752 LIC

Distributed to bookstores by Ingram Publisher Services, (866) 400-5351
Questions about this book? Call us at (303) 442-8792

Version 11.0

OVERVIEW

Your Wedding teaches you how to find the best deals on bridal apparel for the bride and the wedding party. Then, you learn how to shop for your ceremony site, wedding flowers, and invitations. Each chapter gives you in depth money-saving tips and shopping strategies.

Your Reception shows you how to save money on everything from catering to entertainment. Our chapter on wedding photography gives you nine creative ways to save money plus eleven important questions to ask any photographer. You'll also learn how to find the best deals on wedding cakes and wedding videos.

Learn about saving money on a Canadian wedding, with tips and advice on web sites, invitation printers and more.

Advice on how to set up your wedding budget, plus an easy-to-use checklists and comparison charts.

CONTENTS

Chapter 6

Part II: Your Reception

Chapter 7

ICONS

 What Are You Buying?

 Sources

 Best Online Bargains

 Getting Started: How Far in Advance?

 Step-by-Step Shopping Strategies

 Questions to Ask

 Top Money-Saving Secrets

 Myths

 Hints

 Pitfalls to Avoid

 Destination Wedding Tips

So, you're engaged? Well, fasten your seat belts! Soon you will travel through a bizarre and crazy world, where the boundaries of good taste and sane thought are only fuzzy lines. Yes, you've done it now. You have entered the WEDDING ZONE.

See, that's why we are here. We're sort of your tour guides through this wondrous journey of things bridal and ideas nuptial. Of course, right off the bat, you will probably notice a basic difference between this and all those other wedding books and web sites—this book contains actual COMMON SENSE.

Sure, we know we're going out on a limb here but what the heck? Why not write a book you can actually use to plan your wedding? Hey, it's the least we can do. At this point you may have a question: so, who are you guys? Let's put that into bold type.

So Who Are You Guys?

When we got engaged, we did what most newly engaged couples do—seek out advice planning a wedding. We quickly found ourselves overwhelmed with what we call the Wedding White Out—never-ending pictures of bridal gowns, cakes, rings and the like.

And it doesn't take much research to figure out all this white bling is expensive. Yet despite the massive resources devoted today to wedding web sites, apps, expos, books and planners, there is clearly one thing missing: advice on how to throw a fun, memorable wedding . . . without breaking the bank.

That's where we come in—we have spent the last 20+ years researching and writing about weddings. Our emphasis as consumer advocates is how to get the best deal, avoid rip-offs . . . and still have a sense of humor about this bizarre wedding world.

Yes, much has changed since the first edition of this book debuted in 1990. Yep, that is right—1990. Yet what has made this book a best-seller (now in its 11th edition, with 800,000 copies sold) is the old-fashioned way we do research: by talking with brides and grooms and cataloging their creative ways of cutting wedding bills. Then we field tested these ideas by mystery shopping thousands of wedding merchants, from gown sellers to photographers, cake bakeries to florists.

What couple after couple tell us is that planning a wedding today with a myriad of online sources is like drinking out of a fire hose—the information is overwhelming. And contradictory. And confusing.

Another problem: the web is often a mile wide, but an inch deep. Sure, there are many articles online that give you tips on saving on wedding flowers, for example. But the short articles and bullet points don't give you the detail necessary to actually follow through on the advice.

So, that's where this book comes in—we aim to provide a hand-picked collection of time-tested ways to save money on your wedding. And we provide the details necessary so you can act: specific web sites that can be used to save on wedding gowns, detailed lists of affordable flowers, and so on. Your time is tight, so we won't waste it on fluff. That's what the Knot is for. ;)

Our goal is to provide you with a buffet of options to save. For wedding cakes, we have 19 money-saving strategies. Flowers? We've got 30 ideas. Do we expect you to implement all 30 in your wedding? Of course not. But if you cherry pick several tips that work for you and shave 37% off your floral bill, then we've accomplished our mission.

Full disclosure: we make our living by writing this and several other books on parenting (Baby Bargains is the sequel to this book . . . when you are ready for that next stage in life!). We are not wedding planners or consultants, so we have no industry ties. Unlike wedding web sites, we don't take a commission from vendors we recommend. Nor do we try to sell various trinkets from our web site.

Feel free to contact us to ask a question or share a story—see the Contact Us page at the back of this book. And join the discussion on our message boards at BridalBargainsBook.com.

The Four Truths About Weddings No One Tells You

1 So you think your wedding is for you and your fiancé? Ha! Forget it. Unfortunately, weddings often become less a celebration of marriage and more like a huge social torture test for the participants. Parents, and even some brides and grooms, are frequently guilty of turning weddings into spectacles to impress their friends or business associates. Money can become the sticking point since whomever pays for the wedding may feel a divine right to influence the proceedings with their own tastes.

Sometimes, parents or relatives try to make your wedding into the wedding *they* never had (yet always dreamed of). Your friends may be guilty of pressuring you to make your wedding fit some predetermined mold. Put another way, while you may be the stars of the show, you and your fiancé may *not* be the wedding's directors, producers or choreographers.

Recognize this fact early and learn to negotiate without giving ultimatums. Yes, it is YOUR day, but remembering that others (parents, friends, relatives) are on the stage with you may prevent excessive bloodshed.

2 **Weddings always end up twice as large as originally planned.**
If only we had a dime for every couple we met who said "all we wanted was a small, intimate wedding and what we got was a huge affair for hundreds of guests." A wedding often takes on a life of its own, expanding into a hideous creature several times larger than you ever imagined.

This process usually begins with what we call Guest List Inflation. Here the guest list grows because each family simply *must* invite personal friends, close business associates and people whom they haven't seen in fifteen years. The main problem: adding to the guest list has a direct, *negative* impact on your budget.

Several weddings have nearly unraveled when families have insisted on inflating the guest list without offering to help pay for the additional cost. We suggest you and your families be allowed to invite a certain number of guests each. You may find that someone doesn't want to or can't stick to the limits. The offending party must then finance any invites beyond those targets. Negotiations are often necessary to avoid open warfare on this point. Good luck.

3 **Perfect weddings don't exist in the free world.** No matter what anyone tells you, understand that the "perfect wedding" is an impossibility on planet Earth. That's because weddings always involve human beings who, on the whole, tend to be less than perfect creatures.

Now, we know everyone tells you that you must have the perfect gown, perfect flowers, perfect cake . . . or else your marriage will collapse faster than you can say Britney Spears. Don't listen to these demons. Instead, we suggest you aim for a "fantastic" or "wonderful" wedding. Or even just a fun wedding!

Since it's impossible to perfectly script something as complex as a wedding, we say why try? Attendants will miss cues, things will go wrong—if you need any proof of this just search for weddings on YouTube.

Aiming for a wonderful wedding will also give you another benefit—you will probably be able to maintain your sanity.

4 **The "wedding industry" isn't as innocent as it looks.** You might think the wedding industry is a collection of sweet old ladies whose only desire is to help young couples in love, but the reality is quite the opposite. Instead, think of the bridal biz as a hotly competitive industry (used car salesmen come to mind), populated by merchants who are expert at pushing your emotional buttons. Add to that a field of novice buyers—first-time brides and grooms—and you can see where things go wrong.

Humorist Dave Barry once wrote that the motto of the wedding industry is, "Money can't buy you happiness, so you might as well give your money to us." Quite true. Weddings are big bucks.

According to the latest industry statistics, over $50 billion dollars will be spent this year by couples tying the knot. That's billion with a "b." And that's just the wedding and reception—add in another $19 billion spent on gifts and $8 billion on honeymoons and you've got a $77 billion bridal juggernaut. We like to call it the Wedding Industrial Complex. Scary fact: the wedding industry dwarfs many other businesses, including the breakfast cereal biz (a paltry $7.7 billion). Yes, Americans spend more on weddings than on Fruit Loops.

And you can bet your bridal veil that the industry knows EXACTLY how lucrative all these "I Do's" can be. To illustrate this, check out what the publisher of *Bride's* magazine told a trade journal about the wedding industry: "Never before in a woman's life, and never again, is she going to be worth this much money to a marketer. There is no price resistance and she is completely open to new brands," *Bride's* publisher said, adding that the internal tag line for *Bride's* is "Where Love Meets Money."

Of course, we're not against folks trying to make a buck. Hey, sell a quality product or service at a fair price and make a profit—that's America. Yet what makes wedding planning so crazy are bridal merchants who view brides and grooms as human ATMs. And price their products and services like they are coming out of a hotel mini bar.

Other wedding vendors seem at war with their customers, as odd as that seems. Take bridal dress retailers—please! As you'll read in the next chapter, these stores work hard at alienating their key customer (that is, you).

So, you might ask, why? Why does the wedding biz behave like this? Our theory: weddings are a one-shot deal. There are no repeat customers (except for certain celebrities, we suppose). Unlike other industries that rely on repeat business, wedding merchants know you won't be stopping by next month to buy another bridal gown, cake or ice sculpture. And with a fresh crop of new brides and grooms each year, you get a fertile climate for abuse.

So, the mission for this book is to teach you how to separate the good guys from the scam artists out there in wedding land. Yes, there are ethical and honest bridal professionals out there that charge a fair price. Just be aware the wedding business is just that—a business, where folks are trying to make a buck while you tie the knot.

The Goal of This Book: To help you save big money and still have a fantastic wedding!

Here's the take-home message of our book: you CAN plan a fantastic wedding on an affordable budget. And we're going to show you how.

Okay, we realize planning a wedding is a minefield of emotions and consumer pitfalls. And it is easy to get caught up in the bridal whirlwind. That's why we try to keep our perspective about this wedding stuff, and we urge you to do the same. Not maintaining your sense of humor during wedding planning may be hazardous to your health. That's why we've liberally sprinkled what could loosely be described as "humor" throughout this book.

In each chapter we give you Pitfalls to Avoid. As you learn about these bridal scams and wedding frauds, realize that just because you are a bride does not mean you have to be a victim. By using our consumer tips, you can protect yourself from losing hundreds, if not thousands, of dollars and have a good time doing it!

This book is for brides and grooms who want to hire professionals for their wedding. Conversely, we do *not* teach you how to sew a bridal gown or give you a recipe for a wedding cake. Instead, we'll show you how to bypass pricey dress shops and order that designer gown online at a big discount. We'll also show you the secrets to finding an affordable baker, photographer and DJ.

There's no advertising in this book?

There are no paid advertisements in this book. Furthermore, no company paid any consideration or was charged any fee to be mentioned in it. The publisher, Windsor Peak Press, derives its income from the sale of books, ebooks and website subscriptions. As consumer advocates, the authors believe this policy ensures objectivity. The opinions expressed in this book are those of the authors.

So, how much does a wedding cost?

Unless you are a Certified Public Accountant, you may not be inclined to use the words "fun" and "exhilarating" to describe setting the budget for your wedding. As you might expect us to say, however, this is a critical (albeit painful) part of the planning process.

Whether you're spending $100 or $100,000 on your wedding, every bride and groom has a limited amount of money to spend. This means you'll have to make tough choices regarding how you want to allocate your limited resources. For more advice on setting a budget, check out Appendix A at the back of this book.

So, how much does a wedding cost? Nearby are the average costs for a formal wedding for 150 guests. The table nearby lists the actual costs, while a pie chart shows you the biggest expense areas. There will be a quiz on this next week.

AVERAGE WEDDING COSTS

Item	$ Amount	% of Total
Apparel		
Bridal gown	$1,159	
Headpiece, veil	231	
Alterations, accessories	545	
Groom's tux rental	170	
Apparel Sub-Total	**2,105**	**6%**
Rings		
Engagement ring	5,349	
Wedding rings	1,725	
Rings Sub-Total	**7,074**	**20%**
Music		
Ceremony music	490	
DJ at reception	940	
Music Sub-Total	**1,430**	**4%**
Miscellaneous		
Marriage License	72	
Gifts (attendants, fiance, parents)	1,092	
Other Stuff (taxes, tips, etc).	975	
Misc. Sub-Total	**2,139**	**6%**
Ceremony site and officiant	1,078	3%
Flowers	1,813	5%
Cake	545	2%
Reception/Catering	14,180	40%
Photography	2,260	6%
Videography	1,490	4%
Invitations	428	1%
Limo	690	2%
Total	**$35,232**	**100%**

(Based on industry estimates for 150 guests)
Note: percentages do not add up to 100% due to rounding.

BREAKDOWN OF AVERAGE WEDDING COSTS

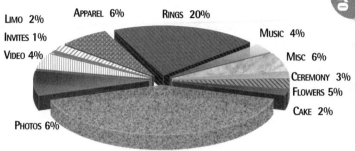

LIMO 2% APPAREL 6% RINGS 20% MUSIC 4%
INVITES 1% MISC 6%
VIDEO 4% CEREMONY 3%
FLOWERS 5%
CAKE 2%
PHOTOS 6%

RECEPTION/CATERING 40%

At this point you might want to catch the next flight to Vegas, but we say "Whoa!" Weddings do NOT have to be that expensive. Let's put that into bold caps: **YOU DO NOT HAVE TO GO BANKRUPT TO HAVE A BEAUTIFUL WEDDING.** Of course, that's the whole point of this book and we'll spend the next 400 pages or so showing you how to cut the cost without compromising on the quality of your wedding. And be sure to read the following section about "average" wedding costs—they are not what they seem!

Of course, where you get married will dramatically impact your wedding costs. Heck, even the cost of a marriage license can vary widely, from a mere $30 in Colorado to $115 in Minnesota.

If you are a bride-to-be in the largest metro areas like New York City or Los Angeles, you may be looking at the above numbers and laughing (or crying). That's because many bridal items in the biggest cities cost at least two to three times the average. Frustrating, we know.

Astute readers may notice that average wedding costs listed above are somewhat higher than the Knot's average wedding cost ($28,427). That's because we include the engagement ring in the above calculation (the Knot omits this cost).

What about bridesmaids' dresses and groomsmen formalwear rentals? Those costs aren't in the earlier table because each attendant typically pays them out of their own pocket. Of course, if you intend to help out a bridesmaid by paying for her gown, start adding to your budget accordingly. In a similar vein, the rehearsal dinner ($1135 on average), ceremony programs ($100), and hair and make-up for the bridal party ($200) are optional items that some couples put in their budgets. Another expense that's not listed above: the honeymoon (which averages about $5100).

Of course, averages are just that—averages. Walk into any bridal dress shop and you'll notice gowns can be $2000, $4000 or more. The same goes for many other wedding items . . . you can quickly spend many times the average in a flash. For example, that $1490 tab for a wedding video assumes a basic package—add in elaborate post-production extras and you can see the total double.

In each chapter, we'll discuss what "average" means for everything from flowers to invitations.

Has there been inflation in wedding costs? Yes, especially with items like food (catering, cakes) and alcohol. But there is good news: some wedding costs have actually DECLINED. No, that isn't a typo. Take the wedding dress: in 1990, it cost $800 to buy the average wedding dress. Given inflation, we'd expect that dress to run $1429 today. BUT—here's the good news—the average bridal gown today is "only" $1159 (the dress itself). So the REAL COST of a bridal gown has actually declined in recent years (thanks to cheaper imported gowns, chain stores and other factors).

Balancing that good news is the reality that some wedding costs have soared—take wedding rings, for example. The average amount spent on wedding rings has DOUBLED in just five years. Why? Are folks buying rings that are twice as big as before? No—soaring costs for precious metals has sharply raised the costs of rings. Another factor: the popularity of platinum rings, which cost 10%-20% or more than gold.

Another way to look at wedding costs is to consider how big a bite a wedding takes out of the average family income. Before World War I, the average wedding cost was one-fourth of the median income for a family. By the 60's, the number rose to one-third. And today? The average wedding this year is 67% of the median annual household income.

The desire to customize or personalize weddings in recent years has led some couples to spend even more on nuptials, driving the designer-end of the bridal biz. And let's not forget the move toward organic or green nuptials. Yes, free-range chicken may be more ethical than a standard wedding chicken entrée—but it will cost you.

Okay, just because many brides and grooms are blowing money faster than a Hollywood starlet, that doesn't mean YOU have to. You found this book, right? So, how can you save? We'll reveal our five commandments for Bridal Bargains later in this chapter. First, here's a quick look at who pays for today's weddings and why averages are misleading.

WHO PAYS FOR THE WEDDING?

BRIDE & GROOM 44%

BRIDE'S PARENTS 42%

PARENTS PLUS
BRIDE & GROOM 14%

Sleight of hand: how surveys inflate "average" costs

Does the average wedding really cost $28,427, as reported by the Knot.com? Or does the popular web site use biased surveys to inflate prices, hoping the wedding industry will look bigger than it really is?

To answer this question, let's look at an excellent analysis of wedding costs by "The Numbers Guy," *Wall Street Journal* reporter Carl Bialik.

Bialik points out an obvious flaw with the Knot's surveys: the average wedding cost is just that—an AVERAGE (or mean) figure.

Ok, we hate to do this, but let's take a trip back to sixth grade and discuss "mean, mode and median." (We promise there will be no painful emotional flashbacks or pop quizzes).

An average or mean can be thrown off if you add in a few expensive weddings. Bialik gives an example: "One $1 million wedding put into the mix with 54 weddings costing $10,000 each would boost the mean to $28,000, although among the 55 couples, $10,000 would seem a much better representation of the typical cost."

A better figure to use to gauge the average cost of a wedding is the MEDIAN—the actual center point of the data, which is less vulnerable to one or two lavish weddings throwing off the average.

Unfortunately, the bridal media don't report median costs for nuptials. But based on previous surveys, we'd estimate the median cost is closer to $18,000 today.

But that's not the only flaw in wedding cost surveys. Consider HOW the surveys are compiled.

The Knot's figures come from an email survey of 17,500 members of their site—note this is not a random sampling of engaged couples, but a group most likely biased toward having a lavish wedding. That's because if you are having a small wedding for $5000, odds are you may never even surf the Knot.

And the Knot's own site metrics underscore the bias: while the Knot has not recently published membership statistics, we estimate that 30% to 40% of the 2.08 million couples who got married last year never signed up for the Knot (the Knot hides some content and tools behind a "members only" wall to encourage registration). Most of the non-Knot couples are mostly likely planning modest affairs. Hence, the Knot's average wedding cost is clearly biased toward expensive weddings.

Bridal media companies use other statistical tricks to make the wedding industry seem more robust than it really is. Example: a few years back, Conde Nast's survey reported that wedding costs have doubled since 1990 (that year, the average cost was $15,208; in 2005, the average was $27,852).

Sounds scary, no?

But Conde Nast FORGOT to factor in inflation. When you use constant dollars, weddings have only gone up 19% in that 15 years period—which is annual growth of 1.1%, even during the 90's. Plenty of other consumer goods have risen much faster than the price of a wedding.

Why do bridal media companies want you to think weddings are lavish and costs are spiraling ever higher? That's because these companies have a vested interest in making weddings look expensive: big advertising dollars. In order to attract millions in ads to their sites and magazines, the Knot and Conde Nast need to promote lavish, expensive weddings.

So, here is the take-home message about average wedding costs:

♥ **DON'T FEEL GUILTY** if you are planning a wedding for LESS than the so-called average: a $18,000 wedding is much closer to the true cost of most weddings.

♥ **IN THIS BOOK, WE REPORT "AVERAGE" COSTS** for items such as flowers, photography, etc. Full disclosure: these are averages, not median prices. Unfortunately, most industry price surveys we found do not give true median prices. So take any "average" price with a grain of salt. Since a handful of expensive weddings can bias the figure, the true median cost for such items is probably substantially less than these figures.

The Fields' Six Commandments for Bridal Bargains

We went up the mountain and came down with these six commandments for brides on a budget. Please repeat after us:

1 The Budget is King. Set a budget and stick to it like a duck on a June bug. Yes, that means making hard choices ... like whether you really need a flower corsage for the wedding cake knife—but, hey, we'll try to point out where to put your money. And where not to waste it.

2 Daylight Savings Time. Timing is everything—and the same goes for weddings. Everyone wants to be married in the peak wedding months of June and August. Do your budget a favor and get hitched in an off-month like October, November, January, February or March. Remember it is also cheaper to get married in the "daylight"—brunch or afternoon weddings are always less than evening bashes.

3 Plan Ahead. Do the math—each year 2 million couples will tie the knot ... but there are only 52 Saturdays each year. The best bargain sites and merchants always book up early. Give yourself plenty of time to comparison shop, get competitive bids and ferret out sales

4 **Undress the Dress.** If you pay full retail for a bridal gown, please give us your home address so we can come over and whack you on the head with this book. Seriously, we found over TWO DOZEN ways to slash that dress bill, as you'll read in the next chapter.

5 **Cut the Cake—and Other Frills.** Brides and grooms pile on the sweets at receptions, but can guests really wolf down a wedding cake, groom's cake AND a dessert table? And do you really need a six-tier confection that looks like a chandelier when a simple cake will do? The same goes for other ridiculous bridal items: wedding favors (guests don't need another dust collector), engraved invitations (other options look just as good at half the cost), or exotic flowers at the ceremony (guests spend much more time looking at your flowers at the *reception*).

6 **Be Prepared to Walk Away.** Don't let wedding merchants pressure you into buying a package you can't afford. Many salespeople in the bridal biz are experts in pushing your emotional buttons (*isn't that $4000 dress soooo beautiful? Don't you want the very best for your wedding?*). Recognize these ploys and don't be bullied! Another key tip: ASK FOR THE MANAGER when negotiating with any merchant. Go right to the top to get the very best deal.

Getting Set, Getting Organized

As with any major project, your first goal in planning a wedding is to get organized. To help, we have published a companion planner to this book, called the *Bridal Bargains Wedding Planner*. This spiral-bound planner contains checklists, to-do lists, budgets and more. We designed our wedding planner to be used together with this book—for example, when we show you how to compare three florists or photographers with a certain set of questions in *Bridal Bargains*, we then provide a worksheet in the *Bridal Bargains Wedding Planner* to do just that. See the back of this book for more details.

Once you start booking merchants for your wedding, you will quickly start collecting quite a bit of paper when planning a wedding. This will easily overwhelm the pockets in any wedding planner. Where should you keep those contracts, proposals and receipts? We suggest going down to a local office supply store and buying a plain accordion file. This costs a mere $5—use the different sections to separate contracts, swatches, receipts and so on.

One reader told us she organized her wedding using a three-ring binder. She hole punched all the contracts and bought pocket inserts for her receipts, photos and fabric swatches. Total cost: $10. If you bought a similar product specially designed for brides with lacy inserts and full color photos, you'd spend as much as $50.

Regardless of the method you use to organize your wedding, keeping all your receipts and contracts in one place is vitally important. Also, make copies of any written correspondence (archive all emails) you have with the businesses you hire. Keeping a journal for cell phone conversations with vendors is also smart.

Although chances are your wedding planning will be a smooth process, if any problems do crop up, you'll be glad you spent the time and money to be so well organized.

The Bridal Clock

The first real crisis of any engagement is the realization that you must accomplish 1.6 million things in about 13 seconds in order to get to the church on time. The second crisis is wondering which of those 1.6 million things you should do first.

To solve this problem, we have invented our BRIDAL CLOCK, below. Think of the numbers of the clock as the sequence of events in the wedding planning process. Your wedding is at "midnight."

Start with reserving your ceremony site (two o'clock). Next, find and book a reception site and caterer. From there, shop for your wedding gown . . . and so on.

In each chapter in this book, you'll find specific advice on how much time you need to order everything from invitations to a wedding cake. Of course, the BRIDAL CLOCK gives you a general sense of how far you've gone—and how much further you need to go until the bewitching hour.

As a side note, you'll notice we did not organize this book in the same order as the Bridal Clock. For simplicity's sake, we divided the book into two sections—wedding and reception.

To be fair, we should also note that many of the bargain tips and advice in this book may require advance planning—it can take up to six

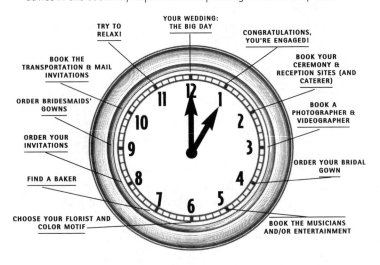

months to order a gown through an online discounter, for example. What if you've just got a few months (or weeks) before your wedding, can you still save money? Of course. Each chapter of this book contains cost-cutting alternatives anyone can use, no matter how much time you have before you walk down the aisle.

Protecting Your Privacy While Planning a Wedding

Marketing to brides and grooms is big business—once you get engaged, you are in the cross hairs of hungry marketers, eager to clog your email box with bridal spam and call your cell phone with the latest pitch.

Consider this email from a recent reader:

> *I'm sure I won't be the only person to mention this, but David's Bridal has started harassing me by phone with telemarketer-type messages, even though I never set foot in one of their stores. I set up an appointment to try on dresses once, then canceled the appointment because I had already bought my dress. I gave them my cell phone when I set up the appointment.*
>
> *Now I keep getting these voicemail messages that are a recording from one of their telemarketers trying to get me to call David's Bridal (between 1-3 times a week, a month after I made my appointment). Totally unprofessional and unheard of from a large chain store. Even places like Best Buy don't do stuff like this.*

Welcome to the world of wedding marketing. Here are a few tips for protecting your privacy—both online and off—while you tie the knot:

♥ **GUARD YOUR PERSONAL INFORMATION BY SETTING UP WEDDING-ONLY EMAIL ACCOUNTS.** Don't hand out your personal or work email to bridal vendors—instead, establish a special throw-away email address on Gmail or Yahoo for wedding-related email.

♥ **DON'T DIVULGE YOUR CELL PHONE OR HOME ADDRESS.** No, the bridal shop does NOT need to have your cell phone to set up an appointment—email should suffice. One clever idea: sign up for Google's Voice feature. This free service lets you pick a phone number and then forward certain calls to your regular cell phone. The free call forwarding feature lets you choose which calls you'll accept . . . or block calls based on the time of day or number that's calling. Use your special Google-only phone number to give out to wedding vendors . . . then turn it off after the wedding. Did we mention this was free? Google Voice has a raft of cool features: voicemail transcription, a mobile app, play your voicemail within Gmail, SMS to email and more.

♥ **BLOCK TRACKING PROGRAMS.** Those free wedding web sites like the Knot or WeddingChannel aren't really free—these sites are tracking your every click so you can be targeted by online advertisers. That's why after you surf the Knot, you'll suddenly see ads for wedding items on unrelated sites like CNN.

Use free browser plug-ins from sites like Ghostery.com and DoNotTrackMe from Abine.com to opt-out of ad networks AND block web trackers.

Once you install Ghostery, for example, you'll now see that the Knot uses not one, or two, but TEN companies to track your every move on the site. Brides.com has 12 web trackers. These companies use cookies, web bugs and other sophisticated techniques to hoover up your personal info. This is then combined with profiles from data mining companies to make sure your browser is stuffed with ads for wedding cruft.

Another way to preserver your privacy is to use a secure browser such as Tor (torproject.org). By bouncing your communications around a worldwide network of relays, Tor prevents sites you visit from learning your physical location. The downside? It can be somewhat slower than a standard browser.

What's new in this edition

So, what's changed with the 11th edition of *Bridal Bargains*? As always, we try to make the book better with enhanced reviews and more bargain tips.

Our secret sauce is reader feedback—and we've got more savvy reader tips on how to save in this edition than ever before. Brides and grooms have shared their favorite money-saving tricks on gowns, catering, photography and more.

New this edition, we cover the growing trend of bridal dress designers that are opening their own factory stores. Also new: we've beefed up our coverage of paperless invites and the latest trends in catering and reception entertainment.

For wedding rings, we cover the myriad of new affordable metals used for men's rings: zirconium, steel, ceramic, wood inlays and more. The good news: many of these styles are much more affordable than the standard gold or platinum ring.

So let's get started with the dress. Turn to the next chapter for our extensive tips and advice on how to save on your bridal gown.

PART 1
YOUR WEDDING

Apparel
Ceremony
Flowers
Invitations

Wonder how you can save up to 70% off those fancy designer bridal gowns? We'll show you how, with our exclusive list of 29 money-saving tips. Before we go there, however, you'll learn the 17 steps to buying the right dress. Next, we'll expose how some dishonest bridal shops rip-off brides, while we teach you how to outfox them.

The Bridal Gown. Is there any icon that better symbolizes a wedding than the bridal gown?

It's hard not to get swept up in all the hoopla and hype when it comes to this dress—yes, you will be photographed in this gown more times than Lindsey Lohan at a court arraignment. (Okay, maybe not that much). And who doesn't want to look spectacular on their wedding day?

After the excitement of announcing the engagement wears off, however, the actual process of shopping for a wedding gown comes into focus. And that's where things can get less than romantic.

We'll spare you all the hype about storybook brides and fairy-tale dresses. Our focus here is on the practical: just how does one shop smart when it comes to buying a wedding gown? And how can you save?

Let's start at the beginning: how much does a gown cost?

What Are You Buying?

At the simplest level, you are buying a dress. But not just any dress. This is a darn expensive dress. The average bridal gown costs $1159. Many of the premium designer gowns sell for much more, topping $2000, $3000 and more.

So what do you think you should get for nearly $1200? Well, before you answer this question, we ask you to shift your mind into BRIDAL MODE. That's because if you think in the REAL WORLD MODE you're going to be in for a shock. For example, if we gave you $1200 and told you to buy a nice party or cocktail dress you'd expect a few things for that amount of money. Fine fabrics like silk? Sure. Quality construction with a lining and finished seams? Why not. How about sewn sequins and detailing? Hey, you'd expect that for $1200! Right?

Well, BRIDAL MODE isn't like that. For $1200, you'll see plenty of dresses with synthetic fabric and shoddy construction with unfinished seams and no lining. Want a sophisticated gown made of silk with a splash of delicate embroidery? Sadly, dresses like that are often way over $2000. Or $3000.

And the price of the gown itself is just the beginning. There are many hidden costs when buying a bridal gown—you'll also need undergarments, a slip, shoes and (optionally) a headpiece/veil. If you think bridal gowns are overpriced, wait until you see what accessories sell for. The "average" headpiece and veil runs $225, while you can add another $300 for other accessories such as shoes, gloves, jewelry, bra and so on. Hence, the total ensemble may cost you $2125. On the next page is a breakdown of extra costs.

And those figures are just averages. Alterations (required for nearly all gowns) can be much more expensive than $250 (roughly the national average). In major cities, brides report to us that some bridal shops are now charging exorbitant "flat fees" for alterations—$300, $400 or more. While that figure covers any changes to the gown, brides who merely need a minor nip and tuck get socked for the full fare. On the other hand, some shops throw in *free* alterations and a pressing if you spend a certain amount of money in the store. (More on alterations later in this chapter).

What part of the country has the most expensive bridal alterations? Our reader email indicates it must be the Washington DC area. Brides report to us that several shops there now charge flat $500 fees for alterations, no matter how little needs to be done to their bridal gowns.

HIDDEN GOWN COSTS

(Sample figures for a typical gown—and those necessary extras)

Gown	$1,159
Rush Charge	50
Alterations	250
Pressing	75
Delivery to ceremony	50
Crinoline/Slip	70
Bra	60
Headpiece/Veil	231
Shoes	85
Jewelry	50
Gloves/Stockings	45
Total	**$2,125**

(Note: in the introduction for this book, we say the average cost of the bride's ensemble is $1935. That's because we don't count two of the above items—the rush charge and delivery to the ceremony, since those are charges most brides don't incur. We also didn't count jewelry, assuming you'll receive this as a gift—hint, hint).

Even if you pay the average amount for a gown and the extras, it's amazing how a $1200 gown can turn into a $2000+ purchase in a hurry. Of course, you don't have to pay that much. Order early (at least six months before the wedding) and you won't pay the rush charge. You can save big bucks by borrowing a crinoline/slip, forget the special delivery to the church (carry it yourself), and buy shoes, jewelry, and other accessories at discount stores. More on money-saving strategies later in this chapter.

We should also note that most shops require a 50% deposit on all special orders. (We'll explain later why most gowns are special-ordered instead of bought off-the-rack.) That can be a sizable financial hit several months before the wedding. The balance is due when the dress comes in. The exception to the half-down rule: some discounters require payment in full when you order. This certainly requires more of a leap of faith on the consumer's part, but the discount (20% to 30% off retail or more) may make this deal attractive.

Sources to Find a Reputable Bridal Shop

Finding a bridal shop is easy—just Google bridal shop and your town name, right? Sure, that will give you a list of nearby shops. But which ones can you trust? Which ones are the most reputable? Here are our tips:

♥ NETWORK, NETWORK, NETWORK. Ask friends, co-workers and friends of co-workers who were recently married for their experiences. Word-of-mouth referrals are valuable.

♥ ONLINE SNOOPING. Bad bridal shops often leave a trial of unhappy customers—many of whom post to the Knot, Yelp, Yahoo and other sites.

♥ Check the BETTER BUSINESS BUREAU. While not perfect, the BBB (bbb.org) tracks complaints for local wedding businesses. You can find whether a business belongs to the BBB, how many complaints they have generated and whether there are any outstanding problems. A red flag: bridal shops with an unsatisfactory rating—if a shop fails to respond to two or more consumer complaints, they get flagged.

Best Online Resources

Here's a scary stat: the Knot.com has 1.3 billion dress pictures online. Ok, we are exaggerating . . . it actually is 1.2 billion.

How can you search for a gown online without losing your sanity? Here are some basic tips:

♥ FOCUS ON THE SILHOUETTE. Most gown search engines let you narrow your search by gown silhouette, neckline and other attributes. Be honest about your figure and focus on the gown that best fits your body shape. There's no reason to stare at strapless sheath dresses if that isn't you!

♥ GO ANALOG. Sure, it is old school, but consider turning off the computer and looking at a magazine or bridal catalog. It's sometimes easier to compare options with old-fashioned paper and ink than pixels.

♥ THERE IS MORE TO THE ONLINE BRIDAL WORLD THAN THE KNOT. Don't forget to surf bridal gown designers—most have elaborate web sites with their complete collections online. For example, Alfred Angelo has 35 pictures on the Knot . . . but the entire collection (120+ gowns) is on AlfredAngelo.com.

Getting Started: How Far in Advance?

Most brides are surprised when they learn how far in advance they must place an order for their gown. In general, most bridal gowns are not bought off-the-rack. You try on sample dresses and then "special order" the gown in your size. It's the special order nature of bridal apparel that takes so long—the *average* dress takes ten to 14 weeks to arrive (yes, that's three to four months). And ordering is just the beginning. When you add in time for shopping, alterations and other necessities, you quickly realize it's best to order your dress five to nine months before the wedding. Let's take a look at the five stages of buying a bridal gown:

1 Shopping. Hey, don't forget that you need time to look for the gown that is just right for you. Sure, you can do this in as little as one day, but most brides we have interviewed said they took two to three weeks. That's because it takes time to visit a handful of the area's best shops and more time to make a final decision.

2 Ordering. Once you place your order, the shop sends it to the manufacturer. Each dress designer has different delivery schedules—some are as quick as six weeks, while others are six months. That's why it's important you know the designer of the gown in order to make sure the gown will arrive in time for your wedding. Some manufacturers offer "rush service," but the extra fee for this may bust your budget. FYI: David's, the country's largest chain of bridal stores, does sell many gowns off the rack—but if your size isn't in stock or the sample is damaged, David's will special order it from their warehouse. This is much like the process for special-ordering a gown from any other bridal shop.

3 Alterations. After the gown comes in, leave another month for alterations. Some shops may be able to do "rush" jobs but the quality may be rushed too. You may have several time-consuming "fittings," appointments with the seamstress where you inch closer and closer to getting the gown to fit just right.

4 Portrait. In some areas, brides have a formal portrait taken before the wedding, which is displayed at the reception. In order to have enough time to view the proofs and get the final print framed, most photographers suggest doing the portrait four to six weeks before the wedding. That means the dress has to be altered and ready to go at that time.

5 **Safety Zone for Mistakes.** Yes, mistakes can happen, especially with gowns. Bridal apparel is most prone to problems since there are more people involved in this process than any other. Orders can be botched at several points between the manufacturer and final delivery. Leaving time (perhaps two weeks) in your schedule to correct problems is prudent.

Whoa! That's a lot of time! The time guideline we recommend is at least six months. If you want an elaborate designer gown, allow for even more time. However, don't panic if your wedding is around the corner. Look for our TOP MONEY SAVING TIPS later in this chapter—many of these strategies can quickly unite you with a gown.

Does the process of special-ordering a gown sound like too much hassle? There is good news: several "off-the-rack" options have sprung up in recent years that enable you to walk out the same day with a bridal gown in your size. And major fashion brands like J Crew and Ann Taylor (among others) offer quick turn around for bridal dress orders (more on these options later in the chapter).

Step-by-step Shopping Strategies

♥ **Step 1:** After you've set the date, sit down with your fiancé to talk about your wedding. The key decision is how formal you want the event to be. Now, bridal web sites have all kinds of crazy rules to tell you what to wear for each formality degree but just remember this: your gown should reflect your ceremony and reception. The gown that is perfect for an intimate garden ceremony held in the afternoon probably won't work at an evening ceremony for 200 close friends at a big church with a sit-down dinner reception following.

♥ **Step 2:** Now that you have an idea of how formal your wedding is, look through those gown pictures online or in magazines. Key in on the elements of the dresses—the silhouettes, the necklines, waistlines, train length, amount of lace, etc. A caveat: take these ads with a grain of salt. What looks good on you (a real bride in the real world) may be vastly different from what you see in online. Keep an open mind.

♥ **Step 3:** Before you head out to local bridal shops, ask your ceremony site coordinator if there are any restrictions on the amount of skin you can show in the sanctuary. Some churches frown on off-the-shoulder, strapless or halter-style gowns—unfortunately, the current bridal fashion now popular on runways. Determining what's appropriate before you fall in love with the "wrong" gown is prudent. If you are determined to wear that bare look, consider ordering extra fabric to make a cover-up (shawl or jacket) to wear for the ceremony. Some gown makers now offer "temple-ready" dresses, which show much less skin. Another note of caution: beware of sheath or mermaid-style gowns if you have to kneel during the ceremony. Most of these gowns don't have slits in the back, making kneeling next to impossible. One option is to have your seamstress add a slit in the back (look inside the gown to make sure a back seam is available).

♥ **Step 4:** Listen to the advice of recently married friends and acquaintances about local bridal shops. Their insights on selection, service and prices may be valuable. Using our other sources mentioned above, draw up a list of three to five stores that offer the gowns you want. Don't forget that a store's service (how you're treated when you come through the door) is almost as important as the selection of dresses.

♥ **Step 5:** In addition to the stores on your list, visit a store or two that sells expensive dresses. Why? This is the best way to educate yourself about quality bridal gowns. Expensive gowns (over $1000 or even $2000) typically feature quality construction, luxurious fabrics and exquisite detailing. Then, when you hit the discounters, warehouse stores and outlets, you can tell what's quality—and what's not. You won't be fooled by gowns marked "sale $490, originally $1000," when the fabric and construction indicate the original price should have been much less. Besides,

Just what is 'couture' anyway?

In the world of fashion, "couture" clothing (in French, literally meaning sewing or seam) typically describes a designer's most expensive line of personally-designed garments. Unlike less expensive "ready to wear" and "bridge" lines, couture clothes are only sold in a handful of stores to a very moneyed crowd. So, what does couture mean in bridal? Absolutely nothing. Bridal apparel makers have so misused and abused the word "couture" that they slap it on any expensive dress (say, over $1000). To us, a couture bridal gown would be personally designed by a famous designer and then handcrafted by a seamstress in the US or Canada. In bridal, however, "couture" dresses have no special pedigree and are often made in assembly-line fashion. To add insult to injury, some bridal retailers slap extra alteration fees on couture dresses (sometimes $400 for a simple nip and tuck). Are these dresses any more difficult to alter than a $500 gown? Nope, there is just the up-charge because it is called a couture gown.

trying on those fancy gowns is fun. But leave your wallet at home.

♥ Step 6: Back to reality. It's time to go shopping for real. Try to visit the stores on your list on any day *other* than a Saturday. Weekends at bridal shops are crazy—everyone tries to shop on Saturday. If you can go during the week (some stores are open in the evening), you'll find better service, less-crowded dressing rooms, etc. Call ahead—some shops require an appointment. (A warning: some shops charge brides "try-on fees" to discourage walk-ins). Don't drop into a fancy bridal shop without an appointment and then get upset at the lack of service. Shop with just one other person (a friend, a relative or even your fiancé) whose opinion you value. Remember to wear undergarments similar to what you plan to wear under your bridal gown; and have your hair in a similar style as what you plan for the wedding. Skip the makeup and lipstick, since that can damage sample gowns.

♥ Step 7: When you visit the shop, be prepared to answer a few questions. The first is probably the most critical: how much do you want to spend? Most salespeople will try to "up-sell" you slightly, so we recommend you under-estimate your price range by 10%. If you really have budgeted about $1000 for a gown (not including alterations and any accessories), tell them you want to spend $800 to $900. Undoubtedly, they'll show you a few dresses closer to $1000.

♥ Step 8: Next you'll be asked about your wedding date and how formal your wedding will be. We recommend you push forward the date about three to four weeks. For example, if your real wedding date is June 15, tell the shop the "big day" is May 15 (or the nearest Saturday to that date). This insures that your gown will arrive (and any potential problems will be fixed) in time. The wedding date will also help determine whether you'll want long or short sleeves, for example. Also, shops ask you what "style" of gown you prefer: Obviously, you won't know all the answers but try to give the salesperson an idea of your preferences. Some shops now put pictures of the gowns they stock in big binders at the front of the store—you're suppose to look through these pictures to pick styles you like before hitting the racks. (A side note: this shouldn't surprise you, but the gowns' manufacturer/designer names are carefully omitted from these pictures).

♥ Step 9: Keep an open mind. Try a few different styles, with a friend taking notes on which gowns you like the best. Be careful of "gown overload:" trying on too many gowns in one day can confuse, blending into a blur of lace and sequins. Our advice: don't try on more than five gowns at each shop. Besides you'll become exhausted.

♥ **Step 10:** Narrow down your choices to two or three gowns. Make an appointment with the same salesperson you talked with on your first visit. Now, it's decision time! Don't be rushed—take your time to make your final choice. Compare prices with discounters (see later in this chapter for sources). If you decide to order from a local retailer, be sure to confirm any extra fees for your gown purchase. (Protective gown bag? Pressing? Shipping?) Get a written estimate for alterations BEFORE you commit to the purchase.

♥ **Step 11:** Congratulations! You've selected your bridal gown! Now, before you put down that hefty 50% non-refundable deposit, ask the bridal shop the questions listed later in this chapter. Get measured (bust, waist, hips and from the base of your throat to the hemline) with a vinyl tape measure and ask to see the manufacturer's sizing chart. Given your measurements (and remember your bust measurement is *not* your bra size), select the gown size that corresponds to the largest of your measurements. Remember you can make a gown smaller but you can't easily expand it. It's important that *you* make the decision of what size to order—don't let the

QUALITY: GOOD VS. BAD

Walk into any bridal shop and you'll be greeted by a sea of white. This dress is $500; this other one is $1200. How about gowns for $2500? What's the difference? The proof is in the details. The more expensive gowns have better fabric, finished seams and built-in crinolines. The following chart summarizes the difference between good and bad quality when it comes to bridal gowns:

	GOOD	POOR
BEADING	SEWN-ON	GLUED-ON
SEAMS	NO VISIBLE THREADS	THREADS SHOW THROUGH SEAMS
INSIDE OF DRESS	COMPLETELY LINED; FINISHED SEAMS	UNLINED; UNFINISHED SEAMS
FABRIC	SILK OR HEAVY WEIGHT SATIN	FEELS LIKE YOU CAN TEAR IT
SEWING	BUILT-IN PETTICOAT OR SLIP	LAYERS SEWN TOGETHER IN SAME SEAM
HEM	HERRINGBONE OR HORSEHAIR HEM	A SIMPLE STRAIGHT STITCH HEM
COMFORT	DRESS IS COMFORTABLE TO WEAR	SCRATCHY LACE OR ITCHY DETAILING

bridal shop make it for you. We'll explain why later in the PITFALLS section.

♥ **Step 12:** If you're unsure whether the shop is an authorized dealer for the gown you want, call the manufacturer (a quick Google search can turn up a phone number). Most manufacturers will tell you if the shop is a legitimate re-seller for their gowns. If the shop won't tell you the manufacturer of the gown, we suggest you go elsewhere. If the manufacturer tells you the shop is not an authorized dealer, the shop may be sewing counterfeit gowns or transshipping the gowns from another source. Ask the owner about this and if you don't get a straight answer, go elsewhere. Don't worry: you may be able to get the dress from another, more honest shop even if the first shop claims they have an "exclusive."

An exception to this rule: many discount mail order and warehouse companies are not "official" authorized outlets, according to public statements by bridal manufacturers. While the discounters often purchase gowns through legitimate channels, the designers don't want to admit that they're selling to them.

♥ **Step 13:** When you place an order, get a receipt with the price, color, size, manufacturer, style number, and most importantly, the promised delivery date. Also, listed on the ticket should be any special-order requests (some dresses can be ordered on a rush basis, with changes to the fabric, lace or detailing, etc.). All these requests cost extra. If the store recommends a size for you, write on the ticket "Store recommends size." Then, if the gown comes in needing extensive (and expensive) alterations, you're in a better negotiating position. When you place your order, also get a written estimate on alterations. Be sure you ask about the store's refund policy, as well as any extra charges for pressing and so on. Since these written details are so important, let's sum up what you want on your dress order form:

Dress description. You want the actual manufacturer's name and style number, not the store's bogus internal code. The price, color, and size should be spelled out.

Special requests. Want extra length? Rush delivery? This should all be on the order form.

Promised delivery date. This can be in weeks or a specific day (on or before X).

Alterations estimate.

Deposit, refund and cancellation policies. Payment info (when the balance is due, etc.) should be clearly stated.

Your contact info. Give the shop your cell number (or your Google Voice number to protect your privacy). If you order online instead of from a shop, the more contact info you can provide the gown seller, the better. (To protect your privacy, insist the shop not sell this info.)

♥ **Step 14:** One to two weeks after you place the order, call the bridal shop for a "confirmed shipping date." The shop usually receives this date from the manufacturer after it places the order.

♥ **Step 15:** Starting two weeks before your dress is due in, call the bridal shop to confirm the date your dress will actually arrive. Delays at the factory (imported lace arriving late, a larger number of back-orders) can delay the delivery of your gown, as well as the bridesmaids'. Bridal shops are usually aware of such delays. Calling ahead will help avoid surprises.

♥ **Step 16:** Hooray! The dress has arrived! Now, inspect the dress carefully *before* you pay the final balance. Gowns have been known to come in with flaws, stains, tears—you name it. Don't rely on the bridal shop to inspect the dress for you (some let problems slip through the cracks). Also, confirm the size of the dress by actually trying it on (or measuring it). Incorrect sizing is a major problem with some manufacturers. *Remember: if you pay for the dress, sign a receipt and walk out the door with the gown, you are accepting the dress as is.* If you do not inspect the dress, take it home and THEN discover a problem, the shop may say "tough luck."

What if you order a gown online? Make sure you IMMEDIATELY inspect the dress and try it on. Any problem should be promptly reported to the gown seller. Most online gown sellers refuse to accept a claim for damage after a certain number of days.

♥ **Step 17:** Alterations. Whether you have the shop or an outside seamstress alter the gown, give the alterations person a firm deadline. Get it in writing. Be sure to confirm the experience level of the seamstress—how familiar is she with bridal fabric? How long has she been altering gowns? See our PITFALLS for more advice on alterations.

No matter where you buy your gown (at a store or online), one service you will probably need is pressing or steaming to get out the wrinkles. What's the difference? First, understand that we use the terms interchangeably in this chapter . . . but there is a difference. Most bridal shops use steamers to get out wrinkles from delicate fabrics; other seamstresses may use a press to iron out tough wrinkles.

We'd suggest steaming for most gowns—bridal fabric is delicate and pressing it could damage the finish. Silk gowns should definitely be steamed. While synthetic fabric gowns aren't as delicate as silk, we still worry about the finish on satin gowns if pressed. A good tip: ASK what method your seamstress will use and make sure it is appropriate to your gown's fabric.

The Ultimate Bridal Gown Glossary

Fiber Content

SILK. This is the premiere wedding fiber for softness, luster and beauty. Silk is made from silkworm cocoons, discovered by the Chinese in 2600 B.C. France became the most famous producer of finished silk fabric, hence the use of so many French names such as dupioni and peau de soie (later in this chapter, we'll define fabric weaves).

Until recently, silk has been an expensive fiber and silk bridal gowns have been equally pricey—most used to cost over $2000. In the last 10 years, however, more affordable silk fabrics (and silk blends) have dropped that price considerably.

Despite increasing competition in silk production, China still makes 70% to 85% of the world's silk. Other countries like Thailand turn out great silk fabric as well.

Silk's use in bridal apparel continues to decline as synthetic fabrics increasingly become more silk-like in their feel and luster.

COTTON. Used as thread and fabric as long ago as 600 B.C., cotton is made from the fibers of its namesake plant. Cotton's popularity in everyday clothes has probably contributed to its absence as a bridal fabric—there's little cachet to a cotton bridal gown. While a few designers use the fabric (woven in sheer or embroidered varieties), it is still rare to see cotton on the bridal dress racks.

LINEN. Made from flax plants, this fiber was first utilized for clothing by the ancient Egyptians. Linen is often combined with cotton or other fibers; by itself it wrinkles badly. As a result, you're more likely to see linen fabric in bridal suits and other informal dresses.

RAYON. Invented during World War II when silk was rationed for use in parachutes, rayon is made from mulberry plant fibers. An affordable fiber, rayon often shows up in blends.

MAN-MADE FIBERS. Nylon, acetate and polyester are those affordable man-made wonders that became unavoidable in 70's fashion. In the bridal world, manufacturers could weave these fibers into shiny or glossy finishes, giving a special look at a lower price. Most affordably priced gowns (under $800) are made of man-made fibers; however, you can still see polyester fabrics in dresses over $1000. While most brides don't think "Hey, I want a polyester bridal gown," most popular bridal fabric weaves such as "satin" and "taffeta" are made of just that. Good news: the increasing sophistication in synthetic fibers is giving natural fabrics like silk a run for its money in recent years.

Fabric Weaves

It is easy to confuse fibers with fabric weaves. Fabric is woven using two sets of threads: vertical "warp" threads and horizontal "weft" threads. The difference in weaves is caused by the types of threads used and by the thickness and texture of those threads. Most bridal fibers (both natural and man-made) can be woven into the wide variety of finishes described below:

BROCADE. Heavy weight fabric woven on a special loom, brocade has raised patterns that give it a contrasting white-on-white or ivory-on-ivory appearance. Commonly designed with a floral pattern.

CHARMEUSE. (shar-MOOSE) A tasty, low fat, non-dairy dessert. Just kidding! Actually, charmeuse is a lightweight version of satin with a softer and clingier look. Charmeuse is a common weave with silk or rayon and has less body than traditional silk fabrics.

CHIFFON. (shi-FON) A sheer, lightweight weave, chiffon may be made from just about any fiber. It is often layered and has an unusual luster.

CREPE. (rhymes with drape) A thin, light fabric with a ridged or finely crinkled surface. New, affordable polyester crepes offer a similar feel and drape as silk crepes. Crepe de chine means literally "crepe from China" and has tiny irregularities in the surface texture.

DAMASK. (DAM-ask) Similar to brocade but of lighter weight.

DUCHESS (DUCHESSE) SATIN. Also referred to as silk-faced satin, this weave weighs less than traditional silk finishes and is usually less expensive as well. Most Duchess satins are a blend of silk and polyester woven into a satin finish.

DUPIONI. (doo-pee-OH-nee) Using coarse fibers of various thicknesses, dupioni is woven into a crisply textured fabric with many visible natural slubs.

FAILLE. (rhymes with "pail"; alternatively pronounced "file") Faille is a ribbed fabric with structure and body. This weave is also seen in bridesmaid's styles today. Most faille is woven from silk, cotton, rayon or polyester.

GAZAR. A variation of organza, gazar provides a sheer effect with more of a stiff or starched feel.

GEORGETTE. A form of crepe with a dull texture.

JERSEY. No not the state, although it's pronounced the same way. This is a machine knitted fabric that can be made of a variety of fibers including silk, rayon and nylon. Typically, jersey is fluid fabric that drapes softly.

MATELASSE. (mat lah-ZAY) This finish gives the effect of embossing, but is actually woven into the fabric to create the texture.

NET, ILLUSION, OR TULLE. This mesh-like fabric is most often woven from synthetic fibers. A recent fad saw several designers adding tulle skirts to their gown designs. Varying weaves can increase or decrease the weight of this fabric.

ORGANDY. A crisp transparent fabric made from cotton.

ORGANZA. Similar to chiffon, but heavier and with more body.

PEAU DE SOIE (skin of silk). (po-deh-SWAH) A heavy, smooth satin with very fine ribbing. This finish is actually somewhat dull in sheen compared to traditional satin.

SATIN. A tightly woven effect that creates a fabric with a beautiful sheen on one side. Typically made in man-made fabrics like polyester, satin is probably the most common bridal gown fabric weave. While satin is most often associated with a high gloss look, it is also available in a matte finish with a toned down glow.

SHANTUNG. Originally known as wild (or natural) silk, this finish has a rougher, nubby appearance. Once associated exclusively with silk fabrics, polyester shantung is now widely available. While similar to dupioni (described above), shantung is usually softer and lighter weight.

TAFFETA. This crisp fabric is often woven from man-made fibers. A close second to satin, taffetas are a favorite for both bridal gowns and bridesmaids dresses too. In the latter, you might find taffeta fabrics with woven moiré patterns.

TWILL. Fibers are woven to create a diagonal pattern.

VELVET. Most folks know this familiar weave, which has a thick nap. Once associated with silks, velvets are now available in cotton or rayon blends as well. A variation of this finish, crushed velvet, is made with a high and low nap to give a shimmering effect.

Laces

Boy, if you thought fabric weaves had funny sounding names, just wait till you check out the laces bridal designers use. Here's a wrap-up of the names you'll encounter:

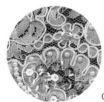

ALENÇON. (al-AHN-son) Probably the most popular of wedding laces, alençon lace has a background of flowers and swags that are re-embroidered along the edges with cording. This lace may be pre-beaded or beaded after it is sewn on the dress.

BATTENBURG. This type of lace is made by stitching a strip of linen fabric into a pattern of loops, then connecting them with thread. Besides bridal gowns, battenburg is often found on table and bed linens.

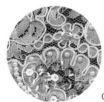

CHANTILLY. (shan-TIL-ee) Flowers and ribbons on a plain net background define Chantilly lace. These details are usually edged with fine cording. Feel free to sing the song now.

DOTTED SWISS. Small circles of flocked fabric over a background of netting typify this lace, which is often used on necklines or layered over skirts (not pictured).

DUCHESSE. This Belgian lace named after the Duchess of Brabant looks like needlepoint.

EYELET. This lace is usually made of cotton, which has perforated holes embroidered around the edges (right).

GUIPURE. This lace has seen a resurgence in recent years. Guipure features a large series of motifs connected by a few threads. Common guipure patterns may be roses, daisies or geometric designs like ovals (left).

RIBBON. A random pattern of ribbon that is sewn over a net background. (right)

SCHIFFLI. (SHIF-lee) A lightweight lace with an all-over embroidered design on a net background. (left)

SOUTACHE. A variation of Alençon. The cording used to re embroider the lace is thicker helping make the lace stand out more (not pictured).

VENISE. (ven-EES) This type of lace is a needlepoint-type design. An example connects small flowers with irregularly placed threads (left).

Questions to Ask A Gown Seller

1 **Who is the manufacturer of this dress?**
As we previously mentioned, some shops try to hide this info. Even if the tags of the dress have been removed, you can still ask them about who makes the dress. This is important for several reasons. First, you can determine if the store is an authorized dealer for the gown by calling the

manufacturer. Second, you know what you are buying—some designers offer better quality than others. If the shop refuses to tell you, or if the salesperson says she just "doesn't know," go elsewhere.

2 **How long will it take to get the dress?** A critical question since the delivery times for different manufacturers vary greatly. If you choose to give the shop an earlier than actual wedding date, be careful here. If you move the date up too early, the shop may not be able to order the dress in time for the early date. In general, it takes ten to 14 weeks to special order a typical bridal gown, although some designers take as little as six weeks and others six months.

3 **What are your payment policies?** Can I put the deposit on a credit card? How about the final balance? This is a very important point, as you'll learn in our next section. Also, confirm the store's refund policy. Nearly all bridal shops have a "no refunds" policy on special-order dresses—even if the wedding is called off or postponed. Read the receipt (or contract) carefully before you sign. Note: some shops are requiring final payment to be made in cash. If this is the case, be sure everything is perfect before leaving the shop with any merchandise.

4 **Can I have a written estimate for alterations?** Before you order, get this in writing. Remember that you do not have to use the store's in-house alterations department (even though they will strongly encourage you to). Quality alterations are extremely important—sadly, there are unskilled seamstresses out there (many at bridal shops). Whomever you decide to hire, try to meet the seamstress who will alter your gown. Ask about her experience with bridal gowns. How long have they been doing this work? Have they ever worked with the fabric and lace on your dress before? If you detect any problems here or can't get a written estimate with delivery time, consider hiring another seamstress.

5 **What free services are available?** Some stores throw in a free "steaming" with all bridal gown orders. Other freebies might include free alterations, delivery to the ceremony site and even wedding coordination (especially when you place a large order with the shop). Some of these services might be offered quietly. Ask and ye shall receive.

BRIDAL BARGAINS 33

❻ **Are there any extra fees for special orders?** As we mentioned earlier in this chapter, some independent bridal retailers are slapping their customers with all kinds of bogus fees and charges. Many such charges aren't disclosed until after you've whipped out the credit card to place an order. So, it would be wise to ask if there is another $20 for shipping or any other creative "fee." Ask for the TOTAL for your order (gown plus any extra fees? Extra size fee? Rush charge? Alterations? Shipping?) to make sure you are getting a good deal.

CONSUMER WARNING

Use Credit Cards Instead of Cash For All Deposits. Here's a little consumer tip that can protect you when ordering a bridal gown: use your credit card (instead of cash or a check) to pay any deposit. Most consumers do not realize that a special federal consumer protection law protects all deposits and payments made with credit cards. The law, called Federal Regulation C, entitles consumers to receive refunds if the merchandise delivered doesn't live up to what's promised.

Specifically, the law says that if you have a problem with the quality of goods or services that you purchased with a credit card and you have tried in good faith to correct the problem with the merchant, you may not have to pay the bill. (As a side note, this only applies to purchases over $50 and if the purchase was made in your home state or within 100 miles of your mailing address). Note: this protection does *not* apply to debit cards or cash advance checks that some credit card companies send their customers.

So what does that mean for you? Well, let's suppose two brides put $500 deposits on the exact same dress at BRIDAL SHOP XYZ in their town. One bride puts the deposit on her Visa (or any credit card) and the other writes a check. Delivery will take four months.

Let us tell you that four months may not seem like a long time to you but it's an ETERNITY to retailers. Much can happen in four months. In fact, BRIDAL SHOP XYZ has now gone out of business. The owner of the shop has left town without a trace. So what's happened to our two brides? Well, the bride who put the deposit on a card will contact her credit card company and, most likely, she will receive a full refund.

And what happens to the other bride who paid with a check (or cash)? Her $500 is probably lost forever. Sure, she can sue the owner in small claims court—if she can find the owner. She can also report the incident (which is technically theft) to local authorities. But, if the shop owner has left town, the bride may never see her money again.

Does this sound far-fetched? Well, it happens more often than you'd think. In one city we researched, for example, no less than ten bridal shops went out of business in just three years! While four closed "responsibly" (they stopped taking deposits and turned their special orders over to other shops in town), the other six bridal shops did not. Their owners took deposits until the day they closed and then quickly left town. We know dozens of brides who lost hundreds of dollars in deposits because they paid cash (or by check) instead of with a credit card.

While there are no national statistics on bridal shops that have closed in recent years, our research indicates there are dozens of retailers that close each year. In addition to shops that close due to the economy, some stores are hit by fires or flooding.

So, what can you do in case your shop disappears?

According to several credit card companies we've talked to, deposits paid with credit cards for bridal apparel (or any wedding-related purchase) are protected by Federal Regulation C. Be aware that the rules vary slightly with each issuing bank. One bank we talked to had a requirement that complaints be filed within 60 days of the purchase. The fact that a deposit isn't really a "purchase" clouds the issue somewhat. Another bank told us they would refund money to a bride under a scenario like the one above even if more than 60 days had elapsed from the date the deposit was processed. Why? In clear cases of fraud (where merchants take off with your money, leaving you gown-less), there is no time limit for you to dispute a charge.

What if you've already paid the bill? It doesn't matter—you may still be able to dispute the charge. What if the shop only takes cash or checks? Go elsewhere. Most bridal shops take credit cards.

Are debit card purchases afforded the same protection? No, debit cards are like cash—you can NOT dispute the charge for a deposit put on a debit card.

The bottom line: use a credit card to pay for all wedding deposits including your gown, flowers, photographer and more.

Destination Wedding Tips

What's the perfect wedding bargain for a beach destination wedding? And how do you transport a gown to a tropical locale? We have the low down:

♥ **Looking for an affordable dress for a destination beach wedding?** Check out J Crew's bridal line, with dresses that start at $295. This simple gown with scalloped lace overlay can be dressed with an affordable headpiece/veil and poof! Instant wedding gown for less than $400.

How do you transport a wedding gown to a destination wedding spot? Very carefully. But seriously—here are our tips:

♥ **First, consider double bagging the dress.** Usually when you buy a dress from a full-service shop, they give you one of those heavy plastic bags made especially for bridal gowns. Consider buying a second bag (they cost from $10 to $25 each) to protect against any rips, tears or splits in the first bag.

♥ **If you're taking the dress on a plane: never check your dress as luggage!** See if you can hang it in one of the garment compartments. If not, lay it as flat as possible in the overhead compartment (you'll have to have the wrinkles steamed out anyway at the wedding location, so don't be too concerned).

♥ **Consider UPS or Fed Ex.** If you can't take the dress on a plane or don't want to be bothered with the hassle, ship it. Leave yourself at least seven working days (double in December) for shipping time. Insure the gown for full value. Send it to a commercial address (that is, the destination wedding hotel, for example).

♥ **Packing**: Stuff bodice and sleeves with tissue paper; wrap in acid-free tissue paper (available at most craft stores); fill the box with peanuts.

♥ **When it gets there.** Find a competent cleaner or bridal shop in your wedding city that can steam your wedding dress for you (note we didn't say press—don't let anyone touch your gown with an iron! The delicate fabric and lace of most gowns rules out ironing. Besides, scorch marks aren't very becoming). Often friends and family can come up with suggestions.

♥ **Hanger hazards.** Lay the dress flat on a bed. DON'T hang the dress for longer than a few hours. The weight of the dress and train can cause it to stretch.

𝒯𝑜𝑝 𝑀𝑜𝑛𝑒𝑦-𝑠𝑎𝑣𝑖𝑛𝑔 𝒮𝑒𝑐𝑟𝑒𝑡𝑠

1 **Purchase a gown online.** Yes, you can buy a gown online—and save a bundle! We found several web sites that sell brand new, name-brand gowns at up to 40% off retail. See the Best Buy section later in this chapter for specifics. Don't want to order your bridal gown online? Well, at least consider it for your bridesmaids' gowns. We'll discuss this in-depth in the next chapter.

2 **Go for a heavily-advertised designer.** If you want to order a dress from a gown discounter, pick a gown from a designer that heavily advertises online or in bridal magazines. Why? It's easier to find a picture of such dresses. Once you know where (and when) a dress was advertised, it's much simpler to get a discount quote. Conversely, pick an obscure designer that rarely advertises and it's darn difficult to price shop.

3 **eBay & Etsy.** Yes, you can use eBay to save on bridal gowns—and headpieces, veils, shoes, tuxes and just about anything else bridal you can think of. Pop the words "bridal gown" into eBay's search function and you'll find 1000+ items up for auction on average. And we're talking about designer brands here folks—on our last visit, we noticed a $3000 silk designer gown by Christos up for auction. The top bid? $425. eBay is for more than just brides trying to sell used gowns—there are online-only bridal shops that offer great deals on eBay. Etsy is another site to look at for affordable gowns, made by small gown makers or importers. (Tip: search Etsy for "bridal gown handmade"). See the Real Wedding Tip box nearby for reader success stories with eBay. And see the next tip for more on saving with eBay.

4 **Buy a gown direct from China.** Why spend $1000 on a bridal gown when you can buy it for just $150? No, that's not a typo. Yes, it is now possible to cut out the middleman and buy your gown direct from China at stunningly low prices. See our Best Buy #2 at the end of this chapter for details.

5 **Haggle.** How can full-price bridal retailers compete with discounters? It's simple: many quietly match prices quoted by web discounters . . . if you ask. These "no frills" discount packages typically offer 20% to 30% discounts if you forgo some of the extra perks shops offer (free pressings, gown bags, and more). The rub: most of these discount deals are completely unadvertised. You have to ask. Also: beware of hidden charges that can turn a discount deal into a bum steer. See the earlier box on hidden gown costs for more on this issue.

6 **Go "off-the-rack."** Chains like David's (reviewed later in this chapter) offer a wide selection of moderately priced gowns with in-stock sizes 2 to 26, as well as women's sizes. Most of David's gowns sell for $600 to $700, about 40% less than the national average. So, are the gowns a great value? No, not really. David's just offers more gowns in-stock in the lower price

REAL WEDDING TIP

eBay Success Stories & Tips

Our readers have been unanimous in their praise of eBay. Here are some of their success stories:

A reader in Florida writes: *"I found my dress on eBay, at a great bargain (I got a $1300 silk dress for only $138!) Granted, many of the dresses on eBay are hideous and should be burned but you can find something nice if you look closely and search well. You can also find veils, shoes, crinoline slips, tuxedo accessories and other items there."*

A reader in Louisville, KY agrees: *"My biggest bargains, thus far, have been found on eBay. I was able to find an Eden silk dress, brand new (but discontinued) for $87, and it is exactly what I wanted! I found my best friend's headpiece for less than half of the price at a salon. And I found my little dyeable flats for $9 (including shipping)."*

Ditto for this reader: *"One of my co-workers found a $3300 Christian Dior gown for just $99. Another friend snagged a designer silk gown (originally $1600) for just $85."*

And the gold metal goes to Catherine C. of Florida: *"I went to a local bridal boutique and fell in love with an Eve of Milady dress that was $6000. I put a reminder on eBay to see if that make and model dress shows up—and sure enough, it did! The Buy It Now price was $3800. I bid $50—and won! With the $20 shipping, I paid a total of $70 for a $6000 dress!"*

If eBay sounds like something you'd like to try, here are some tips:

1. Learn the lingo. eBay has a language all its own—take a second to surf the site's help section to brush up on how auctions work. Learn jargon like NWT—that's an item for sale that is "new with tags."

2. Avoid the tragedy of a missed auction. eBay can notify you via email, instant message or text message for auctions (called Watch Alert). Also: eBay will send you a text message to warn you an auction is about to end.

ranges compared to specialty stores. Quality-wise, a David's $500 gown isn't much better (and some critics would say worse) than those you can find in other stores. And other readers give David's

3. Use credit cards. If possible, never use cash or a check to pay for that winning bid. Instead, pay with a credit card. As we discussed earlier in this chapter, credit cards offer a strong measure of consumer protection against fraud—and that applies to online auctions as well. PayPal offers similar protection with their "purchase protection" policy that offers a full refund in case you don't receive what was promised. This protection covers orders that never arrive, if you receive a different item, an item's condition that was misrepresented or damaged, or a counterfeit.

4. Watch out for subtle clues. Worried that "dream bargain" of a bridal gown will really be a trashed sample? Be careful to pour over the descriptions of items with a fine-tooth comb. Often sellers will leave subtle clues that an item may not be brand new. Email the seller with questions and ask about their return policy.

5. Know thy seller. Look at the seller's feedback. eBay tracks feedback on how sellers have conducted themselves on the site. With one click, you can hear what previous customers say about their experiences. Most sellers try to jealously protect those good ratings—and hence may try to fix any problem you have with the merchandise before you tell the world the seller is a crook.

6. Realize some gown auctioneers are actually bridal shops. eBay isn't just for individual sellers; many bridal retailers have jumped on the bandwagon too. Some stores are desperate to unload their discontinued samples at bargain prices. Yes, these dresses can be steals but be careful—a sample may be trashed from multiple try-ons (try to see detailed pictures of the gown before bidding). And don't think you are safe when buying from an individual—remember that a gown can be altered significantly from its original size. Ask the seller about this issue before bidding.

7. Check with the BBB. A bride in Tennessee emailed this tip. She won an auction for a Maggie Sottero gown from an eBay seller that was a bridal shop. Unfortunately, the shop took her money and never shipped the gown. Turns out the BBB (bbb.org) had 500 complaints on file for this scam artist. While online auction fraud is rare (eBay estimates only one-tenth of a percent of all auctions involve fraud), you still should take steps to check out a seller before bidding.

decidedly mixed reviews on service and delivery. We'll review the chain in depth later in this chapter. Of course, David's isn't the only player in the off-the-rack bridal store business. Gown maker Alfred Angelo has 60+ company-owned stores (alfredangelo-stores.com) that sell gowns off-the-rack.

7 **Craigslist.** Craigslist.org is packed with dress bargains. A search of our local Craigslist site turned up 200+ gowns for sale, including a $50 David's bridal gown (originally $400) and other dresses for half retail. Why do brides sell these gowns? Sometimes weddings are canceled or postponed. In other cases, recent brides who need extra cash are willing to part with their gowns. Most of these gowns are in excellent shape; some have never been worn before. And sometimes you can haggle an even lower price. Of course, you'll need to carefully inspect the gown before buying. Other items available on Craigslist: accessories like crinolines or full slips.

8 **Consider "custom-designing."** If you want a gown that costs over $1000, consider having a local seamstress create a copy of the original. We've seen several beautiful gowns that were custom-designed by talented seamstresses. Why is this a money-saving tip? Well, first a seamstress can often buy the fabric at wholesale (or at a discount from retail). Second, there are no costly alterations—your gown is made to fit. Through several fittings, you can watch the gown take shape and make suggestions along the way. Certainly the labor costs for an expert seamstress can be substantial, but the results can be striking. Total savings here will vary but we priced one exquisite silk Jim Hjelm gown at $2700 retail, which cost only $1400 to reproduce with a local seamstress. The best deals on custom-designed gowns would be on dresses that would retail for $1000, $2000 or more—seamstresses can usually replicate these dresses for far less than what you'd pay in a store. On the other hand, budget polyester gowns that sell for $500 in stores would be hard to duplicate with a seamstress for less money.

9 **Hit a designer sample sale in New York City**. Yes, New York is still the home to many bridal gown designers, a throwback to the days when the entire industry was centered around the garment district in lower Manhattan. When design-ers' warehouses need to be cleaned out, it's sale time! Designer Vera Wang has bi-annual sample sales in New York and Los Angeles (check their blog for the latest schedule). NYmag.com (click on shopping) tracks designer sample sales, updated daily. Another source for sample sale dates: TopButton.com. FYI: Most of these sales are one-day only, first-come, first-serve (although a few sales take appointments). Arrive early for the best deals: up to 80% off retail prices!

10 **Sew it yourself.** We realize this tip isn't for everyone, but if you have a flair for sewing (or know a good friend who does), consider making your gown yourself. Patterns for bridal gowns are readily available at local fabric shops. One such store pointed out to us that the exact materials (fabric, lace, pattern) to make a popular designer dress would cost $300. The retail of this dress was $1500—not counting an extra $250 for alterations. One note of caution: sewing with bridal fabric is challenging so be careful if you go this route.

11 **Buy a "sample" gown.** Bridal shops often sell their samples throughout the year at substantial discounts from retail. Most gowns are marked down at least 50% off, some even more. Since many shops sell most of their gowns by special order, they need these demon-

---

Fabric Sources

Need a source for bridal fabric or trim? Here are some of the sources our readers have cited:

♥ **Hyman Hendler & Sons** (hymanhendler.com) sells fabric and ribbons from both domestic and European sources.
♥ **Dulken & Derrick** (flowersinthecity.com) sells silk flower trim for gowns.
♥ Our readers have also recommended: The Fabric Mart (800-242-3695, fabricmartfabrics.com); Fabric Depot (888-392-3376, fabricdepot.com); McGowen's (908) 965-2298; on Facebook as McGowen's Fabric Outlet.

For further reading: *Bridal Couture: Fine Sewing Techniques for Wedding Gowns & Evening Wear* by Susan Khalje (Krause Publications) is an excellent resource for brides who want a custom bridal gown. Even if you don't want to make a dress yourself, the book includes extensive information on fabrics, laces and proper construction techniques. FYI: This book is now out of print, but still available on Amazon and in local libraries.

strator samples to entice orders. What happens when a gown is discontinued or they need more room for new styles? It's sale time! Some shops have big sample sales throughout the year. However, most shops have a rack of discounted sample gowns year-round. Before you use this recommendation, read our PITFALLS section for special tips on buying a sample dress.

12 **Wear your mom's dress or borrow a friend's gown.** You'd be surprised how inexpensively a seamstress can restore a vintage gown. Even if you spend $100 to $200 to have the gown altered or jazzed up, this will be much less than buying a gown at retail. Borrowing a gown from a friend is another great money-saving option. Total savings = $800 or even more!

13 **The white bridesmaid dress trick** Most brides don't realize that many bridesmaids' gowns can be ordered in white. For a less formal wedding, you can get a plain bridesmaid's gown for just $100 to $200. Beautiful, less-formal gowns (without trains, sequins, pearls, etc.) are available from ready-to-wear clothing designers like Jessica McClintock with prices that start under $200. Jazz up a bridesmaid's gown in white with a detachable train (one bride told us she had a seamstress make one for $25 plus the cost of fabric) and you have a bridal gown at a fraction of the bridal price. One caveat: some designers have tried to stop this trend by charging a penalty fee (an extra $100) for any bridesmaid gown ordered in white. Is white fabric more expensive? Nope, designers just don't want to cannibalize their wedding gown sales. Also: some designers like Vera Wang and Amsale will not sell you a single bridesmaid gown in white or ivory; instead you have to order a minimum of three. That minimum doesn't apply to colored bridesmaids' dresses.

14 **Don't buy a "bridal" gown.** What is a wedding dress anyway but a white gown? You can often save when you shop at places that don't sell "bridal gowns." Many department stores and specialty shops sell white formal dresses—at prices that are significantly less than so-called bridal shops. Shhhh! Don't tell anyone, but these dresses can easily be used as the perfect dress for your wedding.

15 **Check out vintage clothing shops.** A reader in Berkeley, CA shared with us a great bargain shopping tip: vintage clothing stores. In Berkeley, she found a beautiful 1950's wedding gown in excellent condition for just $200 at a vintage shop. Most large cities have such stores; search for "Clothes—Vintage" in your home town or nearby. Want to have a seamstress replicate a vintage gown? We found a great web site on this subject: Sense and Sensibility Patterns (sensibility.com), which has vintage wedding dress patterns, sewing tips, links and more. Another idea: go medieval to save on your wedding gown. RomanticThreads.com has medieval, Victorian and other vintage style wedding dresses. Most gowns are under $500—well priced considering the quality of the fabric and unique designs.

16 Go "new" vintage. A new vintage-inspired gown is another great way to save. What is new vintage? It is a brand new gown that is designed to look vintage. An example: MartinMccrea.com sells 50 styles of affordable vintage gowns for under $1000—and they are all hand-assembled in the US, not imported from China. A reader praised Mccrea's service ("emails are answered promptly and the service was incredibly helpful and friendly") as well as the dress sizes ("true to life and they will custom-size any dress to fit). "The quality of the dress was superb and shipping was only $10," she said.

17 Shop at bridal outlet stores. Scattered across the country are outlet stores for bridal designers and retailers that offer substantial savings. See the Best Buy section later in this chapter for more info.

18 Buy a pre-owned gown. Just like a new car that loses a bundle of cash when you drive it off the lot, a bridal gown has similar steep depreciation. Savvy bargain hunters have found steals in the second-hand gown market.

You can shop on or offline—retail consignment shops dot most major cities. Most second-hand gowns sell for at least HALF their original price tags, depending on the condition. How can you find a good consignment bridal shop? An online source for consignment shops is the National Association of Resale and Thrift Stores at narts.org. Or bypass stores and look online (see sources in the nearby box, Sell That Gown).

As we discussed nearby, Tradesy.com is a general consignment web site that has an amazing wedding section. You can pick up an Amsale dress for 75% off or shop for other name designers. The site let's you zero in on styles like destination weddings to retro, traditional to vintage.

One caveat: there is a limit to how many times a gown can be altered without losing its basic design. Consider how much a dress has been previously altered before you buy. The best advice: if you find a second-hand gown you want, place a small deposit ($25) to hold it. Come back to the shop with a seamstress and let her look it over to make sure alterations can be successful and cost effective. If the second-hand shop has a seamstress, get this evaluation in writing—"the gown had these previous alterations, needs the following work and the cost would be $X." That way if there's a problem, you'll have a paper trail.

19 **Recoup your gown expense—pre-arrange to sell it after the wedding.** Even if you buy a dress at full retail, you can still lower your gown expense by selling the gown after the wedding. Dozens of readers tell us they have pre-arranged selling their gown on sites like Craigslist or on dedicated bridal resale sites (see Sell That Gown box nearby). Even if you recoup half of what you paid, this could still add up to hundreds of dollars.

20 **Swap the fabric.** Fallen in love with a silk gown but can't afford the silk price? You still might be able to afford that gown—just ask if the manufacturer offers the same style in a less-expensive fabric. Not all designers offer this option, but it might be worth asking. You can save $300 or more with a simple fabric swap.

21 **Check the next state over.** A reader in Los Angeles emailed us this tip. She found the same, brand-new designer gown that cost $2200 to special order in LA . . . for just $1300 in a Portland, Oregon shop. Another bonus: Oregon has no sales tax, saving the bride another 9% ($200). Why the major price difference? It's hard to say, but expensive overhead in big cities like LA or NYC sometimes leads to bigger mark-ups. Hence, it may pay to check out prices in a nearby state (check the designer's web site to find the names of other nearby dealers). Remember that if you order a gown in another state and have it shipped home across state lines, you may not have to pay any sales tax. Yes, you have to arrange for alterations on your own, but that typically isn't much of a challenge.

22 **Make a run for the border.** If you live near the Mexican border, look for deals in border towns like Juarez (near El Paso, Texas). There are 33 bridal shops on several blocks of Avenida Lerdo in Juarez selling bridal gowns and bridesmaids for half of retail prices. One tip: a bride suggested NOT telling the shops if you've traveled a long distance—shops tend to charge higher prices to brides who have made major trips to gown shop, figuring you are likely to spend more than brides who live just across the border.

23 **Buy a gown in the "off season."** What's the best time to get the biggest bargains on a wedding dress? Try shopping anytime between Thanksgiving and Christmas. Most bridal shops are absolutely dead in November and December. Hence, many retailers are willing and ready to cut you a deal. Be aware, however, that bargains evaporate after Christmas, as the shops get busy again after all those holiday engagements.

Sell that gown!

Every bride is looking for the perfect dress. So what if you think you've found the "one," only to see another gown you absolutely love? Or another?

It happens. And if it happens to you, you may be in a quandary trying to figure out what to do with those extra gowns.

But don't worry, there are lots of good options for brides who need to thin out their bridal closets. First, you can always list your dress on Craigslist. Yes, folks are often looking for a deal, so you may not get close to the original purchase price. eBay is another option and you can set a minimum price so you don't have to settle for pennies on the dollar. It might take longer to sell, but you'll get closer to what you want.

How about sites that specialize in bridal resales? Here are our top picks: NearlyNewlywed.com, WoreItOnce.com, and PreOwnedWeddingDresses.com. And some general resale sites have excellent wedding sections—Tradesy.com is a good example.

If you decide to resell that extra bridal gown, make sure you can set the selling price and update information including pictures at any time. Most services charge a listing fee of around $25. Be sure to check how long the listing is good for—some last six months, others a whole year . . . or as long as it takes to sell the dress.

NearlyNewlywed.com offers an interesting hybrid service—showroom sales. While you can sell your dress with them online ($25 fee; you get 75% of the sale price), the showroom service allows you to sell your gown in their New York City showroom. This costs $100 and you get 65% of the sales prices.

Make sure the sites protect your privacy—double check the site's privacy policy. Find out how many pictures and how much information you can include in your listing. Some sites limit the number of pictures while others let you go all out. Finally, if you choose a site to list your dress, make sure you check the requirements for photo size limits.

Remember that you need to be very descriptive when you list your gown. Include lots of information and detail on things like train length, type of and amount of lace, beadwork, neckline and waistline style, color, lining, built in crinoline, etc. The more information you give, the fewer questions you'll have to answer.

Finally, if you are feeling generous and don't want to list your gown, consider donating it to charity. See our Real Wedding Tip box on Charity Sale Success later in this chapter.

24 **Hire a student.** Got a fashion school nearby? The Academy of Art in San Francisco (888-493-3261; academyart.edu) refers students and recent graduates who can do custom wedding dresses. One reader told us she got a price quote of $500 (including fabric) for an elaborate gown, which is quite a deal. Search online for nearby fashion schools/colleges to see if one is close to you.

25 **Look for charity sales.** Brides Against Breast Cancer (bridesabc.org), a non-profit foundation based in Sarasota, FL that grants final wishes to women with breast cancer, holds charity bridal gown sales across the country in over a dozen major cities. All gowns are donated by brides (who get a tax write-off) and all the proceeds go to the foundation's work. Over 3000 gowns are sold each year at these sales, held in major cities nationwide. After the wedding, why not donate your gown back to the charity, get a tax deduction and help a worthy cause. We visited a recent sale in our home town and were impressed—as you might expect, there is a large selection of gowns in the 8-12 sizes. But we also saw a large rack of gowns sized 2-6; and another with sizes 18-24. One tip: try on gowns at another venue before you hit the sale, so you can zero in on a particular silhouette and look.

REAL WEDDING TIP

Charity sale success

Reader Jaclyn H. snagged a great deal on a dress at this charity dress sale:

Last night I attended a charity gown sale in New York City sponsored by Brides Against Breast Cancer. The gown sale consists of used gowns donated by past brides, as well as brand new gowns donated by designers. The best part of this sale is the prices. In fact, I purchased a new Anne Barge gown, originally priced at $3,950 for only $1299 . . . the total came out to $1407 with NY tax, but is that a deal or what? More than that though, the volunteers were incredibly helpful and there was even a seamstress who gave wonderful advice. It was a truly wonderful experience, and what makes it even more wonderful is the fact that my money will be going to a good cause.

26 **Go for a knock-off.** Like a David's bridal gown style, but scared off by the chain's customer service reputation? Consider a knock-off of David's called DaVinci (DaVinciBridal.com). Made by Impression (rated later in this chapter), DaVinci's line is a dress-for-dress copy of David's—at prices 20% to 50% below David's. For example, one strapless A-line gown is sold by David's for $900; DaVinci's copy is $550. Sold in specialty stores nationwide, DaVinci also has bridesmaids' gowns for $90 to $160. The quality of DaVinci is similar to David's—that is, most dresses are made of synthetic fabrics and sewn in China. But the value is excellent.

So, is it fair for DaVinci to copy David's? Well, as you'll read later in our discussion of David's, that chain is famous for copying the looks of other designers like Maggie Sottero. Hence DaVinci is merely copying David's copies!

27 **Shop at a place without the word "bridal" in its name.** Sometimes the best deals on bridal are from stores that don't have "wedding" on their sign. Did you know that brands JCrew, Ann Taylor and Anthropologie all have bridal divisions with prices that start at as little as $300?

So, how's the quality? Very good, our readers report. "The dress is fully lined, 100% silk and fits great! The dresses are not that horrible 'bridal cut,' so I actually got a dress in a size that I wear normally! So on my wedding day, I'll feel like a queen and not a cow!" said one bride.

28 **Get your veil at a discount.** Veils, headpieces and tiaras are sold at outrageous prices in retail shops . . . it should be a federal crime to sell a comb with a spritz of pearls and a bit tulle for $300. But that's exactly what you'd see at retail for these items.

There are two key ways to save: sew it yourself or buy it online at a discount. Let's look at each.

Sure, sewing a bridal gown is a massive undertaking but what about a veil and headpiece? The average bridal veil and headpiece is little more than a comb (or headband) with some ribbons, silk flowers and a few fake pearls. Attach a veil and poof! You've got a bridal headpiece. Our advice: make your own. Go to any craft store like Michaels (800-MICHAELS, michaels.com) and pick up the forms and supplies to do it yourself. One reader found rhinestone tiaras at Michaels for $15 to $40 and ribbon edged veils for $15. See the box nearby for success stories.

Okay, you're not a crafty-type person. In that case, buy that headpiece online. Our readers have had great success buying tiaras, headpieces and veils online, at big discounts. Let's look at the best sites:

We've heard several good reviews about **VeilShop.com**, whose well-designed site included detailed pictures, great prices (many tiaras under

$100), videos and the option to order headpieces separately from veils (so you can do your own veil if so inclined). **Wedding–veil.com** is a Colorado-based site with a well-designed web site that makes it easy to shop for tiaras, veils, and more. We liked the detailed FAQ and low price guarantee. One reader gave their service an A+, saying she saved half off on her veil compared to retail prices.

Mary R. of Burbank, CA emailed us a recommendation for **BridalVeilCreations.com**. Her 120" plain edged veil was $68. The site sells veils from $22, or you can customize a veil with a special length, edging and more.

Real Wedding Tip

Make your own headpieces!

Naomi from New York wrote to us about why brides should consider making their own headpieces:

"You mention in your book that most veils and headpieces cannot possibly, in labor or materials, equal the $150-$300 price tag. I tended to agree when I read this, but must admit that I didn't really realize how true this was until I took a visit to a bridal salon. After selecting my gown, I thought it would be a good idea to try on a few headpieces. I did keep an eye on the prices, they ranged from $90 (a comb, a few "silk" flowers, a few ribbon streamers, no veil) to $150 (an elbow tip veil with a slightly embellished comb) to $190 (a "silver" headband wrapped with plastic beads and a few "silk" roses, no veil). How could anyone possibly buy these? Your point, however, was really driven home when I spied a rather simple veil. It was shoulder-length, had no beading, no special finishes, the comb undecorated and as far as I could possibly tell, was made out of plain tulle. You can imagine my reaction when I flipped over the tag. No kidding: $290. I stopped trying on veils at that point.

"A few days later I thought to myself, maybe it's hard to make veils, maybe that's why they're so pricey. Change of mind came quickly after making a trip to my local fabric and crafts store. I bought two patterns, some materials and headed home for an afternoon of crafting. All in all, it was a fun day and at the end I had myself a beautiful, fingertip veil attached to a crown of organza roses and silk lilies. Was it hard to make? No. And the cost of my unique and elegant headpiece? No word of a lie, $40."

Etsy.com is a web site that connects small craftspeople with buyers. Type veil into their search engine and you'll come up with dozens of handmade options at affordable prices.

29 **Rent a gown.** If a groom can rent a tux, why can't a bride rent a gown? RentTheRunway.com has a "For the Bride" section that offers dozens of gowns that can be rented for as little as $50. Example: a Mark & James Badgley Mischka sleeveless gown made of white crinkle chiffon retails for $375, but can be rented for just $100. Accessories like jewelry, purses and more can also be rented.

Another bride from Los Angeles wrote:

"Brides, I am certainly no Seamstress Extraordinaire, but, for gosh sake, MAKE YOUR OWN VEILS! There are all kinds of guides and patterns at craft stores—costume patterns and historical fashion/costumes books also make excellent sources. Unless you want a rhinestone tiara, please skip the (ahem) "professional" bridal veils. For about $12.50 (that's 3 yards of tulle, some fabric glue, thread, trim, and an extra-large comb from the 99¢ store) I will be making a better-quality veil than what I've seen in these so-called 'exclusive' salons. . . and it means more to me personally, too. For example, I am also using 24 faux-pearls from an old, broken necklace once belonging to my grandma. The pearls are far better quality than the plastic monstrosities used today, and have the added bonus of being sentimental."

Finally, Anne O. of San Francisco shared this story:

"I have to pass along the greatest bargain. After much searching for a simple hair comb or headpiece for my wedding, the only one I found that I liked was $325 at an expensive bridal boutique in San Francisco. I found that price outrageous since it consisted of two simple twisted strands of freshwater pearls on a four-inch metal comb. After some research, I found The Bead Shop in Palo Alto, CA (beadshop.com). They sell plain combs and every different type, size and color of beads, crystals and pearls you can imagine. They also have step-by-step instructions online on how to make hair combs, which was great because I am NOT a creative or artsy person in any way. But I was able to buy the comb, and one strand of freshwater pearls for about $40 total. I made my own hair comb in about 30 minutes and it looks exactly like the $325 boutique version!"

Games that Bridal Shops Play

Once you identify local bridal shops you want to visit, the fun begins! It's time to hit the streets! But before you get caught up in the whirlwind of Italian satin and imported lace, take a second to learn about some of the games, tricks and scams you might encounter out there. No, not all bridal retailers play these games, but judging by the email complaints we get from brides, this is a problem with many shops. Let's expose some of the tactics you may encounter while searching for a gown:

1 Mystery Gowns. Many bridal shops rip the tags out of their sample dresses to keep you from knowing who designed and manufactured the gown. When asked, these shop owners simply refuse to tell brides who made the dresses. Why would they do this? We've interviewed many shop owners who basically admit they do it to prevent brides from price shopping their dresses. Hey, they argue, if we tell you the designer, then you'll go down the street to our competitor and get the dress at a discount.

The modern term is "showrooming"—using a retail store as a showroom and then buying the product online or elsewhere for less.

The way some retailers see it, you are supposed to plunk down the money . . . and not ask any questions. Are you getting a designer silk original from Europe—or a cheap polyester copy from China? Who knows? Keeping the designer info secret is a sneaky way for some shops to pass off an inferior gown as a premium product.

What is most perplexing about this deceptive practice is the fact that most brides find out about the shop from a designer's ad online or in a bridal magazine. Designers spend millions trying to get brides to recognize their brand name and for what? To have their retailers tear out the tags is stupid, especially under the guise of stopping "price competition."

Not only is it stupid, it's also illegal. A federal law called the Textile Fiber Products Identification Act of 1963 requires all apparel (yes, even bridal) to be properly labeled. This must include the name of the manufacturer (or their "registered number" assigned by the Federal Trade Commission,ftc.gov) as well as the fiber content and country of origin. Both federal and state laws forbid the removal of these tags. Sadly, many bridal shops openly and flagrantly violate this long-standing consumer law. Why? They know they won't get busted, since the FTC doesn't have any bridal police running around to enforce the rules.

There is one big loophole in the label law, however: shops *can* remove manufacturers' tags as long as they substitute their own tags with the store name and the required information (fiber content, country of origin, care instructions). For imported gowns (the vast majority of all gowns sold in the US are made overseas), this store tag must be sewn into the garment. While this sounds like a big loophole, we've noticed many stores don't even bother to replace tags. They just rip out the designer tags and slap on a hangtag that simply lists the price and an internal store code—and omits all the required information.

You can read more about tag requirements at the Federal Trade Commission's web site at ftc.gov. The FTC has a special publication entitled "Wedding Gown Labels: Unveiling the Requirements" at http://1.usa.gov/XetW7A.

What if you encounter a shop that rips tags and won't reveal info on the dress as required by law? File a complaint with the FTC. The FTC's web site (ftc.gov) has a quick and easy link. The FTC will only take this problem seriously if they receive a good number of complaints from brides. Second, post a message on this to our web site, BridalBargainsBook.com. Click on the message boards and post your story to the bridal gown section. This will warn other readers about such shops.

So, why all the fuss about tags? Without it, you can fall victim to a series of consumer scams we've documented:

♥ **Price Gouging.** By hiding the manufacturer's name, you cannot tell whether you're looking at a designer original . . . or a cheap knock-off made by a copy house. With over 200 manufacturers and importers of bridal apparel sold in North America, there is a WIDE difference in quality of construction, fabric and detailing. We think you have the right to know what you are buying. Tag-ripping bridal shops sometimes try to pawn off affordable tag-less dresses for hundreds *over* the typical retail.

♥ **Fabric fraud.** With the fiber content label torn from dresses, it's hard to say whether the dress you're looking at is silk or polyester. In recent years, many new synthetic fabrics have come on the market that mimic the look and feel of silk. While these fabrics have creative names ("silky satin," for example), they are all polyester or blends. Unscrupulous retailers try to pass off these fabrics as silk.

♥ **Sweatshops and slave labor.** Most bridal gowns are made overseas, typically in Asia. A handful are still sewn in the US, Canada or Europe—these gowns are generally perceived to be of higher quality. When the bridal shop removes a gown's tag that indicates the country of origin, you don't know whether the dress is handcrafted in the USA . . . or mass-produced in a sweatshop in China.

So, what happens when you ask a bridal retailer point blank "Who makes this gown?" Well, some refuse to answer that question. Others say they'll happily tell you the brand . . . AFTER you place down that hefty 50% deposit (which is non-refundable, of course). You'd be offended if you ran into the same practice in an appliance or electronics store, but for some reason bridal retailers think they can get away with it.

What about style numbers? Well, while federal law prevents the removal of manufacturer, fiber content and country of origin tags, there is NO requirement to reveal a gown's style number (a unique number assigned to each dress). Often, bridal shops will tag their dresses with secret codes, not the actual style numbers.

Are designers upset about retailers that rip out their names from their gowns? Well, yes and no. Some designers (Demetrios/Ilissa, for one) have sent letters to their retailers warning them not to rip tags. Most designers could care less. Why? Most bridal gown makers are just concerned with selling samples into bridal stores; they don't care what the retailers do with the gowns after they get them (as long as they pay their bills, of course).

The bottom line: you're probably going to encounter this problem when you gown shop. We found three out of four bridal shops rip tags and violate federal label laws. This happens in both big and small cities, from some of the country's biggest gown sellers in New York and LA to the smallest town in Alabama.

Solution: Find a few dresses you like online and download those pictures. Then walk into the shops listed as dealers and ask to see those specific dresses. If the salespeople say they don't know who makes which gowns, don't believe them. Before you walk out, you may mention to the salesperson that they just lost a big sale.

Another creative solution: look at wedding message boards on sites like the WeddingBee.com. We've noticed that many brides have posted the key to crack the codes at popular shops. (Most shops aren't terribly creative in how they encode the designer and style number info).

Finally, if you can find a RN (registered number) in an otherwise anonymous gown, you can look up who the manufacturer is online. The FTC has a RN look-up web page: http://1.usa.gov/10DuS8a. Pop in an RN and poof! You can discover the designer!

2 **Nickel and dime charges.** So you thought only airlines pile on extra fees? As if bridal gowns weren't expensive enough, some independent bridal retailers have started to add a series of extra charges to inflate your final bill. Examples:

♥ TRY-ON FEES. Hard to believe, but some shops actually charge their customers to try on their dresses! One shop charges their brides $50 for an hour of dress up! Other shops only sock out-of-town brides with such fees (they figure in-town brides are more likely to buy). How do they know you are from out of town? These retailers force all brides to register before browsing the racks—and the registration card asks for your address (as well as other personal information like age, income,

Top 7 Most Outrageous Excuses For Why Bridal Shops Rip Tags

Our email box is always stuffed with brides' gown tales. As a public service, we have been cataloging the most creative excuses used by bridal retailers as to why they rip tags out of their wedding gowns. Yes, these are actual words uttered by retailers to consumers:

1. "The tags are removed to protect the feelings of brides since dress sizes are larger than those in street clothes."

2. "Bridal gown manufacturers forbid us to tell you who makes which dress. So, it's out of our hands."

3. "It's in the computer and that's down, so we don't know."

4. "Designers don't put tags in dresses for copyright purposes (to keep their gowns from being copied) and shops can't do anything about that."

5. "Only the store's buyer knows who makes each dress and she's not telling."

6. "All our dresses are made exclusively for this store in the Orient, so there are no brand names.

7. "We don't know who makes which dress, but if you pay us a 50% non-refundable deposit, we can find out!"

blood type, etc). While try-on fees are typically deducted if you make a purchase, we can't think of any better way to drive brides to chain stores than such bogus fees.

♥ SHIPPING AND HANDLING. More mom-and-pop shops are slapping brides with shipping and handling fees for any special order. Bridal gown? $10 to $20 in shipping charges. Bridesmaids, $5 to $10 EACH. Veils, headpieces, shoes and anything else is $5 or more. We could understand shipping fees if these items were shipped to your home, but that's not the case in Bridal World. Here, retailers charge you shipping to have an item sent from their supplier to the BRIDAL STORE. Then you have to go pick it up! Even more deceptive: shops that claim these shipping charges also cover "insurance." "What girl doesn't want insurance for her gown against damage?" one retailer told us, bragging that their customers have never questioned this. Why this is bogus: ALL retailers must deliver you a gown free from damage, if you special order brand new merchandise. If UPS damages your gown in route from the maker to the store, the shop has to make good on the deal, whether you paid for "insurance" or not.

♥ **ACCOUNTING SURCHARGES.** A Jacksonville, FL bridal shop charges brides a $10 "accounting surcharge" for special orders that are not paid in full at the time of ordering. Never mind that the industry standard for special orders is almost always half down with the balance due when the goods are delivered. (Yes, there are exceptions, but more on this later). Either shops should do the standard half-down deal or require payment up front—surcharges for those who don't pay in full are ridiculous. Another questionable accounting charge: credit card surcharges. Some shops tack on another $5 to $10 for orders paid by credit cards (especially if the order is paid by phone for bridesmaid dresses, for example).

♥ **PENALTY FEE.** Yes, you can save money by ordering a gown mail order or online, but beware of the penalty box when it comes to alterations. In order to punish brides who buy from discount sources, some bridal retailers add special "penalty fees" and surcharges to do alterations on such gowns. Some shops boost their alterations rates 15% to 50% over regular fees or others add a flat $10 to $100 extra charge to alter any dress *not* bought in their store.

♥ **NO SHOW CHARGE.** Want to make an appointment to see gowns at Kleinfeld, one of the largest bridal retailers in the New York area made famous the TV show "Say Yes to the Dress"? First, you'll have to whip out your credit card. If you don't show up for your appointment or fail to cancel within 48 hours, Kleinfeld will charge you a $50 "no show" fee. Yes, amazing but true. Noticeably, Kleinfeld doesn't pay brides $50 if *Kleinfeld* is late, making a bride wait for her appointment.

♥ **STORAGE FEES.** You're getting married in June, but your gown arrives early in March. Should you let the bridal shop store it for you? Unfortunately, many now charge for this service—one bride in Sacramento said a local shop there quoted her $11 *per month* in storage fees. We say don't do it. First, this is an unnecessary expense, especially if you have room at your home or apartment to keep the gown. Second, bridal shops aren't Fort Knox—they burn down, get robbed or flat out disappear. It is probably safer to keep your gown at your own home.

♥ **BAG CHARGE.** You're not going to throw that gown in your trunk, right? Instead, why not protect your gown in our special oversized zippered garment bags? Chains like David's and specialty salons charge brides $10 to $20 for a gown bag. Here's a secret: shops pay just $1 to

$2 wholesale for those bags because they buy them in bulk. That's the bridal biz in a nutshell: how to sell a $4 plastic bag for $20 bucks!

♥ **LIGHT BULB FEE.** Just kidding—but will it be long before some bridal retailer decides to charge brides $25 to use the light bulbs in their dressing rooms?

Why do shops try to zap brides with all these bogus fees? Because they know MOST brides only look at the price of the gown, not the charges for all those little "extras."

We find these nickel and dime charges offensive since they are RARELY disclosed to the bride until the order is written. That way brides will fall in love with a gown before they are hit with the shipping fees, accounting charges and whatever bogus fees a retailer can dream up.

The obvious defense against this is to ask about any extra charges up front, before you start trying on gowns. Yes there are some "legitimate" extra charges—fees for larger sizes, rush delivery, etc. (more on these later). But be careful that your local bridal retailer doesn't try to sneak in some bogus fees on to the final bill.

3 **The Big Fuss.** No matter what gowns you try on, the salesperson that helps you will invariably gush and say something like "That dress is sooooo beautiful!" Sometimes I wonder if I tried on a gown made out of potato sacks, the salesperson would say something like "Wow! That organic look! It's so you!"

As you might have guessed, most salespeople at bridal shops work on commission. Hence, it's to their advantage to get you to buy any gown, preferably an expensive one. The pressure to buy can get even more intense at designer "trunk shows" (see the previous box for more details).

Much of this fuss is to get you to buy NOW. Here is how one retailer advised fellow bridal shop owners on an industry chat board:

> "I have been telling my brides when they find their dream dress to buy it now. They won't find anything they like better and will just keep second-guessing themselves. If they wait to order, the dress just might not be available. Create urgency and doubt. If you wait... you may not get your dream gown. Tell them stories of disappointed brides who waited. Ask for the sale—and pray!"

The bottom line: yes, dresses DO get discontinued. But not overnight—no dress deal is so good you can't even sleep on it (or take a day or two to compare prices online). Don't wait forever (several weeks or months is courting disaster), but don't be pressured into making a snap decision either.

To avoid pressure from shops, bring ONE trusted friend or relative with you whose opinion you value—this ensures a more objective critique. Another tip: consider leaving your wallet at home. That way you're not tempted to rush into a dress decision (and non-refundable deposit) in the heat of the moment.

4 False Discounts. We have found cases of some bridal retailers who mark their gowns over suggested retail and then offer you a "discount." Gee, thanks! For example, we visited one shop that was offering a 10% discount off all special-order gowns. One gown we saw had a price tag of $1500—we later learned the suggested retail for the gown was just $1350. Their big 10% discount knocked $150 off the gown, bringing the price down to . . . $1350.

Solution: Find the actual retail price for your dress. Email any of the dress discounters discussed later in this chapter (such as RKBridal.com

Designer Trunk Shows: Tips & Traps

Bridal gown designers do have something in common with rock stars—occasionally, both go on tour. For dressmakers, these tours include personal appearances at various bridal shops where they are the stars of "trunk shows." But just what the heck are these trunk shows and are they any benefit to you, the bride?

Trunk shows are "limited time" events where designers will show off their complete collection of gowns at a bridal retail shop (or department store). Brides can meet one-on-one with the designer and discuss the right dress for them.

The advantage for consumers is obvious: for once, you can see a designer's ENTIRE line of dresses. Stores can only stock a limited number of gowns; trunk shows give you the whole enchilada. Another big plus: face time lets you ask designers about possible changes to a dress. The result: a customized dress that's right for you.

Of course, that's the upside. Here are some traps to look out for, plus some general tips for getting the most out of trunk shows:

♥ **UNDER PRESSURE.** Trunk shows typically last only two to three days (say, Thursday to Saturday). After that, most of the gowns are gone. If you want to go back next weekend and show the dress to your mom, tough luck. As a result, you feel tremendous and PearlsPlace.com) and they'll tell you the actual retail, along with their discounted price.

5 Elusive Exclusives. Some bridal designers occasionally give one shop in a city an "exclusive" over certain dresses. These dresses are termed "confined," and you can't find them anywhere else in town. Or can you? Many bridal shops skirt these exclusive rules by a process called "transshipping."

We visited several shops that told us they could order *any* gown we want, even if they don't carry it in their store. How do they do this? Transshipping—a bridal shop that does NOT carry a designer line will turn to another retailer who does to place the order.

Is transshipping illegal? No, there is no law that forbids this practice. However, bridal designers HATE transshipping (which lets retailers skirt their minimum stock requirements) and a few force their dealers to sign agreements saying they will not transship. These agreements are then widely ignored by retailers.

pressure to make a quick decision. The best advice: shop extensively before you go to a trunk show. That way you know whether a "here-today, gone-tomorrow" dress is the right one . . . or you need to keep looking.

♥ **FORGET DISCOUNTS.** Given all the hoopla surrounding trunk shows, you might think the gowns would be on sale. Ha! The gowns are almost always sold at full retail. The best you can hope for is to negotiate for changes to a dress design without any additional charges.

♥ **PLAN IN ADVANCE.** Designers typically visit a city only once a year. Miss that one weekend and you're out of luck. Of course, most bridal designers post trunk show schedules well in advance on their web sites (as well as on the Knot's Event Calendar).

♥ **MAKE AN APPOINTMENT.** Some designer trunk shows can be mobbed. The best advice is to make an appointment in advance. Typically, you will be given an hour or two time-slot to try on gowns.

♥ **BE PREPARED.** Just in case you decide to order a gown at a trunk show, make sure you're prepared. In order to take correct measurements, you should bring any special undergarments or shoes you plan to wear on your wedding day.

Why does transshipping happen to begin with? Most bridal shops are small in scale and can only stock ten to 12 lines of bridal apparel. But there are over 200 apparel designers out there, and odds are a customer may want a dress they don't carry. Instead of losing the sale, the shop places the order through back-door channels (typically, a friend who owns a bridal shop that does carry the line). By the way, shops often add a small mark-up for the trouble of ordering a dress from another shop.

By limiting the distribution of certain dresses (or entire lines), designers hope to stop the discounting of their gowns. However, designers also need to sell dresses to make a living—and restricting the sale of a dress design to one shop in a huge city doesn't make financial sense.

In fact, that's why we've noticed many designers talk out of both sides of their mouths when it comes to this issue. While they rail against the evils of transshipping and discounting (keeping their retailers happy), the apparel designers then quietly sell to known transshippers. Others turn a blind eye to discounting since, of course, they end up selling more dresses (and making more profit).

The latest twist to this debate involves online gown sellers. Designers once could control their distribution by just selling to a few small shops, which sold gowns in their local markets. Yet that all has gone out the window with the web—now, shops can sell their goods worldwide, if they wish.

To stop this, some designers have issued "no 'net" policies, forbidding their dealers from selling online. Among the biggest designers to do this are Mon Cheri and Alfred Angelo. Of course, manufacturers once again cheat on this—many (including Angelo) quietly sell to dot-coms while officially banning the practice. Crazy, eh?

What does this mean for you the consumer? Be careful of bridal shops or web sites that promise they can get in "any dress you want." Call the designer to see if the shop/site is an authorized dealer. Check with past client references and the Better Business Bureau to make sure the shop has fulfilled its previous promises. The bottom line: that "exclusive" dress may not be that exclusive. Don't be fooled into thinking it can't be found from another source.

6 Service? What service? The debate over the web versus Main Street usually breaks down to one central point: do you want the absolute rock-bottom lowest price? Or are you willing to pay a bit more to get service from a locally-owned business?

The usual implication here is the local merchant has a large staff standing at the door, waiting to greet you and lavish attention, as they search to find the "perfect gown" in your budget range. Or at least that's the way bridal industry makes it sound.

Fast forward to reality: service even at "full service" bridal shops can often be, well, lacking. As one bride wrote in a blog "Are these folks who write for bridal web sites on meth or am I living in the wrong city? I've been to SEVERAL bridal salons and literally at each one, some salesperson doesn't even ask my name, takes me to a room, brings in 3-4 winter gowns (for an outdoor July wedding) and leaves me alone to find my way into the big dress by myself (isn't it like crawling head first into a white sleeping bag?) Then the salesperson stops by 40 minutes later to see which one I want to buy. Meanwhile, I'm clipping this damn dress myself to keep it from falling off and talking to myself in the fitting room to keep myself from dying of boredom. What's the deal?"

The sad truth: just like many other retail industries today, service at bridal shops is sometimes sorely lacking. We find this especially ironic in light of the ongoing debate about national chains and buying online. Retailers can't expect brides to pay full price when they get far less than full service; no wonder many brides are abandoning independent retailers to order online or even (gasp) shopping chains like David's.

Yes, not all retailers have let service slip. Yet, shops that truly service the bride seem to be more the exception these days than the rule.

Biggest Myths about Bridal Gowns

MYTH #1 *"Considering how expensive those designer bridal gowns are, I assume they are being hand-crafted by skilled seamstresses."*

Wrong. Most so-called designer gowns are made overseas in factories in China or other Asian countries, mass-produced in batches and machine stitched or beaded. Here's how they are made:

First, the bridal manufacturers wait until they receive a certain number of orders for each size (that's why it takes so long to get a gown). Let's say they wait for ten orders of size 8 gowns in a particular style. When the orders come in, they stack ten layers of fabric on a conveyer belt, which are then cut by a laser. Later, machines sew the seams together. Even the lace added to the dress may have been machine-beaded at another location. This partially explains why so many gowns have "quality issues," with unfinished seams, no lining and shoddy construction.

The manufacturing process has more to do with automated assembly lines than seamstresses hand-sewing gowns. As a result, gowns are not custom-made to your measurements but rather are rough approximations that often require additional alterations (read: more of your money).

And China isn't the only place churning out weddings gowns on the cheap. Many bridal dress manufacturers roam the globe searching for cheap labor. The goal is to produce the dress at the lowest cost, not necessarily the highest quality. Many bridal gowns imported from Central

America or Southeast Asia suffer from quality problems that often have to be fixed by bridal retailers.

Yes, there are a handful of bridal gown makers that still hand-sew gowns here in the US, Canada or Europe, although that number seems to be shrinking every year. Unfortunately, you pay through the nose for such dresses—most are $2000 or more.

Are dresses made in the US or Europe automatically better quality than those imported from China? Ten years ago, we might have said yes. But today, improved technology and Chinese production skills have closed the quality gap. Differences between domestic and imported gowns may have to do more with materials than craftsmanship. The few remaining "couture" designers in the US or Europe are likely to use fine silk fabrics and fancy embellishments on their $4000 gowns. Imported gowns from China are most likely polyester gowns with lower-end finishes.

MYTH #2 *"I saw a dress in a bridal store that was made of Italian satin. Is that a luxury fabric from Europe?"*

Actually, no. More than likely it's a synthetic fabric made in Asia. Of course, Italian satin sounds more romantic than, say, Filipino Polyester. But that's what it is—and that points up a common marketing trick in the bridal industry. In their effort to make bridal gowns at affordable price points, manufacturers have to use synthetic fabrics instead of silk. But, most makers know that the words "polyester" or "acetate" don't get brides' hearts racing. So, instead they come up with bogus names like Italian satin, Regal satin, or (our favorite) Silky Satin. Are they made of silk? Don't bet on it. The fabric tag never lies—most of these gowns are 100% polyester.

MYTH #3 *"I am considering ordering my dress from an online discounter. Bridal shops warn me if something goes wrong with the dress, the discounters won't fix the problem."*

Here's a common scare tactic. Retailers say: "If you order online and a problem happens with your order, you are left high and dry." Nothing could be further from the truth. We found many reputable discounters that have excellent customer service reputations and stand behind what they sell. And we've found the best gown web sites will work hard to correct any problem with a dress order. We'll review the best discounters later in this chapter in the "Best Buy" section.

MYTH #4 *"I know brides must always wear white but I've tried on several white gowns that just don't look right for me. Do I have to wear white?"*

No, you don't. Almost all gowns also come in ivory (although this shade varies from designer to designer). But that's not all the color possibilities. Several gowns now are available in subtle colors like platinum (grey), rum pink and "café" (a darker ivory).

Helpful Hints

1 Shopping for a gown is an exhausting process. Take frequent breaks and don't try to squeeze too many shop visits into one day. Limit yourself to two to three stores, leaving time to think about which gown you like most.

2 Sometimes the first dress you try on is the one you buy. The number of brides we've met who buy the first gown they tried on always surprises us. Perhaps the first impression you get from that first gown is the one that most sticks in your mind. Warning: bridal retailers are wise to this phenomenon and, hence, bring out their most expensive gown for you to try on first.

3 Pick your price range carefully. And insist that the bridal shop stay within it. Be aware that some bridal retailers will try to "up sell" you—if you tell them you only want to spend $800 or less, they bring out that "extra special" dress that's $1180 . . . hoping you'll fall in love with it anyway. For that reason, if the shop asks your budget, you might want to low-ball the figure somewhat.

4 Practice the bustle. Once the wedding is over, you will want your train "bustled" for the reception (the train is gathered up and secured to the gown's waistline, making it easier to dance, etc). This is done by hooking the train on to a series of buttons sewn at the back of the gown. A word to the wise: make sure you have someone in your bridal party who knows how to do this, so you aren't carrying around that heavy train all evening!

5 Avoid wardobe malfunctions with strapless gowns. Yes, it is the hip style now—but consider these tips to avoid, uh, problems with strapless bridal gowns. Look for a dress with detachable halter "strings" to wear while dancing. Get the best strapless bra you can afford—make sure it is tight! For women with small busts, consider a silicone stick-on bra to help fill out the gown. Pageant adhesive (brand name It Stays, sold on Amazon) is also a good idea. And consider how a gown is constructed—the best strapless gowns have stitched-in boning that helps prevent slipping.

Pitfalls to Avoid

PITFALL #1: THE GREAT DISAPPEARING BRIDAL SHOP!

"I ordered my gown from a reputable shop that had been in business for years. Imagine my surprise when I turned on the local news and found the shop has gone bankrupt! And now, I have no gown."

Yes, this DOES happen. We have documented numerous cases of bridal shops that have gone belly-up, taking deposits from brides and delivering nothing but empty promises.

And this isn't just a big city problem—we've received emails from readers who report shops that have closed in towns big AND small, in every corner of the US and Canada. Why does this happen? In recent years, bridal retailers have been besieged by new competition, from chains like David's to web sites that discount gowns. This has forced some weak bridal retailers out of business and into bankruptcy.

Big deal, right? Retailers come and go every day, you say. Yes, they do—but when bridal shops fail, it often leads to near riots. As you know, all bridal retailers take HUGE deposits from consumers for "special order" gowns. If a shop fails, all that money goes POOF! The shop suddenly closes (or, more accurately, their landlord pad-locks its doors), leaving brides without deposits or gowns. Word of this closing usually gets out to local area brides, who storm the store trying to get their merchandise. Police have been called to quell rioting brides in several cities who have actually attacked closed bridal stores (and their employees). It isn't a pretty sight.

Now, we're not saying this to scare you. Our message is simple: PROTECT yourself.

As you can guess, it is hard to predict WHICH bridal retailers might fail next, since these small mom-and-pop shops are privately run operations. You can't avoid this problem by picking long-time retailers; we've seen shops tank that have been around for 50 years. And don't expect much help from bridal gown manufacturers—most would prefer NOT to talk about this problem, even if they have put a retailer on credit hold or will only ship them on a C.O.D. basis (obvious tell-tale signs a retailer is in trouble).

The best protection: put that deposit for your gown (or any merchandise) on a credit card. As you read earlier, this is your best defense against take-your-money-and-run retailers. If you leave plenty of time before your wedding when ordering a gown (at least six months), you might be able to reorder the dress through another shop.

What if you order from a shop that disappears? Check the box earlier in this chapter for advice on what to do if the shop you ordered a gown from suddenly vaporizes.

PITFALL #2 BAIT AND SWITCH WITH ADVERTISED GOWNS.

"I fell in love with this dress online. I called the local shop listed as a dealer—they told me they didn't have that design, but had others 'just like it.' This is so frustrating. . . is this a scam or what?"

Well, it happens. Believe it or not, dress designers do not always require their dealers to carry the advertised gown—even if the store is listed in the online ad! While the shop may have other gowns by the same designer, the dress you fell in love with is sometimes nowhere to be found. Usually the shop comes up with some excuse (our favorite is "the designer decided not to cut that sample yet") and then subtly tries to sell you a "similar design we have in stock."

Why do shops do this? Shops lure brides into their store with advertised gowns and then try to switch them to unadvertised or private label dresses. These gowns are sold at bigger mark-ups (since, theoretically, they can't be price shopped, right?). In recent years, this trend has accelerated—many bridal shops are now stocking large quantities of "unadvertised" gowns and a small smattering of advertised dresses just to get consumers in the door.

And here's the latest twist: big bridal gown designers have jumped on the "unadvertised" bandwagon. How? Many designers now have *two* lines of bridal gowns—one that they advertise in magazines and feature on their web site. And a second line of "stealth" dresses that doesn't appear online, in catalogs or magazines. These dresses are pitched as the perfect way for retailers to boost margins.

While we understand why retailers and manufacturers would like to boost their profit margins in a competitive marketplace, resorting to bait and switch tactics to accomplish this is wrong. And we've heard rather blatant stories from brides who allege stores intentionally mislead them when they call regarding an advertised style. "Sure that gown is in stock," says a clerk over the phone. Once you arrive, they announce that the sample "was just sold yesterday. Would you like to see other dresses?"

PITFALL #3 INFLATING THE ALTERATIONS BILL.

"I wear a size 6 in street clothes and I was rather surprised when the saleswoman at the bridal shop told me I needed to order a size 10. In fact, the sample gown was a 10 and it really didn't fit. What size should I order?"

First, understand that bridal sizes do not correspond to real-world sizes. Clothes sold in department stores generally conform to an industry-wide sizing chart. Hence, a dress that's a size four in Macy's is roughly the same dimensions as a size four at Nordstrom's.

Not so in the bridal world. As crazy as it sounds, EVERY bridal gown manufacturer uses its own size chart, which can vary greatly from

BRIDAL BARGAINS 63

Bride's Apparel

designer to designer. Adding to the confusion: bridal gown sizes run small compared to ready-to-wear. If you wear a size 8 at most department stores, you might be a 10 or 12 in bridal apparel. (If the wedding biz were savvy, they'd have it the other way around).

Given the uncertainty surrounding wedding dress sizing, some bridal shops may recommend sizes that they know are too large for the bride. Then, when the dress comes in, guess what? It needs expensive alterations! Here are our tips to make sure you get the correct size bridal gown:

Bridal 911: What happens if your bridal shop disappears?

It is the ultimate dress nightmare: you flip on the evening news and the top story is about a bridal shop that has gone bankrupt, leaving an angry mob of jilted brides sans dresses. Then you realize that's your shop.

While no one has exact figures on how many bridal shops go out of business each year, the anecdotal evidence suggests the number is staggering. The simple fact is that the bridal business is brutal and the turnover rate among shops is high.

Among the more egregious examples: one bridal shop owner in Michigan actually drew a jail sentence when a court determined he and his wife bilked customers out of tens of thousands of dollars (this is a rarity—most bankrupt bridal retailers are never prosecuted for stealing customers' deposits).

So, what can you do? Here are some tips if you've discovered your trusted bridal dress shop has gone Chapter 11:

♥ **Avoid the surprise.** If you can, keep tabs on the shop to make sure it is still in business. Drive by once a month or give them a call to make sure they're still breathing on the other end of the line. While most shops won't announce that they plan to close forever next Tuesday, we have heard of cases where employees have tipped off brides to an impending disaster.

♥ **Time is of the essence.** If there is a problem, you'll need to take immediate steps to protect your deposit and get your dress.

♥ **Beware of confusing press accounts.** Some retailers have put out conflicting statements to the media when they have financial problems. At the outset, they usually promise that

♥ **Don't pay attention to the sample gown.** Most sample gowns are tried on so many times that they stretch—what once was a 10 may now be a 12 or even a 14! Bridal gown manufacturers even warn their own dealers not to rely on sample gowns when sizing a bride!

♥ **Instead, get measured with a vinyl tape measure.** Needed measurements include bust, waist, hips, and from the base of the throat to the hemline (called "hollow to hem"). Don't let the bridal shop use a cloth measuring tape, since it can stretch over time and give inaccurate measurements.

everyone is going to get their gowns—despite the fact that their landlord has pad-locked their doors and the electric company has cut off the power for non-payment. Other shops have posted signs on locked doors announcing "vacations" or "remodeling" . . . during their busiest season (not likely). Don't get suckered by false hopes—most bridal shops that have financial problems don't rescue themselves. They usually just go bankrupt and close forever.

♥ **Draw up a contingency plan.** If there is time before your wedding (say, at least four months), you may be able to order another gown. If there isn't time, scout out the alternatives: you can buy a second-hand gown from Craigslist, have a sample altered to fit, or hit the off-the-rack warehouses mentioned earlier in this book. The best advice is to have a "plan B."

♥ **Contact your credit card company immediately.** You did put that dress deposit on a credit card, right? Well, if you did, it is time to test that federal law that protects credit card purchases. Most banks and credit card issuers will request a written account of what's happened with your dress deposit. Since there may be a time limit on this process, you should do this as soon as possible.

♥ **What about the designer?** Can't you just call up the designer and have them ship your special-order dress direct to you? While that sounds logical, bridal dress manufacturers rarely ride to the rescue of stranded brides. Many are afraid they will offend their remaining retailers if they ship direct to brides. The best hope is to have an unshipped dress directed to another retailer in town.

What if you are measuring yourself for a gown you plan to order online? Keep in mind these measurement guidelines"

Bust/Chest: Lift your arms up and measure around your body, crossing over the fullest part of your chest. When measuring your self, wear only a bra, and make sure not to make tight measurements.

Waist: Measure at your waistline where you normally where your pants. Keep a finger between your body and the measuring tape for an accurate fit.

Hip: Stand with your heels together and measure the fullest part of your hip.

♥ **Ask to personally see the manufacturer's sizing chart.** Each manufacturer has its own sizing chart; a copy is sent to each of their retail dealers. Why is this important?

Let's show you how nutty the sizing process is for bridal gowns. Consider a bride with the measurements of 36, 26, 38 (bust, waist, hips). This woman would wear a size 6 in a European designer, size 10 in a Sweetheart and a size 8 in a Demetrios/Ilissa. In fact, we analyzed the size charts of the top 35 bridal manufacturers and found the above bride would be a size 8 in 3% of the designers' gowns, a size 10 in 34%, a size 12 in 45% and even a size 14 in 18% of the designers. Yes, this very same woman could wear a size 8 OR a size 14, depending on the gown's maker.

The take home message: check that size chart before ordering. Retailers typically have these charts in their stores; web sites like RKBridal.com (click on size charts) have detailed charts for quite a few major gown makers online.

♥ **Given your measurements, pick a size that closely matches your largest measurement.** Why? That's because it's always easier to make a bridal gown smaller; expanding a bridal gown is much more difficult. Make sure the size you pick is clearly marked on the sales receipt.

♥ **Don't get too caught up in the size number.** Some brides we interviewed get personally insulted when the bridal shop tells them they need X size, which is several numbers larger than their street clothes' size. Our advice: don't fixate on that number. Remember, it's the bridal designers who are insane, not you.

To sum up, in our research we discovered that brides encounter problems in this area when they let the shop pick the size for them. Instead of measuring you, some salespeople just guess what your size is. Then the dress comes in and surprise! It needs to be chopped down, say, from a size 14 to a 10. And guess who pays the $200 or $300 alterations bill?

In retailers' defense, however, we should note that some bridal manufacturers are notorious for shipping gowns that are incorrectly sized (that is, too big or small given their own size charts). Mori Lee and Maggie Sottero are two big offenders in this category, but it happens with other designers as well.

So, if your gown doesn't fit, is this intentional fraud to profit on alterations or an "honest" mistake made by unskilled salespeople—or a manufacturer goof? It's hard to say. The bottom line: be careful. If you accept the shop's sizing "advice," write on the receipt that "Shop Recommends Size." If the dress comes in way too big or too small, you have more leverage in negotiating a solution.

PITFALL #4 MANUFACTURER GOOFS ON SIZING.

"I ordered a wedding dress in a size 12. When it came in, it was way too big! Even though it had a size 12 tag in it, the dress was nowhere near those measurements. The shop owner just shrugged her shoulders and told us their seamstress could fix the problem . . . for a hefty charge. What should I do?"

Sizing goofs are a common problem in the bridal biz; we've seen numerous cases of gowns that came in too big or too small even though the tag indicates a "correct" size. In our opinion, the manufacturer is fully responsible for shipping the correct size (that is, a dress whose dimensions match the manufacturer's size chart for the ordered size).

If the order is incorrect, the manufacturer should fix it free of charge. If there is not enough time before the wedding to send the dress back, we believe the manufacturer should pay the shop to alter the gown to the correct size. The bride is definitely not at fault and should never be charged.

In order to protect yourself from this pitfall, make sure all ordered bridal merchandise is inspected and measured when it comes in BEFORE you make a final payment. Try on the gown or use a tape measure to confirm that a garment's dimensions match what was ordered. If you leave the bridal shop without trying your dress on first to check size and quality, you may have little or no recourse if later you discover a defect.

Compounding this rip-off are some shops that refuse to fix defective merchandise. Whether it's the wrong size or botched detailing, we've encountered some merchants who refuse to make good. Some claim "there's not enough time before the wedding to send the dress back." We say that's tough—bridal retailers have a clear responsibility to deliver the right merchandise in the correct size within the time frame promised. The best bridal shops will go to bat for their customers, insisting manufacturers "rush cut" a new gown to replace defective merchandise.

How many dresses come in flawed? One major retailer who sells 10,000 bridal gowns a year told us that, shockingly, two out of every three dresses comes in with a flaw. In about half of those cases, the problem is minor and can be easily fixed. However, the other half include such serious problems as the wrong size or poor workmanship. These must be sent back to the manufacturer to correct.

PITFALL #5 WHOOPS! WE FORGOT TO PLACE THE ORDER!

"I ordered a gown from a bridal shop five months ago. Now the dress is overdue. I've been calling the shop for the last several weeks to find out when it will be in. Finally, someone at the shop admitted they forgot to place my order! I couldn't believe it! And now they won't give me a refund, instead suggesting I buy a gown out of their stock. What should I do?"

When a shop fails to place an order, they are breaking a valid contract and should give you a refund. Instead, some dishonest shops will give you a pitch to buy a sample gown off the rack—that is totally unacceptable. Does this happen every day? Fortunately, no. Yet, we've received enough emails about this problem to warrant this discussion.

Protect yourself by dealing with a reputable shop (find one using the sources we list earlier in this chapter). When you place an order, get a promised delivery date. A few weeks after the purchase, call the bridal shop to confirm the shipping date (they receive this from the manufacturer). The more communication you have with your shop the more likely you will get your gown.

PITFALL #6 BOTCHED ALTERATIONS.

"My bridal gown came in three weeks ago and it was beautiful! However, when I picked it up after alterations, I couldn't believe my eyes! That same gown was a disaster—the seamstress botched the simple hem and bustle! How could I have prevented this?"

Sometimes a shop's "expert seamstress" is a person whose only experience was hemming her daughter's prom gown. No wonder this is one of the biggest problem areas consumers have with bridal shops.

To be fair, bridal gowns aren't the easiest garments to alter. The fabric is slippery and intricately detailed gowns can make even the most simple alterations challenging. Some bridal shops, however, invite consumer complaints by hiring inexperienced seamstresses who then botch the alterations. This is especially problematic around prom season when overwhelmed bridal shops bring in "stringers" to help complete alterations. (One tip: insist the head seamstress do your dress).

Another troubling trend: bridal retailers that sub-contract alterations to another company and then disavow any responsibility if there is a problem. We estimate one-third to one-half of all bridal retailers sub-contract their alterations. How does this work? When you ask the shop for alterations, they refer you to another company that might be right next door. Or they might have an independent seamstress come visit the shop to do fittings twice a week.

All this works fine when things go right. If a problem happens, however, brides tell us bridal retailers suddenly wave open palms and claim they have no control over or responsibility for the seamstress—despite the fact they referred her and perhaps even let her use their shop for fittings.

In general, you can prevent this problem by asking to meet the seamstress before you do the alterations. (If the shop subs out alterations, ask who is responsible if a problem develops.) Ask the seamstress about her experience with bridal gowns. Ask to see the work area. If it looks like a sweatshop or if you sense the seamstress is unqualified, get the gown altered somewhere else. Many communities have free-lance seamstresses who do excellent work at much more affordable rates.

PITFALL #7 SAMPLE GOWNS MAY NOT BE BARGAINS.

"I don't have enough time to order a gown before my wedding. I was thinking of buying a sample gown. What should I watch out for?"

Sample gowns may be a terrific buy—or not. As we explained earlier in this chapter, sample gowns (just like demonstrator models) are cleared out periodically to make room for new styles. Many are marked 20% to 50% (or more) off the retail price.

The big pitfall here: most sample gowns are in less than great shape. That's because most have been tried on dozens (if not hundreds) of times by different shoppers. Sample gowns may be dirty, stained (especially from makeup) and beaten up. We've seen several that have beads missing and lace that is falling off. Furthermore, the gowns are stretched out and often in no way resemble their original sizes.

Of course, the condition of sample gowns varies greatly from store to store—some simply take better care of their merchandise. And the condition of the sample will determine its price. Nearly new sample gowns with little damage may only be discounted by 20% or less.

If you go this route, pour over the dress with a fine-tooth comb. If the shop agrees to clean the gown, get a written guarantee that the purchase is contingent on your approval of the gown after the cleaning. Cleaning a bridal gown is tricky since some dry-cleaning chemicals can damage a dress. An inexperienced cleaner can destroy a bridal gown.

Another tip: don't forget to factor in repairs to your budget. Extensive cleaning and alterations can make a sample gown bargain no deal at all.

Pitfall #8 Salon-style shops.

"I went to a salon where they kept all the gowns in the back. They told me they'd bring out the gowns they thought I would like. Is this kosher?"

We're not big fans of bridal shops that operate "salon-style." In most cases, these shops keep all their gowns out of sight and then ask you for your likes, dislikes, and price ranges. Unless you know exactly what you want, salons can be trying. First of all, the salesperson brings out what *she* thinks you want to see. We've been to several of these salons and they've yet to figure out what I want. Instead, they tend to bring out what they want to sell. We suggest you shop at stores that allow you to see the merchandise. While you can't get a complete picture of what a gown looks like hanging on a hanger, you can tell which detailing (necklines, bodices, beading) you like and have a better feel for prices.

Pitfall #9 Extra charges for large sizes, petites and rush orders.

"Okay, I'm not one of those supermodels. When I visited a bridal shop, all they had were size 10 dresses to try on! Then, they told me they charge extra for 'large sizes!' Is this salt in the wound or what?"

Yes, the bridal industry slaps full-figured brides with a "penalty fee" that can be as much as $50 to $200 or more. But don't feel too singled out, there are also extra charges for petites. The industry claims the extra costs come from "special cuttings" and "increased fabric costs."

One solution: if you're a petite, order a regular size dress and have it altered. Our sources say it just isn't worth it to shell out the extra money to get a petite.

What's most frustrating about large and petite extra fees: only bridal stores charge them. Walk into any department store or leaf through a clothing catalog and you seldom see extra charges for dresses in sizes 18 or 20. And we've never seen such charges for petites. Of the few sites that do have up charges for "women's sizes," the extra cost is maybe $20, not the $200 you see in bridal shops.

Another rip-off: rush charges. Even if your wedding is still three months away, some designers insist on "rush fees" to get you the dress on time. However, just because the manufacturers can't figure out how to sew a gown in less than three months, doesn't mean you should pay a premium.

A solution to this pitfall: consider the alternatives (second-hand shops, eBay, off-the-rack warehouse stores) where you can quickly find a gown, without all the penalty fees. Read more about these options earlier in this chapter.

PITFALL #10 SHOPS THAT HOLD BACK ORDERS.

"I ordered a bridal gown that the shop said would take three months to get in. Four months later, I have no gown and just excuses from the shop. When I ask for a confirmation that they placed the order, I get stonewalled. While my wedding is still two months away, I'm worried."

And you should be. Instead of immediately placing the order with the manufacturer, a shop might hold on to it.

Why? Well, financially-strapped stores may be tempted to use your money to pay other bills—ordering the gown immediately means having to pay their suppliers that much faster. How common is this problem? Even Vincent Piccione, president of Alfred Angelo (the second-largest gown maker in the US), acknowledged how widespread the tactic is. "A major problem that concerns us is retailers who hold on to orders. This is one practice that should be eliminated, thereby putting an end to the root cause of so many horror stories that plague the industry," Piccione said in an industry trade journal.

A parallel scam is something we dub the "involuntary lay-away." In this case, the bridal shop claims it will take much longer than reality to get in a special-order dress. Most designers fill orders within three or four months, with six being the maximum. Yet, some of our readers report shops that claim it will take *eight* or *ten* months to get in their dress. What's happening? Perhaps the shop is using your money to pay their electric bill or other expenses—and plans to order your dress a few months down the line. In a sense, this is like an involuntary lay-away plan, where the shop holds your money for several months longer than necessary.

How can you avoid this problem? First, put the deposit on a credit card. Second, stay on top of the situation. If your dress is due May 1, don't wait for the shop to call you to say the dress is in. Take the initiative and contact the shop to make sure the dress is on time. And don't wait until mid-June to start complaining about a late dress. Yes, it may take a few angry phone calls and emails to get the dress—but don't wait until it's too late.

And what if a shop quotes an eight-month delivery time for a dress? Call around to other dealers or get online quotes to verify delivery time frames. Odds are, you can get the dress much quicker.

PITFALL #11 IT AIN'T OVER IF IT'S OVER.

"My fiancé and I fell on hard financial times and had to postpone our wedding. The problem is I had already ordered a gown. When I contacted the shop, they told me I couldn't cancel the order. Help!"

Most (if not all) bridal shops have "no refund, no cancellation" policies on special-order bridal gowns. Wedding called off? Death in the family? Your fiancé is called to active duty? It doesn't matter—you're still on the hook to buy the dress. That means the shop can also take you to court to force you to pay the balance due on the dress.

If you're merely postponing your wedding, ask the shop if you can get "store credit." At least you might be able to use this in the future.

PITFALL #12 LAYAWAY PROBLEMS.
"I put a bridal gown on layaway at a bridal shop for a few months. After making payments, the shop called to say my dress was now discontinued! My only choice was to take the sample, which was dirty and damaged!"

Layaway sounds like a good idea—in theory. If you don't have the money to buy an item immediately, you reserve it by making monthly payments. While that might work for some items, bridal isn't one of them. Too many things can go wrong when you try to put a bridal gown on lay-away—styles get discontinued, items disappear and worse. Our advice: avoid layaway. If you must put a dress on layaway, only do it for a month or so. Payments for six months or a year can open up a can of worms.

PITFALL #13 BUILDING THE TICKET.
"I feel like I was duped by a local dress shop. The owner added accessory items to my ticket—even though I made it very clear that I just wanted to buy the dress. She said I had to sign the credit card slip before she would give me the itemized list. Upon reviewing the list, I told her that she had incorrectly added a tiara, slip and shoes. To which she said 'too bad, it is a final sale!'"

Building the ticket is a time-honored retail sales strategy—and some shops take this to an extreme. Aggressive sales people try to push around brides-to-be by adding items to the order, whether you agree or not.

The obvious defense: do NOT sign any order form or credit card slip BEFORE you see an itemized list of what you're buying. And don't think this just happens to "dumb" brides—that above quote is a true story from a bride who is an attorney!

Veils: A quick primer

Most bridal veils are described by their length. Here's a breakdown:

BLUSHER/ILLUSION. In addition to the main veil, a blusher is a short, chin-length veil. It is pulled over the bride's face when she walks down the aisle, then pushed back during the wedding ceremony by the groom or father of the bride.

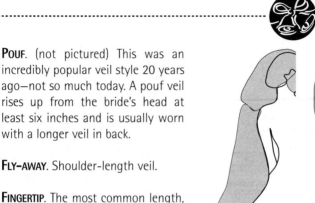

POUF. (not pictured) This was an incredibly popular veil style 20 years ago—not so much today. A pouf veil rises up from the bride's head at least six inches and is usually worn with a longer veil in back.

FLY-AWAY. Shoulder-length veil.

FINGERTIP. The most common length, this one reaches to your finger-tips.

Fingertip

BALLET/WALTZ. Extends to knee length.

Ballet

SWEEP. This style is the same length as the dress skirt.

CHAPEL. 1.5 feet long from waist.

Chapel

CATHEDRAL. 2.5 feet long from waist.

ROYAL. (not pictured) A veil three or more feet long from the waist, matching the length of a cathedral train.

Ratings of Selected Bridal Manufacturers

The charts nearby compare major bridal designers. The rating refers to our opinion of their quality. Our rating system (the key is given below) is based on our extensive research into bridal apparel. We have met many of these designers and evaluated their goods in person, either at trade markets or bridal retail shops.

THE RATINGS

A	EXCELLENT . . . .OUR TOP PICK!
B	GOOD . . . . . . .ABOVE AVERAGE QUALITY, PRICES AND CREATIVITY.
C	FAIR . . . . .COULD STAND SOME IMPROVEMENT.
D	POOR . . . . . . .YUCK! COULD STAND MAJOR IMPROVEMENT.

After the charts: let's talk about our best buys for bridal gowns!

The Top Bridal Designers Compared (A–I)

NAME	RATING	COST	WEB SITE	DELIVERY STANDARD (WEEKS)
Alfred Angelo	C	$	alfredangelo.com	10 to 12
Alfred Sung	B	$	alfredsungbridals.com	11 to 13
Allure	C+	$	allurebridals.com	12 to 16
Alvina Valenta	A–	$$$	jlmcouture.com	14
Amsale	B	$$$	amsale.com	13
Amy Michelson	B–	$$$	amymichelson.com	12 to 16
Anjolique	A	$ to $$	anjolique.com	10 to 12
Ann Barge	B+	$$$	annebarge.com	14
Ann Taylor	A	$	anntaylor.com	1
Birnbaum & Bullock	A–	$$$	birnbaumandbullock.com	12 to 14
Bonny	A–	$	bonny.com	10 to 12
Casablanca	A	$	casablancabridal.com	8 to 10
Chris Kole	B+	$$$	chriskole.com	12 to 14
Christos	B	$$$	christosbridal.com	10 to 14
Claire Pettibone	B–	$$$	clairepettibone.com	12 to 14
David's Bridal	F	$	davidsbridal.com	off rack
DaVinci	B+	$	davincibridal.com	10 to 12
Demetrios/Ilissa	C	$ to $$$	demetriosbride.com	12 to 14
Eden	A	$ to $$	edenbridals.com	10 to 12
Enzoani	B+	$$ to $$$	bluebyenzoani.com	12 to 16
Essense of Australia	A–	$$	essensedesigns.com	11 to 13
Eve of Milady	C	$$$	eveofmiladybridals.com	16
Exclusives by A.C.E.	C–	$		10 to 12
Group USA	B	$	camillelavie.com	off rack
Helen Morley	A–	$$$	helenmorley.com	12 to 16
Henry Roth	B+	$$$	henryroth.com	12 to 14
Impression	B	$ to $$	impressionbridal.com	11 to 13
J. Crew	A	$ to $$$	jcrew.com	1 to 2

NOTES:
RATING: *Our opinion of the designer's quality, value and fashion.*
COST: *The range in retail prices: $=under $800, $$=$800 to $1200, $$$=over $1200.*
CATALOG: *Does the designer have a consumer catalog?*
DELIVERY—**STANDARD:** *The average number of weeks for delivery*
—**RUSH CUTS:** *Some designers offer rush service for an extra fee. Some designers don't offer rush cuts, but have certain in-stock styles for quicker delivery.*
SIZING—**PETITE:** *Designers who offer special petite sizes. Some offer petites for all styles, while others only do petites on a selected number of designs.*

	SIZING			OPTIONS		Key: ●=YES
	RUSH CUTS?	PETITE	LARGE	EXTRA LENGTH	CUSTOM CHANGES	CHARGE FOR COLOR
		●	●	●		
			●			
			●			
			●			
	●		●	●	●	
	●			●	●	
	●				●	
		●	●			
		●				
	●	●	●	●	●	
	●	●	●	●	●	
	●	●	●	●	●	
				●	●	
				●	●	
				●		
			●			
			●			
	●				●	
	●	●	●	●	●	●
	●	●	●	●	●	
	●			●		
	●					●
			●	●		
	●			●	●	
	●			●	●	
	●		●			
	●	●	●			

LARGE: *Nearly all designers offer gowns in sizes 4-20. We classify any size larger than a 20 as a "large size." Some designers just offer sizes 22 and 24, while others go up to a 44. As with petites, only selected styles may be available in larger sizes. Most designers charge extra for large sizes.*

EXTRA LENGTH: *Some designers offer extra skirt length for taller brides for extra fee.*

OPTIONS—**CUSTOM CHANGES:** *Some designers let you customize a dress or offer "custom cuts," dresses that are made to your exact measurements.*

COLOR CHARGES: *Most designers offer dresses in white or ivory for the same price. The few that charge extra for ivory (or for any other color or color combination) are noted here.*

Page 2: The Top Bridal Designers Compared (J-Z)

Name	Rating	Cost	Web site	Delivery Standard (weeks)
Jacquelin	B+	$	jacquelinbridals.ca	10 to 12
James Clifford	B	$$$	jamescliffordcollection.com	16
Janell Berte	A	$$$	berte.com	8 to 10
Jasmine	B	$ to $$$	jasminebridal.com	12 to 14
Jenny Yoo	B+	$ to $$	jennyyoo.com	10 to 12
Jessica McClintock	A	$	jessicamcclintock.com	2 to 6
Jim Hjelm	A-	$$ to $$$	jlmcouture.com	10 to 12
Judd Waddell	A-	$$$	juddwaddell.com	12 to 14
Justin Alexander	B-	$ to $$$	justinalexanderbridal.com	12 to 16
Justina McCaffrey	A	$$$	justinamccaffrey.com	12 to 16
Lane Bryant	A	$	lanebryant.com	1 to 2
Lazaro	B+	$$$	lazarobridal.com	10 to 16
Maggie Sottero	D	$ to $$	maggiesotterobridal.com	20
Marisa	A	$$ to $$$	marisabridals.com	14
Matthew Christopher	A-	$$$	matthewchristopher.com	12 to 14
Mary's	C+	$	marysbridal.com	10 to 12
Mikaella	B	$$	mikaellabridal.com	12 to 14
Mon Cheri	C+	$	moncheribridals.com	12
Monique L'Huillier	A-	$$$	moniquelhuillier.com	12 to 14
Moonlight	B	$ to $$$	moonlightbridal.com	12 to 14
Mori Lee	B-	$	morilee.com	10 to 12
Oscar De La Renta	C+	$$$	oscardelarenta.com	12 to 14
Paloma Blanca	C	$$ to $$$	palomablanca.com	12
Paula Varsalona	B	$$$	paulavarsalona.com	12 to 15
Private Label by G	A-	$	privatelabelbyg.com	10 to 12
Pronovias/St. Patrick	A-	$ to $$$	pronovias.com	9 to 10
Ramona Keveza	B	$$$	romonakeveza.com	12 to 14
Reem Acra	C+	$$$	reemacra.com	10 to 12
Rivini	B	$$$	rivini.com	12 to 14
St. Pucchi	B	$$$	stpucchi.com	16
Simone Carvalli	C-	$$$	simonecarvalli.com	11 to 13
Sincerity	B-	$$	sinceritybridal.com	10 to 14
Stephen Yearick	B	$$$	stephenyearick.com	12 to 16
Sweetheart	B-	$	sweetheartgowns.com	10
Tomasina	A	$$$	tomasina.com	12 to 16
Venus	B	$ to $$	venusbridal.com	12 to 14
Vera Wang	C	$$$	verawang.com	12
Victoria's	B+	$$	victoriascollection.com	12 to 16
Watters	A	$$	watters.com	10 to 14
Winnie Couture	A	$ to $$	winniecouture.com	10 to 12

GOWNS

Key: ●=YES

	SIZING		OPTIONS		
RUSH CUTS?	PETITE	LARGE	EXTRA LENGTH	CUSTOM CHANGES	CHARGE FOR COLOR
		●	●	●	
●		●	●	●	
●			●	●	
●		●	●	●	
●					
	●	●			
●		●	●	●	
●		●	●	●	
●		●	●	●	
●		●	●	●	●
●		●			
●		●	●	●	
●		●			
●		●	●	●	
●		●	●	●	●
●		●	●	●	
●		●	●	●	
	●	●	●	●	
	●				●
●		●	●	●	
		●			●
●		●	●	●	●
●		●	●	●	
●		●	●	●	
●		●			
●			●	●	
				●	
			●	●	
●			●	●	
●		●			
●		●			
●			●	●	
		●	●	●	
●		●	●	●	
●	●	●	●	●	
●		●	●	●	
●	●	●	●	●	
●		●		●	
●		●	●	●	

SPOTLIGHT: BEST BUY #1

THE BEST DISCOUNT GOWN WEB SITES

Yes, you can save big bucks on bridal gowns and bridesmaids dresses on the net. In this section, we'll review our picks of the top places on the web to buy gowns. How much can you save? About 20% to 40% off retail. But before you fire up the browser and surf for dress deals, consider these facts:

1. Like most ecommerce, selling bridal gowns online is evolving. Sites range from those with in-depth pricing information to others that are merely one-page ads with little detail. If you're looking for fancy web sites with on-line pricing guides, you'll be sorely disappointed. Price quotes are given out via the phone or email. And forget about online ordering. When you want to actually buy, most sites call or email with an order.

2. When shopping a discounter, do your homework first. Gather information on colors and options. After narrowing down your choices to just your top picks, *then* contact a discounter for a price quote. This is only fair, since hogging a discounter's time only reduces the response rate for everyone. We know some brides that have carpet-bombed discounters with email requests for 16 dress quotes . . . or with color questions that could be easily answered on the designer's web site.

3. Our biggest beef with these web sites is that (at this point) they are all run by *local* bridal shops—there is no Amazon of bridal. And it is hard to tell long distance whether the shop is reputable just by the look of their Web graphics. Ecommerce is a totally different business than retail—you have to deal with shipping logistics, long-distance customer service and all sorts of other complications. We'd like to see someone have at least three years experience doing this operation (selling dresses online) before we'd give our hard-earned cash as a deposit.

4. Remember that discount deals are typically for mail-order customers only. Most bridal web sites that sell gowns also operate physical stores. So does that mean you can get a discount deal via email and then go to the store and get the same price? No, special web prices are almost always for folks who *don't* come into the store, try on gowns and use the store's alterations services. While most web sites don't explicitly say this, several brides have confirmed these policies.

5. Another caveat: many gown designers and manufacturers are livid about web sites that discount their dresses. Some have threatened to cut off accounts who sell through an "unauthorized 800-number or web site." While most of the designers' protests are mere saber rattling (few have actually cut off 'net sellers), there is a risk—albeit small—that your gown order could be caught in the crossfire.

6. See if the site will do a price match. The web is a very competitive world. If you find a site you'd like to work with but you get a lower quote from another source, give them the chance to match it. Most sites have a policy of meeting or beating their competition.

7. Don't order if time is tight. Be aware that many sites say they can ship items like bridal accessories in "7-10 business days." That is the time to *process* your order and typically does NOT include the actual shipping time . . . which can add another week, depending on your distance from the shipper. If time is tight, it might be better to buy an item at a retail store than take the chance on an online order.

8. You have to arrange for alterations and steaming on your own. That means finding a local seamstress or alteration service. Most dresses are packed rather tightly in their shipping boxes; the resulting gown will probably be wrinkled. Buy a portable steamer at Wal-Mart or Target to get the wrinkles out.

Can a dress be let out?

What if your gown arrives and it's too tight? Can a bridal gown be let out? As we noted earlier in this book, the general rule of thumb is to order a gown that's slightly larger than your measurements. Why? It's easier to make a gown smaller (that is, take it in) than the opposite direction. Of course, there are exceptions to this rule. Some designers actually leave room in the seams to enable a gown to be taken out. What if there isn't any extra fabric? Well, the only solution then is to make a "gusset," a piece of fabric inserted into the dress to give extra room. If that sounds complex, it is—only skilled seamstresses should attempt this alteration. A gusset may change the way a dress looks, sometimes for the worse.

So, here's our advice: be careful out there. Confirm the web site is an *authorized dealer* for the brand you want. Only a handful of web sites are actually authorized dealers of the manufacturers they claim to sell. A wise move: call the designer or manufacturer *first* before you order. (Remember that some web sites may be authorized under their parent retail shop's name, not their on-line address—ask the site how they would be listed in a designer's records). Finally, use a credit card for all deposits and final payments.

Our round up of discount gown web sites, in alphabetical order:

♥ **DORI ANNE VEILS** DoriAnneVeils.com (888) 344-6009. Despite the name, this company sells more than just veils—Dori Anne Veils discounts bridal gowns, bridesmaids, and accessories at 20% to 40% off retail. Owner Debra LaSpina Goldwater started as a veil designer in 1997 with a shop in California's Bay Area; she soon expanded into bridal gowns, maids gowns and other accessories. The web site is detailed, with an online quote form, sizing advice and more. **Rating: A–**

♥ **eBRIDALSUPERSTORE.** eBridalSuperstore.com offers to beat their competitor's lowest price by 5%. Their two dozen lines include such major brand names as Alfred Angelo, Watters and Mori Lee. We liked eBridalSuperstore's "advanced search," which lets you focus on specific designer labels, price range, gowns that are stock and more. Find a style and the web page indicates which sizes and color are available, along with a pop-up size chart. Prices range from 10% to 40% off retail. The site also carries bridesmaids (including Bill Levkoff and Bari Jay) as well as accessories like shoes, slips, crinolines, gloves and more. Feedback on this site has been positive. **Rating: B+**

♥ **LIGHTINTHEBOX.** LightInTheBox.com is unusual among bridal discounters: it is a Chinese company that went public in 2013, selling shares on the US stock market. It sources gowns direct from China and then sells them to customers worldwide. LightInTheBox is a strange site that combines wedding apparel with electronic gadgets and home and garden items. The average wedding dress on LightInTheBox is $209. Delivery takes three weeks. Reviews for this site have been mixed. While the quality of the sewing is good, we saw scattered complaints about orders arriving late, the wrong size shipped, etc. Customer service at LightInTheBox is polite, but tends to stonewall complaints, say readers. So it is a mixed review for LightInTheBox—if you have plenty of time and a strong will, then we say go for it. Otherwise, there are other choices out there with less heartburn. **Rating: C+**

♥ **NETBRIDE** NetBride.com; (866) 638-2743. NetBride.com is the online outpost of Minneapolis-based bridal retailer Rush's, which has been in business since 1948 (online since 1995). NetBride carries a wide variety of brands of both bridal and bridesmaids, including such better labels as Marisa and Mon Cheri. NetBride's site is a cut above its competitors: we liked the online sizing charts, price quote request, and yes, even an online order form. The site notes which dresses can be ordered quickly if you need a dress immediately and they offer to match all competitors' price quotes. Feedback on NetBride has been quite positive—brides tell us they like NetBride's speedy response to quote requests and overall good customer service. NetBride's track record at the BBB is also clean, racking up just one complaint in the last three years. **Rating: A**

♥ **PEARL'S PLACE** PearlsPlace.com; (504) 885-9213. Pearl's Place was one of the first bridal shops to open an online outpost. The Metairie, Louisiana shop specializes in the "better" couture labels, the ones that are hard to find at a discount anywhere else online. Pearl's has been in business since 1971 and online since 1998. Discounts are 20% to 30% off retail, which is impressive considering the couture name brands.

We like the web site's navigation including their extensive listing of designers. Unfortunately, you still can't order online—you'll need to call the number above and speak to a customer service representative. Email is available to brides who have questions for the company.

Some brides complain that the physical store in Metairie is quite a zoo to visit. But if you are ordering online, that isn't a factor. Judging from our reader feedback, brides are now happy overall with the service and prices at Pearls. FYI: Pearl's deposit policy is half the *original retail price* of the gown (not half the discounted price). **Rating: A**

♥ **PRICE LESS BRIDALS** BargainWeddingGowns.com; (818) 442-9888. The online offshoot of a Southern California bridal shop by the same name, Price Less has a huge inventory of "recently discontinued wedding gowns at 65% off retail." The company touts their in stock size range and notes they especially carry gowns in large sizes. A reader who ordered her gown from Price Less said she was happy, even though the gown was a little late (Price Less waived the shipping fee, however). "Price Less is a little harder to get in touch with than Pearl's—that is they don't answer their email as quickly and you have to nag them a bit," said the bride. "But the dress I received was very pretty and for $350, it can't be beat." Another interesting note: Price Less is one of the few web discounters that also occasionally hosts eBay auctions. **Rating: B**

♥ **RK BRIDAL** RKBridal.com; (800) 929-9512. This New York City-based retail shop hosts an attractive, easily navigated online site that offers to match and beat any online price you find by five percent. You can get a

Bride's Apparel

price quote for dresses from 50 manufacturers. Many of the lines are upper-end, couture dresses that are hard to find at a discount. One plus: RK's price quotes include shipping and delivery charges. RK Bridal has a shop in New York's garment district at 318 West 39th Street (between 8th & 9th Ave.), although most of the prices there are not discounted like they are on the web. In business since 1985, RK gets mostly positive marks from our readers. **Rating: A**

FIGURE 2:

A sampling of some of the bargain sites for wedding gowns, maids and more.

GOWNS

♥ **Other sites recommended by our readers.** Angeri.com is an online boutique that sells overstock couture dresses from designers like Givenchy, Amsale and Vera Wang. Sample deal: a $4000 silk designer dress for $699. The site stocks sizes 2 to 16, but we noticed the selection at either extreme of the size spectrum was limited, as you might expect. All the gowns are new and were either runway samples or designer overstock. We noticed recently they began offering to consign gowns for brides or shops. They charge a listing price for consignment gowns but the seller keeps the entire sale price

At first glance, you'd think a site like **Stump's Party** wouldn't have anything to offer brides. But a sharp-eyed reader spied tiaras and other headpieces (stumpsparty.com, then click on weddings) at great prices—she got a $150 tiara for just $30.

What about other sites on the web that sell gowns? Yes, we realize

PROS AND CONS

Should you buy a dress from local retailer or an online discounter? Here is a summary of the pros and cons of each option.

OPTION	PROS	CONS
DISCOUNT	GREAT PRICE: 20–40% OFF RETAIL	SOME REQUIRE UPFRONT PAYMENT WHEN ORDERING
	NO SALES TAX; NO PUSHY SALESPEOPLE	MUST KNOW EXACT DRESS YOU WANT
	INDIE SEAMSTRESS CAN BE MONEY-SAVER	MUST COORDINATE ALTERATIONS YOURSELF (HASSLE)
	NO MESSY BRIDAL SHOPS	LONG-DISTANCE RELATIONSHIP VIA PHONE OR EMAIL
	GET DRESS SHIPPED DIRECTLY TO YOU	MUST STORE DRESS YOURSELF
RETAIL	FULL SERVICE OFTEN INCLUDES ALTERATIONS	FULL RETAIL PRICE . . . AND SOMETIMES MORE
	CAN TRY ON DRESSES	LIMITED SELECTION
	PAY HALF DOWN; HALF WHEN DRESS COMES IN	SERVICE SOMETIMES SLIPS AFTER THEY HAVE YOUR MONEY
	EXTRAS LIKE PRESSING, GOWN STORAGE AND PAYMENT PLANS	DID WE MENTION YOU PAY FULL RETAIL PRICE?

there are at least a dozen more sites out there, but we didn't review them here. Why? The sites above had the best feedback from our readers and the longest track records. If you are considering ordering from a site we haven't reviewed, first go to the Better Business Bureau's web site (bbb.org) to check the site's track record. Then look at the message boards on our site (BridalBargainsBook.com) as well as those of the Knot and Wedding Channel. Do a search of those boards to see what experiences other brides have had with the site.

SPOTLIGHT: BEST BUY #2

CUT OUT THE MIDDLE MAN: CHINA DIRECT GOWNS

It's a time-honored strategy to save money: cut out the middleman and get a better price.

The bridal version of this is buying a gown direct from China via eBay or a manufacturer's web site at an unbelievably low price. How low? How about $100 or $150 for a bridal gown like you see in stores? No, we're not making that up.

How is this possible? First, a quick history lesson. Until the 1980's, most bridal gowns sold in the US were made in the US. Storied designers like Bianchi and Priscilla (among dozens of others) actually had dress factories in places like Boston, New York or San Francisco.

That ended long ago, as production moved off shore. Today's hot bridal gown makers (just about any name brand you see online or in magazines) don't really make anything at all—they are gown importers. After designing a dress, they farm out production to a gown manufacturer in China (the US designer doesn't own the Chinese factory). The dress is shipped to the designer's distribution center in the US and then, finally, to a retailer.

Every time the dress changes hands, it gets marked up. According to industry sources, we estimate that a $1,000 bridal gown you see in stores actually costs just $50 to make in China. The importer buys it for $100 and then re-sells it to a retailer for $500. The retailer marks it up to $1,000, the final price you see as a consumer.

But who needs the designer and retailer anyway? What value do they really add to this process? After all, once the gown lands in the US, it can be UPS'd direct to you, bypassing the importer and retailer. Chinese gown makers apparently have been pondering that as well—and several have set up eBay accounts and web sites to sell gowns direct to brides.

And given these prices, we can see why this is suddenly the hot bargain trend in bridal. $30 for an A-line dress with a touch of pearls? $50 for an off-the-shoulder dress with a beaded bodice and chiffon overlay skirt? Yes, those are real prices, not typos!

We've interviewed over hundreds brides who've bought gowns direct from China. Based on their experiences, here is our advice:

♥ **Where to look.** See the following box on Chinese copycats for a list of the top gown sellers. Some sellers have extensive eBay stores; others like 1Koo.com and Lilywedding.com

♥ **How much can you save?** Most gowns are under $300. So the savings is about 50% to 80% off what you see in stores.

♥ **What about shipping? How much time do I need to leave to order?** Shipping is usually extra, another $30 to $100. It takes about 2-3 months for a gown to arrive at your doorstep. A word to the wise: leave plenty of time for customs delays!

♥ **Is there a language barrier?** All of the above web sites and eBay stores are in English—but if you want a special request or custom alteration, you may have to deal with a Chinese customer service agent with limited English skills. Set your expectations accordingly.

♥ **How's the quality?** In our opinion, good. Now, if you buy a $200 knock-off of a $2000 dress, is it exactly the same? No, the fabric on the $2000 designer original is probably silk or other luxury fabric. The $200 version is probably made of a basic polyester satin. Will the beading, lace and detailing be exactly the same? No. But you could argue: who can really tell? Most brides we interviewed have been pleasantly surprised with the quality of fabric, stitching and detailing. Does that mean you won't need alterations? Of course not—you'll still probably have to make an adjustment here or there to the gown. But that's true for a gown you buy anywhere.

♥ **Is there a place to swap info with other brides on which Chinese sellers are best?** Wedding message boards on the Knot, WeddingBee and other sites are good place to check out a site's reputation. And we have a forum on our site as well (BridalBargainsBook.com; click on Community and then the Bridal Bargains forum).

THE EMPIRE STRIKES BACK:
DESIGNERS WIN RESTRAINING ORDER AGAINST CHINA COPYCATS . . . OR 20 DRESS WEB SITES BRIDAL DESIGNERS WISH YOU NEVER SURF

In the long running battle between bridal designers and copycats, the designers scored a victory in 2012 when they won a temporary restraining order against 45 online merchants.

The American Bridal & Prom Industry Association, a trade-group made up of bridal manufacturers and retailers, filed a federal lawsuit against the online gown sellers, claiming they were "victims of a massive Internet counterfeiting scheme to advertise and sell counterfeit products."

The suit claims the gown sellers, most of which are based in China, tried to mislead consumers with "identical and/or confusingly similar" web site names to the designers' brands. The sites are also accused of using copyrighted gown photos without permission.

An example is the web site Moncherybridal.com, which sounds close to the web site for Mon Cheri Bridals (Moncheribridals.com).

Chinese gown sites sell an estimated 600,000 knockoff gowns a year, a lawyer for the bridal trade group told the New York Times in 2013.

The restraining order enables bridal designers to seize the knockoff companies' web domain names as well as funds held by third-party payment processors like Paypal. As a result, several of the web sites have gown out of business. Below is a list of the Chinese gown sellers targeted in the lawsuit that are still in business as of this writing. The industry group says it will expand its lawsuit to include more sellers.

We can see both sides of this argument. China has been notorious for exploiting Western intellectual property and their flagrant abuse of trademarks and copyright does damage domestic companies, without a doubt. Bridal designers certainly have the right to defend their trademarks and copyright-protected intellectual property (namely, gown pictures used for advertising).

At the same time, as we've discussed earlier, there is no federal protection for bridal gown designs. While lace patterns can be protected by copyright, dress styles are NOT (legislation to do just that has languished in Congress).

So it is a novel legal strategy to hit these web sites with attack based on counterfeiting, since the dress designs themselves are not protected. In our review of top copycat gown seller web sites, we conclude most Chinese gown sites do not promise they will ship you a designer XYZ gown, even though the pictured dress looks much like designer original. The Chinese dress will not have the manufacturer's tag and so on. So where is the counterfeiting?

It is true that bridal gown industry is rife with copycats—but so is the entire fashion biz. Once a name brand designer shows a $3000 gown with a distinctive pattern of, say, 273 beads in a swoosh pattern at the back of the dress, you can be sure other lower-end designers are fast at work creating "their version" of this new style. And then Chinese sellers will copy their copies.

In our opinion, this legal attack on Chinese gown sellers is futile—by their own admission, the bridal gown makers say there are 2000 to 3000 sites that sell copycat gowns online. There is nothing that will stop companies from closing down one web site and then opening with a new domain the next day. What is likely to happen, however, is consumers may get caught in the crossfire—dress orders may be cancelled and deposits seized. And that chaos may be exactly what the bridal gown makers want, in order to scare consumers away from shopping online.

The bigger issue here is ecommerce. Bridal gown makers and shops have been slow to embrace ecommerce, wanting instead to protect their lucrative retail business. The consumer would benefit more if the gown makers spent less on lawyers and more on adapting their business model to the 21st century.

Here is a list of the Chinese gown sellers that were cited in the lawsuit. Or put another way, here are 20 discount dress web sites the gown designers hope you never surf:

9Dresses.com	BigDayDress.net
Brideslee.com	DHgate.com
DinoDirect.com	DreamProm.com
ElleDream.net	EliseBridal.com
FishInTheSky.com	Kelly-Prom.com
Milanoo.com	Micwell.com
SeasonMall.com	Tidebuy.com
Soobest.com	Tbdress.com
FaryBridal.com	Dress-Market.com
AliExpress.com	PhoebeBridal.com

Late update: As of press time, all the above web sites were still in business. Hence, the designers' efforts to shut them doesn't look to be very effective. And remember, just because the above sites have been accused of copyright infringement, that doesn't mean they've committed any offense. While we would urge caution in ordering from any online site that ships direct from China, we've heard from many readers who are more than happy with the gowns ordered from the above sites.

SPOTLIGHT: BEST BUY #3

BRIDAL OUTLETS

Read me first: outlet locations are constantly changing. Be sure to call these locations FIRST before heading out! If you find an outlet that is no longer around—or a new discovery that you'd like to share—email us at authors@bridalbargainsbook.com.

With an outlet mall in just about every corner of North America, it seems you can find any product at less than retail—sweaters, cookware, electronics, you name it. But what about a bridal gown?

Surprisingly, there ARE bridal outlets out there . . . they just take some effort to find. Most are NOT in those fancy outlet malls on the interstate. Instead, bridal outlets are located in off-the-beaten path locales. Here's our look at the best bets:

♥ **"1385 BROADWAY"** (BridalBuilding.com) used to be one of the best places to find a gown deal in New York City. We say "used to be" because the scene there has changed much over the years.

In the heart of Manhattan's garment district, the building at 1385 (and 1375) Broadway used to house the showrooms and offices of the country's top bridal designers. In years past, the designers used to quietly open to the public on Saturday . . . and shhh! The prices were discounted!

In more recent years, however the Bridal Building has changed quite a bit. First, many major gown manufacturers have abandoned the building (and New York's high rents) by moving their showrooms out of the city. In their place, we've seen several smaller designers and seamstresses move into the Bridal Building. In some cases, these smaller salons are selling overstock samples from major gown makers; other times, they are selling their own creations.

So, is it still worth it to trek to the Bridal Building? Well, if you live in or near (or plan to visit) New York City, you might as well go look. It can't hurt. We found some of the deals impressive—one designer bridal gown in excellent condition was originally $1300, marked to $600. Our readers report one major bridesmaid designer sells their $250 gowns for just $120 on Saturdays.

But . . . you might find similar deals from other discount sources we list in this chapter (like RK Bridal, the web site and store in the Garment District reviewed earlier). So, educate yourself on designers, prices and selection before you go to the bridal building. And don't forget to factor in the price of parking and tolls for not only the initial visit but also any follow-up fittings.

The Bridal Building isn't the only place to get bridal gown bargains in New York City. If you are looking for a couture gown without the couture price tag, check out the **BRIDAL GARDEN**, 54 West 21st St., Suite 907 (bridalgarden.org). This non-profit resale bridal boutique sells couture bridal gowns and gives the proceeds to children's charities. You can find overstock and resale gowns here from such labels as Reem Acra, Ulla Maija and more. Many of these $5000 gowns are on sale for $2000 or so. Don't go here looking for a dress under $1000, however. Brides tell us the pickings are slim in that price range.

♥ **JESSICA MCCLINTOCK** (jessicamcclintock.com) has one California outlets for her popular line of bridal apparel: South San Francisco (415-553-8390, 25 15th St.). Both outlets carry past-season styles of bridal gowns, bridesmaids' dresses and all kinds of accessories. And the prices? Wowza.

McClintock's outlet is hit or miss—we hear reports of great bargains and then others find little to nothing. We recently visited and were impressed. We saw dozens of bridal gowns (priced from $60 to $100), plus bridesmaids' dresses, flower girls, party dresses and more. Most of the bridal gowns were discounted 50% to 80%, but we understand periodic sales offer even better deals. We've heard of brides who found $10 formal bridal gowns (no, that's not a typo). While the deals weren't that fantastic when we were there, we did notice a large rack of informal gowns on sale for just $80. You can then buy a separate train ($20 each). Top off your bargain ensemble with a pair of white shoes with lace trim, on clearance while we visited for just $5 a pair. Wow.

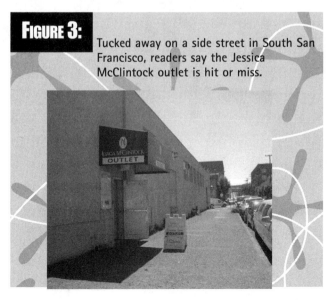

FIGURE 3: Tucked away on a side street in South San Francisco, readers say the Jessica McClintock outlet is hit or miss.

Most gowns we saw at the McClintock outlet were sizes 8-14, although a few 4-6's and 16-20's were floating around. Surprisingly, the dresses were in pretty good shape—most were in protective bags and had very little damage or wear. Watch for those end-of season clearances for the best deals (you can put your name on their mailing list to get notices).

Don't expect any service at the outlet—the staff is "rude, nasty," said one reader. Others note that there is but one large dressing room where you try on clothes with "a bunch of women half naked." But "this is the place to find that diamond in the rough," said another reader and we agree. Where else can you find a decent wedding gown for $75?

♥ Vows Bridal Outlet (BridePower.com) in Watertown, MA (866) THE-GOWN specializes in selling overstock and close-outs from top designers like Vera Wang and Pronovias. You'll see these top names at prices 50% to 70% off retail although dresses are only available in sample sizes

Factory stores: new twist on outlets

Beset by competition and faltering retail dealers, bridal gown manufacturers have rolled out a new weapon to fight chains like David's: the factory store. Demetrios kicked off this trend with the launch of "Brides by Demetrios" in California. The designer then opened 22 more stores in 15 states. Call Demetrios at (212-961-5222 or check their website (demetriosbride.com) for the latest locations.

So what are these factory stores? In a way, these stores are a hybrid between discount outlets and pure retail locations. The best advantage for consumers is selection.

Demetrios loads his stores with his ENTIRE collection (over 250 styles), in sizes 4 to 26. Unlike regular bridal shops that may just carry a few styles in a line, factory stores let a manufacturer showcase their entire line. Of course, if you don't like the Demetrios look, this isn't the place to shop. Brides by Demetrios stores only stock Demetrios bridal gowns (along with bridesmaids dresses, accessories and all the other usual stuff). Overall reviews from brides are positive. The gowns are great, but service can vary from store to store, so we recommend you check Yelp reviews for the store in your area before making an appointment.

Unfortunately, prices are typically at full retail. But we have heard from readers that the Demetrios stores will match price quotes from online discounters, so it may not hurt to ask. And (usually 12s). We visited the store and found it to be well stocked and the service (as reported by our readers) is excellent. Don't live near Boston? Check out Vows online at BridePower.com. You can browse their collection online and even purchase dresses direct from the site.

♥ **MORE OUTLETS:** A reader in California praised the **HAVEN BRIDAL MART** (bridalmegamall.com) in Folsom, CA (near Sacramento): "The whole experience was outstanding. Great prices and caring service without any pressure to buy. The place was spotless and the dresses in super clean condition.

The **GLAMOUR CLOSET** (GlamourCloset.com) is a San Francisco-based boutique (now with stores in Los Angeles and Chicago too) that sells overstock wedding gowns for 25% to 75% off retail—labels include Vera Wang, Lazaro, Carolina Herrera and more. One bride said she snagged a $6300 gown for $900; others praise the service ("friendly, but not

they will occasionally send out a 15% off coupon. Of course, while you might pay full price, you also get full service (on-site alterations are available at most stores). Another tip: look for sale racks at factory stores. Demetrios stores have a large selection of discontinued dresses that are $299 to $699, about 30% to 50% off retail.

Of course, Demetrios isn't the only designer going the "factory store" route. Jessica McClintock has for years operated her own stores in 13 states. Even industry stalwart Alfred Angelo has opened over 60+ company stores (go to alfredangelo.com for the latest locations). One bride posted to our message boards the bargain she found there—a $650 gown marked down to $199!

Yes, even designer Pronovias has opened a company store— the Barcelona-based bridal company operates a six-floor flagship store at 14 East 52nd Street in New York City.

The latest designer to join the trend is Casablanca Bridal, which opened a flagship store in Newport Beach at Crystal Cove in 2013. Mid-price designer Impression Bridal opened "premier stores" in Texas, Georgia, Oklahoma and West Virginia in the past year.

All of this is good for consumers, in our view. Factory stores give brides another option for gown shopping and piece of mind in knowing the store is manufacturer-owned. Whether these stores will be aggressive with pricing and special sales remains to be seen, but expect to see more in the coming years.

pushy") but the store's popularity can mean a long wait for a dressing room. And while the gowns are discounted, most are still $1000 to $2000 (occasional sales bring lower prices). Since these are sample gowns, most of them are size 8, 10 or 12.

David's Bridal: Not Recommended

What a long strange trip it's been.

David's, the country's largest chain of bridal shops (300 and counting, DavidsBridal.com), has changed dramatically from their humble beginnings in South Florida in 1990. When we first visited David's in Tampa in 1993, they were known as "David's Bridal Warehouse." And a warehouse was what it was—rack after rack of gowns sold "as is" at deep discount prices. The crammed-together inventory, lack of dressing rooms and harsh fluorescent lighting gave David's all the ambiance of a Kmart.

How times have changed. We recently visited a David's in Colorado and boy, things *are* different. The airy, 10,000 square foot store featured high ceilings, tapestry carpet, subtle lighting and a HUGE dressing area with wall-to-ceiling mirrors. It's no wonder David's has dropped "warehouse" from their name—it looks like a regular (albeit big) bridal salon.

What hasn't changed are the gowns—David's still sells most gowns off the rack. Unlike traditional stores that stock only sample gowns and force you to wait months for a "special order," most of David's business is cash and carry. You see a gown, find your size (they stock sizes 2 to 24), pay for it and then walk out the door. What a concept.

Over time, David's has strayed from its off-the-rack roots: more and more of David's gowns are special order. Now, nearly a third of the chain's business is special order.. Nearly all David's bridesmaids sales are also special order. And the chain has added more premium (read: expensive) merchandise.

So, what exactly is David's selling? Well, these are not designer-brand dresses. In fact, ALL the gowns in David's are their own "private label" or in-house names. David's has plants in Asia that churn out copies of all the hip styles featured on bridal web sites. And the prices are attractive: most synthetic fabric styles are $300 to $1200; the average is $500 to $600.

David's has tried to boost the designer cache in their stores in recent years. In addition to selling their own in-house labels, David's has snapped up the brand names of defunct bridal designers like Galina, White by Vera Wang and Melissa Sweet. At the top end, David's offers the Oleg Cassini collection, which gives David's an entree to the premium gown market with styles running $950 to $1650.

So, how's the quality? At David's you get what you pay for—a $500 dress is clearly not in the same quality league as one that is $1200. The initial quality of David's gowns is good; it is what happens after they sit in the stores for a while that is the problem (more on this below). All in all, we thought most of David's dresses were comparable in price and quality to other low-end bridal designers like Mori Lee and Alfred Angelo.

Okay, you might be wondering, why is David's "not recommended"? As we just finished discussing, their quality (at least initially) is decent. And the prices give a good value. So, here are our concerns:

♥ **Spam, spam, spam!** The moment you walk into David's, you are implored to "register" your wedding with a cheerful consultant. And once David's has your personal info, expect to receive an avalanche of junk mail, spam and come-ons from just about every wedding vendor in America. You can read it yourself in the fine print of David's privacy policy, posted on their web site. A word to the wise: if you decide to purchase anything at David's, give them only the minimal personal info needed (a cell phone, for example, to notify you of the arrival of a special order). Don't give out your mailing address, especially if you just are buying something cash and carry.

♥ **Trashed gowns.** Among the biggest complaints we get about David's from consumers is the condition of their merchandise. "Deplorable" is often one word we hear; "disgusting" is another.

The bottom line: David's off-the-rack strategy means gowns are tried on multiple times before purchased and that takes a toll on the dresses. So, what is David's answer to brides who complain their dream dress is dirty? They can special order a new, clean version!

Well, that brings us to the next issue with David's: we still get numerous complaints about the chain's "special order" process—orders arriving late, wrong, damaged or worse. This happens with bridal gowns, bridesmaids' dresses and more.

David's is in deep denial on this: a spokesperson for the chain told us there are "no problems" with special ordered merchandise.

Our general advice for David's: unless the item is actually in stock at the store, don't buy it.

♥ **Service, or lack thereof.** You don't have to look hard to find complaints about David's service. Wedding message boards are peppered with stories about rude salesclerks, botched alterations and big pressure to buy.

It's that last issue that really bothers us—you might expect the hard sell when shopping for a used car, but some David's salespeople have mastered this for bridal. One Tennessee bride emailed that when she told a David's sales clerk that she wanted to sleep on a gown deal, the sales-person said the dress probably wouldn't be there the next day. After suc-cumbing to the pressure to buy today, the salesperson proceeded to write up the order—and then added shoes, veil, tiara, bra and slip to the sales order! The bride clearly told the clerk she just wanted to buy the dress. "I can't tell you how upset I was with how I was talked to and treated," said the bride.

A former David's employee echoed that experience—she told us David's salespeople are trained to sell a slip, bra, shoes or headpiece with

Big Fashion Brands Turn to Bridal

One of our time-honored tips to saving money on a wedding is shopping at stores that don't have "bridal" in their name. A perfect example is bridal attire offered by fashion brands like J. Crew, Ann Taylor and Anthropologie's BHLDN division. Here's an overview.

J. Crew started selling bridal gowns in 2004 with just a handful of bridal gowns and bridesmaids dresses. Today, they sell over 40 designs (including some on closeout). Prices range from $395 to nearly $3000. Fabrics include silk chiffon, cotton and cotton/silk blends, silk taffeta, and more. Styles don't have trains to speak of and they are rather simple with minimal detail. But price, selection and the ability to return your gown if it doesn't fit make this a great option. And by the way, the sizing is based on J. Crew's size chart so you don't have the huge hassle of translating a bridal size to your street size.

J. Crew has wedding specialists available via email or by phone. These folks help keep you organized, follow up on orders and answer questions about styles, shipping, sizing and more. They'll even try to find you a dress that is out of stock. These wedding specialists are also available in some stores, including Chicago, Los Angeles, Atlanta, New York and other major cities. We found J. Crew's bridal site to be well designed, complete with a fabric glossary, dress fit guide and a color swatch page (wed-ding specialists can also order swatches for you).

Ann Taylor (anntaylor.com) has expanded their bridal col-lection to over 35 gowns in recent years. Dresses range from $500 to $1500 for floor length gowns, less for cocktail style dresses. They also offer separates: skirts and tops. Like J. Crew, gowns are simple designs without trains. Fabrics range from every gown ... and they are chastised by a manager if they don't. It's no surprise that brides tell us they get heavy sales pressure to purchase these extras at hefty prices. "I always thought it was pretty disgusting that we had to sell these extras at full price after so many women had tried them on," said the employee. And while David's stresses appointments, they never turn away walk-ins. "Whoever shows up first will get a 'consultant.' A rush of walk-ins will overwhelm consultants, who then have to handle five or six brides at a time."

Even David's seems to acknowledge its service is, uh, underwhelming.

silk to cotton to man-made fabrics. Sizes are available up to 14. The Ann Taylor bridal gown pictured at right is $650. Ann Taylor has also added a bridesmaids line with 14 styles, (one of which is floor length) in silk dupioni, silk chiffon, jersey and lace. Price: $150 to $265.

Finally, Anthropologie, (anthropologie.com), the upscale sister chain to Urban Outfitters, has developed a bridal line called BHLDN (BHLDN.com). The style: heirloom looks in a range of lengths. Gown run the gamut from dresses that look like they stepped off of Grecian paintings, Art Deco styles, 19th century Empire gowns and more (an example is pictured right). Prices range from $600 to $3600. Sale gowns are available for as little as $300. Fabrics range from silk organza to silk/cotton blends to cotton and more. BHLDN does require an additional shipping charge of $15 for bridal gowns.

Bridesmaids, flower girl and mother of the bride dresses are also available from BHLDN. Bridesmaids range from $220 to $500. Accessories like shoes, purses, lingerie and jewelry are also sold on the site. If you live in Chicago or Houston, BHLDN also has a couple stores so you can actually try on the gowns.

BRIDAL BARGAINS 95

In a little-noticed blog, a David's marketing consultant admitted the company's own internal survey found "the service wasn't so good" and complaints were on the increase in recent years.

To be fair to David's, we should note that many comments on David's service are bi-polar—folks either love or hate the place. And their vice president of marketing told us in an interview that the chain has implemented an extensive training process to improve service.

We wonder, given the general decline of service at many retailers, what can we expect from a chain like David's? Is it likely the chain has an impossible task: hiring clerks at $7.50 an hour (plus commissions to sell a service-intensive product like a bridal gown? That said, the fish rots from the head first—it is David's corporate office that sets the tone for the chain . . . and the emphasis on high volume sales is driving many of the complaints about the stores.

♥ **Ethics.** Finally, we are most concerned with the behavior of the chain when it comes to advertising and marketing. Take their $99 bridal gown sales. David's spends tens of millions of dollars on advertising each year (and racked up $1.3 billion in sales) and much of their promo effort went to plug these events, held three to four times a year. The problem? Brides complain that when they arrive at these "sales," all they find is a few trashed sample gowns at $99. True, all other bridal gowns and some bridesmaids are marked down $50 to $300 off during the sale. Yet, if you advertise $99 gowns, you better have a decent selection of, say, dresses at $99.

Alterations are perhaps the biggest flash point for David's customers—while folks run hot or cold on David's merchandise or service, there is almost unanimous loathing for David's alterations services, in our research. Just about anything that can go wrong does . . . botched, late, poor-quality alterations and so on. And since most bridal gowns need at least some alterations, this is a major shortcoming of the chain. Of course, just because you buy a dress at David's does NOT mean you have to get it altered there. Our advice: take it elsewhere.

So, what's the bottom line? Frankly, we can't recommend this chain. The volume of complaints is so overwhelming that we can't recommend any of our readers give David's their hard-earned money. We expect a market leader like David's to set an example for other bridal retailers when it comes to customer service and satisfaction . . . instead, the chain sets new lows for the industry.

Yes, David's accounts for about a third of the bridal market—one out of every three brides will get their gown there. And for brides with special needs (say, getting a large size gown in a hurry), David's may be the only choice. We applaud the chain's recent addition of a women's size line (David's sizes now go to 26W). FYI: In 2012, David's was sold for just over a billion dollars to a private equity firm.

But, overall, it comes down to this: is David's a bargain? Is this a store we'd recommend to our readers? No, on both counts. You can find similar quality gowns from makers like Mori Lee and DaVinci for less money than David's. And given the feedback we get about the chain's service, special orders and alterations, we simply can't send our readers down that road.

What if you want to ignore this advice and purchase a dress at David's? First, only buy items that are in prefect condition *and* in stock so you can leave with them that very day—don't "special order" anything. If a dress is damaged, don't buy it—David's may promise you they can fix or clean whatever is wrong; don't bet on it. Finally, if you buy a dress at David's, get it altered somewhere else—you'll save both your money and your sanity.

And watch for sales reps trying to "build the ticket." As we discussed earlier, some David's sales associates will add all sorts of accessories to your bill—without your permission. Check over the final bill carefully and insist David's remove any extras.

Gown Preservation: The Dirty Little Secret of the Bridal Industry?

Bridal gowns in dress shops take an incredible amount of abuse. Make-up stains, filthy hemlines, lace that gets dirty—repeated try-ons can turn the most beautiful white gown into a mess.

So, if a bridal gown gets stained, do dress shops send it out to one of those expensive, national gown cleaners? Or even a local dry cleaner? Nope, here's the surprising secret: most bridal shops just pop that dirty gown into a washing machine in the back of the store.

No, that wasn't a typo—many dress shops simply wash bridal gowns in a regular washing machine to remove dirt, make-up stains and other signs of wear and tear. Now, we find this highly ironic since many of these same shops pitch their customers to use very expensive, nationwide "gown preservation" companies that charge $150 to $500 or more to "preserve" the gown after the wedding. In a business where "custom-ordered" gowns require $300 in alterations and accessories like veils are grossly overpriced, this is probably the final insult to brides who have traversed the wedding industry.

Just what do these gown preservation companies do for all this money? Well, just ask reader Shelley Brown-Parish of Hampton Falls, NH. On the advice of the bridal shop where she bought her gown, she paid $250 to Nationwide Gown Cleaning Service of Flushing, NY to clean and preserve her $3800 Scaasi wedding gown using their "Zurcion" method. The allegedly clean gown was returned to her in a sealed box, along with a notice saying if the box was opened, the company would not guarantee the dress.

Four years later, Brown decided to sell the gown and took it to a local consignment shop. When the box was opened, she was horrified. "The entire gown had changed color from white to ivory," she said, noting it had "large yellow stains all over the dress, blue ball-point pen marks on the front and on the train, and also had blood stains where the gown had been fastened to the tissue in the preservation box." Nationwide Gown Cleaning (which also goes under the names Continental Gown Cleaning and Prestige Gown Cleaning) said they'd re-clean the gown and have it back to her in two weeks.

One year later, Brown still didn't have her dress.

After complaining to the Better Business Bureau and bringing her story to the *Boston Globe*, the company still refused to return her dress. So, she sued them. After a local TV station picked up the chase, she *finally* got the gown back, which was still dirty and now smelled of cigarette smoke! The dress is now so famous it was featured on a national talk show on wedding scams as an example of what can go wrong with these gown preservation companies.

Thankfully, the Federal Trade Commission took action in this case. The FTC sued Nationwide (Prestige) Gown Cleaning, charging them with false advertising and deceptive trade practices. Specifically, the FTC charged that Nationwide/Prestige broke the law by claiming its Zurcion method was the only method by which dresses could be cleaned—and for failing to disclose to consumers the conditions of its warranty (which forbids brides from opening their gown boxes). A year later, Nationwide signed a consent order with the FTC and agreed to stop these practices.

So what lessons does this have for other brides?

First, we think this whole "gown preservation box" scheme is a rip-off. According to the National Association of Resale and Thrift Shops, over 80% of bridal gowns brought into re-sale shops to be consigned in their original, unopened, sealed boxes are found to be dirty. These national gown preservation companies are duping brides into thinking their gowns are being preserved when evidence shows they're not even being *cleaned*. Here's our advice for brides who want to preserve their gowns:

1. Don't. If you're saving the dress for your daughter, you're assuming the dress will fit her, not have yellowed or be out of style. That's a slim chance. A better idea: donate your gown to the charity gown sale run by the Brides Against Breast Cancer foundation (see earlier in this chapter for details). Donating your gown not only gives you a tax deduction, but also affords another bride a good deal—and all the proceeds go to breast cancer patients. Check their web site at BridesAgainstBreastCancer.org for details.

FIGURE 4: Forget expensive gown cleaners—donate your dress to a worthy cause and get a tax deduction to boot
(BridesAgainstBreast Cancer.org)

2. We recommend consigning your dress at a local re-sale shop as soon as possible after the wedding. Or try selling your gown on Craigslist or eBay. Why? Styles change and dresses start to age quickly. Take the money and put it towards a savings account for your first child.

3. Clean and preserve it yourself. Most bridal gowns are made of synthetic fabrics (polyester satin is common) that can be cleaned in a washing machine. Yes you read right: a regular ol' washing machine. Cold water, a gentle cycle and a pure detergent (no fabric softeners or bleach) is best. Some bridal shop owners first spray the inside and outside of the dress with Shout or Spray 'N Wash. Hang dry on a plastic hanger. Note: before washing, you should test any beading or pearls. Place one bead/pearl in cold water for ten minutes and see if it disintegrates (some designers use very cheap pearls). If it passes the test, you can clean the gown at home.

4. After the dress is clean, wrap it in a clean, dry, white cotton sheet. If you want to stuff it with tissue paper, make sure it's acid free paper (available from local arts supplies or craft stores or stores like the Container Store, containerstore.com). Put it in an acid-free box (also available from the sources above) and store it in a cool dry place—no attics or basements.

5. If this sounds too daunting, take/send it to a reputable clean-

er. If you decide to use a local cleaner, be sure to check references and the Better Business Bureau. Another tip: if the gown is expensive (over $1000), insist that the shop only release the gown when you show a photo ID.

We do recommend a national resource for gown preservation: Professional Cleaners (professionalcleaners.com; 800-690-2146). Owner David Glausha is a seasoned pro when it comes to gown cleaning and preservation.

In a recent **Wall Street Journal** article that tested different gown preservation cleaners, the Cranky Consumer recommended Heritage Gown Preservation (heritagegown.com). The company charged $310 to clean the test gown. One negative: turnaround time was seven and a half weeks.

One final caveat—even if you do all the above steps and use that acid-free box, there is no guarantee that the dress won't yellow. Whether you pop that dress in the Maytag or send it to an expensive gown preservation company, there is still a good chance it will discolor over time.

Whew! We're at page 100 already? Wow, how time flies. Now that you've learned all the tricks to saving on a bridal gown, let's move on to the attire for the bridesmaids and the groomsmen. That's up next!

Pop quiz: can you name 14 ways to find a bridesmaids dress that won't break the bank? And does not look hideous? We reveal the answers, plus discuss the hottest maids' designers and the best online deals. Finally, let's not forget the groom— we'll take a look at tuxedos and several ways to cut that expense.

Bridesmaids' Gowns

What Are You Buying?

Remember the movie "27 Dresses?" Yes, the best part of that movie about a woman who was a bridesmaid 27 times was seeing those horrid gowns! Okay, we know you're not going to do that to your bridesmaids and we're here to help you make that happen. You can avoid the cheap poly-ester fabric, ugly colors, absurd detailing . . . and your bridesmaids will love you for it.

Traditional bridesmaids dresses are designed to be "disposable," worn for only one day and then burned—yet they are sold at prices that are far from disposable. Most bridesmaids' dresses range from $100 to $250 (the national average is $140), although you can find maids gowns for as little as $70 from discounters. On the upper end, the "couture" bridesmaids' designers expect you to shell out $400+ for their creations. And, of course, those figures don't include expensive alter-ations—er, "custom fitting."

The good news: today you have great alternatives to those low quality, high-priced traditional dresses. In fact, right off the bat, we'll review some new options for your bridesmaids that will make them love you for your amazing taste without breaking their bank accounts.

Getting Started: How Far in Advance?

Most bridesmaids' gowns take two to four months to special order from bridal shops. If you are getting married in popular summer months, give yourself a little more time. In general, once you have selected the bridal gown, begin the search for bridesmaids' apparel. What if you don't have four months? Most of the major bridesmaids makers offer "rush service"—a limited selection of styles available in about six to eight weeks.

Web sites, like those mentioned later in this chapter, take only a week or two to ship most in-stock gowns. And don't forget David's (reviewed in the last chapter). This chain does carry some in-stock maids' gowns in a variety of sizes.

Factor in time for alterations. That can take a couple weeks as well. Depending on the store you by from you'll need at least a month and as much as five or six months to order ahead.

Step-by-step Shopping Strategies

♥ **Step 1:** After buying your bridal gown (and hence deciding on the setting and formality of your wedding), start the search for bridesmaids' gowns. Shopping for bridesmaids' dresses before you find your gown will only be distracting.

♥ **Step 2:** Take into account your bridesmaids' ability to pay for the dress. (Traditionally, the bridesmaid pays for her gown plus alterations and accessories.) Are your bridesmaids cash-strapped college students or corporate lawyers earning six figures a year? Obviously, this is a big factor in your decision.

♥ **Step 3:** Given the financial condition of your attendants, start the shopping process. Follow much the same steps as for finding a bridal gown. Look at fabrics, finishes, and styles.

♥ **Step 4:** When you decide on a gown, announce your decision to the bridesmaids. Make sure each bridesmaid is individually measured and receives a written receipt that specifies the manufacturer, style number, size and delivery date.

♥ **Step 5:** Be sure to leave two weeks or more for alterations—even longer if the dresses have to be shipped to out-of-town bridesmaids. Get written cost estimates on any alterations before the order is placed.

Top Money-saving Secrets

1 **Package discounts.** If you order your gown from a bridal shop, they may offer a discount if you order all the bridesmaids' dresses there as well. This discount can range from 10% to 20%. Sometimes this is negotiable, so ask. (Always check prices with a couple of sources to make sure you are getting a true discount).

2 **Check out the discounters.** The discount gown web sites reviewed in the last chapter also sell bridesmaids and even flower girl dresses. Typical savings run 20% to 40%, depending on the brand.

3 **Sew your own.** What's a bridesmaid-style dress, anyway? A basic dress pattern with little detailing or fuss. And can't you just buy typical bridesmaid fabrics like taffeta or crepe at a fabric store? Yes, you can. We've heard from several brides who had their favorite aunt sew their bridesmaids' dresses. While not a solution for everyone, this concept has its merits. One bargain tip: if you go this route, sign up for Joann Fabric's mailing list. Readers say Joann regularly sends out "1/2 price on anything" coupons to their mailing list, making fabric a bargain.

4 **Pick a color, any color.** Instead of forcing all the bridesmaids to wear the same dress, just give them a color (a swatch is best) and then have them buy separate dresses. Sure, they won't exactly match in style, but who cares? Let the bridesmaids shop their favorite dress shop and find a style that they can wear again. (One tip: suggest to the maids a basic style or skirt length). Obviously, you can't be a control freak to follow this tip, but it might be worth a shot. A truly kind bride might even let her brides pick *any* dress they like regardless of color; this trend comes to us courtesy of our European cousins who don't do the matchy-matchy.

5 **Hit the department stores.** Okay, we realize you haven't been in a department store for a while. But don't over look these retail dinosaurs—many offer surprisingly good deals on maids' gowns. One big reason: recent bridesmaids fashion looks much like the "dressy" gowns already stocked by departments stores. Even better: department stores offer much lower prices (and higher quality) than bridal shops. One reader emailed us to point out that Bloomingdales has many bridesmaid-looking dresses that are available off-the-rack or orderable in different colors, sizes, lengths, etc. She hit a sale and got her dresses for just

$60 each. Even if you pay full price (about $100 to $200 at most stores), you can at least try on several styles, colors and sizes right in the store. Plus you don't have to wait for an eternity for a "special" order to arrive—most department stores will track down different colors/sizes at nearby locations.

6 **Buy the gloves at a discount.** Don't pay high retail prices for bridesmaids' gloves—we found an online discounter, Dina's (bridalgloves.com) that offers a 20% to 30% savings off nationally advertised gloves. Here's how it works: to identify the gloves, you provide a picture you've seen online or the bridesmaid dress info (style, color, etc.)—Dina's does the rest. Most gloves (made by the same companies advertised in bridal magazines) are only $16 to $35 a pair. The same company also discounts matching handbags and other maids' accessories.

7 **Do it online.** Besides the web sites we mention later in this chapter, consider Bloomingdales by Mail (Bloomingdales. com), Talbots (talbots.com), Spiegel (Spiegel.com), even JCPenney (jcpenney.com). Remember, you can return dresses from these manufacturers with little or no hassle.

Maids' accessories can also be purchased online at a discount. Purses, gloves, jewelry, and hose are all available at a myriad of online sites—you don't have to buy these a t full retail.

8 **Avoid rush cuts.** Bridesmaids' dresses are expensive enough when ordered at full retail. Add in that extra "rush" fee (incurred when you order a dress with less than two to three months before your wedding) and you'll see the price rise another 20%. Web sites also charge more for express shipping. Don't delay making this decision as you plan the rest of your wedding

9 **For shoes, go surfing.** Avoid retail stores and their $200+ price tags. The web has many discount sources for dye-to-match satin shoes. In addition to those sources mentioned in Chapter 2 (see the Accessories box), Based on reader reviews, we'd recommend DyeableShoeStore.com, which has shoes that start at an amazing $40. Here's how it works: you purchase the desired size shoe in white satin and have them shipped to you to confirm sizing. Next, send them back to the website with a swatch of fabric in the color you want. DyeableShoeStore.com will then custom dye the shoes to match.

What if you want to have someone else dye the shoes? You don't have to go to a fancy retail shop and pay through the nose for dyeing. Our advice: go to a shoe repair shop instead. They charge $10 to $20 a pair for dyeing—and don't forget to negotiate a discount if you have more than four pairs.

A few notes about dyed-to-match shoes: the dye is NOT waterproof. If you are planning an outdoor wedding, remember wet grass can cause the dye to run and stain. It is also difficult to get every last shoe to match; and the color may look different in outdoor light compared to indoors.

10 **Don't shop in a store with "bridal" in its name.** Many specialty stores have great deals on dresses that would work well for bridesmaids.

11 **Hit outlet stores.** Many of the stores we mention in this chapter have outlet stores. Check the web site Outlet Bound (web: outletbound.com) to see if one is near you. Example: Group USA has 12 outlet stores in the US including Miami and Dallas. Ann Taylor has over 90 outlets across the country. Don't forget Nordstrom's Rack stores as well. We've seen multitudes of dresses suitable for bridesmaids on sale in their stores. You could find them for as little as $30 each.

12 **Skip the accessories.** Bridesmaids' designers have been turning out all manner of matching accessories like shawls, purses and shoes in recent seasons. The prices, however, are outrageous. One designer now pitches matching purses for $64 and satin dyeable shoes for up to $170! Shawls and wraps add another $30 to $60 to another famous maids designer's dresses. And try to avoid needing a shawl or wrap by selecting a bridesmaids style that isn't so bare to begin with. Finally, just skip some superfluous items altogether. Do your bridesmaids really need a $64 handbag dyed to match their chartreuse gowns?

13 **Try the Rack.** If you have a Nordstrom department store near you, odds are you also have a Nordstrom Rack. That's the clearance outlet for merchandise that didn't make it in the store. One reader emailed us this incredible story: she found her bridesmaids' dresses at

Alteration-friendly maids gowns

Here's something no one tells you about bridesmaids gowns: some are easier to alter than others. Bridal retailers tell us the best bridesmaids dresses (that is, easiest to alter) are made by Alfred Angelo, Bridal Originals and After Six. The worst? Mori Lee, Levkoff, McClintock and Bari Jay are the most difficult, thanks to a lack of seam allowance and other construction shortcuts.

Nordstrom Rack for just $14.95. Nope, that isn't a typo. "Every year they put dresses on sale—racks of them! Ours were periwinkle matte satin strapless sheaths. The sizes ran from 0 to 14!" What if you have a tough-to-fit bridesmaid? The same reader said she solved that problem by buying TWO gowns (at $15 each) in different sizes and then had a seamstress piece them together for a tough-to-fit maid. Go to Nordstrom.com to find a Rack near you.

74 Look for flash sales. Limited time "flash" sales on designer clothes, shoes and housewares, are all the rage now in the fashion world—and many of these sales would work for bridesmaids dresses and accessories. Sign up with sites like IDEELI, MyHabit and HauteLook, then you'll get daily emails featuring all kinds of great deals.

BRIDESMAIDS OPTIONS

Why spend $200+ on a bridesmaids gown from a bridal shop when you can get a similar gown from a department store or catalog at HALF the price? Here's how several options compare to the standard issue bridesmaids dress found in bridal stores (we used a Levkoff gown for comparison):

WHERE	WHAT	PRICE	FABRIC
LEVKOFF (AT A BRIDAL SHOP)	STRAPLESS A-LINE DRESS	$210; OTHERS $145-$270	POLY SATIN
DRESS BARN DRESSBARN.COM	ASYMETRICAL DRESS CRYSTALS AT SHOULDER	$86; OTHERS $46-$148	POLY
WHITE HOUSE WHITEHOUSEBLACK MARKET.COM	CROSS BACK MATTE JERSEY	$158; OTHERS $150-$300	POLY
BLOOMINGDALES BLOOMINGDALES.COM	STRAPLESS A-LINE FLOOR LENGTH DRESS	$210 OTHERS $125-$1000	POLY

Notes: As you can see, the biggest advantage to ordering a standard "bridesmaids dress" like a Bill Levkoff design from a bridal shop is the wide availability of sizes and colors. Yes, some mail order sources sell large sizes (above a 16 or 18) . . . but extra length is rarely available. Colors are also limited—if your heart is set on a particular odd hue, a standard bridesmaids dress might be the only solution. Another

maids

An example: on IDEELI we found a silver strapless cocktail dress regularly $365 for $119. It was available in sizes 2-8 plus size 12. Yes, supplies and sizes may be limited so it may work best for small wedding parties. And you'll want to make a very quick decision since items go fast. But if you can save your bridesmaids as much as $250, it may be well worth the effort.

Helpful Hints

1 **Don't go shopping with a committee.** If you want to make the process of shopping for bridesmaids' gowns go as smoothly as possible, just take along ONE friend or relative. Too many bridesmaids (each with their own opinions and tastes) will only complicate the decision. Make the

COMPARED

Sizes	Comments	Returnable?
Sizes 4-28 some styles in 38-42	available in 32 colors Delivery: 12-14 weeks. shipping included	Are you kidding?
Sizes 2-12	One color; Delivery 3-8 days shipping $7-14	Free returns to stores; exchange or refund
Sizes 00-16	One color; Delivery 7-10 days shipping $14-$15	Free returns to stores or $7 by Mail
Misses (2-12)	Two colors; Delivery 3-9 days shipping: $18	Yes, exchange or full refund

advantage to standard bridesmaid gowns: they guarantee the dye lots will match if you order several gowns. Of course, you pay for that, almost TWICE the price of mail order options. Plus delivery is much quicker using mail order and department stores, a matter of days versus 12-14 WEEKS for a standard issue bridesmaid gown.

decision and announce it to the other bridesmaids. Don't expect every-one to love your choice (and, unfortunately, some bridesmaids may be tacky enough to tell you about it to your face). If you want to see evi-dence of why shopping for bridesmaids dresses-by-committee is a bad idea, just watch about any episode of TLC's "Say Yes to the Dress."

2 **Take your hardest to fit bridesmaid with you.** So, which bridesmaid should you take along with you? Let's be frank: every-thing looks great on the bridesmaid who models in her spare time. It's a smarter bet to take another bridesmaid who is, uh, the most challeng-ing to fit.

3 **You may be on the hook for deadbeat bridesmaids or groomsmen.** Here's a nasty surprise: some bridal retailers are forcing brides and grooms to sign contracts that say they are responsi-ble for payment on ANY dress purchase or tux rental by their wedding party. Yes, when your flaky maid of honor fails to pay the balance due for her gown order to the bridal shop, YOU could be on the hook.

Pitfalls to Avoid

PITFALL #1 SQUARE PEG, ROUND HOLE.

"Help! I want my bridesmaids to wear this slinky dress I saw online, but when we went to order, none of the girls fit the size chart! The bridal shop recommended a size 14 for a girl who normally wears a size 6. When the dress comes in, won't she be socked with expensive alterations?"

Do you have the body of a supermodel? Well, we sure don't. But, unfortunately, most bridesmaids dress manufacturers have size charts that are designed for bizarre, alien woman with exaggerated Barbie Doll figures. Giraffes with breasts.

Take, for example, that above story. The bridesmaid in question had measurements of 36" bust, 29" waist, 37" hips. Now, look at the size chart for one of the U.S. and Canada's biggest bridesmaids designers.

	\multicolumn{9}{c}{SIZE}
	4	6	8	10	12	14	16	18	20
Bust	33	34	35	36	37	38.5	40	41.5	43.5
Waist	24	25	26	27	28	29.5	31	32.5	34.5
Hips	36	37	38	39	40	41.5	43	44.5	46.5

So, what size would YOU order? Let's see, the bridesmaid's bust (measured at the fullest part of the chest; this is NOT her bra size) would fit into a size 10. BUT, look at that waist—it needs a size 14. And the hips? Try a size 6.

Because it is always easiest to alter IN a dress (instead of letting it out), we recommend ordering the size that corresponds to the bridesmaid's LARGEST measurement. That would indeed be a size 14. As you'll note, however, this will require significant alterations, as the dress will have to be taken in a couple inches at the bust and hips.

This problem has grown in recent years, thanks to those new, body-hugging styles churned out by bridesmaids' designers. Those slinky dresses are definitely a step forward fashion-wise, but all this haute couture has run head long into the reality of women's bodies. The fact is many bridesmaids just don't fit the bizarro size charts. As a result, some are being socked with HUGE alteration bills to remake (or drastically cut down) these gowns.

What makes this problem even more complex is the fact that each bridesmaid designer has just ONE size chart. This chart covers a wide range of dress styles, from a loosely fitting empire-waist gown to a body-hugging sheath. If you go for an empire-style dress (which is tightly fitted in the bust), the measurement that counts the most is, of course, the bust. But if you plan to have your maids don a sexy strapless number, watch out—those waist and hip measurements will be critical.

One thing you can be sure of: almost all bridesmaids' dresses require alterations. Even if a bridesmaid exactly matches the size chart, she'll still probably need some minor alterations (a skirt hem, a bodice tuck here and there). That's because these dresses are not custom-made to your measurements—heck, sometimes they don't even correspond closely to the size chart itself.

What if your bridesmaids are "off the chart," that is they don't closely correspond to the size charts? Do yourself and them a favor: DON'T order maids dresses from a bridal shop. Instead, consider some of our alternative dress sources. Stores like J. Crew and Talbot's carry a wide range of sizes and (here's a shocker) actually let you return a dress that doesn't fit.

PITFALL #2 DISINTEGRATING BRIDESMAIDS DRESSES.

"I ordered five bridesmaids dresses from a major designer. When they came in, I was shocked! Every single dress was defective. All of the dresses came out of the boxes with threads hanging from every seam and the seams all pulled and puckered. The buttons and loops on the backs of the dresses fell apart when the girls tried to button them. These had to be sewn on four of the five dresses one half hour before I was to be married! The most appalling defect of all was the detailing on the front of one of the dresses. It was sewn on crooked and had to be taken off and reat-

*tached by a professional dressmaker. While my maid of honor was up at
the altar next to me, we could actually hear her dress popping apart."*

Yes, it is no wonder the bridesmaids dress is the biggest joke in the
fashion business. What's most frustrating about this purchase, however,
is the "bait and switch" tactics of the largest bridesmaid manufacturers.

Here's how it works: the bridesmaid *samples* you first try on at the
bridal shop are always pristine and perfect. But what about your special
order? Somehow, the quality then slips—and drops through the floor.
Consumers we interviewed describe the workmanship on many of these
dresses in one word: abysmal. And it's not just on the cheap dresses; the
ones described above cost $260 each, according to the bride.

Invisible zippers are an example of the quality problem with bridesmaids' gowns. Yes, these disappearing zippers (seen on such hip lines as
After Six and Dessy) are supposed to make gowns look more fashionable. The only problem: they break. Some shops have been so frustrated
with invisible zippers (insiders call them "miserable zippers") that they
are replacing them during alterations.

Overall, the best advice we can give is to order early. Leaving enough
time will enable the shop to fix the problems. Another idea is to by-pass
the standard bridesmaid dress entirely. Select dresses at a department
store or from a web site and have the last laugh.

PITFALL #3 SIZING PROBLEMS.

*"Our $300 bridesmaids gowns arrived yesterday and NONE of them fit
the girls! Some were too big, others too small. What happened?"*

Yes, you carefully shopped for bridesmaids' gowns and made sure
you ordered the correct sizes for all the girls after comparing their measurements to the designer's size charts. But then the gowns came in and
whamo! Nothing fit. What happened?

Here's a dirty little secret of the bridesmaids dress biz: sometimes,
your "special order" gowns won't fit. That's because the bridesmaid
manufacturers goof with the sizing. Among the worst offenders: After
Six/Dessy, Mori Lee and Bari Jay.

What makes this more frustrating is there is little rhyme or reason
to the incorrect sizing—some gowns come in too big; others are too
small. Then, adding insult to injury, some dress designers (notably Mori
Lee and Bari Jay) take an "it's YOUR problem" attitude toward sizing
goofs. Hard to believe, but these manufactures think you are getting
such a deal on their gowns that they refuse to fix any problems, leaving
shops and brides scrambling to alter miss-sized gowns. (On a positive
note, even though After Six/Dessy is guilty of miss sizing, the designer
is at least willing to fix problems).

PITFALL #4 CLASHING COLOR MOTIFS.

"I was a bridesmaid in a wedding recently. The bride picked out lovely peach bridesmaids' gowns. Unfortunately, the church was all decorated in bright red—all her pictures looked like 'Night of the Clashing Circus Clowns!' It wasn't pretty."

Be careful when you select the bridesmaids' gowns to take into account the decor of your ceremony and reception site. Many of your wedding pictures will have the site as a backdrop. Try to pick a color that is pleasing—and doesn't clash with the decor. Hint: if you are marrying in a church, ask the officiant what types/colors of hangings and alter cloths they use during your wedding month.

PITFALL #5 DYE LOTS MAY VARY.

"I would like to order bridesmaids gowns from two different stores (in different towns). The shop owners all have told me that they won't guarantee that the colors will match, since the fabric will be from different dye lots. Is that true? Could you really tell the difference?"

If you've got bridesmaids scattered across the country, it may be tempting to have them go to a local bridal shop to order their dress. Our advice: don't. It is true that dye lots can (and do) vary from one batch of dresses to another. The only way to insure they will all match is to order them from the same source at the *same time* (out-of-town bridesmaids will have to get their dresses by mail and have fittings done locally).

Would you really be able to tell a difference in the dye lots? It's hard to say. That depends on the color and fabric—some styles might show more of a color variation than others. It's not worth the risk.

Are gown knock-offs legal?

It's a time-honored tradition in fashion: ripping-off your competitor's hot selling design. While we see frequent design-stealing in bridal gowns, it's a virtual epidemic in the world of bridesmaids' designs, where one "hot" style quickly appears in several different versions from different makers. And guess what? It's completely legal. Copyright laws do NOT cover apparel (except for logos and certain patterns of lace). Hence it is completely legal to buy a knock-off gown or to have your aunt (or any seamstress) sew a copy of a hot style.

This same advice applies to any extra fabric you order (to make a flower girl's dress or shawls for the ceremony, etc). Order the fabric at the same time you order the gowns.

PITFALL #6 SIGHT UNSEEN COLORS.

"I ordered $300 bridesmaids dresses in 'blue onyx' from a local bridal shop. The only problem? I didn't see the color chart or a swatch before ordering. The shop had samples in green and burgundy, but only a catalog picture of the blue. When the dresses came in, I was shocked. The color looked nothing like the picture and was terrible!"

Since bridal shops carry a limited amount of inventory, you may be tempted to order a bridesmaids dress in a color you can't see. You may want a dress in "cranberry," but the shop only carries the same style in a "hunter green." And even the same color can look different in certain fabrics (velvets versus chiffons, etc.).

The best protection is to insist on seeing a color swatch or color chart to make sure it is what you want. Catalog/online pictures can be notoriously unreliable—funky lighting in the photo or simple variations in printing can make a "deep plum" dress seem more like bright purple.

The quote above is an actual email we received from a New Jersey bride. Unfortunately, she was stuck with dresses she described as "god-awful ugly." (Actually, she used more colorful language than that, but you get the idea.) The bridal shop asked the manufacturer to fix the problem and guess what? The manufacturer refused, saying, "That's what 'blue onyx' is supposed to look like."

The bottom line: make sure you see the color(s) in the fabric(s) you want before committing to a special-order bridesmaids dress.

PITFALL #7 MARK IT UP TO MARK IT DOWN.

"The bridal shop where I bought my gown offered a 10% discount on maids dresses. That sounded great until I did some price shopping. I found the shop was marking up the gowns over retail before they gave me a 'discount.'"

Fake discounts are a problem in the bridal industry. We've talked with retailers who confess to the "mark it up before you mark it down" scam—shops will price dresses OVER retail before they give you a so-called "discount." A word to the wise: do some price shopping before you commit to any package deal.

Another trend: no-name bridesmaids dresses. More and more retailers are now carrying "stealth" bridesmaids' gowns by no-name manufacturers. Don't look for those gowns advertised online—these makers keep a very low profile. The gowns are typically knock-offs of designer dresses, sewn cheaply and sold to retailers at low wholesale prices. Retailers then can feel free to mark-up no name gowns to whatever they want, since it is so hard to price-shop these dresses.

What's worse: some shops do a bait and switch with no-name dresses. We've seen several reports of bridesmaids who ordered a name brand gown and then got a no name knock-off. One bride ordered a Levkoff dress and got an Alexia copy.

How can you prevent this? Be sure you get a written order ticket that indicates the manufacturer's name. Some shops only put their bogus in-house codes on order forms, making it hard to prove what was promised. When the bridesmaids' dresses come in, check for the designer's label. A telltale sign of the knock-off scam are maids' dresses that come in missing designer labels (legit designers like Levkoff almost always put tags in).

Your best defense against all these scams: buy from non-traditional sources like web sites, department's stores and non-wedding shops. Often prices are comparable or cheaper, quality is great and service problems are few.

Flower girl dresses: where to get the deals

Sure, those matching flower girl dresses are cute, but do you really want to pay $180 for a dress for a five-year-old girl? No, you don't have to spend a three-figure sum to get a cute flower girl gown. Here are our bargain tips:

♥ **Department store holiday and Easter sales.** After Christmas and Easter, look for deals on dress-up clothes for girls—most of these gowns can double for a flower girl. And you'll save 50% or more by hitting those sales. Hint: also check out the communion dresses for the smallest flower girls—again, much more affordable than the $100+ dresses you see in bridal stores.

♥ **Go online.** Readers found sites like eBay have terrific deals on dresses your flower girl can wear. Many dresses are under $35. Another site to check out: Dapperlads.com (formerly Dandylasses.com). The discounts aren't huge on this site but the dresses are exceptional and most are priced below $75.

Best Online Bargains

What's the advantage to buying your bridesmaids gowns online? Here is the run-down:

Everything is returnable (except some sale items). Sizing charts are easy to use and understand, often the same as real-world sizing. So if you know what you wear at Ann Taylor, for example, your bridesmaid gown will be sized the same. Dresses can be mailed to individual bridesmaids directly and shipping is usually pretty affordable. Finally, great looking dresses do go on sale on these sites for as much as half off, although they may have only limited sizing.

The negatives: you can't always see the dresses before you buy them (some chains carry bridal and bridesmaid styles in a limited number of locations). But many sites will allow you to order a swatch, which helps you get an idea of the color and fabric. Also sizes can be limited. If your maids have a wide variety of body types and sizes, a traditional bridal shop may be able to help you find matching gowns to suit everyone. You may still need to have dresses altered meaning your maids will have to find a local seamstress to help.

Here are reviews of the best online retailers for bridesmaids' dresses:

Ann Taylor *anntaylor.com* Ann Taylor's foray into weddings includes a decent-sized collection of potential bridesmaids dresses at excellent prices. All the dresses are silk in finishes like georgette, taffeta and dupioni. Some styles are rather basic, while others add nice touches like sashes, ruffles, and fabric flowers. You'll find halter necklines, strapless looks and sweetheart designs. Prices range from $150 to $365, although most are in the $200 to $250 range. Sale dresses are available for as little as $90. Sizing ranges from 00 to 18.

Ann Taylor's website has lots of excellent information for bridesmaids. They have a fit guide, fabric glossary and style and fashion tips. Shoes and other accessories are also available. **Rating: A**

BHLDN *BHLDN.com* A few years ago, Anthropologie (sister chain to Urban Outfitters) contemplated entering the bridal market. Rather than adding a wedding category to Anthropologie, however, they opted for a completely separate site: BHLDN.com (short for beholden). Decidedly upscale in its offerings, BHLDN dresses range from $220 to $500. Fabrications include silk/cotton blends, silk gazar, cotton lace and more. Fans of the Anthropologie vibe won't be disappointed in these dresses. **Rating: B**

Brideside *Brideside.com* Are your bridesmaids scattered around the country? Wish you had the experience of the communal bridesmaids shopping trip, complete with fashion show? The solution may be Brideside.com. You can shop many of the brand name bridesmaids gowns, including Alfred Sung and Dessy, place them in your virtual "closet" for friends to see and even order a sample of your favorite choices for only $10. When the dresses come in, Skype your friends and set up a fashion show of the options you've chosen. Sit down with a glass of Merlot and critique the dresses together. Then you can order the top style for your bridesmaid; Brideside ships the dresses directly to each maid. The only downside: prices are regular retail. And we found the site a bit frustrating to navigate; they could use an FAQ on the ordering process. Those concerns aside, Brideside offers an interesting option for bridal parties scattered in different states. **Rating: B-**

Dress Barn *dressbarn.com* How about a bridesmaids dress for as little as $40? Dress Barn has special occasion dresses that would work very well for bridesmaids. Prices start at $40 and range up to $100. The day we visited the site, they were offering a "buy 2 dresses, save $10" promotion. One of our favorites: a metallic blue floor length sheath with crystal accents for a mere $92. The dress was lined with built in bra cups, unusual for a dress at this price. Sizes range from 4-24 plus petites 4-16. **Rating: A-**

J.Crew *jcrew.com* J. Crew has more styles of bridesmaids' dresses than most other chains. We like how they categorize the dresses by fabric and by style. For example, they offer fabric collections like cotton cady, liquid jersey, silk taffeta, tulle and eyelet. Style silhouettes include strapless, halter, shift, a-line and empire. Most of their designs are pretty short with only a few floor length options. The overall look is trendy and prices correspond accordingly. Most dresses hover around $250 with long lengths going up to $365.

Colors are unique (misty rose shade rather than pink, for example) and fabrics and finishes quite fashionable. We wish they had more affordable designs—a few are under $200, but not many. **Rating: A-**

The Limited *thelimited.com* The Limited offers only a few limited options that could be used as bridesmaid dresses. On the plus side, all were priced under $100. Styles are simple in above-the-knee lengths. All their gowns are polyester. Overall, the prices were affordable, but the limited styles and fabric is disappointing. **Rating: C+**

Two Birds Bridesmaid *TwoBirdsBridesmaid.com* Two Birds is the originator of the convertible bridesmaid dress. Basically, these dresses come with long strap/ties that can be tied in a huge variety of ways. By twisting, knotting and draping the straps you can convert their designs from strapless to halter to cap sleeve to one shoulder and more; there are 15 different options, all showcased online. As for the dresses themselves, the fabric is a poly/jersey blend and comes in four different silhouettes: classic, chiffon, rosette and high-low. The gowns are available in over 20 colors and prices start at $260. The web site is really amazing: it shows each dress in any of the different strap styles and colors so you can see all the options. Swatches are also available. Dresses take 12 weeks to make and shipping is $7 to $15 per dress. FYI, Nordstrom also sells Two Birds' dresses. **Rating: B+**

White House/Black Market *whitehouseblackmarket.com* As you can imagine with a store whose theme is black and white clothes, the brides-maids' dresses from White House/Black Market (WHBM) are somewhat monochromatic. The only dress with color was one wine colored option—perhaps perfect for that Valentines weekend wedding. Selection is limited and ranged in price from $150 to $398 with a mix of cocktail lengths and floor-length. The styling is very sophisticated and up scale although the fabrics are nothing to write home about. **Rating: B+**

♥ **Other sites recommended by our readers.** Who's got the lowest prices for bridesmaids' gowns online? We have to give the award to **ShopShop** (a.k.a., CyberGown.com; shopshop.com). Their maids begin at the unbelievably low price of $49! Other dresses run $59 to $259.

Looking for women's sizes in bridesmaids' gowns? Check out Roamans (roamans.com) which offer sizes 12W to 44W. The selection is pretty good and prices are reasonable. Another reader recommended **Jessica London** (JessicaLondon.com) as a good source for plus size maids at discounted prices.

The $59 bridesmaids dress

Can you really buy a bridesmaid's dress for $59? Yes, you can. **ShopShop.com** (we briefly mentioned them earlier in this chapter) has well over 50 bridesmaids dresses that start at just $49. What do they look like? Who cares at this price! Just kidding—they look just fine. No, we're not talking the latest couture here, but these are some decent basic dresses. And did we mention the price? Your maids will thank you for not forcing them to pay $300+ for a maids gown that will be thrown away after the wedding. Sizes 4 to 28.

Another reader recommended **CybernetPlaza.com** as a good source for cheap bridesmaids gowns. "They have true sizing, good quality and decent styling. The best thing is that none of us paid over $80 for a dress!" Prices start at $49.

Ratings of Selected Bridesmaids Designers

With over $800 million worth of bridesmaids dresses sold each year, there is certainly no shortage of options to consider. Besides manufacturers that just make bridesmaids dresses (After Six/Dessy, Jordan), there are many bridal gown designers that make maids' dresses too. But who has the best quality? The best value for the dollar?

To answer those questions, we intensively research all the different brands, designers and manufacturers. We attend industry wholesale markets to view runway shows and inspect garments. We also talk with retailers about which dresses are best . . . and worst. Finally, we hear from you, the reader. Our email box is always open to hear your comments.

The chart nearby compares the top 20 bridesmaid dress designers. The rating refers to our opinion of their quality.

Tuxedos

Nowhere are the wedding etiquette rules sillier than for men's formal wear. For example, they say you MUST wear a black tux with tails for a formal wedding after six in the evening. If you don't, the vengeful WEDDING GODS will strike you down, ostracize your family and charge obscene amounts of money to your credit cards.

Now if your wedding is before six you can wear a gray or white short coat . . . but not if the moon is full. And, of course, you must follow the omnipotent "formality" rules that dictate proper dress for weddings that are very formal, just plain formal, semi-formal, pseudo-formal and the dreaded para-formal.

Just kidding.

We believe all this is nonsense. Grooms and groomsmen should wear whatever they believe is appropriate. Who cares what time of day the wedding is? If your wedding is an informal ceremony in a local civic rose garden, you don't have to wear a tuxedo. We know we might incur the wrath of Emily Post for saying this, but hey, do what you want to do. If you look good in a double-breasted tux, wear that. If you don't, look for another style. You get the idea.

Continued on page 120

Bridesmaids designers compared

NAME	RATING	COST	WEB	SIZING Petite	Large
After Six	A-	$$	aftersix.com		●
Alfred Angelo	C	$$	alfredangelo.com	●	●
Alfred Sung	A-	$$	alfredsungdresses.com		●
Alyce Designs	B-	$$ to $$$	alyceparis.com		●
Amsale	B	$$$	amsale.com		●
Ann Taylor	A-	$$	anntaylor.com	●	
Bari Jay	B+	$$	barijay.com		●
Belsoie / B2	A-	$$ to $$$	jasminebridal.com		●
Bill Levkoff	A-	$$ to $$$	billlevkoff.com		●
Chadwicks	A	$	chadwicks.com	●	●
David's Bridal	D	$ to $$	davidsbridal.com	●	●
Davinci	A-	$	davincibridal.com		●
Dessy	B+	$$$	dessy.com		●
Eden	B+	$ to $$	edenbridals.com	●	●
Impression	A-	$ to $$	impressionbridal.com		●
J Crew	A	$$$	jcrew.com	●	
JC Penney	A-	$	jcpenney.com	●	●
Jessica Mclintock	B	$ to $$	jessicamclintock.com		●
J Hjelm Occasions	B+	$$$	jimhjelm.com	●	●
Jordan	C	$$ to $$$	jordanfashions.com		●
Lazaro	B	$$$	jlmcouture.com	●	
Laundry	B+	$$$	laundrybyshellisegal.com		
Mori Lee	C+	$	morilee.com		●
New Image	B	$$$	billlevkoff.com		●
Siri	B	$$$	siriinc.com		
Talbot's	B	$$$	talbots.com	●	●
Vera Wang	C	$$$	verawang.com		
Watters	A	$$$	watters.com		●

NOTES: RATING: *Our opinion of the designer's quality, value and fashion, based on our own hands-on inspections and surveys of bridal retailers.* COST: *The range in retail prices: $=under $140, $$=$140 to $200, $$$=over $200.* WEB: *The designer's web site.* SIZING—PETITE: *Designers who offer special petite sizes. Some offer petites for all styles, while others only do petites on a selected number of designs.* LARGE: *Nearly all designers offer gowns in sizes 4-20. We classify any size larger*

Key: •=YES

EASY TO ALTER?	COMMENTS
•	Good quality; excellent web site with online color swatches
•	Not the cutting edge of fashion, but good value. 46 colors.
•	Big on separates. Made by Dessy/After Six.
	Quality is average; delivery is good. Prices a bit high.
•	Fashion forward, but sizing is limited.
	Generous return policy; matching shoes, accessories.
	Can be difficult to alter; fashion above average.
	B2 is simpler with lower prices, less fancy fabric.
•	Fashionable yes and quality has improved. Huge selection.
•	Most under $150; limited colors but good value.
	Complaints and snafus mar rating; do offer maternity styles.
	Knock-off David's maids gowns at lower prices.
•	Quality is above average, but prices are steep.
	Basic traditional styling, good value.
•	Separates a mainstay here; fashion good. Sizing inconsistent.
•	Yes, you can actually wear these again! High price, but all silk.
	Basic styling. Great prices. Only some styles have extended sizes.
	Above-average quality; not-so-great customer service.
	Good quality, great styling. Very expensive.
	Entry-level "Joanie G" line is best value; quality is average.
	A $300 maids dress? Too pricey for only average quality.
	Designed by Liz Claiborne's Shelli Segal, but made by Levkoff.
	Knock-off fashion, low quality but low price. Slow delivery.
	Division of Levkoff has slightly better quality, fashion.
	Many styles available in different fabrics; difficult to alter.
	Pricey, but mostly silk fabric. Limited colors. Look for sales..
	Overpriced and limited sizes. Did we mention overpriced?
•	Fabrics, styling, color choice above average. A bit pricey.

*than a 20 as a "large size." Some designers just offer sizes 22
and 24, while others go up to a 44. As with petites, only selected styles may be available in larger sizes. Most designers
charge extra for large sizes.* **EASY TO ALTER?** *Based on our interviews with 150 seamstresses, which bridesmaids dresses are
easiest to alter? A lack of seam allowance or other construction shortcuts can be make a dress difficult to alter.*

What Are You Buying?

Actually, most grooms and groomsmen *rent* formal wear for weddings. Imagine what would happen if men had to shell out the same kind of money that bridesmaids spend on those horrendously ugly bridesmaids' gowns. There would be mass revolts and street rioting. Fortunately, for national security's sake, most men's formal wear is rented. Typically, the groomsmen are financially responsible for their tuxedo rentals, so basically you and your fiancé's only expense is the groom's tux. Here are the three basic options for men's formalwear:

***1* Rent.** Good news: you CAN rent a stylish tux for your wedding. Yes, until a few years ago, most tux shops just offered cookie-cutter styles (you could have black or black). Now, the $1.6 billion tux business has received a fashion injection, thanks to Hollywood's influence on formal attire. You can still rent a black tux, but now you can choose from styles with pointed lapels, brocade vests and long satin ties. Yes, you can even rent a white linen tux.

Rentals account for 70% of the tux market (the rest of the guys will purchase a tux). When you rent a tux, you get just about everything: jacket, pants, cummerbund, shirt, tie, cuff links, and, of course, shirt studs (little jewelry that covers your buttons). Notice what's missing? No, not underwear. If you answered "shoes" give yourself extra points. While most tuxes rent for $100 to $175 (an average is $150), the shoes are often $20 to $30 extra. Of course, it's more expensive in major metropolitan areas (like New York City, where tux rentals can top $200, $250 in Washington DC). A small deposit/damage waiver ($10 to $25) is required to reserve a tux. There are three types of places to rent formal wear:

♥ **CHAIN STORES.** Large formalwear chains (such as MensWearhouse.com, Josbank.com and JimsFormalwear.com) are located across the U.S. They basically offer similar styles and brand names. Service can range from helpful to dreadful. Most of these chains don't carry any stock at their stores—a central warehouse is used to dispense the tuxedos. Hence, it's difficult to decide which style is best for you by just looking at mannequins or a catalog. To try on a particular style, you must ask the shop for a "trial fitting." For no charge, most shops will bring in a style in your size. The only disadvantage is that this requires a second visit to the shop, rather inconvenient for those of you who lead busy lives.

♥ **BRIDAL SHOPS.** More and more bridal shops are now renting tuxes. However, instead of stocking tuxes at their store, they use a service, which supplies them with rentals. Hence, the way you pick a tuxedo is to look through a book with pictures of tuxedo-clad models. On the up side, the bridal shops may cut you a deal if you buy the bridal and bridesmaids' gowns from them. On the down side, while bridal shop employees may know a lot about bridal gowns, they may know diddly-squat about men's formal wear.

Tux Shopping Tips

In the old days, tux shopping was rather simple: if you were planning a formal evening wedding, you wore a single-breasted tux. Daytime or less formal affairs called for cutaways, strollers or morning coats. Now, that's all been thrown out the window—guys are wearing all sorts of tuxes during all times of the day. So, perhaps the best advice is to get a tux that best matches your body. Here are some ideas, given different body types:

♥ **Short, stocky guys.** Jackets with slim shawl collars are a good bet. Stick with a single breasted look with a low button. You don't need any of those broad-shoulder Euro-style tuxes; that would be overkill. Instead jackets with natural shoulder lines are best. For pants, avoid styles that have too much break on the foot (which creates a sloppy look); instead, try reverse double-pleated trousers.

♥ **Short, slender guys.** Skip the double-breasted styles and look at single-breasted jackets with a low button and wide lapels.

♥ **Tall, slender guys.** These folks have it easy—just about everything works. Double-breasted tuxes with those Euro-style broad shoulders are fine, as are those hip three-button styles that close high on the chest. Trousers can have more break at the foot.

♥ **Tall, stocky guys.** Jacket length is a tough one here; try styles with shawl collars. Consider a jacket with a bit of room to allow for movement. Stick with traditional looks here.

♥ **Other tips.** Vests are a popular alternative to cummerbunds these days. Be sure to ask whether the vest is a full back or half-back (full looks better if you take off your jacket during the reception).

♥ **INDEPENDENT SHOPS.** Occasionally, we find an independent tuxedo rental shop, one that is not affiliated with a national chain. We often are impressed by the quality of service at these outlets. Furthermore, independent shops may carry a wider selection of styles and designers. You can also find some great deals. For example, Tux-Xpress in Scottsdale, Arizona (tux-xpress.com) rents designer-brand tuxes for $38 to $120, far below the prices of the chains.

2 **Buy.** If you expect to need a tuxedo again for a fancy party or corporate banquet, it may pay to buy. That's because most tuxedos cost $300 to $500 to purchase (although you can find several at discounters for $200 or less). Considering rental fees of $100+ a pop, this might be a good investment. See the money-saving tips in this chapter for places on the web to buy a tux or accessories.

3 **Go with your own suit.** Especially for less formal weddings, it is perfectly acceptable for the groom and groomsmen to wear dark suits.

Tuxedo Basics

Tuxedo jackets are classified by the style of lapel. There are three different types: notched, peaked, or shawl (see right).

Most tuxes are also single breasted but you'll find a few double-breasted styles as well. Morning coats or "cutaways" (right) and strollers are not technically tuxedos. Both are intended to be formal looking without the satin accents that denote formal evening events. Strollers do not have extended tails (like morning coats) and mimic charcoal grey or black suits. Morning coats and strollers are typically worn with vests and four in hand ties (see lower left) not bow ties and cummerbunds.

Tuxedo shirts are available in two different styles: wing collar and spread collar. Occasionally you still see tux shirts with a banded collar. A spread collar is appropriate with either a bow tie or a four-in-hand tie, but stick with bow ties for the wing collar.

The most formal option for a tuxedo is white tie. This merely means the bow tie is white and the tux has tails. You could also wear gloves and even a top hat to complete the look.

A note about suspenders: if you need a way to keep pants on, a belt is not the answer with a tux. Stick with suspenders instead.

Best Online Bargains

Just like in the magazine world, groom's issues often get short shrift on the 'net. Here are some good links to help:

♥ **MYOWNTUXEDO.COM.** Looking for a deal on a tuxedo? Consider My Own Tuxedo, a site that sells both gently worn used tuxes and new designer outfits. Prices are within the range of many rental tux shops. Consider buying a new After Six Mystique coat for a mere $39. A Ralph Lauren Black Barrington IV jacket was $39. Trousers, shirts, vests, cummerbunds, ties, shoes and jewelry are sold separately. Even when you add it all up, it's often less than the rental price at most places! And they have many tuxes on sale as well. Sizing options range from boys size 3 to men's 70L.

♥ **MENSWEARHOUSE.COM.** If you just want to look at current styles, check out MensWearhouse.com. The site offers its unique "Build a Tux" feature. You start with the coat and pant style you like, select a shirt, vest/cummerbund and tie. Then choose shoes and accessories. Your "paperdoll" guy then showcases the look you've chosen. They also have pre-styled looks you can start with and then tweak, as well as a video gallery of looks for inspiration. To rent, you'll want to visit one of the Men's Warehouse stores (they have over 900 locations in the US).

♥ **OTHER SITES TO CONSIDER:** Tuxedos.com, FCGI (fabiancouture.com), Tuxedos.com, and Santana (santanaapparel.com) are additional sites to check out.

Getting Started: How Far in Advance?

Boy, this varies greatly from area to area. In small towns, or for less popular months, you can shop one to two months before the wedding. However, you may need to reserve your tuxedos three to four months before the wedding in larger cities or for popular summer wedding months. If you have out-of-town groomsmen, you may want to leave extra time to get their measurements. FYI: leave extra time for tux shopping if it is prom season (April and May)— shops are extra busy then.

Money-saving Secrets for Tuxedos

1 **Package discounts.** Almost all tuxedo shops offer a free tux rental with the rental of four, five or six tuxedos. In some cases, tux shops distribute coupons good for $10 or more

tuxes

Wedding Party Apparel

off each rental. Our advice: always ask about group discounts.

2 **Skip the rental shoes.** Why? Those cheap rental shoes can be awfully uncomfortable. Instead, wear your own black dress shoes if you have them and save $25.

3 **Surf for discounts.** ETuxedo (etuxedo.com; 888-879-7848) is a large discount seller of tuxes, with prices starting at $90. Even if you don't want to buy a tux online, you can use this site to compare accessory prices like tie & cummerbund sets, cuff links, or shirts. Another site for tux shoppers is CheapTux.com, which offers discounted tuxes as well as accessories at half off retail.

4 **Consider tux alternatives.** In years past, if you wanted to buy or rent a tux you had limited choices—typically just a handful of formalwear stores or bridal shops rented tuxes. Now, there is some competition. Men's Wearhouse is now the biggest tux renter/seller in the U.S. You can rent a tux from one of nearly 1000 Men's Wearhouse stores (In Canada, Men's Wearhouse goes under the name Moore's). Rentals run $140 to $160 (including shoes). Or you can buy a tux at Men's Wearhouse for around $230 for a wool single-breasted style. Jos. A Banks has also added tuxedos to their clothing mix (josbank.com).

5 **Look for coupons.** Speaking of Men's Wearhouse, look for a coupon for this chain at local bridal shows or online at menswearhouse.com. Specials vary, but when we lasted looked, there was a $20 discount. Other chains offer periodic coupons as well—sign up for a store's email newsletter or scan bridal web sites for the latest deals. One tip: coupon code site RetailMeNot.com tracks the latest Men's Warehouse deals.

6 **Buy used.** What do chains that rent tuxes do with the tuxes when they are done renting? They sell them at substantial discounts, starting at around $100. (FYI: most new tuxes start at $200 and range up to $500.) And the quality? Most are in good shape. Yes, you want to inspect the garment carefully. But most designer rental tuxes are made from quality fabrics that hold up well over the long term.

7 **Skip the tux altogether.** Chance are the groom and groomsmen have already decent looking dark suits. So why not have them wear a dark suit, white shirt and coordinate a tie/pocket square combination? Their only expense is the new tie and pocket square.

Helpful Hints

1 Try on the entire tuxedo when you pick it up.
From personal experience, we can say that trying on
that tux at the shop is the best thing you can do. At a recent
wedding we attended, the store called the bride to tell her they were
closing early and she needed to pick up all the tuxes. Unfortunately,
some of the tuxes did not fit properly. Those unlucky guys had to call
the shop after hours and get someone to come back to the store to fit
them. Thankfully, the store was happy to accommodate them, but it
would have been a mess otherwise.

Here are some questions to ask yourself when trying on a tux:

♥ Is the tux the correct color and style?

♥ Can you button the top jacket button and still comfortably move
around? A too-tight jacket will have wrinkles and feel uncomfortable.

♥ Are all the buttons and jewelry accounted for? You'll most likely have
button studs (five or six) and a pair of cufflinks. Unless you're receiving these as a gift the most common ones available with rental tuxes
are polished black. Keep the little plastic bag they come in so you can
return them to the shop.

♥ Do the shoes fit and match? You don't want to be uncomfortable all
night long! And make sure that you're getting the same style as
everyone else. Remember this is all about making people match (at
least most of the time).

♥ Is the neck comfortable on the shirt when closed? No need to suffer,
guys!

♥ Check the length of the sleeves and pants:
1. Trouser style pants: should break midway between the top of the
shoe and brush the top of the heel in the back.
2. Tuxedo style pants: no break (because the satin stripe should fall
straight), they should brush the top of the shoe
3. Jacket sleeve: should fall at the middle of the wrist bone when
arm is hanging loosely at your side
4. Shirt sleeve: should be 2" longer than the jacket sleeve when arm
is hanging loosely at your side

**2 Give a copy of the list of questions above to your grooms-
men, best man, and groom.** You won't be there when the guys

in your wedding pick up their tuxes. So make sure they know what to look for and questions to ask when they try on their tuxes. You'll save yourself (and them) some grief, especially if they don't know what they're doing!

3 **Move up deadlines.** A groom emailed us this tip. Frustrated by his procrastinating groomsmen (who were late for fittings), he suggested other grooms fudge the measurement deadline. For example, tell them they must get measured six weeks before the wedding even though the real deadline is just four weeks. That way you'll have a buffer zone for foot-dragging guys.

4 **Ignore the "black tie invited" pressure.** Some bridal web sites and retailers are suggesting you put "black tie invited" on your invitations. Is this to encourage your guests to dress up? Or to merely line the pockets of tuxedo rental places? Whatever the motivation, we should note that *Crane's Wedding Blue Book* (the bible of invitation etiquette) says that it is NOT proper to specify the type of dress on an invitation. "The formality of dress is indicated by the time of day (of the wedding). After six o'clock is considered formal." Putting "Black Tie Invited" or "Black Tie Optional" is confusing and not necessary.

5 **Consider renting an extra shirt for summer outdoor weddings.** A bride called in this excellent tip—if you plan a summer outdoor wedding, consider having the groom and groomsmen rent an extra tuxedo shirt. That way they can change after the wedding into a fresh shirt for the reception.

Now that you've squared away the attire for the entire wedding party, it's time to move to planning the actual ceremony. Up next, everything you need to know about booking a place to tie the knot.

Here's a surprise most folks don't plan for—rental fees for ceremony sites can run hundreds of dollars, even when you belong to a church or temple. In this chapter, we'll discuss a group of often-overlooked wedding ceremony sites that are extremely affordable—plus we'll give you six important questions to ask your site coordinator.

Selecting a site for your ceremony first requires a decision on the type of ceremony you want. Wedding ceremonies are divided into two categories: religious and civil.

1 Religious ceremonies. Religious ceremonies (69% of all weddings), of course, are most likely held in a house of worship. Requirements for religious ceremonies vary greatly from one denomination to another. Pre-marital counseling is required by some religions; others forbid interfaith marriages. Often the rules are established by the church or temple's local priest, minister, pastor, imam or rabbi. Call your local house of worship for guidelines and requirements.

2 Civil ceremonies. About one-third (31% to be exact) of all weddings are civil ceremonies. Legal requirements vary from state to state, but usually a judge or other officiant presides over the ceremony. Customs and traditions vary greatly from region to region. For example, we spoke to one hotel catering manager who worked in both Boston and Austin, TX. In Boston, she told us nearly 75% of couples had a civil ceremony on site at the hotel. Just the opposite was true in Texas, where most weddings are held in a church with only the reception following at the hotel.

Religious vs. Civil: It's All a Matter of State

Interestingly enough, the split between civil and religious ceremonies varies greatly from state to state. According to federal government statistics, the state with the largest number of religious wedding ceremonies is West Virginia. In that state, a whopping 97% of all weddings are religious ceremonies. On the other end of the spectrum, South Carolina leads the nation in civil ceremonies (54% of all weddings), perhaps due to the state's large military population.

So what happened to Nevada, where the large number of Las Vegas weddings probably would rank that state #1 in civil ceremonies? Well, Nevada was omitted from this study for reasons unknown.

Other states with a high number of civil ceremonies include: Florida (45%) New Hampshire (40%), Hawaii (36%), New York (35%), as well as Maine, Georgia and Virginia.

Which states have a large number of religious wedding ceremonies? Besides West Virginia, those states include Missouri (91%), Nebraska (84.2%), Michigan (83.9%), Pennsylvania (83.7%), Idaho (83.5%), California (83.1%).

What Are You Buying?

When you book a ceremony site, you are not only purchasing use of the site for the wedding but also time for set-up and teardown of the decorations. Now we say *purchasing* because many sites charge fees to use the facilities for a wedding. One bride we interviewed was surprised that the church they belonged to charged her over $900 in fees for her ceremony. Of course, these fees often go to reimburse church staff and to pay expenses like utilities, clean up, etc. Unfortunately, some churches use weddings to subsidize other less-profitable operations. Anyway, the fees vary widely from site to site but the charges tend to be more in larger cities.

What if you are not a member of a church but you want a church wedding? Well, some churches allow non-members to use their facilities for weddings . . . but with a few catches. First, the fees are normally higher. Second, members get first shot at dates, so non-members may not be able to book a wedding until, say, three months in advance.

Whether you're planning a civil or religious service, the officiant typically gets paid an honorarium. Sometimes this is in the form of a donation to the house of worship. Other church employees (organist, choir) may require separate payment that covers not only their performance at the wedding but also any prior rehearsals. Independent clergy typically charge $250 to $500 for a typical wedding ceremony.

Sources to Find a Great Ceremony Site

There are several great sources to find affordable sites.

♥ **ONLINE.** Yelp is a favorite site for the best venues in most cities, both big and small. Search "wedding" and then select the "venues and event spaces." Yelp's user reviews are helpful, of course. Example: a search of wedding venues in Seattle on Yelp yielded 48 listings, including multiple sites with 10+ user reviews.

♥ **LOCAL VISITORS/TOURISM BUREAUS.** An often-overlooked resource, these governmental or non-profit resources keep databases of local facilities that are available for weddings and receptions. A local Chamber of Commerce or Historical Society office may also have more leads.

♥ **LOCAL PARKS DEPARTMENTS.** Parks departments administer most city and county parks and historical areas. Ask them which sites are most popular for wedding ceremonies.

Sources to Find an Officiant. If you're planning a civil ceremony, where do you find an officiant? Here are some thoughts:

♥ **VENDOR LISTS.** Many reception sites (including parks departments) have "vendor lists" that list everything from florists to photographers. Often, you can find officiant names on such lists.

♥ **WEDDINGMINSTERS.COM** This site lets your search for officiants by city/metro area, state or region.

♥ **CRAIGSLIST.** Sure, it sounds a bit odd—but many officiants (including ministers and justices of the peace) list their services on the local boards of Craigslist.

♥ **NON-DENOMINATIONAL CHURCHES.** Such houses of worship (example: Unitarian churches) may have officiants who are willing to conduct religious ceremonies for couples who are not members of the church. A side comment: we should note that technically the Unitarian church is NOT non-denominational. The Unitarians do not restrict people from being married in their churches based on previous or current religious affiliation. This is really called "non-creedal." Just an FYI.

Best Online Sources

Finding a ceremony site on the web can be a bit tricky—many religious and smaller sites don't have web pages. But many venues that offer both ceremonies and receptions (so-called catering halls and facilities) can be found online. Example: WeddingLocation.com contains listings for venues for all 50 states with photos, details on wedding packages and more.

Getting Started: How Far in Advance?

Especially for popular wedding months, start your search for a ceremony site as soon as you have selected the date. Prime dates can book up to a year in advance—there are only so many Saturdays in June. However, be aware that popular months vary by region. For example, in the South, December is a particularly popular month. In Arizona, and many areas of the desert Southwest, spring months (such as April) are almost as popular as the hot summer months. See the chart later in this chapter for a list of the most and least popular months for weddings by state.

Be aware that religious restrictions may rule out certain times of the

FIGURE 1:

A search of Yelp for reception sites in Atlanta yields 16 possibilities. Yelp has wedding resources for cities across the U.S.

year. For example, Catholics and Greek Orthodox avoid marrying during Lent in March. Jews don't have weddings during the High Holy Days (usually in September or October).

Questions to Ask of a Ceremony Site

1 **Do you have my wedding date available?** Yes, it's an obvious question, but probably the most important one. It is easy to forget there are many *other* brides and grooms competing for the same slots on a Saturday afternoon.

2 **What are the restrictions, set-up times and clean-up requirements?** Many sites have put these items in writing. One local church we know has so many guidelines that they filled a 72-page book! Make sure you are fully aware of these details to avoid any surprises.

3 **Are there any rules regarding candles or flowers?** Some facilities ban candles outright. Others forbid the throwing of rice or birdseed after the ceremony. We've even heard of one church that required the altar flower arrangement be "donated" to the church after the ceremony. One reader emailed us to explain that some congregations, particularly in the Northeast see this type of donation as a sort of "thank you" from the bride for the church community's support.

REAL WEDDING TIP

Church ceremony fees can add up

"I would just like to comment on a substantial wedding cost which I did not see addressed in your book. After I got engaged, I called the Episcopal Church I have attended since I was a little girl and booked a date in May. I have always assumed that I would be married there, and so I did not give this aspect of planning the wedding much thought. Recently, I received an information packet from the church that included a price list. Imagine my surprise to learn that getting married at my local church will cost approximately $2,000 ($750 for rental of the church and the rest in fees to various people needed to perform the service). I had not counted on this expense, and frankly, was quite surprised by it. To make matters worse, when I tried to call other Episcopal churches in the area, the wedding coordinators refused to disclose any prices unless I had the rector of my official church call and give permission for me to be married there."

4 **Who will be my contact?** In order to prevent miscommunications, make sure you find out who is the wedding coordinator. This person will be an invaluable referral source for other wedding services.

5 **What kind of equipment must be rented for my wedding?** Don't assume that something in the sanctuary or at the site is included in your rental of the facility.

Most/Least Popular Months

STATE	Most Popular	Least Popular
New England:		
Maine	August, July, June	Jan., Feb., Mar.
New Hampshire	Oct., June, Aug.	Jan. Mar., Feb.
Vermont	July, August, June	Jan., Mar., Feb.
Massachusetts	Oct., Sept., June.	Jan., Mar., Feb.
Rhode Island	Sept., Oct., June	Jan., Feb., Mar.
Connecticut	Oct., Sept., June	Jan., Mar., Feb.
Middle Atlantic:		
New York	Sept., Aug, June	Jan., Feb., Mar.
New Jersey	Oct., Sept., June	Jan., Feb., Mar.
Pennsylvania	Oct., June, Sept.	Jan., Feb., Mar.
East North Central:		
Ohio	June, July, Sept.	Jan., Feb., Mar.
Indiana	June, July, August	Jan., Feb., Mar.
Illinois	June, Sept., Oct.	Jan., Feb., Mar.
Michigan	August, June, Sept.	Jan., Mar., Feb.
Wisconsin	June, Sept., Aug.	Jan., Feb., Mar.
West North Central:		
Minnesota	June, Sept., Aug.	Jan., Mar., Feb.
Iowa	June, August, Sept.	Jan., Feb., Mar.
Missouri	June, May, Oct.	Jan., Feb., Mar.
North Dakota	June, July, August	Jan., Mar., Feb.
South Dakota	August, June, July	Jan., Mar., Feb.
Nebraska	June, July, August.	Jan., Feb., Mar.
Kansas	June, July, May	Jan., Feb., Mar.
East South Central:		
Kentucky	June, July, May	Jan., Feb., Mar.
Tennessee	June, July, Dec.	Jan., Feb., Mar.
Alabama	June, July, August	Jan., Feb., Nov.
Mississippi	June, July, Dec.	Jan., Feb., Nov.
West South Central:		
Arkansas	June, July, August	Jan., Feb., Nov.
Louisiana	July, June, Oct.	Mar., Feb., Jan.

How early will the site be available for decorating? Will the
air conditioning or heat be turned on at that time? Your florist
may need to access the ceremony site several hours before your wedding. Confirm that heat or A/C will be running to make it easier for vendors to work (and to avoid damage to delicate blooms and other decor).

Can we schedule a rehearsal time? Ideally, the wedding
rehearsal is held a day or so before the actual ceremony. However,

for Weddings *by* State

STATE	Most Popular	Least Popular
Oklahoma	June, August, May	Jan., Feb., Oct.
Texas	June, July, August	Jan., Nov., Feb.
South Atlantic:		
Delaware	Oct., Sept., June	Jan., Feb., Mar.
Maryland	June, Sept., Oct.	Jan., Feb., Mar.
Wash. D.C.	June, Sept., Oct.	Feb., Jan., Mar.
Virginia	June, July, May	Jan., Mar., Feb.
West Virginia	June, July, Aug.	Jan., Mar., Feb.
North Carolina	June, July, May	Jan., Mar., Feb.
South Carolina	July, June, May	Jan, Feb., Mar.
Georgia	June, July, April	Jan., Feb., Mar.
Florida	Dec., June, April	Jan., Mar., Sept.
Mountain:		
Montana	July, June, August	Jan., Feb., Mar.
Idaho	August, July, June	Jan., Mar., Feb.
Wyoming	July, August, June	Jan., Mar., Feb.
Colorado	June, August, July	Jan., Mar., Nov.
New Mexico	June, August, May	Jan., Sept., Feb.
Arizona	June, May, Apr.	Feb., August, July
Utah	July, August, Sept.	Jan., Feb., Oct.
Nevada	July, August, April	Jan., Mar., Nov.
Pacific:		
Washington	August, Oct., July	Jan., Feb., Dec.
Oregon	August, June, July	Jan., Feb., Mar.
California	June, Sept., July	Jan., April, Feb.
Alaska	August, June, July	Jan., Mar., April
Hawaii	May, July, August	Jan., Mar., Feb.
US (TOTAL)	*June, July, August*	*Jan., Feb., Mar.*

*Note: Months are listed in order of popularity. For example, "July, August,
June" means that July is the #1 month, followed by August and so on. The
least popular month is listed first, followed by the second least popular
and so on. Source: US Dept. of Health report.*

some sites have strict rules and times for wedding rehearsals—you may even have to do it the morning of the event. The rehearsal lets everyone know where they are supposed to stand, the order of events and so on.

Questions to Ask an Officiant

1 **What is the expected honorarium, donation or fee?** When is this normally paid?

2 **Are there any travel charges or other costs?** If you're planning a wedding at a non-religious site (hotel, home, etc.), you may want to confirm these details.

3 **Is any pre-wedding counseling required?** Some churches require couples to attend pre-wedding counseling. Others require the couple to promise to raise their children in that religion. Before you are asked to make any commitments, ask the site coordinator about this matter.

4 **Do you provide the ceremony/vows or can we write our own?** Are you familiar with the wedding site?

5 **Are you licensed to perform wedding ceremonies in this county?** And will you file all the necessary paperwork (marriage license, etc.) with the county?

6 **Will you attend the rehearsal?** If so, is there an extra charge for this time? Another issue: ask the officiant when he arrives at the ceremony site and how long he will stay afterward. This is important to coordinate with your photographer. If you are marrying in your or your family's church or synagogue, it is customary to invite the clergy member (and his/her spouse) to the reception.

Top Money-saving Secrets

1 **Consider a civic site.** Many sites run by your city (parks, rose gardens, etc.) have lovely facilities available for wedding ceremonies. Best of all: most of these sites are rent for a very small fee. For example, we've found rose gardens and historical parks (complete with gazebo or chapel) that cost under $500. The National Park Foundation (nationalparks.org) is a good place to start.

2 **Call around to different sites.** Yes, fees can vary widely from facility to facility.

3 **Consider becoming a member.** Many churches charge less for weddings of members than non-members. Hence, consider joining the church where you'll be married. Of course, you'll be making a commitment to that house of worship, which is something not to take lightly. Don't simply join a church to get married there—that isn't fair to houses of worship that count on members to continue their involvement, both spiritually and financially.

4 **Ask about discounts.** For example, some churches and temples offer discounts on wedding invitations as a fundraiser.

5 **Have a friend officiate.** In most states it is fairly easy to become licensed to perform weddings. Have a friend or relative get licensed and perform the ceremony as a gift. A reader in San Diego emailed us about that state's "Deputy Marriage Commissioner for a Day" program. For a modest fee (some counties don't charge at all), you can have anyone perform your ceremony! If you live in California contact your county for specific rules. Essentially, your friend writes a letter to the court requesting this, and then a judge swears your friend in for that specific day. Check with counties in other states to see if a similar program exists for your area.

6 **Take a tax deduction.** Certain fees paid to a church or synagogue for a ceremony may be considered a charitable contribution; check with your tax preparer about deducting this off your taxes. You may have to be a member of the church or temple in order to take the deduction. Also: if the ceremony site requires you leave behind flowers as a "donation," this may also be tax deductible.

7 **Go historic.** The National Park Service's National Register of Historic Places database (nrhp.focus.nps.gov) is a good place to find historic places to tie the knot. And here's the hidden bargain of these sites: you can often bring in an off-site caterer to provide food and alcohol. This is typically a big savings of hotels or country clubs.

8 **Bed and breakfast deals.** BnBFinder.com is a good source for small inns and bed and breakfasts—many of these facilities are a deal for smaller weddings. Plus you can get lodging discounts for out of town guests.

9 **Get artsy.** Local art museums are a fantastic find for wedding ceremonies and receptions. Try artcyclopedia.com/museums-us.html to unearth good options near you.

10 **College campuses.** Many universities and colleges have chapels and receptions centers that are available for rent. Example: the ballroom at the University of Louisville's Shelpy Campus runs $1200—plus there are discounts for alumni, students and employees. Like historic sites, the money-savings secret here is usually tied to bringing in an affordable caterer.

Destination Wedding Tips

♥ **Marriage license 411.** Getting a valid marriage license used to be quite a chore if you were being married overseas. But there is good news: more countries are putting their marriage license info online. And some countries (notably in the Caribbean) have relaxed rules and regulations in order to spur more destination wedding biz.

♥ **Lean on that wedding coordinator.** Most folks who marry abroad do so at a resort—and most of those resorts now have full-time wedding coordinators. We've found most of these professionals to be very knowledgeable about local marriage license requirements . . . but it's always smart to double check!

♥ **Be aware that local customs may forbid religious ceremonies for non-residents.** Other countries have convoluted rules for what makes a wedding legal. For example, in Mexico, only civil marriages (in front a judge) are considered legal.

♥ **Consider the secret home ceremony.** If getting a marriage license in a foreign country is too much of a hassle, then consider this tip: get married quietly at home at a courthouse before you go. Then you re-take your vows at the destination wedding spot. Of course, the guests don't know this isn't the real wedding—the legal one was back in the U.S.!

Once you've nailed down the location for your ceremony, it's time to think about flowers. Next up, we'll give you the scoop on saving for all things floral for both the wedding and reception.

## Chapter 5

A rose is a rose . . . except when you're shopping for flowers for your wedding. Then a "bridal" rose is suddenly eight times more expensive than a regular rose. With the average floral bill for weddings topping $1800, there have to be some creative ways to stretch that budget. We came up with 30 cost-cutters. Plus, in this chapter, we also translate "floral speak" and give you eight floral "best buys."

What Are You Buying?

Flowers are more than petals, stems and leaves. When you contract with a professional florist, you are buying their expertise and creativity. Not only is the florist's knowledge of flowers important but also their understanding of colors and contrasts. Florists must be able to come up with a floral motif to best complement the bride, the bridal gown, the bridesmaids' colors, the ceremony and the reception. To synthesize these elements and the "feel of the wedding" (a formal sit-down dinner versus an informal barbecue) takes talent. Lots of it. Your tastes and desires are key here, and a florist who understands a couple's individuality is the best choice.

There are three basic categories of flowers that you are buying:

♥ **PERSONAL FLOWERS.** The bride's and bridesmaids' bouquets, corsages for the mothers and house party, and boutonnieres for the men.

♥ **CEREMONY SITE FLOWERS.** Altar flowers and/or aisle arrangements (ribbons, candles, pew markers).

♥ **RECEPTION SITE FLOWERS.** Guest book table, table centerpieces and the cake table. Other floral expense areas may include the rehearsal dinner and any other pre-wedding parties.

Average total costs: $1813 covers the total floral bill at most weddings, according to industry estimates. In the largest cities (such as New York or Chicago) the flower budget can easily zoom past $3000 or even $10,000 for lavish affairs. Deposits range from nothing (the exception) to as much as 50% of the estimated bill. Many florists ask for $50 to $100 to reserve the date. The balance is usually due one to two weeks before the wedding (because many florists must order the flowers in advance from their suppliers).

Sources to Find an Affordable Florist

Since there are three general types of florists out there, we thought it might be helpful to explain the differences, and then detail where to find the one that will work best for you:

1 **Cash 'n Carry.** These shops basically specialize in providing an arrangement for Mother's Day, or a friend's birthday. They usually don't do many weddings and may not have as much experience with such a special event.

2 **Full service.** Weddings, online orders, and special events are within a full-service florist's repertoire. A majority of florists fit in this category, although some are better than others at weddings.

3 **Specialists.** Some florists specialize in one aspect of the floral business, such as corporate affairs. Obviously, those who specialize in weddings are your best bet. Those that don't may have little incentive to do a good job since they don't target that market anyway. Don't assume that your neighborhood florist, who has done great arrangements for you at Christmas and other times, will be best for your wedding.

Where to Find Florists Who are Wedding Specialists

♥ CEREMONY SITE COORDINATORS. Ask the person who coordinates (or books) weddings at your church, synagogue, etc. for florist recommendations. This is a great source since they often see florists' work up close and personal. They also know the florists who have been late to set up and those who have not provided the freshest flowers or best service. If your ceremony site coordinator doesn't have any recommendations, call around to a few popular churches in your area. Odds are you'll turn up some valuable referrals.

♥ PHOTOGRAPHERS. Many have opinions as to which florists offer the best service and which don't. However, since a photographer's contact with florists is limited to the final product at the wedding, they may not have insight into a florist's bedside manner.

Flowers 411

Don't know a gladiolus from a glamelia? Does the word "phalaenopsis" make you think of a rare skin condition? (Actually, it's an orchid). Don't fret--you can get a crash course in bridal flowers by surfing the web. Here are the best sites we found to answer these and other floral questions:

♥ ABOUT FLOWERS (aboutflowers.com) is a web site designed by the flower industry (the Society of American Florists—SAF) for consumers. They offer an extensive flower library to help you research a myriad possible flowers and colors. You can click on individual photos for an enlargement and informative details on the different blooms. Check out the Photo Gallery section for bouquet ideas and the Flower Meanings link to add a twist to your wedding flowers. Looking for a SAF florist in your area? Visit NationalFloristsDirectory.com.

♥ Visit the CALIFORNIA CUT FLOWER COMMISSION (ccfc.org). Check out their wedding bouquets (under Flower Lovers button) for ideas as well as their color chart which calls out blooms in different color ranges. We loved some of the unique ideas for bouquets (a floral "purse" anyone?). A seasonal availability chart is handy too with not only information on which flowers will be available for your wedding date but also how long they last when cut, what kind of special care the blooms might require, and the flower's meaning.

♥ **IF YOU PLAN TO PRODUCE YOUR OWN ARRANGEMENTS** or have a friend do it, google your city along with "flowers wholesale" to find a local source. Some wholesalers refuse to sell to the public while others don't have such restrictions. Another source: flower growers. Contact the Association of Specialty Cut Flower Growers (ASCFG) at (440) 774-2887 (web: ascfg.org) to see if there is a grower in your area. Some growers even offer wedding design services.

Getting Started: How Far in Advance?

Book a florist up to six months in advance of your wedding. In larger cities, some florists may even require more time. For most towns, however, many florists consider three to six months notice adequate. Remember that you can put down a small deposit further in advance and then talk specifics at a later date.

FIGURE 1: AboutFlowers.com provides a good overview of flowers with detailed pictures and information.

Step-by-step Shopping Strategies

♥ **Step 1:** First, you must have the time, place and apparel selected before you can get an accurate bid from a florist. The bridal gown is crucial—everything flows from this design element. The colors of the bridesmaids' gowns are also important.

♥ **Step 2:** Choose two to three florists to visit, using the sources mentioned earlier. Make an appointment with each and leave about one hour's time to discuss the details.

♥ **Step 3:** Be sure to bring swatches of the bridesmaids apparel and a picture of the bridal gown you have selected. Give this to the florist so they'll remember what the dress looks like when they actually make the bouquet. Also, it will be helpful to bring any pictures of flowers/designs you like.

♥ **Step 4**: Look through actual photographs of previous work. Don't settle for FTD design books or floral magazines. Identify flowers and designs that fit your wedding's style—unadorned wedding gowns can be set-off by a lush bride's bouquet. Similarly, a simple bouquet may better compliment an ornate wedding dress. See if the florist attempts to understand your tastes and desires instead of merely telling you what you must have.

♥ **Step 5:** Get a written proposal specifying exact flowers to be used. Each item (brides bouquet, corsages, etc.) should be priced individually. Get this *before* you place any deposit with the florist.

♥ **Step 6:** Pick your top florist choice and ask to visit one of their weddings during set-up. On your visit, check to see if they are on time and organized. Also, look to see how fresh the flowers are. Do you find the designs pleasing (keeping in mind that the other bride's taste may be different from your own)?

♥ **Step 7:** If you believe an on-site meeting at your ceremony or reception site is necessary, now is the time. Finalize the details.

♥ **Step 8:** Get a written contract that spells out the following:

The date of the event (if it is not a Saturday, have the actual day noted, i.e. Sunday).
Set-up time and place.
Specific flowers for each item (roses for bridal bouquet, orchids for mothers' corsages, tulips for bridesmaids, etc.). Don't forget to list

the colors chosen for each flower element as well—bridal white roses or red gladiolus.

Any special instructions. If you want open roses, include that in the contract. If you are ordering a flower girl hair wreath have the florist write down the girl's head measurements on the contract.

Emergency contact numbers for the florist (including cell phone).

Specific payment information including deposits as well as refund/cancellation terms.

As you get closer to your wedding, there may be some modifications (more corsages, etc.). Make sure any changes are in writing.

♥ **Step 9:** If you're having a large or complex wedding, a pre-wedding floral check-up may be necessary. Here you'll meet with the florist about one to two weeks prior to the date to iron out any last minute details/changes, etc.

Questions to Ask a Florist

1 **Is my date available?** If it is, check to see if a deposit is necessary to hold the date. Also ask if there is any consultation fee.

2 **Do you have actual photographs or samples of your past work?** It's important to see the work of the actual florist, not airbrushed photos from a generic floral book. There is no better way to see if their style complements your tastes and verify just how skilled they are.

3 **Is there a delivery or set-up fee?** Watch out—this can be a substantial extra charge. Most florists will charge a delivery/set-up fee especially if you have either complex flower arrangements or a site that is a long distance from their shop. If the charge is high, consider finding a florist closer to the site or cut back on the complicated decorations.

4 **Do you offer any silk or dried flower arrangements?** This may be important to you if you want to save your bouquet or want an unusual look for a table centerpiece. Sometimes these two options may be less expensive than fresh flowers, especially for some exotics like orchids.

5 **How many weddings do you do in a day?** The biggest problem with some florists is that they become over-extended—trying to do too many weddings in one day. A florist can probably do two or three weddings a day if the events are held at different times and/or the florist has plenty of help. If the florist's schedule looks crowded for your wedding date, they may arrive late or deliver the wrong flowers (or worse). Look for someone focused on your wedding . . . not just your wallet.

6 **Are you familiar with my ceremony/reception site location?** If not, will you visit it with me? It may be a good idea to introduce your florist to the ceremony or reception site if they've never seen it. Ask if there is any charge for this on-site visit.

7 **What rental items do you have? How are they priced?** Some things you may want to rent include candelabrum, aisle standards, or urns. The best florists charge a fair fee for any rentals. One way to verify this: compare prices with a local rental store. A common mark-up for florists is about 10% for their time to coordinate this detail. If you would prefer to rent the items yourself because you can get a better price, be sure you have the time to pick-up and return the items.

8 **Can I attend one of your weddings during set-up for a look at your designs?** Here is another way to determine how professional and talented your florist is. You'll need to visit during set-up and leave before the wedding party arrives. Try not to interrupt the florist or their staff while they work (save your questions for later). Look for timeliness, freshness and beauty of the flowers, and how well the florist and staff work together.

9 **What time will you be at my ceremony/reception sites to set-up my wedding?** Confirm this time constantly throughout your planning. Many florists set up weddings a couple hours in advance. If this is the case with your wedding, be sure the temperature at the site is not too hot for the flowers—you want them to look fresh at wedding time. Some ceremony sites might have a refrigerator to store personal flowers until you arrive. Confirm this detail with both your site and florist.

10 **Will you merely drop off my flowers or stay through the ceremony?** The degree of service here differs dramatically from florist to florist. Some just drop off the flowers at the ceremony and leave, while others stay to pin on corsages, make sure nothing is missing, etc. There may be an extra fee ($50) for this service, especially for large weddings; however, this may be a worthwhile investment.

11 **What happens if the flowers I pick aren't available for my wedding?** How will you determine what flowers to substitute? A related question: What is the policy if I want to add extra items (such as another table centerpiece or boutonniere) at the last minute?

Top Money-saving Secrets

1 Get the LED out. Table floral centerpieces can cost a small fortune . . . so how can you add pizzazz on a budget? Use LED floral lights in a vase with marbles—the look is dramatic, but the price ($2-$3 per light) is a steal. Another idea if you want to skip marbles: vase filler (ColorFill, $7 per two-pound bag) and a LED light make for a striking look!

2 Don't use a florist who charges a consultation fee. Most florists do NOT charge a consultation fee, however, beware of those who do. You can find plenty of great florists who will talk to you for free; don't spend time with the few that charge such fees. (Some florists tell us they charge consulting fees to "weed out" brides who are just window shopping.)

3 Choose a wedding date that is not near a holiday. As you may well realize, all roses are outrageously priced in February, thanks to Valentine's Day. So if you want roses, don't plan on a wedding at that time. Also, December is an expensive time to buy fresh flowers since the supply is limited and the demand from holiday events is high. On the other hand, brides have found Christmas weddings are less expensive for *ceremony* flowers since the church may already be decorated.

4 Seasonal and regional flowers can be great bargains. Today's floral market is truly global: while most roses are imported from Ecuador, other blooms come from places as far flung as Holland and New Zealand. Yes, a florist can get in flowers from halfway around the world, but it's important to remember that seasonality still affects availability *and* price. Example: tulips are typically abundant from December through April and as such are fairly inexpensive. If you want them in July, however, you will pay a premium (three times the low-season price) since they may have to be flown in from South America.

5 Turn over a new leaf. Cambridge, MA floral designer Hiroko Takeshita (HanayaFloral.com) gave us this great tip: use large, accordion leaves to add volume to bouquets. The leaves cost a fraction of pricey blooms!

Another idea: all greenery bouquets. Creative, modern bouquet designs incorporate succulents and other greenery with no flowers at all. Commonly referred to as "hen and chicks," succulents are shaped

like roses (see picture). This tip can help you save as much as $100 over traditional roses.

6 **Avoid exotic flowers.** Of course, what's considered an "exotic" flower may vary from region to region. For example, in the Southwest, lilies of the valley (see picture) are very expensive and difficult to find. Yet in the northern part of the US, where they are common, they may be very reasonable. Exotic flowers such as pricey orchids imported from Hawaii are usually expensive no matter where you live.

7 **Use silk flowers to replace expensive, fresh varieties.** Even dried flowers may be affordable alternatives. All-silk arrangements may not be much less expensive if you have them made by a florist— their charge for labor may be expensive no matter what type of flower they use. However, you can save money doing it yourself or substituting silk exotics (like orchids) for real ones.

Here are some top picks for online silk and dried flower bargains. A best bet is Save-on-Crafts (save-on-crafts.com). For dried flowers check out these two sites: Dried Flowers R Us (driedflowersrus.com) and Dried Flowers Direct (driedflowersdirect.com).

8 **Consider paper flowers.** Yes, it sounds like an elementary school art project, but paper flowers have definitely come a long way! You can learn to make your own or purchase them from crafts people on sites like Etsy.com. Making them yourself will certainly cost a lot less: crepe paper is as little as $2.50 per sheet plus wire and floral tape. But even if you have your personal flowers made for you, it can be affordable. Example: a made-to-order 10" bouquet made with six blossom peonies and 14 roses in pink and cream, with stems wrapped in lace. Price: $75 plus shipping on Etsy (flowerdecoration.etsy.com). And the designer can custom-make it to suit your colors and flower choices.

9 **Instead of big (and expensive) bouquets, carry a single flower.** This works well with long-stem varieties like calla lilies and roses. If you (the bride) want to carry a bouquet, consider having the bridesmaids carry single flowers.

Here's a really unique idea borrowing on money saving idea #8: a gigantic single flower made of crepe paper. We know, it sounds weird, but bear with us. You can make a paper rose with stem and greenery from crepe paper for as little as $25. You'll find the directions and color photos here: *http://bit.ly/16nrNev/*. You can even use a huge blossom as the centerpiece for you reception tables—just sit them flat in the center of each table. Talk about simple, stunning and cheap.

10 **Limit the number of attendants.** This is just basic math: the more attendants, the more flowers, the higher the final cost.

𝒯𝒶𝒷𝓁ℯ 𝒸ℯ𝓃𝓉ℯ𝓇𝓅𝒾ℯ𝒸ℯ𝓈 ℴ𝓃 𝓉𝒽ℯ 𝒸𝒽ℯ𝒶𝓅

Talk with any florist and you'll quickly realize how table centerpieces can greatly inflate the final bill. If you have ten tables to decorate, the cost of flowers, greenery and a vase can easily run $100 per table. And elaborate centerpieces with extensive flowers and rented stands can soar above $200 each.

How can you save on this item without looking cheap?

♥ **POTTED PLANTS AT HOME DEPOT.** Five bucks goes a long way at Home Depot. One reader decorated her tables with $5 pots of spring flowers like daffodils and tulips. Obviously, what plants and flowers are available will vary depending on the time of the year. Tip: ask a Home Depot manager what flowers are set to arrive the week of your wedding. Ask them if they can order in specific colors or plants you want, plus set them aside when they arrive so you can get first choice.

♥ **GO WITH MORE FOLIAGE THAN FLOWERS.** The more foliage you add to table centerpieces, the fewer flowers you will need. On average, foliage is much less expensive than flowers. Another idea: bare branches with strategically placed single flowers—a Japanese cherry blossom look. Or if you have forsythia or other flower shrubs available on your wedding date, consider these branches placed in tall glass vases.

♥ **BASKETS WITH GOURDS AND SILK LEAVES.** For a fall wedding, this would be a fitting theme. One bride in Massachusetts told us she found baskets on sale at Pier One for 50% off. By scouting out grocery stores, craft stores, and nurseries, she found gourds, mini pumpkins and silk leaves in fall colors to fill the baskets. Total cost: $21 per basket. How about a fall wedding centerpiece of autumn-colored leaves in glass vases? Colorful, yet affordable for fall.

77 Spend your money where people will see it. Most wedding
ceremonies are relatively short (about 30 minutes); therefore your
guests will be spending most of their time at your reception. We suggest
that you spend money on flowers at the reception rather than at the
ceremony. You'll be able to enjoy them more at the reception and so will
your guests. At a typical wedding, ceremony site flowers are the biggest
expense, but you see them for the shortest amount of time!

12 Share and share alike. If there is another wedding scheduled
for the same day at your ceremony site, share the floral

♥ **COLORED WATER.** If you are using clear glass containers to hold
flowers, add a few drops of food coloring to the water.

♥ **EDIBLE CENTERPIECES.** Instead of flowers, have your caterer stack
piles of fruit (in coordinating colors, of course) in the center of the
table. For example, an arrangement of strawberries with chocolate
dipping sauce or powdered sugar would be nice. Another idea:
dessert centerpieces. Instead of a large, expensive wedding cake,
beautifully decorated but smaller cakes could serve as your centerpiece. Without the elaborate stacked cake you should be able to
save some money here.

♥ **CYBER FLOWERS.** Yes, you can order fresh flowers from the
Internet delivered to you via Fed Ex the day before your wedding.
You may not want to design and arrange all your flowers for
your wedding, but you could buy 150 gerbera daisies from Brides
N Blooms (bridesnblooms.com) for $175. Find affordable con-
tainers and you've got casual, fresh floral centerpieces (at just
$12 per table, assuming ten stems per arrangement). More on
this option later in the chapter.

♥ **NO FLOWERS AT ALL.** How about table centerpieces that are just
photos of you and your fiancé through time? Start with baby
pictures, through childhood into adulthood including your dat-
ing and engagement time periods. Chances are parents already
have lots of framed pictures that can be used. This gives your
guests get a little timeline of your lives to enjoy and you won't
have to spend much money at all.

♥ **WATCH THE HEIGHT OF TABLE CENTERPIECES.** High table centerpieces often cost TWICE the price of low designs. Go with all low
designs or mix up high and low to save.

arrangements with the other bride! Splitting the cost here could be a major savings. Use neutral hues like whites and creams to avoid any color clashes.

13 **Balloons!** Forget the florist and call a company that does balloon arrangements. You might be surprised at how inexpensive balloons can be. We priced balloon table centerpieces at $15 to $50 each—you'd have to spend twice or three times that amount to get a similar look from fresh flowers. One tip: balloon centerpieces look best in reception sites with high ceilings. For more ideas on affordable table centerpieces, see the nearby box Table Centerpieces on the Cheap.

14 **Renting plants and other greenery as filler.** A great money-saving option, this may save you from buying tons of flowers for a reception or ceremony site that needs lots of decoration. Check local nurseries and party stores for rental greenery.

Another idea: buy cheap greenery at places like Home Depot. Many sell large potted plants for a fraction of what a florist would charge. Use blooming plants as table centerpieces or larger greenery (trees) to fill in blank spots at the ceremony or reception sites. Best of all, at the end of the reception, you can give them away to guests or reuse them in your own garden. One bride told us she purchased an assortment of potted, flowering plants at a local nursery. The cost for 12 plants (covered in foil for a festive look) was only $100.

Also: ask about RENTING vases for table centerpieces instead of buying. We priced a 28" tall Eiffel Tower glass vase at $130 to purchase. On the website SimplyElegantWed.com, we could rent one for $8.50. Savings: over 90%. A 50% deposit is required at most rental stores.

15 **Recycle!** Reuse some of the ceremony arrangements and bouquets at the reception. The bridesmaid's bouquets can be used to decorate the cake and guest book tables. Some altar arrangements can be moved to the reception site (although there may be a delivery fee).

16 **Luxe for less.** A popular floral trend is to tightly cluster a large number of flowers in a mass or ball for bouquets. The problem? A mass of roses or orchids can quickly drain your budget. The solution? Use affordable bloom (mums, gerbera daisies or Peruvian lilies) for the same tight look and save 35%. Thanks to San Francisco floral designer Nancy Liu Chin (nancyliuchin.com) for this great tip.

One impressive look we've noticed lately: scads of baby's breath (gypsophila) gathered into ethereal bouquets, garlands and wreaths. We know, you're thinking of the stuff used in you high school prom corsages, but when used alone and in huge amounts, the effect is awesome. And cheap—bridemaids bouquets start at about $20. And since they're only one flower, you could probably put together bouquets yourself without much trouble.

17 **Consider arranging the flowers yourself.** It's not that hard, especially if you have a friend or relative who can lend a hand. An entire package of wedding flowers can be ordered online (see Spotlight: Best Buy later in this chapter for online sources) for as little as $400. Silk flowers are another option; many craft

stores like Hobby Lobby (reviewed later) sell do-it-yourself supplies or you can use their in-house arranging service. Another source for do-it-yourself blooms: farmer's markets. We'll discuss this in tip #24. A good book on this subject: *The Frugal Florist: Do-It-Yourself Flowers on a Budget* (Klingel, $22)

18 **Scale-down the pew decorations at the ceremony.** Consider using just greenery or bows instead of fresh flowers. Some brides have eliminated this decoration altogether. Another option: craft stores will teach you how to make the bows yourself. One handy product is the EZ Bowmaker from EZ Bowz (available on Amazon and craft web sites). This simple device enables you to make professional-looking bows for pew decorations, table centerpieces and more. The cost is $14. Why pay a florist hundreds of dollars when you can do it yourself for pennies?

19 **Pick the general color scheme** and let your florist buy the most affordable flowers available the week of your wedding. Obviously, you must feel very confident in your florist to go this route. Specifically rule out any flowers you don't want but try to remain flexible—this isn't a tip for control freaks. Flower prices fluctuate so greatly from month to month; take advantage of this by having your florist pick the best bargains.

20 **Call a local horticultural school.** A bride in Ohio wrote to us with this great tip—she found that the students at a local horticultural school would arrange the flowers for her wedding for free. She paid for the flowers (only $200) and they did all the labor—a great deal! Go to Gradschools.com and search for "horticulture" to find programs in your state. Another idea: craft stores and community colleges often have classes in flower arranging. If you don't have time to take a class, see if the students will take on your wedding as a class project.

Another thought: hire an instructor from a local horticulture school to design your wedding flowers. They often moonlight for private parties and are very experienced as well.

21 **Check the church.** Yes, some churches arrange flowers. A reader told us at her Episcopal church in Chicago, the Altar Guild can make beautiful arrangements for as little as $100.

22 **Costco.** A great way to save! Costco offers a series of wedding flower packages starting at just $230. We'll take an in-depth look at Costco's wedding flower services later in this chapter.

23 **Local flower growers.** You might be surprised at the wedding services offered by local growers. For example, Flinthill Flower Farm in Maryland (301-607-4554) not only grows flowers but also offers a design service. Here's what reader Sara Markle told us about her wedding flowers from Flinthill: "I toured the farm to see what kinds of flowers were in season and had a good time working with the owner deciding on the arrangements. He was easy to work with and found ways to reduce my costs. I didn't compare costs with a regular florist, except that I got one quote from the florist who supplies my church. That person quoted $250 for one altar arrangement. From the farm, I got *two* church arrangements for $150.

"In all, I spent about $1200 for my bouquet, a headpiece, three maids' bouquets, seven boutonnieres, four corsages, two large church arrangements and one small church arrangement, four large arrangements for the reception, 21 table arrangements, and delivery and set up costs."

24 **Don't forget after–Christmas sales.** One reader found twinkle lights, bows and candles at 50% off and more. She recommended hitting Wal-Mart, Target and other discounters' after season sales to find gold candles, silver ribbon, bells and more. Use your imagination! Many "holiday" items can be re-used at a wedding. After Easter, you can find pastel ribbon and other décor marked down.

25 **Farmer's markets.** This is a great resource for fresh, locally grown flowers. In our hometown, we found local growers selling flowers at prices that can only be described as a steal—a dozen roses for $6, a large mixed bouquet for $7. Pop into Home Depot for some containers (a steel watering can for $15? a galvanized bucket for $10?) and you've got ceremony or reception site decor on the cheap.

Some of our readers have hit a farmer's market the day of or day before the wedding and loosely arranged the flowers for a fraction of the cost of a professional florist. Be sure to have plenty of supplies on hand (like floral foam, rubber bands, ribbon, scissors and clippers). And don't forget to have a cool place to store your creations before the wedding.

Another option: wholesale floral markets, which are held year round. One reader told us that the Los Angeles Flower District (laflowerdistrict.com) is an entire block of flower growers and importers. Yes, the main business of the district is wholesaling flowers to florists, but many vendors will sell direct to the public as well—they prefer cash only. The prices are phenomenal ($18 for two dozen roses) but feel free to haggle. Don't accept the first price you're given.

26 **Ask your reception site if they have votive candles.** Sure, your florist can supply votive candles . . . but some charge up to $5 each! Instead, see if your reception site has votives. Most will let you use them for free or a nominal charge, typically much less than a florist.

27 **For bridesmaids bouquets, turn up the volume!** Choose flowers with large blooms—peonies in spring, for example. Why? You'll need fewer flowers overall to make a bouquet. Three or four flowers with large blooms will be much less than a bouquet of small bloom flowers like roses.

28 **Take a tax deduction.** If your church or temple requires you to leave behind altar decorations, check with your tax preparer to see if it is a gift-in-kind and hence tax deductible.

29 **Order candles online.** See the box on online candle sources at the end of this chapter.

30 **Purchase "like" flowers.** Flowers are cheaper when you purchase them in bunches (typically 25 stems). If you stick with a limited number of flower types, you cut your bill, California florist Corinne Thomas told us (Corinne's shop is in Westlake Village, CA; WestLakeVillageFlorist.com). Example: bouquets and arrangements with one or two flower types will be much less expensive than arrangements with four to six different flowers.

SPOTLIGHT: BEST BUYS

For some lovely yet affordable flowers that won't bust your budget, we've compiled a short list of flowers that can be used to fill out arrangements. Be aware that certain flowers may be more affordable in various regions of the US. Ask your florist for local recommendations. Also, seasonality may affect the prices of certain flowers.

♥ **ALSTROEMERIA LILIES.** These are miniature lilies that come in over 20 different shades. Some flowers are even multi-colored. Because they are small, they look best in bouquets, hairpieces, on wedding cakes or in table arrangements.

♥ **CARNATIONS.** Ah, the old standby. These are a great pick for altar arrangements since they fill out space without great expense. They come in a wide variety of colors, but we don't recommend the dyed ones—stick to natural colors. Some varieties are also available as miniatures if you want to add them to table arrangements or bouquets. These are very "heat-hardy" too for those of you in hot climates.

♥ **CHRYSANTHEMUMS.** More commonly referred to as mums, these flowers are also great filler for altar arrangements. They add oodles of volume to your arrangements without costing a great deal. These flowers are available in a wide range of colors from white to bronze. Some even look like simple daisies in pink, yellow or white.

♥ **FREESIA.** Another small delicate flower with a pleasant scent, freesia can be used as a wonderful substitute for the more expensive stephanotis (a traditional "bridal" flower). They come in white, yellow, pink, orange, lavender, and red.

♥ **GERBERA DAISIES.** These giant-sized versions of common daisies make wonderful and colorful bridesmaids' bouquets. They also have long stems and can be used successfully in table and altar arrangements. They come in incredible colors from plain white to deep fuchsia. Pastels are also available; there are even "miniature" gerbera daisies that can be used in boutonnieres.

♥ **GLADIOLUS.** These long-stalked flowers are covered in bright blooms. They look especially nice in altar or buffet arrangements to add height. Individual blooms can be used as glamelias (ask your florist to see an example). Colors range from white to pink to deep, true red.

♥ **HEATHER.** This dusty-pink flower has tiny spikes of bell-shaped blossoms. Many florists use heather as an affordable boutonniere or in corsages. The price is about $2 per stem. Heather is a traditional flower at Scottish weddings.

♥ **HYDRANGEAS.** Because hydrangeas are so large (six inches across for just one!) they make excellent bouquets and centerpieces. You might need only three to five stems to create a full, lush look. They come in off white, pink, blue and lavender.

♥ **LISIANTHUS.** Available in white, pink, blue and purple, lisianthus is a delicate, multi petal flower with dark center. It is longer lasting than roses making it a good value.

♥ **STATTICE.** Fabulous filler flowers for bridal bouquets, these clusters of tiny white or purple blossoms are reasonably priced. Other fillers that are inexpensive include Queen Anne's Lace and "stock," a long-stalked flower with copious blooms. Stock has another bonus: they have a great fragrance.

Best Online Bargains

Ever wish you could order flowers at wholesale prices direct from the grower? Thanks to the 'net, you can. Here are some tips before we review our top picks in this category.

1. Do a small test order first, a few months before your wedding. That way you can evaluate the flower quality, color and delivery. You can also see how long it takes certain flowers to open. A multi-color bunch is a good idea to see variations in hues.

2. Plan in advance. You may need the flowers to arrive a few days before your wedding to insure they open in time. Warm water speeds this process, but it can still take a few days.

3. Be sure you have adequate supplies for arrangements. If you or a friend is arranging the flowers for your wedding, be sure to locate the appropriate supplies. From water tubes to vases to floral foam, the necessities are vast. Save-On-Crafts (save-on-crafts.com) is a great source for floral supplies as well as most craft and hobby chains.

4. Remember you don't have to go whole hog. If the thought of doing ALL your floral arrangements via the web is scary, consider doing merely the table centerpieces or other decor at the ceremony or reception site. Then hire a professional florist to do the personal flowers (bouquets, corsages, etc.).

Here's our round-up of discount floral web sites:

♥ **2G Roses** *freshroses.com* 2G Roses was one of the first online flower wholesalers. The Watsonville, CA grower has been in business since 1974.

2G's web site is a floral bargain hunter's paradise. 2G sells much more than roses—you can order lilies, orchids, tulips or hundreds of other available varieties. And the prices? Roses start at as little as $1.25 each. You can order flowers in individual bunches (say, mini calla lilies, 20 stems for $68) or select one of several bridal packages. For example, the "Premium All Rose Wedding" features enough roses, greenery and filler flowers to make eleven table arrangements, ten boutonnieres, six corsages, five bridesmaids' bouquets, one bride's bouquet and a head table arrangement (available in 18 colors). Price: $600, including shipping (FED-EX overnight to insure freshness). Order that many flowers from a

---

REAL WEDDING TIP

Green your wedding flowers

At first blush, flowers may seem like the most anti-green element of an eco-friendly wedding: many wedding blooms are grown with tons of pesticides and flown in from halfway around the world.

But there are many ways to green the flowers for your wedding. First, think local—use locally grown, in-season blooms to reduce the impact of flying in flowers from Holland. Bonus: this is usually less expensive. See the money saving tip earlier in this chapter on farmer's markets and local flower farms—both are great ways to find local growers.

If there are no local sources, consider online options like OrganicBouquet.com, which bills itself as the "largest online provider of eco-friendly and organic floral gifts." The web site only buys flowers from certified organic growers. Many of our recommended online flower web sites discuss their flowers, how they are grown and where. Some are even certified by outside environmental organizations as being responsible growers.

---

retail florist and you'd easily spend twice that amount of money.

Items are also available a la carte. And you don't have to limit yourself to roses. We counted at least 36 floral varieties available in June alone.

2G's web site clearly explains their packages and how to order and they also have a great FAQ to answer your questions. Most handy was a chart that listed flower availability by month—that way you can tell exactly what blooms are available for, say, an October wedding.

Here's what one bride told us about experience with 2G Roses:

"I used 2G Roses for all of my bouquets. The service and quality was excellent. They even confirmed my order over the phone before placing it. A friend and I made "hand-tied bouquets"...another tip out of your book. I would like to add that area florists started at about $85 a piece for one hand-tie bouquet. For about $350, I made my bouquet, three bridesmaids, two mother of the bride/groom corsages and I don't know how many boutonnieres and other arrangements!"

♥ **Brides N Blooms** *bridesnblooms.com* Even though Brides N Blooms has "brides" in their name, they don't really have bridal packages per se. They do offer a couple "floral combinations" under the Mix & Match category that would work well for weddings. For example, you could order combo boxes with mini callas and roses plus greenery for $345 to $430, up to the "over the top" box with callas, mini callas, cymbidium orchids and roses for $970. Other flower options include hydrangeas, lilies, iris, gerbera daisies, even stephanotis (25 flowers for $50). Browse the site by color to find interesting options. Remember, not all flowers will be in season for your wedding. Do-it-yourselfers will also find supplies at Brides N Blooms including bouquet forms and vases plus greens for filler. Brides N Blooms has a minimum purchase of one box of anything. So you could actually buy one box of 30 long stem calla lilies and have everyone carry these simple blooms for just $100. Brides N Blooms now offers a design service (bridesnbloomsdesigns.com) as well as the do-it-yourself supplies.

♥ **Costco.com** *costco.com* Remember our advice about shopping for wedding items at stores that do NOT have wedding in their name? Here's a case in point: when you think wedding flowers, Costco (the membership warehouse chain) probably doesn't come mind first. But the chain has moved big-time into weddings, so much so that they are now touting their bridal wares, both in the store and online. Go to Costco.com (click on Gift Cards, Tickets & Floral) and you'll find several packages for brides (all flowers are shipped direct from the wholesaler to your home). For example, the Simply Elegant Wedding Rose Collection for $400 includes one bridal bouquet, two bridesmaids bouquets, six corsages, six boutonnieres, three centerpieces and one rose petal bud. They even throw in a toss-away bouquet. Note these are FINISHED bouquets and arrangements, not loose flowers! Additional packages include a Sunflower Collection, Garden Wedding Collection, even a Wedding Calla Lily Collection and more. Prices start at $200 and go up to $750. Minor quibble: if you are not a member of Costco, there is a 5% surcharge on orders. A membership runs $50 for a year.

♥ **The Flower Exchange** *theflowerexchange.com* Readers of our past books have recommended the Flower Exchange, a Miami-based wholesaler whose web site has roses in perhaps the most number of color variations we've seen. Just click on white roses and you'll be able to choose from ten varieties. Another great option: garden roses (seasonal availability). These have bigger, more old-fashioned blooms. Prices are good overall. For example, hydrangeas start at $4.95 a stem, stargazer lilies at $18.65 per bunch of five and roses at $1.10 each. They also sell floral supplies like vases, bouquet holders and water tubes.

The Flower Exchange will also make your wedding bouquets and other items if you don't want to do the arranging yourself. These "wedding boxes" include ten to 28 pieces. For example, the ten-piece option has one bridal bouquet with matching groom's boutonnière, one maid of honor bouquet with matching best man boutonnière, one bridesmaid bouquet and matching groomsman boutonnière, one toss away bouquet, an extra boutonnière and two corsages for $398. That's a steal! Shipping for orders under $150 is $30 via FedEx, but for orders over $150 the shipping is free.

♥ **Fresh Petals** *FreshRosePetals.com* Fresh Petals was first recommended to us by a reader. She told us she had found their prices to be excellent, as well as their service. Their long stem roses are as little as $1.10 a stem. Shipping prices are affordable and are waved if you buy three different products from the site. A bunch of 25 roses was $73.59 including shipping. Of course, like 2G, Fresh Petals sells much more than roses. Their web site lists at least 20 other flowers, including gardenias, orchids and lilies. Fresh Petals has about five wedding packages. For example, their do it yourself package in one of six color schemes costs $184. For that price you'll get 50 long stem roses, 20 stems of spray roses, 20 stems of seasonal flowers and 2 bunches of greens plus two packages of assorted rose petals. The larger package ($276) adds another 25 roses, 10 spray roses, 10 seasonal flowers and one more bunch of greens. Wedding garlands are also available in ten-foot lengths for $110. Great for decorating arches or tables.

♥ **Rainforest Rose** *rainforestrose.com* If you are set on roses, Rainforest Rose sells only farm-direct Colombian roses (over 50 varieties in 15 colors). The web site offers a special wedding collection that includes bouquets, boutonnieres and centerpieces. The bridal bouquets are $75 to $85, bridesmaids $45, and centerpieces (without vase) are $47 each. Other flowers are available including orchids, lilies, hydrangeas and more. Photos of rose colors (15 choices) can be found in the Rose Gallery and you can buy the roses in bulk to design your own arrangements. For example, 250 red roses would cost $261 in bulk. Orders much be received at least seven days in advance, longer for special orders. A big selling point for Rainforest Rose is their Rainforest Alliance certification. Rainforest Alliance is an international nonprofit dedicated to the conservation of tropical forests. This certification ensures Rainforest Rose buys flowers from Columbian farms that don't damage the rainforest.

FIGURE 3:

Cut out the middle man and order your flowers wholesale! A sampling of web sites that you do just that.

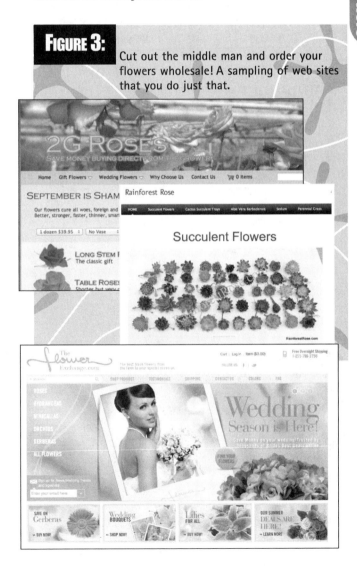

Biggest Myths about Wedding Flowers

MYTH #1 *"My mother insists that we have lots and lots of flowers at my wedding. Is this really necessary?"*

Bridal web sites often picture weddings with flowers dripping from the ceiling and crawling along the floor. Some florists feed this perception by suggesting superfluous floral items like "cake knife corsages" (believe it or not, a special flower wrapped with a bow around the knife you cut the cake with), "hairpiece flowers" and arrangements for the gift table. We are not making this stuff up. Does the gift table really need a floral arrangement?

Among the more ridiculous examples of floral price gouging from our readers: $20 for petals for a flower girl's basket (that doesn't include the basket, nor rose petals—just regular flower petals) and $50 for a small floral wreath for the flower girl's hair. Those were actual prices quoted to a Chicago bride by a local florist. The same bride told the florist to keep the quote under $1500. The florist's final bid: $1900.

MYTH #2 *"I figured on spending only about $500 on my wedding flowers. Given the cost of arrangements I've sent friends, I assume this is a good estimate."*

Most flowers are cheap. Most florists aren't. What you are paying for is the florist's talent, skill and overhead. The manual labor needed to create beautiful bouquets and arrangements (not to mention delivery and set-up) is what costs big money. We should note that some exotic flowers (orchids, etc.) are pricey exceptions: they virtually guarantee an astronomically high floral bill.

Helpful Hints

1 **Look for ideas on Pinterest.** If you haven't visited Pinterest, you've likely been sitting on an orbiting spacecraft for the last two years. But forget about looking at cute dog pics or the latest in cool shoes, focus on weddings. You'll find an unbelievable number of ideas from handmade paper flowers to cascading floral backdrops to peacock feather boutonnieres. Another site with great ideas: OffBeatBride.com. We loved the Lego themed boutonnieres and other unique ideas on this site.

2 **Put your deposit and balance on a credit card.** We have heard occasional stories of couples that hired a florist to do their flowers only to have the wrong flowers delivered. Or worse, the florist went out of business. Although these are rare occurrences, it's best to be safe. Special consumer protection laws protect deposits put on credit cards. See Chapter 2 (Apparel) for more details.

3 **Keep an open mind.** Instead of setting your heart on a particular design or flower, let your florist come up with some suggestions. Because florists work with flowers so closely, they may be aware of some options that are really terrific. Especially when choosing colors, listen to your florist's ideas and look at some of his/her past work before you make up your mind. You might be surprised!

4 **Confirm any restrictions on flowers/decorations.** Some churches prohibit candles and still others "request" that you donate the altar arrangement to the church. Reception sites may also have similar rules, especially regarding the throwing of birdseed or flower petals.

5 **Go European.** Check out European bridal magazines and web sites for creative ideas. We've noticed those publications feature more unique designs than their American counterparts. Some sites to consider: WeddingandWeddingFlowers.co.uk and YouandWourWedding.co.uk

6 **Head measurements for floral wreaths.** One bride emailed us this tip: if you order floral wreaths for the flower girls or bridesmaids, make sure to give the florist head measurements so she have an idea how big (or small) to make the wreaths. Her florist failed to get this detail, and the resulting flower girl wreaths were so big they could have been worn around the girls' necks.

7 **Label the personal flowers.** Here's a tip from a bride who learned this lesson the hard way: have your florist label the personal flowers (bouquets, corsages, boutonnieres) with the names of the intended recipient. That way you know who gets what at the wedding—and you avoid that messy scene when Aunt Bunny "accidentally" takes that special corsage you had made up for your mother-in-law. Don't laugh, this can happen to you.

8 **Ask the florist to pin corsages and boutonnieres on your wedding party.** One bride was frustrated that her florist just dropped off the flowers without taking a minute to help everyone pin on their corsages, boutonnieres, etc. Ask up front if your florist will be available to help. It will relieve some of the stress right before the wedding.

Pitfalls to Avoid

PITFALL #1 THE MERCEDES SYNDROME.

"I was at a florist the other day discussing my wedding when another bride pulled up in an expensive car. All the sudden, the florist's employees started chattering about how rich she was and how they'd have to triple the bill for her flowers! They were kidding, right?"

Maybe not. We once interviewed a florist who admitted charging more for wedding flowers depending on what type of car the bride drove up in! Apparently, brides who arrived at the florist's studio in a fancy ride look like they could afford to pay more for their wedding flowers. While that sounds absurd, think about it—when you walk into a flower shop, do you see any prices for bridal bouquets? Nope, most flower proposals are worked up on the fly, where a florist "estimates" what items cost due to the flowers used. Or perhaps how deep the client's pockets appear.

We've never tested this theory scientifically, but we wonder what would happen if two brides arrived at a floral shop to price bridal arrangements. One drives a Mercedes; the other a Kia. Guess who gets charged more? One bride in Oklahoma told us her florist's eyes lit up when the bride slipped and mentioned her fiancé was a doctor. Suddenly, the florist insisted she fly in exotic Asiatic lilies for the wedding. And the bill soared concurrently.

Then there is the mom syndrome. Several brides we interviewed noticed that when they brought their moms with them to the florist, the final tab went up. The assumption: if mom is along, mom must be paying . . . so let's pile it on! One bride noticed her florist's proposal was much higher than a friend's, despite the same quantity/quality of flowers requested for both weddings. The difference? Her friend went alone; the first bride brought her mom to visit the florist.

Similar to this is the "marriage markup," where simply telling a florist it's a wedding causes and increase in the price. To test this theory, ABC's 20/20 news magazine show hired actors to play an engaged couple planning a wedding and a brother/sister couple planning a 40th birthday party. They both visited the same florist asking for the same rose table centerpieces. The quote they received was quite revealing: for the wedding $300 per centerpiece. For the party, $250 each. So for ten tables, the wedding markup was an extra $500.

So a word of advice when floral shopping: don't flash that big diamond engagement ring. Dress in baggy clothes. Don't bring your mom. Pretend you're brother and sister. And take the bus.

PITFALL #2 "FTD COOKIE-CUTTER" WEDDINGS.

"I met with a florist for my wedding and was extremely disappointed.

All they showed me were boring FTD design books. The few real photos I saw featured bouquets that all looked the same."

Some florists try to make every wedding fit a "cookie cutter" mold. Instead of keying on the individuality of the bride and groom, they merely suggest stiff, formulated designs that are uninspired at best and dreadful at worst. We find "cash and carry" florists most guilty of this offense—they simply don't care enough about weddings to try harder.

PITFALL #3 PLASTIC BOUQUET HOLDERS.

"We attended a fancy wedding and were surprised at the bouquets. Beautiful flowers were stuck in plastic holders that just looked cheap!"

Plastic bouquet holders have become a crutch for many lazy florists. Instead of hand tying and hand-wrapping the bouquets, some florists simply stick flowers into floral foam inside plastic holders. Besides looking cheap, poorly inserted flowers can actually drop out of the plastic holder!

Some florists insist plastic holders are necessary since they provide a water source for delicate flowers. Other florists point out plastic holders are a cost-cutter for crescent or cascade bouquets, since they don't have to wire each individual bloom. That's great, but as they say, show us the money—we often found little savings with florists that use plastic holders.

If your florist uses plastic holders, insist the plastic be covered with green floral tape and/or ribbon. Another idea: you can camouflage a holder by wrapping it in satin fabric or by using leaves. Or choose a florist that hand ties and hand wraps the bouquets. A small tube of water can be attached to delicate flowers needing moisture.

PITFALL #4 HEAT-SENSITIVE FLOWERS.

"My friend got married last summer in an outdoor ceremony. Unfortunately, the heat caused the flowers to wilt and even turn brown."

If your wedding is in the summer, watch out for flowers that are vulnerable to extreme heat. Some flowers with this problem include stephanotis and gardenias (very expensive flowers to begin with). Ask your florist for flowers that can withstand the heat and still look fresh. As a side note, we heard from one florist who uses an "anti-transpirant" spray such as Bloomlife Plastic Wax or Crowning Glory (see right) on delicate blooms. These  products seal in the moisture so flowers don't wilt as fast—a good tip for brides getting married in August!

PITFALL #5 MARTHAHOLICS.

"I fell in love with a bouquet I saw on Martha Stewart Weddings web site. The flowers were phenomenal and I wanted my florist to copy it exactly. But when my florist called to find the source for the flowers, they told him they are from Martha's garden and not available commercially! Bummer!"

Yes, Martha is still a major trendsetter these days, but sometimes she forgets to let brides in on a secret: the supplies she uses are often hard or impossible to find. Or the "Martha look" may be impossible to replicate without hours of labor by a florist. If you've got your heart set on a Martha design, realize you may have to make compromises or shell out big bucks.

Trends

♥ **BOUTONNIERES BEDAZZLED.** The groom and groomsmen are so short-changed! The only flowers they wear are boutonnieres, and frankly, that's more than they probably want anyway. So why not something to fit their guy personalities? How about a Lego Indiana Jones for your swashbuckling groom? Or a steampunk combination of gears and flowers? We even saw a My Little Pony option for those "Brony" groomsmen.

♥ **CAN THE CORSAGE.** Yes, the tradition for moms and grandmothers has always been the ubiquitous corsage, worn pinned to the chest or on the wrist. But that's always seemed awkward—you crush it when you hug someone or it itches your wrist and you take it off. So here's a new trend: mini bouquets for mom. Imagine mini gerbera daisies or roses tied up with ribbon to match the moms' dresses. And bouquets make a great keepsake when dried.

♥ **GREEN.** Brides are choosing to use a lot more greenery in their bouquets. It's a great way to save money and unusual greenery like dusty teal succulents or bright green colored flowers (think button mums) contrast beautifully with the white of the bridal gown or the jeweled tones of a bridesmaids dress.

♥ **SINGLE BLOOMS.** Consider a bouquet consisting of a single type of flower. We've seen some stunning examples including a dozen hand-tied maroon mini calla lilies or a big puff of lavender hydrangeas, accented by satin ribbon. Brides are also cutting back on the many different types of flowers in table centerpieces as well, sticking with just a few types but in larger quantities.

♥ **BLING FOR THE BOUQUET.** Let's talk shiny! You can add in glittering broaches or pins to your bouquet, or wrap it with metallic ribbon and strings of pearls. We've even seen tiny faux gems glued to the centers of the flowers for a dash of sparkle. And don't forget the groom's boutonniere. It can incorporate a bit of bling to set your man off from the rest of the groomsmen. More recent additions to bridal bouquets: feather accents, seed pods and berries.

♥ **ACCENT WITH FLOWERS.** Flowers are not just for bouquets anymore. You can see them as hair accents, shoe accents or even on matching purses for the bridesmaids (if you don't want to ruin the purses, florists can design a detachable accent piece). One cool idea: a floral "pocket square" for the groom instead of a boutonniere. The florist glues tiny flowers to a cardboard form that will then slip into the groom lapel pocket leaving the flowers to peek out like a traditional pocket square.

♥ **SMALLER, COMPACT BOUQUETS.** Forget the loosely tied designs or the flowing cascades of the past. These days, brides want a tightly tied bouquet with a ton of blooms. If you want to add a bit of flair, some florists can add a few tendrils of greenery to soften the look.

♥ **UNIQUE FLOWERS TO ACCENT YOUR BOUQUET.** Tired of roses and orchids? Try unique (yet affordable) blooms such as chocolate cosmos, kangaroo paws (see right), fiddlehead ferns.

Thanks to Alice Norwick of Petals by Alice (PetalsbyAlice.com) for her insight into trends in the wedding flower industry.

SPOTLIGHT: ROSES

Types of Roses
"Where do florists get roses? Will they be the lame blooms I see at the grocery store? How can I be sure to get the best quality?"

Florists buy roses from wholesalers. Wholesalers, in turn, buy them from a variety of sources. Most roses sold in the US are grown in Columbia and Ecuador. Roses are sold by length as the quality of the blossom is related to the length of the stem. The longer the stem, the better the blossom.

Color Options
"I requested bridal white roses from my florist for my bridal bouquet, but the bouquet I saw on my wedding day looked pinkish rather than white.

Was my florist substituting the wrong flowers?"

Definitely not. One thing brides should understand about colors in the floral business is that they can be very deceiving. For example, a red rose isn't actually a true red. And a "bridal white" rose isn't really all white; rather it's a creamy white hue with a pink- or peach-tinged center. Gather several bridal white roses together in a bouquet and the overall look may be more pink or peach than you expected. If you have any doubts about color, request a sample of the flowers you are interested in to see the hue in person.

When looking at flowers online, keep in mind that colors may vary depending on your monitor. That's why it's a great idea to purchase samples of the flowers you're interested in before your wedding day. Some sites offer specific samplers, others do samples on request.

One interesting final note on roses: color has little or nothing to do with prices. You might expect unusual hues (lavender, for example) to cost more, but in reality the wholesale price is often the same.

Unique Ideas

♥ **Hold the rice.** The traditional rice thrown at the newlyweds has been declared "environmentally-incorrect" (birds eat the rice; birds die). So, couples have been replacing rice with flower petals, bubbles and so on. Another alternative to consider: Amazing Butterflies (amazingbutterflies.com; $65 to $95 per dozen) offers brides the option to release butterflies at the end of their ceremonies or receptions.

A side note: releasing butterflies is controversial (environmentalists don't like it). Yes, please use common sense and don't release them at a January wedding in Michigan—they'll all die! One site mentions that the air temperature must be at least 72° for the butterflies to take off.

A recent bride wrote to us with her idea for a dramatic send off. As wedding favors, she gave the guests printed matchbooks. They then used them to light sparklers (provided by the bride) at the end of the wedding as the couple left the reception. A few cautions: fireworks may be illegal in the city or town where you're getting married—check first. Also, if you live in a drought area, avoid any fireworks. And don't let small children play with sparklers. Have buckets of water handy to douse the sparklers after you've left. (Check Chapter 7, Reception Sites, for more info about fireworks—we'll detail how one bride capped her reception with a mini-fireworks show).

There is a downside we discovered with the sparkler idea: at a wedding we attended, the wind blew ash onto a guest's suit quickly burning a hole in the guest's wool jacket. Consider suspending this idea if the wind picks up!

SPOTLIGHT: CRAFT STORES

MICHAELS ARTS AND CRAFTS STORES
(800) MICHAELS
michaels.com

One of the best sources for silk flowers and wedding supplies in North America has got to be Michaels Arts and Crafts stores. With over 900 stores in the US and Canada, Michaels provides not only a large number of attractive, affordable silk flowers, but they also have in-store arrangers who can do all the arrangements at affordable rates.

For example, when we visited a Michaels store, the floral department told us most custom silk bouquets range from $50 to $100. Pre-made silk bouquets start at an amazing $8 for a small roses-only round bouquet. Larger versions are $13. Wow! This is a great savings when compared with the average fresh bouquet from a retail florist—which can run up to $200 or more.

Michaels stores also carry other accessories for do-it-yourself brides. They have supplies with which to make veils and headpieces ($10 to $20), tiaras ($20 to $45) wedding cakes toppers, favors (Jordan almond 16 oz. bag $8), unity candles ($35-$40) and other wedding items. They carry accessories ranging from ring pillows to do-it-yourself invitations to cake knives as well.

One Michaels web site (michaels.com), besides the standard store locator, you'll also find craft projects posted on-line, complete with supplies lists and instructions. We saw several bridal projects that could be used to make favors, table centerpieces and more. There's also a "crafts calendar" that lists in-store classes.

HOBBY LOBBY
(405) 745-1100 Web: hobbylobby.com

Hobby Lobby is an expanding national chain of craft stores with some attractive offerings. The stores carry all the usual bridal supplies like silk flowers and ribbon. We saw pre-made silk bouquets for $15 as well as headpieces for $13 to $40. Unity candles were $20 to $40 and cake toppers were $13 to $30.

But don't limit yourself to the wedding aisle at this store. We discovered clay pots (for garden style table centerpieces) for only $1. Looking for gifts for children in your wedding party? Don't pass up the funky picture frames and craft kits for kids. Overall, we think Hobby Lobby is one of the best do-it-yourself wedding resources you'll find in the country.

FLORAL DICTIONARY

Lilies

♥ **Calla**
Huge, long white flowers on thick stalks (as in Katherine Hepburn's ". . . the calla lilies are in bloom.") Smaller versions (called mini calla lilies) come in a variety of colors.

♥ **Rubrum**
Star flowers come in colors from white to peach to deep maroon.

Rubrum Lily

♥ **Lily of the Valley**
Small, white blooms that look like tiny bells. This flower is affordable in northern climates but quite expensive in other parts of the U.S. For a picture, see "Top Money-saving Secrets" earlier in the chapter.

Orchids

♥ **Dendrobium**
Miniature orchids that come in sprays, may be used individually or as trailing pieces.

♥ **Cymbidium**
Smaller than Japhet orchids with a curly edge only at the center.

Dendrobium Orchid

♥ **Japhet**
Large orchids with a curly edge all over, often have yellow throats.

♥ **Phalaenopsis**
These are round-edged orchids that are white with reddish throats. Their delicate nature makes them best for corsages as opposed to bridal bouquets.

Miscellaneous

♥ Stephanotis

Small, white flowers with star-like petals and a deep throat (we've been told that these can discolor in extreme heat).

Stephanotis

♥ Anthurium

One of the few "true red" flowers, this has a heart-shaped bloom with a large stamen.

♥ Peony

Another large blossom that is quite popular for wedding flowers. They are typically available in white with pinky/peach centers. Peonies are only available for a short time in spring and early summer.

♥ Anemone

Startlingly bright purple, pink or red with black centers, anemones make a great addition to bridesmaids' bouquets.

♥ Iris

Not your mother's garden iris, these blooms are

Anemone

slender and delicate in deep purple or white with yellow throats. A cool combination: purple iris with tiny yellow oncidium orchids.

♥ Star of Bethlehem (ornithogalum)

Multiple blooms of white, star-shaped flowers on long stalks

♥ Sunflowers

Yellow petals with black/brown centers, these can be quite large and are often found at summer farmer's markets.

Star of Bethlehem

♥ Snapdragons

Available in assorted colors including white, pink, yellow, orange and burgundy. Tall spikes that would work well in ceremony or reception arrangements

♥ Agapanthus

Blue to purple in color and arranged in a ball shape of tiny flowers topping a tall stalk.

Agapanthus

Candles and ribbon at a discount

Yes, candles do add ambience to a wedding or reception. But many invitation sites sell candles at obscene prices. Of course, our smart readers never pay retail. Here are their picks for best discount candle sites:

- ♥ **Oriental Trading Co.** (Orientaltrading.com): votives, unity candles floating candles.
- ♥ **Wax Wizard** (Waxwizard.net): floating candles, votives, unity candles.
- ♥ **Gen Wax** (Genwax.com): floating candles, votives, unity candles.
- ♥ **Bridal Shop Store** (BridalShopStore.com): floating candles.

Our favorite discount ribbon sites:

- ♥ **C.O.D. WHOLESALE** (codwholesale.com)
- ♥ **Ribbon Trade** (ribbontrade.com)
- ♥ **Idea Ribbon** (IdeaRibbon.com)

## Chapter 6

In this chapter, we'll tell you about a printing process that can save you 50% or more on your invitations. Then, check out discount sources for invites. Next, we'll show you the five-step shopping process for finding invitations, and share several of the latest invite trends.

What Are You Buying?

Buying invitations is a little like buying a meal at an a la carte restaurant. In other words, everything is priced separately: the appetizer, salad, entree, and dessert. With invitations, the entree is the basic invitation design itself (the paper style and the printing). Thankfully, the price does include the envelopes (two for very formal invitations or one for more informal options).

There are also other "accessories" available but these are priced separately in addition to the original invitation. Here are some options and a short description:

♥ **RECEPTION CARDS** announce to the guest the location and time of the reception.

♥ **RESPONSE CARDS** (also known as R.S.V.P.'s) are just as they sound—a card that asks guests to tell you whether or not they can attend. An envelope (with your return address printed) is included with each response card. Most couples put postage on the response card envelopes to encourage their guests to respond.

♥ **COLORED INK** is available from almost every manufacturer (you can often choose among as many as 30 or more hues). High-end printers usually don't charge an extra fee for colored ink.

♥ **ENVELOPE LININGS** add a little flair and color to invitations.

♥ **YOUR RETURN ADDRESS** can be printed on the back flap of the envelopes.

♥ **INFORMALS**, used mainly as thank-you notes, are blank cards with your names printed on the outside.

♥ **PROGRAMS, PEW CARDS, AND OTHER ENCLOSURES** may be additional items to consider . Programs ($50 to $250 per 100) list all the participants in the wedding ceremony and tell guests the order of the service. Pew cards are used to differentiate between guests who are to be seated up at the front of the church (reserved seating) from those who should be seated farther back (general admission). Maps are included for weddings with many out of town guests or if guests are going to a separate reception site after the ceremony.

A word on invitation sizes. Most wedding invitations are rectangles; a typical size is 5" by 7". In recent years, new popular styles include square invites (7" by 7" or their smaller cousins, marquis at 5.5" by 5.5") and something called "tea length" invites that are the size of this book (4" by 9"). Remember that larger square invitations may require additional postage.

FYI: A wedding isn't just a single event. You may have a wedding engagement party, a shower (or two!), bridesmaids' luncheon and many more events that precede the big day. Anything from a simple email to a casual paper invitation may be required for these events. Some invites will be the bride's responsibility (like the bridesmaids' luncheon), some may be friends (showers) and some will fall to parents (engagement parties, rehearsal dinner). Usually, a casual paper invitation with phone number for RSVP will work fine for these events. You could also include them in a wedding newsletter, web site or Facebook page.

Average total costs. The average couple pays about $428 for paper invitations and other stationery needs (for a wedding with 150 guests). But you can spend as little as $100 . . . or as much as $1500 for top-of-the-line engraved options. The average deposit is 50% down with the balance due when you pick up the order (if you order from a retail store). When ordering online, complete payment is due when the order is placed.

Where to Buy Invitations

There are three basic options for buying invitations. You can purchase them online, offline or do-it-yourself. Here's an overview:

♥ **ONLINE.** A myriad of companies have sprung up in recent years to offer wedding invitations online. Later in this chapter we'll review some of the best online options.

There are three types of online retailers:

1 **Traditional stationery dealers/buying services.** These are companies that offer the same brand names as brick and mortar dealers. Instead of looking through invitation catalogs, you browse thumbnails online to see details and prices. Often, you have to call these guys to place an order, so there is still a personal service aspect. The downside: it can be quite exhausting to shop online. You'll be clicking thumbnails for hours looking through designs. And some sites have hundreds of possibilities! See reviews of our top stationers later in this chapter.

2 **Direct from the manufacturer.** Most major invitation printers have web sites for direct orders. There is often an 800 number to call for help on wording or other questions. Prices are often 40% off similar retail invitations. Quality varies widely—we suggest asking for sample invitations of designs you're interested in so you can compare papers. Don't forget to check for a money back guarantee. Also, many of these manufacturers have quick turn-arounds of as little as two to three days—perfect if you are in a hurry. Here are a few manufacturer direct sites:

TheAmericanWedding.com
InvitationsbyDawn.com
ReavesEngraving.com
Invitations.BedBathandBeyond.com (Rexcraft)

3 **Paperless.** If you're interested in saving a few trees, these all-electronic options are an alternative to the traditional printed invite. Paperless wedding invitation sites let you pick an e-invite design that is then sent your friends and family, complete with "digital" envelope. We'll review a few of these sites in the Best Online Bargains later in the chapter.

♥ **OFFLINE.** If you're interested in the old school method of purchasing invitations, you'll likely visit a few invitations stores and look through a series of books with invitation samples. Here are the typical retail sources for offline invites:

1 Stationery shops. Google "Invitations" or "Wedding Invitations" in your town and you'll find a smorgasbord of places, from party stores to gift boutiques. As dealers for major invitations printers, these shops carry a selection of sample books containing examples of each invitation. Brides choose a design from these sample books and then place an order. Hands-on service is one of the chief advantages to this route—most stores can help you with etiquette/wording questions and, perhaps more importantly, deal with any problems that crop up with the printer. Of course, you pay for this service with full-retail prices and few discounts.

2 Places you wouldn't think of. Some churches and synagogues offer invitations at discounted prices as a fundraiser. We've even heard of several companies that offer invitations as a perk for their employees. One bride who worked at Xerox told us she was able to order invitations through the company at a substantial discount.

Another great source is "out of home" stationers. These businesses operate from home-based offices and, thanks to low overhead, usually pass along savings from 10% to 20%. You still get service with these stationers, just no fancy retail shop. As with any merchant you deal with for your wedding, you'll want to make sure the company is reputable by checking with the Better Business Bureau (bbb.org), contacting references, etc.

Some department stores with bridal registries also sell invitations, as do offset printers. A few local printers actually print their own invitations while most send the orders along to the same national printers you'll see in stationery shops.

♥ **Do It Yourself.** You design your own invite, either with help from a web site, by buying an invitation kits with laser compatible paper or by using design tools like Adobe Illustrator and buying your own paper. We'll share some of the best paper and kit suppliers with you later in this chapter.

Sources to Find Stationers

♥ **Yelp:** If you're looking for a traditional retail stationer in your hometown, Yelp is an excellent resource to check.

♥ **Online:** Next, let's look at the best online sources for invites.

Best Online Bargains

Ann's Bridal Bargains *annsbridalbargains.com* No rela-
tion to this book, Ann's site highlights invitations for less
than $1 right up front. This site has free invitation samples,
an e-newsletter mailing list, and free wedding web sites. Ann's guarantee: they'll match any lower price you find out there.

Invitation designs start at a mere $50 per 100 for the simplest of white
cards up to $169 per one hundred for a Separate-n-Send design. Over
330 options are available and range from contemporary to traditional,
Seal-n-Send to traditional cards to print-your-own options.

We love the prices here. If you want a truly affordable paper invite, this
place has a wide selection. We've seen a lot of these designs from other
sources and know that the paper quality is only average. Some designs
are pretty flimsy, so you may want to stick with panel cards for a better-
looking invite. **Rating: B**

eInvite *einvite.com* With nearly 1000 invitation designs, eInvite allows
you to see an exact typeset copy of the invitation with colored ink, lettering and sizes online. Once you choose an invitation, you can click the link
to personalize it. Then the site allows you to enter your personal wording,
choose an ink color and letter style, then click again to view the changes.

Immediately, you'll see a life size version of your wedding invitation
exactly as it would be printed. Once you decide on the invitation, you can
simply click to send it along to the printer. One note of caution: after you
purchase the invite, the design goes directly to the printer. Be sure to
proofread carefully because it becomes difficult if not impossible to recall
it once its sent to the printer.

If you have any etiquette concerns, eInvite offers a wedding etiquette
guide, FAQ, glossary of terms and more. The site has four shipping options
from UPS Ground to Next Day Air. Check for occasional free shipping
offers. Samples of most styles are available for a small charge.

Prices start at about $83 per 100 for a simple panel style. And you can
sort invitations by popularity, color or price. This helps you avoid having
to search through oodles of invites to find one in your price range.

eInvite is easy to use and we love the display proofs. We think it's prudent to ask for a sample of invites you're interested in before you place your
order. Overall all, the site is easy to use—eInvite is a keeper. **Rating: A**

evite *evite.com* This site offers over 100 wedding themed e-invitations
for free. Yep, you read right—free. And it's ridiculously simple. Just pick
from one of their many options (or you can design your own), fill in info
about the event (you can even include a map), type a message to your
guests if you'd like, add your guests' emails addresses . . . and hit send. For
the paperless bride, this is a great option. And if you don't have much

time, evite makes sense.

Style-wise, evite's invitations are more casual/modern—many are photo designs. For example, one design featured a photo of two wedding rings and some ribbon. Or the scrabble theme with the works "to have". Some designs are cartoony and might be more appropriate for a shower or bridesmaids' luncheon.

Evite has an extensive FAQ section with advice and help on creating and editing invitations, managing your guest list, reminders, troubleshooting and more. We are impressed with their options and, of course, the price: free! **Rating: A**

pingg *pingg.com* Pingg offers its own take on paperless invites. They have a basic service, which is completely free. This allows you to choose any design with your own wording and photos, which can then be sent to your guests at no charge. Then, if you want more, they offer an upgrade to pingg Plus for $10 to $70 depending on which extra features you want.

Pingg Plus includes an ad-free web site for your event, digital envelopes, the ability to send to a larger number of guests (250 to 2500), customized URL, extended designs from their library of over four million images, and ten to 20% off "Postal pinggs." What's a Postal pingg? This is an additional service that will send paper invitations to your guests in addition to the virtual invitations. The cost: $2.50 per invite. The pitch: these paper invites can be a "keepsake" for your guests.

Pingg bills itself as a more unique e-invitation site because of their emphasis on design. They actively encourage artists, photographers, illustrators and anyone else to submit designs to the site (which probably explains how they ended up with four million images!). You can choose designs based on a favorite artist, theme, holidays and more. Designs run the gamut but all are pretty casual looks. **Rating: B+**

Paperless Post *paperlesspost.com* Paperless Post has a unique way of charging customers to use their web site: they charge users for "virtual stamps" to email each card, invite, announcement or save the date card. So this site isn't free. But you won't see any advertisements on the site (like you will on evite.com, for example), and you get 25 free coins when you sign up.

Additional coins are available starting at for $5 per 25 coins. Larger quantities are available up to 5000 coins for $325. The more you buy, the cheaper each coin gets. Compare that price to the cost of sending real paper invites through the Post Office and it's quite a deal! As an alternative, you can buy coins that allow for extra customizations like envelope liners and logos. And you qualify for free stamps when your friends join the site.

But what about the invites? They are impressive—a bit more sophisticated than the options on evite. You'll see decorative boarders, virtual ribbons, colored backgrounds ... everything that is available in print invitations is here. Once you choose a design, you can write the wording yourself or get help with traditional wording from the site.

Then you can choose images (if it's a photo card) and finally you pick the envelope. If you have some of those coins you'll have the ability to line the envelope or add other custom touches. If you need to make changes, you can even if the card has already been sent. You can also track emails that have been delivered but not responded to yet and resend invites.

FAQ's are available under the Help button as well as info on getting started, managing your email list, tracking, customization and troubleshooting. The site is not always intuitive, but after a little wandering around, it gets easier to figure out. Overall, it's an attractive option for paperless invites. Paper invitations are also available **Rating: A-**

Indian Wedding Card *indiaweddingcard.com* Recommended by a reader, this site has unbelievably unique designs. You won't see these papers and styles anywhere else. The prices are surprisingly affordable with orders shipped within two to 14 days. Delivery to the US takes three to six days once they are shipped.

For example, we found a gate folded design with tassel tie in 6 different colors. The design was an exotic embossed floral and paisley style accented with gold in red, maroon, cream, blue, green or brown. Prices: $1.65. The inside pages (called inserts) are golden textured sheets and the envelope incorporates touches of color as well.

The site has an extensive FAQ, which is helpful since the order process is different from most other invitation web sites. For example, they will recommend the color of silkscreen printing for each design. Their FAQ states that the site's proofing team chooses the appropriate color for the invitation based on their extensive experience. But they will allow you to choose your own color if you want. Samples are available for most designs and there is a charge ranging from $2 to $20 per card depending on how fancy the design.

Perhaps the coolest option we saw was scroll invitations. Most scrolls are printed with the invitation and included in their own decorative box. Yes, this would be quite a bit more expensive to mail than a paper invite, but if you were having a small wedding and wanted to splurge, this would be amazing. (Scrolls are also available without boxes for as little as $1.50 each.) Prices go up to $9 each for the fanciest—velvet printed fabric with silver support bars and tassels, silver and gold metal case and gold and silver embossed paper. These invites must be seen to be appreciated. **Rating: A**

BRIDAL BARGAINS 175

Wedding Paper Divas *weddingpaperdivas.com* Wedding Paper Divas is an off-shoot of Shutterfly, the photo storage and gift web site. The two sites have a similar feel, with an easy to use format, detailed advice and FAQs. And Wedding Paper Divas offers wedding web sites just like Shutterfly's photo storage sites.

Divas sells regular thermography, letterpress and engraved invitation options. Styles range from vintage to modern with a smattering of traditional designs as well. If you don't mind a little do-it-yourself, the site has pocket invites and layered options that require some assembly. Prices for traditional invites start at as low as $1.25 each per 100, while letterpress invites can be as much as $6 per invite.

Costco has a deal with Wedding Paper Divas to supply invitations for Costco members (warehouse.stores.weddingpaperdivas.com). They sell the same invitations but at a 20% discount—a great deal. You have to go to Costco's web site and click on Floral then Invitations and Announcements to get the special price. **Rating: B+**

Zazzle *zazzle.com* Amid a site that carries everything from iPhone cases to t-shirts, Zazzle also quite a few wedding invitations in variety of sizes. Yes, the paper can be somewhat flimsy, depending on the style, but they are cheap and lightning quick.

The site allows you to shop by theme, color or season. For example, if you're having a summer wedding, you'll find invites decorated with summer flowers, summer scenes (a swing with lovebirds), butterflies and other summer motifs. Prices start at around $1 per invite. Most of the

FIGURE 1: Costco members can save 25% off the price of invites at Wedding Paper Divas.

INTRODUCING COSTCO IN-WAREHOUSE PICK UP
Pick up qualifying orders at your local Costco when it's convenient for you.

designs are available in different sizes and different papers.

One of the best things about Zazzle is their detailed info online: the type of envelope that comes with the invite, how many paper types and colors you can choose from (there is an up-charge for some variations) and how much the postage will be to send one of those invitations.

We ordered invitations recently from Zazzle for an anniversary party and were impressed with how easy it was. Design the wording online, see a digital proof and send off your final choice. Shipping is quick (about a week) and they guarantee their work—no questions asked. **Rating: A-**

Best Bargains: Buying Services

If your invitations needs are complex and you need advice on wording and accessories, consider a buying service. Here are some of our favorites:

♥ **Elegant Brides Invitations** *eleganterides.invitations.com* This invitations website offers a 30%-40% discount on invites from a wide number of manufacturers. Options include Jean M, Styleart, Checkerboard and more. Save-the-date cards, do-it-yourself invites, photo invites and recycled paper designs are available as well. We like how the site organizes wedding invitations by designer and type. So if you're looking for a pocket invitation, you can bypass looking at non-pocket designs. The Before You Order section is a great overview of the options from each designer. You can view an invitation proof online and get a proof mailed to you for a small fee. "Efficient, quality service," said another reader. Call Elegant Brides directly for help ordering your invites. **Rating: B+**

♥ **Invitation Hotline** *invitationhotline.com* Here's a great option for traditional bridal invites from well-known manufacturers like Encore, Checkerboard and more. Over 90 albums are available to choose from, including such premium brands as Encore and Elite. Owner Marcy Slachman told us the company also offers calligraphy and other custom accessories (maps, seating cards).

Marcy also noted that expensive lines are adding lower priced options—so you get the quality at a lower price, although styles will be less extravagant. She also mentioned that brides are turning to response postcards to save money on envelopes and postage.

You can submit an online quote request—just include the book name and style number. Marcy will help troubleshoot any etiquette or wording questions. Delivery takes about two weeks from the date the order is placed. Faster delivery is available via overnight services. **Rating: A**

♥ **You're The Bride** *yourethebride.com* This company has "great prices and very honest service," says a reader who said the site saved her $300 on her invites. The well-designed site sells Birchcraft, Stylart and other brands at a 35% discount. Free samples are available. A plus to the site: the Invitation Tutorial. This audio presentation steps through all you ever wanted to know about invitations. Tracie Morris, who owns the site, is a certified wedding consultant. Her site includes lots of tips on how to plan your wedding as well. **Rating: B+**

REAL WEDDING TIP

How many people should you invite?

Here's a classic dilemma: Your reception site holds 150 people . . . so, how many guests should you invite? 200? 175? Or just 150?

This issue points up one of the mysteries of wedding planning: estimating possible response rates to a wedding invitation. The answer . . . it's anybody's guess.

Your response rate will be based on several factors. How many out of town guests are invited? Odds are you'll have a higher rejection rate from folks who have to travel a great distance. What about the time of year? Weddings near major holidays may also suffer from lower response rates, since guests may be out of town on vacation.

A parallel issue to this is the response (or RSVP) card, where folks are asked the simple question "will you be attending?" Yes or no? Heck, they even get a postage-paid envelope that makes a response painless. The sad fact: many guests simply don't pay you the courtesy of using them. Perhaps they're too busy; perhaps they don't want to offend you by saying no. Whatever the reason, it can be very hard to tell just HOW MANY people will actually show up to your wedding.

We think it's fair for the bride and groom to contact wayward guests to see if they are coming. Blame it on the caterer, who needs an approximate count two weeks before your wedding. If the acceptance rate seems lower than expected, consider sending off a second wave of invitations to those friends or relatives on the B list.

If you want some help keeping track of invitations, RSVPs, dinner choices, gifts and the like, check out **WeddingControl.com,** a free database for brides. Record guest list info, dinner choices and so on. Then you can access any guest on the list easily to track information about them like gifts and thank yous. New on the site, now you can track your budget and seating assignments.

Best Do-It-Yourself-Invitation Bargains

Do it yourself invites can be one of two options: invitation kits with blank paper, or self designed (on a program like Adobe Illustrator) with unique papers. Great tips on making your own invites can be found on Paper-Source.com. Here are some paper suppliers we recommend for couples who are interested in designing their invites:

Art Paper	artpaper.com
Dew Drafting	draftingsuppliesdew.com (vellum paper)
First Base	first-base.com
Geographics	geographics.com
LCI Paper	lcipaper.com
Marco's	marcopaper.com
Paper & More	paperandmore.com
Paper Direct	paperdirect.com
Paper Source	paper-source.com
Paper Studio	paperstudio.com
Southworth	southworth.com

If you'd rather not cut, paste, print and tie your invites but would prefer to just laser print them, consider do it yourself invitation kits. These typically come in a box with invites, envelopes, and enclosure cards (use for RSVP, etc.). You'll likely have to buy more than one box for medium to large size weddings. Most kits include anywhere from 25 to 50 invites and enclosures. Here are some of our readers' favorite sites to find wedding kits:

My Gatsby	mygatsby.com
Formal Invitations	formal-invitations.com
My Expression	myexpression.com
Cards and Pockets	cardsandpockets.com

Getting Started: How Far in Advance?

There are five steps in the shopping process for invitations: Overall, we recommend ordering invitations at least three to four months before your wedding.

1 **Shopping**. While it may sound easy to shop for invites online, it can be overwhelming. And sometimes seeing sample invites in person (that is, in retail stationery stores) gives you a better feel for paper quality, printing styles and so on. Give yourself time to see invite samples, whether in a store or by mail.

2 **Ordering**. This varies greatly by printer. Generally, it can take anywhere from ten days to two months to order invitations. Most orders take two to four weeks, although some companies offer rush service.

3 **Mistakes**. We suggest you leave a two-week "buffer zone" in case your invitations come in with errors. One stationer told us that one out of every three orders comes in with mistakes from the printer. "Quality control" seems to be a fuzzy concept with some invitation printers.

4 **Addressing**. Considering how busy you probably are with work and wedding planning, leaving four weeks here is prudent. If you choose to hire a local calligrapher, most take between one and three weeks to complete a job.

5 **Mailing**. Everyone knows how efficient the US Postal Service can be. Give yourself plenty of time. Mail invitations to out-of-town guests at least six weeks before the wedding. For in-town guests, mail at least four weeks before the event. If your wedding is on or near a holiday, consider mailing even earlier so your guests will have time to make plans.

Step-by-step Shopping Strategies

♥ **Step 1:** Determine the number of invitations needed. Here's a quick quiz: if you're inviting 200 people to your wedding, do you need 200 invitations? Answer: no—you send only one invitation *per household*. And since most of the folks you invite will be couples, you probably need about 100 invitations. (There is one exception to this rule, however—if a guest's child is over 18 and living at home, he receives his own invitation.)

♥ **Step 2:** Confirm the place and time of the wedding and reception. Also, verify the spellings of the facilities and names of participants. (We heard one story of a bride who didn't know how to spell her fiancé's middle name—the resulting invitation was misspelled!

♥ **Step 3:** Determine your overall wedding style. For example, an outdoor afternoon wedding followed by a barbecue reception will probably not have a formal, engraved invitation. On the other hand, a formal wedding with a sit-down dinner reception at the Four Seasons isn't the time for embossed hearts and flowers on parchment paper. The invitation is your guests' clue about what to expect. To decide how formal your wedding is, consider time of day, formality of dress, and reception style. At the same time, you and your fiancé's personalities should also be reflected in the wedding invitation.

♥ **Step 4:** Decide on an invitation budget. Prices range from $35 to $1000 per 100 invitations. The average spent on invitations is $600 (including enclosures and thank you notes).

♥ **Step 5:** Once you find a stationer (either online or offline), look at their sample books or catalog. First, decide on the paper. Forget the wording, type styles, and ink colors. Instead, look at the paper design and quality. (If you are shopping online, request a sample of the paper to see it in person). Here's an inside tip: for almost all invitations, any style of type, wording and colors can be put on any paper design—so focus on the paper first. Paper grades and weights largely determine the price: inexpensive invitations use lightweight 24 lb. paper, while more expensive brands use heavier (up to 80 lb.) stock. Papers made of 100% cotton are usually more expensive than wood pulp options, but give a more elegant look.

♥ **Step 6:** Next, consider the printing. Decide on the ink color, lettering style and printing method (engraving or thermography). Sometimes the design of the invitation limits the choice of printing method.

♥ **Step 7:** Given the paper design and printing that best fits your reception, choose an invitation in your price range. Don't forget to factor in the cost of extras including napkins, place cards and maps if you want them.

♥ **Step 8:** Order at least 25 more invitations than your actual count in case you decide you need more later (you may want a few for keepsakes, etc.). Also, order extra envelopes in case of addressing goofs (calligraphers often ask for 10% extra for mistakes). After the order is written, proofread very carefully before the order is sent off. This is a critical step to catch any errors.

♥ **Step 9:** When the order comes in, proofread again and count the number of invitations to be sure you received the amount you ordered. Do this before you leave the store or as soon as the invites arrive by mail. Stationers have only a three- to five-day window allowed by printers to catch mistakes. Online invitations have varying return policies, but most only allow 15 to 30 days.

Questions to Ask about Invitations

1 **How many different lines do you carry?** A wide assortment of styles and brands not only gives you more choices (and price ranges) but also a clue to how serious the retail stationer is about her business. Since stationers must purchase those sample books (at a cost of $45 to $300 a book), the number they carry indicates their commitment to wedding invitations.

2 **Given my wedding and reception, what is your opinion of having response cards?** Response cards (an extra expense) encourage your guests to let you know whether they will attend the wedding. However, in some regions of the country (parts of the South and Southwest) guests often don't send in their response cards because they prefer not to "disappoint" the bride by saying no. In other regions, particularly the Northeast, response cards are considered a must and are routinely returned by guests.

A retail stationer in your area should be able to give advice on this if you are uncertain. Even if you do choose to send response cards, you may only receive as few as 30% back. We recommend response cards when you are inviting a large number of guests and/or are having a very expensive meal. If you are only planning a cake and punch reception or are having fewer than a hundred guests, response cards may not be needed. Remember that response cards also require their own stamp, raising your expenses accordingly. Yes, you can put your email address on the RSVP card, but always give guests the option of responding by mail.

A plus to paperless invites: some allow you to send a gentle reminder to your guests who have not responded. And it may be easier to get a response if they can simply click a button.

3 **Can I see some samples of actual invitations?** This is one way to separate the part-time stationer from the full-time professional—the latter typically has many actual samples on hand. The best mail order and web sources also provide samples of invitation designs upon request (either for free or at a nominal charge). Don't look at the style or color of the samples. Instead key in on the wording and the overall composition. Is the effect pleasing? Are the lines of type proportionate to the paper size? Is the type correctly aligned on the paper? If the invitation wording looks awkward, you may not want to trust your invitation to this business.

Occasionally, you'll come across a site that charges for samples. If the paper and/or designs are unique, this is understandable. Other sites limit the number of samples you can order for free. Beyond that number they may charge you so choose the designs you request carefully.

4 **Who is responsible for any errors that occur?** Some retail stationers may not offer to fix errors, whether you made them or they did. The true professional will take care of anything that goes wrong, regardless of who is responsible. If ordering online, be sure to read sale terms carefully. You'll want to note how the site handles errors, reorders and extra envelope requests.

5 **Can I see a proof of the invitation? Some printers offer this at a very small cost (about $10 to $20).** If you have a large order or complex invitation, this might be a prudent way to go. One trade-off: requesting and approving a proof will add more time to the process, but still may be worth it for the peace of mind. Digital proofs are available from many online sources for free. There is usually a charge for a physical proof of the design.

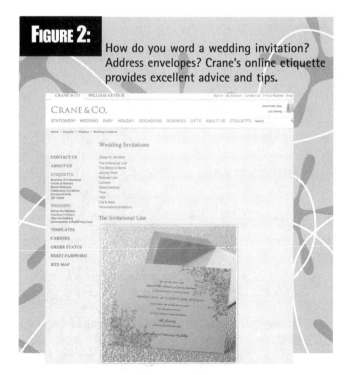

FIGURE 2:

How do you word a wedding invitation? Address envelopes? Crane's online etiquette provides excellent advice and tips.

Top Money-saving Secrets

1 Paperless invites. Who needs paper? Just email your invite. You save trees *and* money—what a deal! In the earlier reviews of favorite paperless websites, you'll note most are free. And these sites offer options for wedding web sites, methods of tracking invites and responses, options to re-contact guests who haven't responded, send save-the-date cards, thank yous and anything else you can think of. Even sites that charge a fee for emailing are still considerably more affordable than snail mail invites.

2 Order from a professional stationer who discounts. See the discount sources earlier in this chapter.

3 Skip the extras. As you've read above, there are quite a few different accessories and extras available to match your wedding invitation. Instead of ordering separate reception cards, consider printing "Reception Following" at the bottom of your actual invitation (obviously, this only works if you are having the wedding and reception at the same location!). This could save about 15% off your bill. Also, skip envelope linings and response cards if you don't see a need for them. To see how all these charges add up, let's look at the sample costs for an invitation with black ink from Carlson Craft, a major brand we'll review later in this chapter.

INVITATION PRICING EXAMPLE
Carlson Craft Invitation
(PRICE FOR 100 INVITATIONS)

Basic Invitation	$102.90
Return Address on Flap	34.00
Reception Card	52.90
Response (RSVP) Card	64.90
Lined Envelopes	25.60
Informals (Thank You Notes)	52.90
TOTAL	$333.20

As you can see by this example, the original invitation is a fraction of the total bill; note how the "options" can double or triple your final tab.

4 Choose thermographed invitations instead of engraved. Right about now you may be wondering what is thermography. Let's take a quick look at the difference between the two printing processes. Note: we aren't talking about the style of script or the quality of the paper; this is just the actual printing process.

Engraving is the Rolls Royce of printing. Until the 1970's (when thermography became widespread), this was your only choice for invitations.

Both engraving and thermography create raised printing. However, with engraving, a copper or steel plate is etched with the type and design. These etchings fill with ink and are forced against a die, lifting the ink out of the plate and creating a raised image on the paper. The paper is left with an impression from the back (called a "bruise").

Thermography is often used to simulate engraving. A resinous powder is dusted over the ink while it is still wet. The paper is then heated, the powder melts and fuses with the ink, swelling to create a raised surface. While metal plates may be used, this process is much less expensive (up to 50% or more). Another advantage to thermography: this process also allows you to use a wide variety of ink colors and type styles. Thermography has become extremely popular, thanks to better production quality. The process is virtually indistinguishable from engraving, except there is no dent (or bruise) on the back of the invitations. All the mail-order catalogs/web sites listed later in this chapter offer thermographed invitations.

5 **Buy an embosser with your return address instead of paying extra to get this printed on the back flap.** The cost of an embosser is about equal to or less than the return address charge in many cases—the advantage here is you can use the embosser again. You can order an embosser at most office supply stores or sites like this:

Officedepot.com   Officemax.com
Stampco.com   Staples.com

6 **Order your stationery needs all at once.** Many printers offer quantity discounts if you order the invitation and any extras

REAL WEDDING TIP

Engraved invites without the engraved price

A reader in Maryland found Reaves (reavesengraving.com) saved her big bucks over Crane engraved :

"I saved $900+ on my engraved wedding invitations thanks to Reaves. I used their card stock verses Crane's (I couldn't tell the difference) because the watermark wouldn't show anyway. I was so pleased with their work, service, prices and overall GREAT attitude!"

(thank you notes, RSVP cards) at the same time.

7 **To save on postage, don't buy an oversized invitation.** Oversized invitations require more postage. Also, an invitation with lots of enclosures (reception cards, response cards, maps, etc.) will be more expensive to mail since it will probably exceed one ounce in weight. (A smart tip: before you do the mailing, take one invite to the post office to get an actual weight with all enclosures). Remember that response cards or postcards require their own stamp, too. Pockets may add weight as well.

8 **For engraved invitations, consider alternatives to Crane.** The Cadillac of engraved invitations, Crane (see review in the next section) charges about $500 to $1000 for 100 engraved invitations. But what if you desire engraved invitations, yet can't afford the Crane price? There are several affordable alternatives. For example, Reaves Engraving (877-9REAVES or 910-369-2260; web: reavesengraving.com) charges just $426 for 100 engraved invitations on Crane paper. (It's even less for engraved invitations on their own in-house stock—$166 per 100). FYI: Reaves also offers calligraphy.

Another alternative: use a discount buying source like Invitation Hotline (800) 800-4355 (see review earlier in this chapter). They offer a variety of manufacturers with engraving options for up to 30% off.

9 **Postcards**—a great way to save on money and postage for RSVP's! Instead of a response card (which needs a separate envelope and a first-class stamp), consider a response postcard. One bride told us she whipped up a response postcard on her computer and had it copied on double-sided cardstock at a local copy shop. Total cost: $15 per 100. And then the postcards only require a 33¢ stamp. A basic response card with envelope costs about $50 per 100 and requires a 46¢ stamp. Your savings: $48.

10 **Design it yourself on a computer.** Got a computer and printer? ED-iT (ed-it.com) offers a wedding invitation software program that allows you to design and print invitations, announcements, response cards, pew cards, reception cards, place cards, maps, thank you notes, programs and even envelopes. The software helps with wording, offers "perfect typesetting" and has a built-in guest list manager. Six invitation fonts are available or you can use your own fonts. This Windows-only program costs $30. They also offer a Try-Before-Buy feature that allows you to use the program for 30 days free (the only trick: they add "for evaluation use" to every print out so no, you can't really use it without paying). The only downside, the site is still stuck in the late '90's. They really need to upgrade it with a little more zazz.

Yet another do-it-yourself software option called *Printing Press Pro Extreme* is available from Mountain Cow (mountaincow.com; see picture). This kit offers a built in address book as well as original fonts for a wide variety of looks. It will help you design invitations, guest cards, place cards and more as well as address envelopes. Printing Press also allows you to import photos. The price: $150 for the standard option, $102 for a Platinum Deluxe version and $200 for an deluxe version that includes the ability to add illustrations.

If you plan to print your own invitations and need advice on wording, consider *Crane's Wedding Blue Book* by Steven Feinberg. This 150 page paperback answers just about every wedding etiquette question there is when it comes to invitations—wording, addressing, assembling and more. The book is available in libraries or online at Crane's web site (crane.com). See Figure 2 on page 183.

11 **Cut the second color.** Sure, it might be tempting to set off a small embellishment on your invitation in a second color, but watch out! Two colors add dramatically to the cost of any invite—raising the price by 50% or more. One trick to achieve the same look: choose a different SHADE of the same color, instead of a second color. Some custom printers and invitation designers can use a darker hue of the same color to give that second color look . . . without the second color price.

12 **Get creative on the accessories.** When you buy invitations, you're more than likely to be pitched on buying all those little bridal accessories like guest books, plume pens and other doo-dads—at high retail prices.

Our advice: to save, get creative. One reader from Toronto told us her inventive idea for a guest book. She went to an arts and crafts store and purchased a picture matte (16x20) and an archival-quality gold pen. "At the wedding, each guest signed their name on the matte. I used the matte to frame a photo of us and got a beautiful and unique keepsake." Total cost: $12. Compare that to fancy guest books that can run $50 or more.

Another idea: Reader Mary O'Rourke wrote to tell us that they forgot to take their guest book to the wedding—so they grabbed some permanent markers and had guests sign a table cloth! She said, "The idea was a hit. Our guests wrote such nice messages, much more than they could have in a guest book. Today, we have it hanging in our office room of our apartment and we read it constantly."

Looking for a source to print maps? A reader recommended WeddingMapper.com. The company describes itself as "an interactive and personalized guide to your wedding." The end product will provide guests and wedding businesses with information on all your wedding events plus things to do in the wedding city. This includes museums, the rehearsal dinner location, restaurant recommendations and more. The best part? It's free!

Instead of using traditional invitation printers to print her napkins, one reader found this deal: Oceans of Roses (OceansOfRoses.com—click on Miscellaneous) sells 100 personalized cocktail napkins for about $35.

13 Compare prices. Many of our readers have noticed that dozens of web sites often sell the exact same invitations at different prices. Don't order from the first site you visit without checking the competition.

14 Check out warehouse clubs. An example: some Costco warehouse stores (web: costco.com) offer name-brand invitations at a 20% discount. We discussed Costco's invites earlier in this chapter.

15 Consider Seal and Send invites. Seal-N-Send.com offers a unique twist: an "all-in-one" invitation that includes a perforated response card at the bottom. No separate envelopes—just a postcard your guests can easily return. And the invite doesn't have an envelope either—just fold, seal and send. Prices range from $100 to $280 per 100; choose from over 100 styles. A great option to save money and paper.

Helpful Hints

1 For large weddings, engraved invitations may be a better bargain. While thermography is generally cheaper than engraving, there is an exception. After you get beyond 300 to 350 invitations, the reverse is often true. For example, we priced 400 thermographed invitations from a major printer at $575. The same number of engraved invitations from a discount buying source was $566. Not only is it cheaper, but you also get a bonus: some printers like Jenner (jennerco.com) will fold and stuff the invitations into envelopes—that's no small task. Another tip: while mail-order catalogs have great prices on orders of 100 or 200 thermographed invitations, their price advantage drops as the quantity grows. You may find a better deal on large orders (over 300) from a local stationer.

2 Consider addressing options. Many stationery shops and even web sites today offer envelope addressing services for busy brides and grooms. They'll take your guest list, feed it into a computer and then voila! Addressed envelopes ready to stamp and mail. While some services still use a pen-based addressing machine (like Inscribe), more and more are turning to computerized output from laser and ink jet printers (occasionally a stationer will offer hand calligraphy). Which is best? Consider the paper type before making a decision. If your envelopes are not made from paper that is laser printer compatible (ask the stationer or catalog to find out), go with an ink jet printer service. Why? The laser printer toner might rub off at the post office, making the invitations undeliverable. Ink jet printing is preferable since it sticks to the envelope better.

3 **Factor in the limits of the postal system.** Invitation printers love to sell brides all sorts of new looks. But before you pay, make sure your invitations are post-office friendly. An example: wax seals. They sure look neat on envelopes, but they can gum up the post offices' processing machines. The result: at best, the wax will smudge. At worst, the invitation gets jammed in the machine, shredding it beyond recognition. The best advice is to only use wax seals on the *inside* envelopes.

Along the same lines, watch out for invitation fads. Example: bows, ribbons and fabric appliqués that extend off the card. Sure, they look neat . . . BUT they have to be stuffed into an envelope and sent through the postal system. The result may look nothing like what was intended.

Finally, ask the post office to hand cancel your stamps. That way your invitations aren't machine canceled with an ugly postmark.

4 **If you don't like the flimsy paper from low-end manufacturers, check out single panel cards.** The card stock used to make single panel invitations is much more substantial than many of the papers used for the folded designs in mail order catalogs. You'll give your guests the illusion of better quality invitations and spend a fraction to do it.

Biggest Myths About Invitations

MYTH #1 *"I thought it would take 15 minutes to write up my invitations order at the stationer. Boy was I surprised when it took nearly two hours!"*

That's right! Many folks think writing an invitation is easy—until they actually try it. In reality, finding the right combination of words and type styles that make an aesthetically attractive invitation is challenging. That's why just writing up an invitation order can take an hour or more. Using a professional retail stationer or calling a catalog's customer service department will make this process go easier. As we mentioned earlier, *Crane's Wedding Blue Book* (available in stores or online at crane.com) is a good source for wording advice.

MYTH #2 *"I assumed when we ordered our invitations that extra envelopes would be included—is this true?"*

Nope, many printers send the exact quantity of envelopes as invitations ordered. If you want extra envelopes, they must be ordered in advance (there is a small additional cost). Why is this important? Well, if you're addressing your own invitations, it pays to have extra envelopes in case of mistakes. Even calligraphers will request you supply extra envelopes.

Pitfalls to Avoid

PITFALL #1 UNDER-ORDERING OF INVITATIONS.

"When I first ordered invitations, I ordered exactly enough for the people on my list. Later, my mother came up with some long-lost relatives, and I had to go back and reorder another 25. I was shocked at the extra expense!"

If you guess wrong and need more invitations, the set-up charge to reprint more invites will be tremendous. For example, let's look at a sample invitation order from a popular brand. The total for 100 invitations is $204.50. Let's assume you're a smart bride and decide to order extras, say 125 invitations. The total would be $246.20—a $41.70 difference. However, if you order only 100 now and find out later you need 25 more, the total cost will be $363.50. Wow! Ordering 125 in the first place would have saved you $117! As you can see, ordering extras in your original order is much more cost effective. That's because the set-up charge for additional orders is the same as for the original order. There is no cost savings on invitations if you go back later to order more.

PITFALL #2 ORDER SNAFUS.

"I ordered invitations online from a site recommended on a wedding web site. Boy, am I sorry—the order came in with several mistakes and the whole design looked out of whack."

Sure, mail-order invitation sites offer great prices, but do you get what you pay for? We've heard stories from brides who felt burned when their invitations arrived, looking nothing like they expected.

The reasons for this are many. In some cases, the composition (how the type is aligned) is off, due to a mistake in the printing process. Other times, the vendor made a goof with spelling or wording. Later in this chapter, we'll review the companies we think are most reliable—including those who offer an unconditional guarantee, the best bet for getting what you want.

PITFALL #3 WHEN INVITATIONS ARE JUST A SIDELINE.

"The bridal shop where I bought my gown offers invitations at a 10% discount. However, the salesperson who helped me didn't seem to know much more than I did about how to write up the order or word the invitation."

Competition in the invitation business is intense. Many bridal businesses (particularly bridal and tux shops) offer discounted invitations as an add-on service. The discount is usually 10% to 20% off retail. The problem: many of these businesses are inexperienced with invitations. Their selection and knowledge of invitation printers is limited and service by low-paid clerks is lackluster. Many also lack the skills to word the invitations correctly.

Another twist on this pitfall are stores that advertise "up to 50% off" on wedding invitations. The catch: you have to order five bridesmaids dresses (or rent five tuxes) to get the discount, which only applies to the invitation itself—response cards, maps and other accessories are full price. Hence, you might get a better deal on the *whole* invitation order from an invitation site or retail stationer who discounts.

Nancy Gresl from Milwaukee wrote to us about her frustrating experience ordering invitations at a local tux store:

"We first planned to order our invitations from the tux store, as they offered us a 30% discount since we are getting our tuxedo rentals from them. I had already decided on an invitation I found in the Now and Forever catalog (N&F), but since the tux shop offered 30% off, I thought I would try that.

"First, 30% is off of *the store's* price. But the *regular* price on the N&F site was almost equal to the *discounted* price at the tux shop. Bottom line: the total savings was only about $20 for 225 invitations with inserts and thank yous! Plus, the tux shop had a $35 shipping fee! Their selection of font types was also not as broad as N&F, and I was told I could not adjust the font point size for various parts of my wording. After trying three proofs with the tux shop, I canceled my order—wasting almost three weeks. I then called N&F and was told that if I sent/faxed a detailed description of my invite wording with the point sizes noted, they had no problem printing my invitations in various font sizes. I faxed an order, had my proof a day and a half later, approved the proof on Thursday, and had my entire order the following week using their two-day shipping! My invitations look wonderful. And this was so easy to do."

PITFALL #4 LAST MINUTE CHANGES.

"My church just called to say that we have to move up the time of our ceremony by one hour. The problem is I've already ordered invitations. Can I make a change?"

Not without incurring some big charges. First, understand that most invitations orders are submitted to the printer within 36 hours. Once received by the printer, it is very difficult to change or stop the order. If changes can be made, there is always a charge. For example, one big printer we researched charges $10 "per inquiry" and another $10 per change.

PITFALL #5 THE REVENGE OF THE ETIQUETTE POLICE.

"I just got in my invitation order and got a big surprise. With no warning, the printer had changed my order to fix an alleged 'etiquette error' in the wording! This is ridiculous."

Hard to believe, but it is true that some printers will change the wording on invitations to conform to "proper etiquette" as they see it. The only way you can avoid this problem is to tell the stationer that you want the wording (and any capitalization) to be printed exactly as you specify. Checking a box on the order form or noting it in some other way usually accomplishes this (which can be in very small type, buried at the bottom). You must also indicate if unusual spellings of names (like Henri instead of Henry) are correct. That way the printer won't substitute their etiquette rules or spelling corrections for your finely crafted prose.

PITFALL #6 PET POSTAL PEEVES.

"My stationer told me the invitations would cost just 46¢ to mail. However, after I added two maps and took the invitations to the post office, they said it would be 86¢. As a result, we have to shell out another $50 in postage."

This is why we recommend taking your invitation (and all the enclosures) to the post office and getting it weighed before you buy all those cute "love" stamps. Start adding maps, response cards or other enclosures and you'll notice the postage bill soars.

Another interesting twist on this problem is a story we heard from an Austin, Texas reader. A local wedding company there was advertising an "addressing, stuffing and mailing" service for just $1 per invitation. Sounds great, eh? The problem was the service didn't tell brides they were mailing their invitations *bulk rate*. The post office treats bulk rate mail as a very low priority, to put it charitably. As a result, some of the brides' invitations arrived six weeks after the wedding—others didn't arrive at all. As it turns out, it's illegal to mail invitations (or any personal correspondence) bulk rate and the post office may have confiscated the invitations. The best advice: *always* mail invitations first class.

Pitfall #7 Outrageously priced accessories.

"I was so excited with the savings on invitations from a mail-order catalog, I decided to order a slew of accessories too. Yet when I visited a local shop, I saw some of the same products at much lower prices. What's going on here?"

Ah, you've discovered the secret moneymaking machine behind mail-order invitation web sites and catalogs. While the invitation itself is very affordable (perhaps as much as 50% less than retail), the prices on accessories can go through the roof.

Look through most mail-order invitation sites and you'll see plenty of superfluous stationery items (pew cards, save-the-date cards) as well as pictures of "suggested accessories," including matching napkins, programs, unity candles, cake toppers, toasting glasses, garters—even swizzle sticks printed with the bride and groom's name. Yet the prices can be amazingly high. We found much better deals on these items online, at party stores, gift shops or other local stores. And then there's the whole question of whether you really need a matching "gold guest-book pen with heart-shaped, rose-etched Lucite base" for $40. The best advice: comparison shop before you buy. See the previous chapter (Chapter 5, Flowers) for affordable accessories such as candles, decor and more.

Trends

♥ **Pockets.** Wedding invites with pockets for reception/RSVP cards are increasingly popular. Of course, there is a downside: pockets make invites heavier . . . and more expensive to mail. Also, consider the do-it-yourself challenges when assembling pocket invitations. Some require gluing which may be best left to the professionals.

♥ **Paper that shimmers.** Pearlescent papers that shimmer are hot. An example: Stardream papers from Italy have a smooth surface with a metallic glow and come in several different colors. This paper is coated and laser printable (or can be used with traditional invitation printing like thermography). Another trend: paper with sharply beveled or chiseled edges.

♥ **Save the date cards.** These range from simple postcards to more elaborate options that cost $1 each. Save the date cards have become increasingly popular, as couples seek to give their guests a heads up for an upcoming event.

♥ COLOR AND MORE COLOR. Gone are the old days of simply white or cream invites. Now color is the rage: from jewel-toned envelope linings to colored ink for the printing itself. Some invitation printers are now doing TWO ink colors on one design.

A big part of the color trend: colored papers. From chocolate brown to copper to baby blue, the choices are endless. Add a metallic ink like gold or silver (especially to dark colors) and the designs really pop. And look for reversed color pallets with reception cards. For example, you might choose a chocolate brown invite with cream ink—then this is paired with a cream reception card with brown ink.

♥ UNIQUE PAPER FOR DO-IT-YOURSELF KITS. **Invitesite** (invitesite.com) offers brides unique papers in a do-it-yourself kit. Kits include handmade papers, printable papers, instructions and accessories. For example, Algonquin comes with gate-folded bronze floral embossed exterior surrounding a shimmering champagne invite all tied together with a light blue satin ribbon. To complete the look, a sprig of pressed blue larkspur decorates the design for $3.00 per invite (minimum order of 50). What makes this unique: the designs look hand-crafted rather than mass produced. What excited us most about Invitesite: finally, a company has made sets of invitations that are compatible with laser or inkjet printers but also look truly unique. If the kits don't interest you, Invitesite can provide the printing for you at an additional cost. InviteSite.com also offers a selection of eco friendly designs.

♥ RIBBON. More than just a tied bow, ribbon accents are being employed on invites in creative ways: a decorative banner, ribbons with texture (organza, for example) and more.

♥ BELLY BANDS. Yes, invitations are still layered with vellum and wrapped in paper folders, but a new trend is to add "belly bands." These accents, often vellum strips, wide ribbons or contrasting paper, wrap up your invitations. Some belly bands are printed with the couple's names. Just remember, as with most ribbons, belly bands and other accents, *you'll* be the one assembling them. Leave time for this!

♥ **ELABORATE PATTERNS.** We're seeing quite a lot of heavily patterned invites inspired by Indian mosaics and Middle Eastern tiles. Colors are rich and include deep reds, golds and purples among others (see nearby example). The effect is opulent and exotic.

SPOTLIGHT: FAVORS

Like many wedding traditions, favors have a colorful if not somewhat mysterious history. Here is some background:

Where did favors originate? Popular mainly on the East Coast and in California, wedding favors have had a long, rich history. When we say rich, we really mean royal. In fact, in France in the 16th century, nobility and royalty gave valuable gifts (usually of porcelain) to their wedding guests as mementos of the occasion.

In the middle of the 16th century, almonds came to Italy from the Far East. These almonds were very expensive and became popular to give as favors to guests at royal weddings. To preserve these almonds, a sugar-coating was added—Jordan almonds were born.

In the 17th century, three almonds, painted in bright colors and wrapped in bridal veiling, were given to guests as a symbol of fertility. Why three almonds? From the union of two comes one—a baby. The veiling meant that the guests shared the couple's happiness.

What about favors in the US? Favors in America are most popular with ethnic communities (particularly Italians). Favor manufacturers tell us that nearly 25% of their orders come from just three states, Pennsylvania, New York and New Jersey. Some couples in these states order elaborate favors that can cost $20 each. Elsewhere, potpourri is a more popular choice. While favors are also common in the Southeast (Georgia, Florida, the Carolinas in particular), brides in the Midwest, Northwest and Southwest rarely give favors to guests.

Here are some sources for favors on a budget—as well as some unique ideas for favors submitted by our readers:

♥ **Nashville Wraps** (nashvillewraps.com) offers amazing wholesale prices on items like metallic favor bags, tulle, ribbon, candy boxes and more. How about a sheer mini bag in pastel colors for $2.00 each? Fill them with treats and you've got an affordable favor. Look for closeouts at even better prices.

♥ **Hercules Candies** (800) 924-4339 or (315) 463-4339 (web: hercules-candy.com) is a New York-based candy maker that's been selling hand-made chocolates for 100 years. Their extensive brochure lists dozens of chocolate favor options. Each is customized with the bride and groom's name and wedding date on the box holding the chocolates. Prices start at $1.75 per box for the 2-piece versions. Other options are available. The samples we tasted were great.

♥ **Eco ideas.** An Ohio bride told us she gave away flower seed packets as favors to her guests. Cost: 17¢ per packet. One source: the Tender Seed Company (web: favorswithseeds.com) sells customized seed packets, some with ribbons and pearls, for $.65 to $2.25.

♥ **Candy Wrappers.** And what about candy bar wrappers with the bride and groom's name and wedding date? Moosie Wrappers (web:

5 favors for under $5

Everyone can usually agree: when it comes to favors, things you can eat usually outweigh a trinket that collects dust. So here's our take on five favors for under $5:

♥ Add a Southern voice to your wedding with **Aunt Sally's pralines**—a box of 72 pieces is $142 (less than $2 each; auntsallys.com)

♥ Custom caramels are the specialty of **GoodKarmal.com**—a Budda Box for $5 contains two caramels in a kraft box tied with a satin ribbon. You can also customize the box for $1 more.

♥ Whoopie pie favors? Yes you can! **WannaHavaCookie.com** sells a dozen of these treats for $21 ($1.75 each).

♥ Cupcake truffles from **TruffleTruffle.com** come in two-dozen varieties and run $2.50 each. Try the apple pie truffle for a July 4th wedding or Earl Grey for British-themed nuptials.

♥ Salt-water taffy in galvanized beach buckets make for a fun favor for beach weddings: under $3 each from **Shrivers.com**.

moosiewrapper.com) sells the wrappers for only 89¢ each for 36 to 149 wrappers. Discounts on larger quantities are available. You buy the candy bars then slide the wrappers over them. If you want the bar and wrapper together, the charge for a minimum of 24 bars starts at $1.79 each.

♥ Reader Elizabeth Jaust suggested an altruistic wedding favor: **give to your favorite charity.** "I am making a donation on behalf of the wedding to the Susan G. Komen Breast Cancer Foundation. They give you a card to place at each table. It just seems nicer than giving out 100 little wine bottles that nobody keeps. Also, my mother passed away from cancer and this seems like a nice way to celebrate her. And you don't have to give a large gift. It can be like 50 bucks or so. Contact the foundation at komen.org."

♥ Kathy LeFevre invented a great idea for wedding favors: **a family recipe cookbook.** She started a company called Friends and Family Cookbooks (friendsandfamilycookbooks.com) that creates custom cookbooks. Just hit up all your relatives for their favorite recipes and send them to the site (you can enter the recipes online via their web site). You can also add up to 60 family photos. Friends and Family will put it all together for you starting at $9.70 each for the first 100 copies with 100 recipes. Yes, it's a bit expensive, but they will take all those recipes, organize them and design the book for you. And, Kathy points out, you'll only give one cookbook out per family, not per person, so the cost isn't as much as you think. The result is a unique favor that folks won't toss after the wedding is over.

♥ **eBay**. Reader Joely Macheel sent an email about buying favor supplies on eBay: "I purchased 72 undecorated bubbles (3 boxes of 24) for $6.00, a favor-maker for $11.50 and 144 ribbon roses for $3.50. eBay is my savior!"

♥ **Ribbons, at a discount.** Check out Chapter 5, Flowers for a listing of discount ribbons sites.

♥ **Two words: Oriental Trading.** Their famous web site (OrientalTrading. com) is the mother lode of cheap favors. Examples: 50 white organza wedding favor bags for just $10.50. Or two-dozen wedding bubbles for $7.25. The site will even personalize items. The only caveat: watch out for shipping costs, which can sometimes run more than the items!

Now that you've got the invitations covered, it's time to move on to the reception. Up next, we'll cover catering, photography, music and more.

Notes

PART 2
YOUR RECEPTION

Receptions Sites
Catering
Photo/Video
Cakes
Entertainment
Etc.

The choice of a reception site can make or break any wedding budget. In this chapter, we'll explore 17 ways to save—including some ingenious places that brides and grooms have discovered to hold their receptions. Plus, we'll give you the seven most common pitfalls with reception sites and how to avoid them. Finally, we'll take a candid look at the pros and cons of the five most common sites.

What Are You Buying?

There are two basic categories of wedding reception sites: places where you just rent the hall (and bring in an outside caterer) and others that have on-site catering, like hotels, country clubs or catering halls. Therefore, you are basically buying the following services:

♥ **EXCLUSIVE USE OF THE FACILITY.** Either you are charged a flat fee for a certain period of time or there is an hourly rate. Obviously, rates vary with the amount of ambiance. An historic restored mansion will cost much more than a local union hall. Most places require a booking deposit, which can be several hundred (or thousand) dollars. A second deposit (to cover any damage or clean-up) may also be required at some sites.

♥ **CATERING** (food, beverages, service and rentals). You typically have two choices: use the site's in-house caterer or bring in an off-site caterer. When a site has an in-house caterer, there is often no "room charge"—the facility makes its money from the catering. Unfortunately, some sites not only charge you for the catering but also tack on a facility rental fee. We cover wedding catering in-depth in a separate chapter later in this book.

The Big Trade-off: Ambiance vs. Great Food. In a perfect world, a reception site would offer both a beautiful setting AND great food. In reality, there are typically trade-offs. A restaurant may offer a stunning view of the city, but only mediocre food choices. On the other end, catering halls may have a sterile "wedding factory" atmosphere, but they have receptions down to a science. A site that lets you bring in an outside caterer (and hence, allows you more control over food quality) may be the perfect compromise, but these sites can be hard to find.

An important factor: "Good lighting" isn't often on the list of things brides and grooms consider for a reception site ... but it should be! Why? Consider your wedding photography. You'll probably be spending a pretty penny for pictures from your wedding—and good lighting is a key requirement for such photos. Ambient or natural light is best. Look for sites with lots of windows. If you are planning an evening or candlelit reception, consult with your photographer for advice (hint, you might need to double the number of candles or add lighting to a dance area).

Average costs. What does a wedding reception cost? As you might remember from Chapter 1, we quote the average cost as $14,180 for 150 guests. That figure covers not only the facility but also all the catering (food, beverages, labor, rentals, etc). What makes this confusing is that some sites include the site rental fee with the catering (hotels, for example). Of course, you often have to meet a rather hefty minimum spending amount. Other sites charge you a flat or hourly fee and let you bring in your own caterer. Prices for those types of sites are all over the board, from free (a church hall in some cases) to thousands of dollars for a historic inn or home.

The basic rule is that more money buys you more ambiance—the prettiest sites always cost more than a nondescript hall. But there are exceptions ... we'll discuss how to find affordable sites that still have zing later in this chapter.

Sources to Find a Reception Site

Finding the right reception site for your wedding may be the most challenging task you face. That's mainly because of the big bucks involved here—the reception (and, specifically, the catering) is the most expensive part of getting married. Here are some top sources to find affordable sites.

♥ **WEDDING COORDINATORS AT YOUR CEREMONY SITE.** Yes, these folks probably have talked to hundreds of brides over the years. They might be able

---

REAL WEDDING TIP

How to get reception sites to call *you*!

One Minneapolis bride found that her local visitors' bureau went way beyond the call of duty to help with her wedding plans:

"I don't believe your book does enough justice to this great resource that I tapped into—the local Convention and Visitor Bureaus (CVB)! This is an especially great resource if you are having a lot of out-of-town guests. I conacted the Minneapolis CVB several weeks ago, first to ask if there was any major convention or event going on the weekend of my wedding. Then they asked what type of event I was planning, so I broke down and told them. Lo and behold, the representative said she would transfer me to the CVB's "wedding coordinator." This woman was a Godsend! She immediately asked for key info about my event—the dates, how large a space I would need, type of reception—and most importantly, how many hotel rooms I would need. (This is the key here because the goal of any CVB is to fill hotel rooms!)

Then, the wedding coordinator said she would create a blast e-mail to all the hotels in the area, effectively putting my event "out for bid." Since all the hotels would know other hotels got the same information, it creates a bit of competition. Sure enough, hotels started calling and emailing ME, instead of the other way around! They gave me great room rates, room blocks, reception space info, etc. I settled on a large downtown business hotel that offered me room rates of only $109 with free guest parking, and a full reception package at $43 per person, including an open-bar cocktail hour, hors d'oeuvres, champagne toast, seated dinner, and free parking for the guests. I even negotiated a lower food and beverage minimum and a $3 per person discount on the wedding package.

I would have never thought to even call this hotel, because it is upscale, and I thought it would be way out of our budget! I'd urge all brides to call their local CVB—especially if you need a block of hotel rooms. They also can give you free city guides and maps for out-of-towners. Please pass this tip onto other brides, especially those getting married in large metro areas!"

reception

to give you the "word on the street" for several reception sites.

♥ **CATERERS.** Most off-site (or independent) caterers are well aware of the best local wedding reception sites. That's because their livelihood depends on the existence of facilities that let outside caterers come in for receptions. Call around to a few local caterers to find leads.

♥ **RECENTLY-MARRIED COUPLES.** Ask your co-workers or friends if they know anyone who was recently married. These couples are often more than willing to share their research and experiences about reception sites.

♥ **VISITORS/TOURISM BUREAUS AND LOCAL PARKS DEPARTMENTS.** If you are looking for a civic site (such as an historic home), your local visitors/tourism bureau or chamber of commerce may have some suggestions. Many local parks departments book civic sites (like gardens and parks). See the nearby box for one bride's experience with the visitor's bureau in her town.

♥ **ONLINE.** Sure, you can use those big wedding web sites to quickly screen venues. Of course, you realize that sites pay for these listings— and that many hidden gems are not listed.

Many of our readers tell us they get valuable feedback on venues from online message boards focused on specific cities. Sites like UrbanSpoon.com provide user-generated reviews of restaurants, many of which also have banquet facilities for weddings.

♥ **BRIDAL SHOWS.** Yes, bridal shows can be a source for reception sites. Large expos with many vendors are your best bet. Reception sites often set up booths and hand out food samples and menus.

Best Online Sites

♥ **OneWed.com** has an easy-to-use vendor search by zip code—search for vendors by various distances away from your location. Of course, this site as all the standard fare you see on other wedding sites (message boards, do-it-yourself wedding web sites, checklists, etc). The site's blog is among the better bridal blogs out there, frequently updated with new ideas. **Rating: A-**

♥ The **Wedding Mapper** (weddingmapper.com) enables you to show guests where the ceremony, reception and guest hotels are, all on a Google map. Share the map with others via email or embed it in a wedding web page. Also cool: "real weddings" chronicles the venues and vendors used by local brides and grooms. **Rating: A**

Getting Started: How Far in Advance?

Don't delay the search for your reception site. As soon as you have confirmed your ceremony site, start the search for a reception facility. Time is of the essence. Most cities have a shortage of great reception sites; prime dates in the spring and summer often go quickly. In the South, December can book up to a year in advance for popular Christmas weddings. For spring/summer dates, booking a site nine months to a year in advance may be necessary.

Of course, the city you live in can require even more advance planning. Case in point: Washington, DC. DC brides and grooms not only compete with other weddings for scarce sites, but also political and charity events. No wonder hotel receptions in DC book up to a year or more in advance. Historic sites in the Capitol are an alternative, but most are small in size.

Step-by-step Shopping Strategies

♥ **Step 1:** Figure out how many guests you want to invite. Then look for a site that fits that capacity. Many

Finding the best hotel deal

If you are having many out-of-town guests, you may want to put them up at one hotel. Most hotels will negotiate a discount room deal for a block of rooms . . . but how do you know you are getting a good deal?

First, start with the hotel's web site. Look up the room rates for a weekend in a similar time of year. Be sure to check ALL the hotel's rates: AAA, AARP, government, advance purchase and so on. You'll notice some hotels can have a dozen or so rates for the very same room.

Next, compare room rates on travel sites like Travelocity and Expedia. Kayak.com also compares rates across several sites.

Finally, also check the Priceline rate. How do you do this? Go to BiddingForTravel.com, a site that posts winning bids from Priceline.com users.

Start negotiating with the hotel based on the lowest online price you see, even if it is a Priceline.com special. Speak with the hotel's manager—document the best rates you found with copies of online deals. If you are having your reception at the same hotel, the hotel should be giving you their very best room rate!

couples make the mistake of doing this the other way around—picking a site first and then having to adapt their guest list around its size.

♥ **Step 2:** Using the above sources, make appointments with three to five of the top prospects. Confirm the availability of your date before making any trip. Bring a friend or your fiancé along to help inspect the facilities.

♥ **Step 3:** When you visit a reception site, look carefully at the facility. Can the room really hold all your guests comfortably or does it look cramped? Is the lighting on a dimmer system? How will guest traffic flow around buffet tables, the dance floor, etc.?

♥ **Step 4:** Ask for the manager! Try to meet the catering manager (if the catering is done in-house). Honestly discuss your budget and suggest the manager custom-tailor a menu for your reception. Read the catering chapter to make sure you cover all of those details. Get a detailed price breakdown—in writing—on *everything* (food, beverages, service, centerpieces, linens, china, etc.).

♥ **Step 5:** Ask to see the site set-up for a wedding. It's sometimes hard to imagine an empty ballroom dressed to the nines for a wedding reception. Here's a good way to get a more realistic impression. Ask to visit just before a reception is about to start. Check the traffic flow—for buffets, see if the layout of the food stations makes sense. Does the staff seem organized, or are they running around at the last minute in a panic? Check the math—is the dance floor large enough for your guest list? (See discussion nearby for more on this topic).

♥ **Step 6:** If the site has in-house catering, ask for a taste-test of the food. The quality of food varies greatly from site to site, so asking for this is a wise precaution. Most sites offer taste tests at no charge; of course there are exceptions. Some brides and grooms have emailed us with stories of sites that refuse to do tastings. We usually wonder what those facilities are trying to hide.

♥ **Step 7:** After visiting several sites, make your decision and put down as small a deposit as possible. Sign a contract that includes the date, hours, rental fee and any other charges and approximate guest count. Be very careful to get any verbal promises by the site ("oh, sure we can decorate that landing with flowers for no charge") in writing in the contract. As with any wedding, details may change. Make sure you get any alterations to the original menu or site plan in writing (keep a log of conversations, archive all emails, etc.).

♥ **Step 8:** Get the site coordinator/catering manager's name in writing in the contract. Confirm that this person will be there at your reception. If there are problems, you'll need this contact to troubleshoot any last minute issues.

♥ **Step 9:** Keep the lines of communication open. Remember you might book the site up to a year (or more) before your wedding. Checking back periodically with the site's manager (a call every couple months or so) is prudent to avoid any surprises (oh, did we mention we sold the facility to the Society of Professional Motorcyclists last month?).

Questions to Ask of a Reception Site

1 **How many guests can the space accommodate?** Typically, the capacity is given in two numbers, one for a buffet/hors d'oeuvres (or standing) reception and one for a sit-down dinner. Be careful about these figures—sites often fudge capacity numbers or give "approximate" guesses. Don't forget to account for any buffet tables or dance floors; these all take space.

2 **How many hours are included with the rental fee? What are the overtime charges?** Be sure to ask about whether set-up and clean-up time is included in the stated hours. Some sites don't count this time "on the clock," while others do. Because some sites do more than one wedding a day, be careful there is adequate time between events. A money-saving tip: book the time you realistically need for your reception and avoid costly overtime charges.

3 **Is there an in-house caterer or a list of approved caterers?** Or can you bring in any caterer? Obviously, hotels have in-house

Dance floor math

How big should the dance floor be for your wedding reception? An industry rule of thumb is 2.5 square feet per guest. Hence, a 100 guest wedding would require 250 square feet; 200 guests would be 500 square feet and so on. FYI: some sites quote dance floors by their dimensions, so you'll have to do the math: a 20 x 25 dance floor is 500 square feet. One hint: err on the side of making the dance floor smaller if you have to choose between two sizes. A more packed dance floor encourages more dancing and adds to the energy of the event.

caterers (that's how they make the big bucks). But many other sites are also picky about this—after a sloppy caterer burns them, a site may restrict brides and grooms to a list of "pre-approved" caterers. In case you can't find a caterer on their approved list that meets your specifications, ask if you can bring in another one.

4 **Are there any cooking restrictions?** For a site where an outside caterer is brought in, check the kitchen facilities. Some sites restrict caterers from cooking on-site and just allow the warming of food that is prepared elsewhere. Make sure you confirm with your caterer to see if the kitchen facilities are adequate.

5 **Is there a piano available?** Obviously, bands don't cart around a baby grand with them to every reception, so ask the site coordinator. Don't assume anything is free. Ask the site about any extra charges to prevent surprises.

6 **What else is happening at the site the day of my wedding?** Some sites book multiple events during the same day, even when the site can't realistically handle that many people. And we're not just talking about hotels. We've even seen smaller sites (restored mansions, catering halls) try to cram two or more weddings into a facility. Any site that tries to do more than one wedding a day is a wedding factory; approach any such facility with caution. Will you have to compete with a noisy convention of insurance agents that has a 10-piece band in the next room? Will your party have to share a bathroom or other facilities with the other wedding? Press the catering rep to give you exclusivity over the facility. Or at least, insist on a layout of the parties that minimizes overlapping noise.

7 **Are there any union rules we must follow?** In some states (particularly the Northeast), union work rules may force certain restrictions on sites, including the serving of food and set-up of any audio equipment.

8 **What are the minimums?** Watch out—some sites may require you to pay for a minimum amount of catering, no matter how many guests you have. Such minimums are common during peak wedding months (typically, May through September).

9 **How late can we play music?** Some facilities have a curfew for music. Be sure that doesn't conflict with your plans to dance the night way.

10 **Are there any insurance requirements?** According to our reader email, there are some reception sites out there that require other wedding vendors present at your event (DJ, band, photographer) to carry liability insurance. We're not sure why this is the responsibility of the bride and groom to check out, but it might be a good question to ask. If a vendor you want doesn't have liability insurance, inquire as to whether your (or your parents') homeowner's insurance will cover the event.

11 **Are there any "caterer surcharges"?** Some sites which let you bring in a caterer will then slap that vendor with an extra surcharge—a percentage of what you are spending on food and beverage. This fee is a major rip-off and rarely disclosed—that is, until the caterer passes it along to you in the form of an additional charge of 7% to 15%. We'll discuss this more in the Pitfalls section later in this chapter.

12 **What are the parking options/costs?** Some sites have free parking; others require valet parking. Venues with limited parking may require you to hire a shuttle service for your guests. Remember any fee for parking is negotiable—at a minimum, see if you can bargain for a lower rate. Whether you pay for the parking for your guests or not, make sure there is adequate parking (also consider parking for vendors like your photographer and musicians). Weather may factor in your decision on whether to have valet parking. For home weddings, see if you can rent a nearby church or community center parking lot so you guests aren't jamming up the local residential streets.

Top Money-saving Secrets

1 **City sites.** Fortunately, most sites run by municipal governments aren't trying to make a killing on weddings. Hence, city sites are the most affordable reception sites you can find. For example, in Austin, Texas, a nice city-owned clubhouse that holds 150 guests in a park that offered stunning skyline views was available to rent for just $850 for 7 hours. That's no typo—$850 and you bring in your own caterer. Another similar-sized facility run by a private company in the same town costs $3500 to rent for four hours. Obviously, the ambiance of these city sites (clubhouses, recreation centers, parks, gardens) is different than a downtown hotel or catering hall, but, hey, they are great bargains.

2 **Choose a site where you can bring in a caterer.** In every city we've researched, there are always a handful of sites where you can rent the facility and then bring in an "off-site" caterer. Often, this is where the big savings are found—see our chapter on catering for more details.

3 **Ask for the manager**. Skip the sales rep and head to the top—ask for the manager at a venue to get the lowest price. If you want to haggle (or even simply ask "is this your best price?"), it's best to deal with the manager or owner of a venue. The manager may go under different titles—at a hotel, this could be director of catering. At a country club, it might be food and beverage manager . . . you get the idea. Yes, that friendly sales rep may be all smiles . . . but it is the *manager* who can really cut a deal.

4 **Consider an off-peak time.** Everyone wants to get married on a Saturday night in June. If you pick a time with less competition, you can often negotiate better rental rates. Many sites have stated discounts for Friday or Sunday weddings. (The down side to this tip: some wedding vendors like photographers may charge an extra fee to work on Sundays.) If you still have your heart set on a Saturday wedding, consider less popular months of the year (basically anytime other than the summer). Many sites have stated discounts for such off-months. A reader in Seattle did point out a negative to having a wedding on a Friday night: traffic. She was a bridesmaid in a Friday night wedding that was held up by a traffic jam—"even the photographer who left way earlier, was late because of traffic." Keep this in mind when you schedule your wedding.

5 **Your house.** Hey, at least the facility is free. But be aware that you may have to rent chairs, tables, etc. and this will add to the tab. You may also have to pay a mover to store your furniture for the weekend. If you plan to pitch a tent in the backyard, the expense can go even higher (see the box Tent Rental 101 later in this chapter for tips and advice). Of course, even when you factor in all these expenses, the savings of a home wedding instead of holding the reception at a pricey hotel may put you ahead overall. Between 10% and 20% of all receptions are held in private homes.

6 **Consider your ceremony site.** Many houses of worship have attached reception halls. In fact, almost one-quarter of all receptions occur at churches or temples. One key reason: rental rates are particularly affordable. We'll have more on this option later in this chapter.

7 **Have a reception lunch or brunch instead of dinner.** The biggest expense of most receptions is catering, and the most expensive meal to serve is dinner. Wedding lunches or brunches often are much more affordable. What's the cheapest time of day to tie the knot? A two o'clock wedding—guests will already have eaten lunch and are not expecting dinner. Hence, a reception with cake, punch and light hors d'oeuvres is all that's needed . . . and 40% to 60% less expensive than a full dinner. Check the catering chapter for more tips to save money on this big budget item.

8 **Restaurant receptions.** Many restaurants have banquet rooms that are prefect for a wedding reception. These may be a great alternative to pricey hotels or catering halls. A bride in Chicago provided us with some cost comparisons: she priced a reception at a gourmet French restaurant in Des Plaines at $65 per person. That's for a chicken or steak dinner. Compare that to fancy Chicago downtown hotels, where a similar reception starts at $175 and can go up to $300 per guest. Another bonus: most restaurants don't charge "room fees" or other bogus charges. And the food may be higher quality than a hotel or catering hall.

9 **Join the Navy.** Just kidding. But, do you have any relatives or friends who are active duty or retired military? If so, you may have access to a wide range of possible reception sites at military bases. One bride in Cape May, NJ discovered she could rent a wonderful Officer's Club of the local Coast Guard base since her father was a retired naval officer. The cost? A mere $25 per hour.

10 **Check nearby small towns.** A bride in Lexington, Kentucky emailed us this tip. She found a reception site in nearby Paris (a 15 minute drive) that was charging 40% cheaper rates than in-town options. "The historic building offered the outdoor intimate garden we were looking for," she said. Another tip for historic sites: barter. If you've got any skills, offer the caretaker of these sites a trade. One groom offered to fix some broken doors and shutters on a historic site and received a reduced rental rate.

11 **Tell them you are planning a retirement party.** A Connecticut bride called in this tip: she found a restaurant with a nice banquet room that was perfect for her 50-guest reception. Instead of telling them it was a wedding reception, she said the party was a family reunion. The result: she was able to get a great price for a complete sit-down luncheon, estimating she saved about 20% off a similar "bridal" package. Two weeks before the reception, she told the restaurant it was actually a wedding—too late for the restaurant to raise the price!

12 **Consider a business hotel.** If you like the convenience of a hotel reception but not the cost, check out hotels that cater to business travelers. Why? Most are dead on the weekends . . . and may be willing to cut a deal for a wedding reception. A bride in Los Angeles discovered the savings could be dramatic. She priced a 250-guest reception (four-course sit-down dinner, cocktail hour with open bar and appetizers, beer, wine and a champagne toast) for $8300 at a Wyndham hotel that caters to business travelers. "That's pretty amazing considering that this is in Los Angeles," said the bride, adding, "I don't feel that we are giving up on the quality either. The food is excellent." An additional bonus: she got a special weekend hotel room rate of $100 for out of town guests, which is a steal in LA.

73 **Go to college.** Got a university or college in town? If so, that's a great place to look for reception site bargains. Many such institutions have alumni halls, faculty clubs and other facilities that are available at very affordable rates. And you don't always have to be a student or alum to book a site.

𝒯𝑒𝓃𝓉 𝑅𝑒𝓃𝓉𝒶𝓁 𝟣𝟢𝟣

Yes, renting a tent for a home wedding can be pricey, but there are some basic points to remember:

♥ There are four types of tents: frame tents, pole tents, pop-ups and party canopies. **Frame** tents have no center poles, using a lightweight metal frame covered with vinyl for support. Since they require minimal staking, frame tents are best for decks and patios. **Pole** tents are more traditional, with pole supports both on the perimeter and in the center. These types of tents require extensive staking. Some folks think pole tents are more festive looking; pole tents are probably the best option for large receptions. **Pop-up** and **party canopies** are do-it-yourself alternatives to pole tents with collapsible frames and offer shelter against sun or light rain.

♥ Which one is the most affordable? Pop-up and party canopies are the cheapest options. Frame tents tend be more expensive than pole tents. A large company that rents tents in New England charges $900 for a frame tent that is 30' by 60' feet (this would hold 144 people seated for dinner). The same size pole tent is $750. Other elaborate pole tents with sidewalls can top $5000 depending on the options. At the top end, in the Northeast, it can cost $15,000 to rent a 50x80 tent that holds 200 guests—that includes lighting, flooring, heating, delivery, set-up and tear-down. While it might run $8000 for the same tent without all the extras, remember that a tent for large crowds will probably be more expensive than holding the same event in a hotel or catering hall.

14 **Get creative.** We're constantly amazed at the inventive sites couples can find to hold their receptions—aquariums, airports, zoos, laundromats, you name it, it might be possible. If you want an off-beat site, the web is your best friend. Readers say they've found great site possibilities from web sites such as FieldTrip.com (which focuses on such Eastern states as Connecticut, New York, New Jersey, Delaware, Maryland and Pennsylvania) and HereComesTheGuide.com (California, Chicago, New York).

15 **Write it off.** Many reception sites are non-profits that will allow you to write off some or all of your rental fee as a charitable donation. One bride told us that her contract with The Chapel of our Lady in Cold Spring, New York specifically noted that the donation required to use the site was tax deductible because the fee "helps to preserve the beauty" of this historic restored building. We should note that the key to deducting these dollars is HOW the site refers to the fee—if it

♥ **How big of a tent do I need?** A good general rule: you need 15 square feet per guest at receptions; for ceremonies the suggested size is eight square feet per person (assuming chairs, a center aisle, podium and/or stage).

♥ **Accessories** can add comfort—for a price. Sidewalls with windows are an option for larger tents, as are air conditioning and heating. If a tent is placed on a lawn, sub-flooring and carpeting can protect sod. Most folks rent a dance floor and add some basic lighting to create a mood.

♥ **Surprise**: you may need more than one tent—the caterer may need a separate tent for food prep, tents may be needed for walkways, etc. Other surprise expenses: some towns require you to pull a permit for your tent. Some tent companies handle this detail, but always confirm.

♥ **Key questions to ask:** What exactly is included in the price? What are the extras? Some companies include set-up and takedown in their fees; others price this separately. Be sure to confirm any extra charges for weekend delivery and special fees like a "drying charge" should it rain on your event. Also ask: Are tents deodorized? How early is the set-up? Do you have insurance? Get a written agreement that covers ALL these details.

The Marriage Mark-Up

Do you wonder if the price suddenly goes up when you mention the word "wedding" to a reception site? We've always been suspicious that folks planning retirement parties, birthdays or any other type of event get quoted LOWER prices than brides and grooms.

Our suspicions were confirmed when Boston NBC affiliate WHDH-TV did a story on the "Marriage Mark-Up." The TV station did a simple test—they called eleven Boston-area reception sites and asked how much they charge for a wedding. Then they called back and asked for a retirement party. Now, to be fair, the station made sure it was asking for the same size party on the same date.

The results? Eight out of eleven places quoted the station the "marriage mark-up." One site said a retirement party would be $65 per person, but $90 for a wedding. Another said brides and grooms have to shell out 20% more. And those prices didn't include any special items like a wedding cake.

In Atlanta, one major hotel quotes a $10,000 minimum for a wedding, but just $7500 for retirement parties. Another facility in San Francisco quoted us an $18,000 estimate for a wedding with 125 guests; the same size party for a family reunion was just $9000.

Another example: on ABC's *20/20* in 2013, producers called 13 New York City DJs, first posing as a bride and then as a friend planning a 40th birthday party. The dates, times and services were exactly the same. Ten out of the 13 DJs quoted higher prices to work the wedding; an average of 46% higher than the birthday party.

So, what can you do? Our advice would be to just "forget" to mention you are planning a wedding when you first request menu packages and pricing from a venue. Just say you are planning a party or event. It's clear that hotels and other reception sites have special "bridal package" menus that are quite pricey. What they DON'T show you is their regular menu packages with lower-cost food options. You'll be in a better position to negotiate a deal if you have ALL the facility's menus and pricing info, not just the expensive "bridal" options.

is a donation or contribution, it may be tax-deductible. If the fee is a rental charge (where a service is provided), the fee may NOT be tax deductible. Ask your tax preparer for details.

16 **Get historical**. Speaking of historic sites, don't overlook historical societies. Many rent out their facilities as a way to further their preservation mission. Elizabeth S. of Texas said she found an incredible bargain by going this route—a local historical society rented her their rose garden, covered gazebo, reception hall for four hours for a grand total of $180. Nope, that's no typo. $180 for the complete site and she could bring in her own caterer. Now that's a great deal.

17 **Light it up**. Spice up an otherwise average site with lighting. Memphis caterer Jaime Newsom (Social Butterflies, SB-Events.com) uses pin spots to light up wedding cakes and other food stations. The cost of pin spots for a wedding cake: $50 from a rental company. Dramatic lighting can make an average site look like a much more expensive venue.

Pitfalls to Avoid

PITFALL #1 UNWRITTEN PROMISES.

"I booked my wedding and reception at an historic home. The wedding coordinator there told me all the wonderful things they would do for my reception at no charge. For example, they said they would decorate the gazebo for free if I brought them the fabric. Then, wouldn't you know? My contact person left and the owner of the site refused to fulfill the promises she made! I was furious! The only problem was I couldn't prove a thing since nothing was written down!"

Well, this is perhaps the most common complaint we hear about reception sites: unfulfilled promises. To get you to book the site, some unscrupulous site managers will make wild promises they never intend to keep. Another problem: the person you first meet with quits or is fired before your wedding. This happens more than you might think. A word to the wise: get every last promise and detail *in writing* in the contract. This protects you from dishonest salespeople or from changes in personnel. If promises are made after the contract is signed, get them to write a note (a fax or email will do) putting the promises in black and white.

PITFALL #2 MENU GOOFS.

"My wedding and reception was at a popular hotel in our town. We spent hours going over the menu but what was served at the reception in no way resembled what we ordered. Worse yet, then we couldn't find anyone from the catering department to fix the problem! What happened?"

Sometimes the bureaucracy at hotels and other reception sites can lead to snafus. Perhaps the catering manager "forgot" to inform the kitchen of your menu. Maybe the chef just had an extra 200 Chicken Cordon Bleus left over from a banquet the night before. In any case, you deserve a refund or the site should offer a fair reduction in the bill as compensation for their mistake.

As for fixing a problem the night of the wedding, good luck. While you might be able to have the maitre d' contact the catering director, there may be little that can be done at that moment. Another wise idea: if the catering director or representative won't be at the reception, get their cell or home phone numbers.

PITFALL #3 KICK-BACKS AND CATERING MANAGERS.

"My site's catering coordinator gave us a list of recommended musicians. I found out later that the bands who were on the list paid to be there. Is that kosher?"

Kickbacks (or "referral fees") are a reality when it comes to the wedding biz. Obviously, not all sites demand a kickback to be featured on their recommended vendor lists. And there are certain parts of the country (ahem, New Jersey and New York, we are talking about you) that you are more often to find this issue.

Our message: protect yourself by independently checking out any "recommended." That means calling references, checking with the Better Business Bureau (bbb.org) and searching wedding message boards for any consumer feedback on the vendor. Trust but verify!

PITFALL #4 BETTER SAFE THAN SORRY.

"My fiancé and I wanted to book this civic site since it had sentimental meaning to us. The site coordinator told us we 'had dibs' on the site because we had inquired about it first. They only book one year in advance, but we were told we didn't have to get our deposit in immediately. Guess what? We just discovered they gave our date to another bride who came in on the first day it was available!"

Some site coordinators may tell you "there's no need to rush" to put a deposit on a site, but you might want to do otherwise. There's no guarantee that a date will be held for you . . . especially when another bride shows up with deposit money in hand. The best advice: book it now, show them the money (place the deposit) and get it in writing.

PITFALL #5 CATERING SURCHARGES.

" I was perturbed to learn recently that the reception site I have booked for my wedding charges caterers a percent fee for 'use of the site.' In

other words, once the total catering fee is determined, an extra 7% of this total must be paid to the reception site. This cost of course, is passed on to me. This was nowhere reflected in my contract with the reception site and it seems pretty underhanded to me. The caterer I'm working with however, explained that technically the fee is imposed on the caterer as the price of doing business at the site, that all sites do this and that in fact 7% was very reasonable. Is this typical? Is this LEGAL when I've already paid $2000 to rent out the space!"

Some reception sites "forget" to disclose this fee when booking. It also appears nowhere in the site's contract. And, of course, many caterers simply pass this fee along to you as an extra charge. (In one case we researched, a caterer simply refused to work with a bride at a site that charged a 15% commission, since she didn't want to pay it either.)

One bride discovered a 20% surcharge when she booked a national park in Maryland—the National Park Service's food service contractor demanded a huge 20% fee if she used an outside caterer (the contractor didn't have the capacity to cater events like weddings). This fee is on top of the rental charge the park service levies for use of the facility.

How can you prevent this from happening to you? Be sure to ask about any catering surcharges or commissions BEFORE you book a site that allows outside catering. And if a site fails to disclose this fee, you should be entitled to a full refund on your deposit if you decide to cancel.

From a legal point of view, such sites are on very shaky ground. The sites cannot impose a fee on a third-party (the caterer) because you've contracted with the site for a reception. What's next? Charging the DJ an "electricity fee" when he plugs in an amplifier? Slapping the baker with a "cake fee" because they are delivering a wedding cake to the site?

PITFALL # 6 COOKIE CUTTER RECEPTION SITES.

"My friend was convinced to have her wedding at a 'one-stop-shopping wedding emporium.' They touted their experience with weddings and promised that my friend wouldn't have to lift a finger—everything would be done for her. But the meal was only mediocre, the band played the music too loud (and too much disco) and we all left early. The $157 a plate price seemed a waste."

Popular on the East Coast, wedding halls like to promise the moon, but often deliver much less. Our advice: comparison shop these sites on an apples to apples basis. The bride who wrote that email noted she was able to price out an elegant reception at the Four Seasons with spectacular food and great service for much less than the wedding emporium's price. While it may be convenient to go with a wedding hall, the better deal may be to steer clear of such establishments.

PITFALL #7 BALLROOM SWITCHEROO.

"We reserved a hotel ballroom for our reception six months before our wedding. When we went to put down the deposit, we were told "Oops! Sorry...we moved you to a smaller ballroom to make room for a convention that day." The hotel's contract has a clause that states they retain the right to change the ballroom, even up to a day before the wedding. Is it just me, or does this policy seem absolutely ridiculous?"

Yes, this is certainly a problem with hotels and other sites with multiple ballrooms. Our advice: if they can't guarantee you a specific room, don't show them the money. Never sign a contract with such a clause.

Helpful Hints

1 Kids' buckets. If you plan to have children at your wedding, consider doing what one reader did: she made up kids' buckets (start with cheap, plastic sand buckets) and filled them with 99¢ coloring books, crayons and small games. "They were waiting on the tables at place settings for kids. As a result, moms and dads didn't have to entertain their kids. I still hear thank yous to this day!"

2 Check back occasionally. Bridal shops aren't the only ones to go out of business suddenly; sadly this can happen to reception sites too. We heard from a Michigan bride who reported two reception sites near Ypsilanti closed during a recent six-month period; couples were left scrambling to find alternatives. While this is still rare, it might be prudent to call your reception site every other month to make sure they're still around.

3 Box up meals of guests that don't show up. If you paid for 100 prime rib dinners and only 97 guests showed up, then ask the caterer to box up those extra meals! If not, they go into the trash (or into the mouths of waiters). Note: some county health department rules may prohibit you from taking food off the premises.

4 Choice can be a pricey option. Some folks like to give their guests a choice of entrees—say fish or chicken. That's nice, but watch out: some sites will charge you the HIGHER meal price no matter what option the guest chooses. It might be less expensive to just pick one menu and forget the choice.

5 Practice your poker face. Just like when shopping for a home or car, don't appear too excited when visiting reception sites. Many sites are willing to negotiate their prices if they know what your exact budget is. But if you act as though you *must* have the site for your wedding or else, they may think they've got you and don't have to negotiate.

One reader told us that she was surprised that so many hotels she visited were willing to meet her budget to get the business. Don't be afraid to haggle. Just because a site's price sheet says their weddings cost X doesn't mean it's the price *you* have to pay!

6 **Check with a local convention or visitor's bureau** to make sure a major convention or event is not scheduled during your wedding weekend. Many visitors' bureau web sites have convention calendars.

A Look at the Six Most Common Reception Site Types

This section will explore the pros, cons and costs of the six most common places for receptions: hotels/catering halls, private and country clubs, civic sites, home weddings, church weddings and (our favorite) miscellaneous sites.

HOTELS/CATERING HALLS

Catering halls and hotels may seem like an obvious choice as the site for a reception—both have spacious banquet rooms and full-service catering staffs to take care of every detail. On the East Coast, catering halls host as many as half of all wedding receptions. Meanwhile, in the South, hotel ballrooms are often the only choice for a bride who is inviting 300 or 400 guests. While hotels may only account for 10% to 20% of receptions nationwide, they often host the biggest and most lavish receptions in many cities. Here are the pros and cons of having your wedding reception at a hotel or catering hall.

The Good News

♥ **ALL-INCLUSIVE PACKAGES.** When you have a reception at these facilities, all the rentals (tables, chairs, serving pieces, bars, dance floors, etc.) are generally included in the price.

♥ **LARGE WEDDINGS.** For large weddings, hotels or catering halls may be the best choice. That's because their big ballrooms can accommodate large parties up to or over 1000 guests. Most other sites have peak capacities at about 200 to 300 guests.

♥ **CLIMATE CONTROL.** In areas of the country with harsh weather, climate-controlled ballrooms are a plus.

♥ **DISCOUNTS ON ROOM RENTALS, HONEYMOON SUITES.** Most hotels are willing to negotiate a discounted rate for a block of rooms. If you have many out-of-town relatives, this may be a big plus. Some hotel packages also throw in a honeymoon suite gratis—a nice touch. One caveat: make sure to double-check the hotel's "special" rate to see if you're really getting a deal. More than one bride has told us they discovered the "special group rate" was no different than the regular room fees available online.

♥ **SPECIAL WEDDING RECEPTION PACKAGES.** Many hotels and catering halls have special catering packages for wedding receptions. Unfortunately, these are sometimes more expensive than their a la carte choices! Why? The extra labor needed for a reception versus other functions might be one answer. Or maybe it's just extra profit (call it a "bridal" package and the price rises 30%). Be sure to crunch the numbers for different packages to see which is the best deal. On the other hand, some facilities aggressively pursue weddings by offering many freebies—you'd be surprised at the big difference in costs from one site to another.

♥ **DIETARY RESTRICTIONS.** For those couples that need kosher catering, hotels are often a best bet. Hotels must meet certain standards before they are certified Kosher. Call a local synagogue or rabbi to get a list of approved facilities.

♥ **I DO TOO.** Some hotels and catering halls can also host a lovely ceremony. One West Coast hotel we researched has an outdoor garden and gazebo for ceremonies. At a catering hall we visited in New Jersey, lush gardens offered several ceremony site options. The convenience of having everything at one location may be a big plus.

♥ **ADVICE ON ENTERTAINERS, FLORISTS, BAKERS, ETC.** Catering managers at hotels and catering halls often have their pulse on the best wedding bands and entertainers. Use their experience, but be careful of some who take kickbacks from "recommended" services. (See Pitfall #3 earlier in this chapter for more info.)

The Bad News

♥ **DRAB INTERIOR DECOR.** Some sites look like they were decorated in Early Eisenhower.

♥ **THESE SITES CAN BE DARN EXPENSIVE.** While hotels and catering halls offer all-inclusive packages, you definitely pay for this convenience.

Case in point: sky high minimum food and beverage fees for premium nights. A bride in Chicago told us one exclusive hotel there has a $30,000 minimum charge for a Saturday night in May! Another famous Michigan Avenue hotel charges $180 to $280 per guest just for food and beverages. And that's before they slap you with an 18% mandatory gratuity and 9.25% sales tax. Even if you don't get married at the most chic hotel, your wedding budget at any hotel can suffer death by a thousand cuts. Hotels are skilled at taking $12 bottles of wine and charging you $80. Another famous hotel chain charged couples $35 for a gallon of fruit punch.

♥ **FROZEN FOOD.** Perhaps the biggest problem that plagues many hotels and catering halls is poor quality food. These sites often buy frozen food that can be quickly prepared. Ever seen those mini-quiches at a hotel wedding reception? Hotels can buy these and other popular buffet items in bulk. Pop them in an oven and presto! Dinner's ready! Obviously, pre-fabricated, frozen hors d'oeuvres simply don't compare to freshly prepared dishes.

♥ **BUREAUCRACY OF CATERING DEPARTMENTS.** From busboys to waiters to captains to catering assistants to managers, the multi-layer manage-

---

REAL WEDDING TIP

Don't pay rack rate!

A recent bride had advice on working with hotels for accommodations for guests:

"Even if you don't need ANY banquet/catering services, most hotels will happily negotiate a group room rate for your hotel guests. When my Matron of Honor got married four years ago, she talked the Omni in San Antonio into a fantastic group rate for her wedding guests. For my wedding, she made a bunch of calls on my behalf and did the same thing at a Houston Marriott: our rate was less than half the best weekend rate and was valid for the entire week of the wedding. Business hotels are dying for business on weekends. Also, remember December and January are really good times to get deeply discounted room rates at many hotels—the holidays are busy for banquets/parties, but not for room occupancy. Just make sure your guests are really coming BEFORE you guarantee a room count—most hotels charge steep penalties if you use fewer room nights than you guarantee."

ment of catering departments can be vexing. Ask if the catering manager (or the contact person you planned your event with) will be at your reception.

♥ **WEDDINGS CAN BE LOW ON THE PRIORITY LIST.** Especially in December, hotels are distracted with corporate holiday parties on large budgets. Competition with convention and reunion business can also be a headache.

♥ **REMEMBER THE CATERING REPRESENTATIVES ARE ON COMMISSION.** The more money you spend, the more money they make. Hence, we find many hotels and catering halls pushing exotic (and expensive) foods to jack up the tab. Many hotels also "suggest" expensive wines and other liquor.

♥ **BE CAREFUL OF NICKEL–AND–DIME CHARGES.** Never assume that anything is free. Extra charges could include valet parking, special table skirting, ice carvings, a dance floor, corking fees, cake cutting charge (see catering chapter), food station attendants, and any audio equipment (a microphone for toasts, for example). Also, silk flower table centerpieces and special linens or china may be extra. Compare the estimate on centerpieces with your florist's bid to get the best deal.

What Does a Hotel/Catering Hall Reception Cost?

Reception packages vary widely. Hotels and catering halls in downtown areas tend to be the most expensive (and also expect to pay extra for valet parking). In suburban areas, rates are somewhat less and these sites tend to be more aggressive in their competition for wedding business (since they can't rely on downtown convention traffic). In our research, we've found packages that start as low as $45 per person for a buffet at an Oklahoma hotel and go up to $500 per person for a complete sit-down dinner at a posh New York City catering hall. In general, most sites are in the $50 to $150 per person range for basic receptions (not counting liquor). In the biggest cities (New York, Los Angeles, Chicago, Philadelphia), you can expect to pay twice to three times more. Add in a big liquor tab and you'll see the total costs soar. In San Francisco, top downtown hotels now charge $20,000 to $45,000 minimums for food and beverage. And considering those same hotels charge $125 to $230 per guest for reception dinners, you'll be hitting those minimums real fast.

PRIVATE/COUNTRY CLUBS

reception

Think you have to be a member of those fancy country clubs and private clubs to hold a wedding reception in their facilities? Not always. In fact, many clubs welcome non-members with open arms! That's because weddings often bring in badly needed revenue. We define private and country clubs as any site that has membership requirements or restrictions. While you may have to be a member at some sites, others just require a "member-sponsor." Still others don't have any requirements at all.

Types of Clubs

1 Business clubs. Located downtown on top of skyscrapers, some business clubs have a restaurant open for lunch each day and space to host meetings and receptions. Various professional organizations (i.e., Engineers' Clubs, Doctors' Clubs) may own and operate these facilities. Such sites vary widely in appeal (we saw one Engineer's Club that looked like it was decorated by, well, engineers) but are generally more open to wedding receptions. Most likely, you must use the club's in-house catering.

2 Military clubs. If someone in your family is a retired or active duty military, you may have access to a military club facility in your area. Rates are usually very affordable.

3 Country clubs. These sites normally have a golf course and several acres of landscaped grounds. Here, the clubhouse is the focal point for receptions. Lush grounds can make beautiful backdrops for photos. These sites may be the most restrictive; many require a member (who can be a friend or just an acquaintance) to at least "sponsor" the reception. Sometimes, this sponsorship is just a token technicality where the member assumes responsibility in case you don't pay the bill and flee to Peru. In most cases, you must use the country club's in-house catering.

4 Civic/Social clubs. Elks Clubs, Garden Clubs, Federation of Women's clubs, Junior Leagues, Junior Forums—each of these organizations may have facilities they rent for receptions. Typically, you must bring in an outside caterer. Prices and quality are all over the board: Elks Clubs and Veterans of Foreign Wars (VFW) Posts, for example, are often quite affordable but offer rather Spartan decor. Other clubs are located in historic buildings that are beautiful but also carry a hefty price tag. Membership requirements are usually non-existent.

The Good News

♥ **MORE PERSONAL SERVICE.** These facilities have less of that "wedding factory" feel you find at hotels or catering halls. One reason: less bureaucracy. Many sites have fewer people to deal with and this sometimes improves customer service.

♥ **BETTER AMBIANCE.** Unlike the drab and sterile decor of many hotels, country and private clubs are usually set on beautiful sites—golf courses are definitely easier on the eyes than parking lots. Downtown business clubs perched atop skyscrapers may offer spectacular skyline views.

♥ **SOME CLUBS PERMIT OUTSIDE CATERERS.** While business and country clubs usually have in-house catering, some clubs let you bring in a caterer of your choice—this can be a fantastic savings (see our catering chapter).

The Bad News

♥ **YOU MAY HAVE TO BE A MEMBER.** Frequently this depends on the local economy. If the club is in need of funds, they may allow non-member wedding receptions. However, if the club is flushed with members, they will limit the use of the club to members only.

♥ **IF YOU AREN'T A MEMBER, SOME CLUBS REQUIRE YOU TO HAVE A MEMBER-**

Discount chair covers

Yes, most rental places rent chairs, but what if you want a fancier look? Some folks like the look of chair covers. But the price? A reader in New Orleans was stunned when she priced out chair covers from a local party store. Her suggestion: BBJLinen.com, a Chicago-based company that rents chair covers and other linens at very affordable rates. BBJ Linen's rates are often HALF the price of other rental companies. Also try Be-Seated.com, another site with great prices (they service several metro areas and ship nationwide).

Another tip: when shopping for chair covers and table linens from local companies, watch out for shipping. Some companies charge for this, others don't. "Many times I found a company that wanted to charge me $7.50 for a chair cover, another $3 for a sash and then slap shipping on top of that," a reader emailed us. By shopping around, the same reader found chair covers for $2 each including sash.

SPONSOR. Here, a member of the club must "sponsor" your reception, agreeing to attend the event and pay for it if you skip town. If you have a friend who is a member, great. If you don't, some clubs may negotiate around this point—perhaps by requesting a larger deposit. We've found that some clubs will find you a sponsor if you don't know one!

♥ **FOOD QUALITY CAN VARY WIDELY.** Some clubs have gourmet chefs on staff that create wonderful dishes. Other clubs may not and their food quality is, at best, as good as that of an average hotel. Ask for a taste test to confirm this detail.

♥ **EXPENSIVE RECEPTIONS.** Some clubs can be just as, or even more, expensive than hotel weddings. Overpricing of liquor is a common problem. Just like hotels, club catering managers receive commissions based on the total amount you spend—giving them an incentive to inflate the tab. Many clubs also add on a high gratuity, similar to hotels.

What Does it Cost?

Well, it depends. Fancy country clubs may be just as expensive as the prices we quoted above for hotels and catering halls. Other clubs, that don't have in-house catering, just charge a rental fee for the facility. These can be a major bargain.

CIVIC SITES

A "civic" site is any reception facility that is owned and administered by a city or municipal agency. Almost always, you must bring in your own caterer. Some civic sites have a recommended list of caterers that you may have to choose from. Be aware that some sites may have time and beverage restrictions (no liquor) and others require you to hire security officers. Civic sites are usually the best bargains. Why? Subsidized by taxpayers, these sites are seen as a public amenity (instead of a profit generator).

Types of Civic Sites

1 **Parks, gardens, amphitheaters.** Often quite affordable, these sites are usually administered by city parks departments. Some sites even have clubhouses. If you decide to have an outdoor ceremony or reception, make sure you have a backup plan in case of inclement weather.

2 **Recreation centers, civic centers, town halls, conference centers.** Quality varies greatly with these sites (some are spectacular while others are dumps), but they are usually quite affordable.

3 **Sites owned by universities or colleges.** These sites include faculty clubs, alumni halls, chapels, etc. You might be surprised at the sheer variety of spaces available for rent on a college campus—they are rarely advertised and can be great bargains. One limitation: you may have to be an alum (or know one) to book the site. Also, many of these facilities will require you to use their in-house caterer.

4 **Museums.** Rare but available in some cities, these sites may be quite expensive and even require you to be a "museum patron" (i.e., make a hefty donation).

The Good News

♥ **LOW COST AND UNIQUE LOCATIONS.** Most of these sites are very affordable. And you can't beat the ambience of a local rose garden . . . or a museum stocked with priceless art.

♥ **BRING IN AN OUTSIDE CATERER.** Off-site caterers can save oodles of money and offer creative, delicious menu options. However, you may be required to pick a caterer off an "approved" list.

The Bad News

♥ **VERY POPULAR SITES BOOK UP QUICKLY.** Since civic sites are so affordable, they are also very popular. Many book months in advance.

♥ **EQUIPMENT RENTAL EXPENSE CAN BE HIGH.** Some of these sites might require you to bring in tables, chairs, serving pieces, etc. This could be a significant expense.

♥ **MAKE SURE THE CATERER IS VERY FAMILIAR WITH THE SITE.** Some brides and grooms find hiring and dealing with an outside caterer challenging—increasing the complexity of the event by adding another person in the loop. Another limitation: civic sites' lack of kitchen facilities may affect a caterer's ability to do the function.

HOME WEDDINGS

Yes, we can always tell when it's wedding season in Boulder, Colorado. Pick any road that winds its way up into the foothills and you'll see several handmade signs directing guests to a remote location for the nuptials of "Spense and Lisa," "Cheyenne and Bob," and so on.

Home weddings are big here, as they are in other parts of the Rockies. While only accounting for 6% to 10% of all receptions in the US, Boulder seems to be the center of the universe for home nuptials and receptions—half of all weddings here are at home, according to our estimates. Perhaps it's the nice summer weather or the views of the Continental Divide that convince brides and grooms to tie the knot at home. Or maybe we're just cheap—the price ($0) to use your own home is right for many folks.

The Good News

♥ **AFFORDABLE RECEPTIONS.** Let's be honest: home weddings can be had cheap. Whether you have friends and family help with the food or order a meal from a restaurant or catering service, home weddings are a fraction of the cost of receptions at traditional sites like hotels, catering halls and private clubs.

♥ **NO SCHEDULING CONFLICTS.** If you want to have a wedding in June on a Saturday night, you may discover that so do many other couples in your area. The competition for reception sites during popular months may lead you to consider a home wedding.

♥ **SMALL WEDDINGS.** Unless you live in Bill Gates' house, the average home can only hold a minimal number of guests (usually under 100). This is a plus and a minus. While you may not be able to invite everyone you'd like to, you do have the perfect excuse for cutting down that guest list.

The Bad News

♥ **RENTALS, RENTALS, RENTALS.** Planning a home wedding for 75 guests but you don't have tables and chairs for the crowd? You'll need to rent them, along with plates, silverware, glassware, serving pieces, bar set-ups and more. Afraid it might rain on your parade? Renting a tent can set you back $800 for a simple tent or $20,000 for a fancy model with air conditioning, lighting and more. As you can see, the money you save on catering with a home wedding may be partially eaten up by a big rental bill.

REAL WEDDING TIP

An Amazing Send-off

We are impressed with the resourcefulness of our readers and none more than Robin Holzer of Houston, TX. She was determined to have real fireworks at her wedding reception and shared her story:

This one may be beyond the scope of Bridal Bargains, but I managed to arrange a five-and-a-half minute professional fireworks display (set to music) for the end of our wedding reception. The process was fraught with red tape, but here's a summary:

In most jurisdictions, all pyrotechnic displays are strictly regulated by state and local fire codes. Conveniently, the Texas state code is available online. In Texas, only licensed professional operators may legally discharge fireworks. The operator must carry minimum liability insurance ($1 million) for the event.

A fire marshal must review the site plan prior to issuing a permit for the fireworks display, and one or more fire marshals must be onsite to monitor the actual display and sweep the area for fallen embers afterwards. Fourth of July fireworks displays are typically "aerial" and go upwards of 400 feet. A "close proximity" display is smaller and goes only 150 to 200 feet in the air. Outside of city limits, we could get a five-minute display with 200-250 shells/minute for $1000. Inside the city, the same close-proximity display ran $2500-$3500.

Brides on a budget should consider "gerbs," which are small (4 to 6 feet) "fountains" of shooting, colored sparks (see the end of the movie "My Best Friend's Wedding" for a visual). Remember that even tiny sparklers and gerbs require a permit from the fire marshal in many jurisdictions.

We found licensed operators online—there were only three in Houston. The big operators are considerably more professional than the small independent guys, though the little guy IS cheaper. And the big guys WILL do small displays (except around July 4 and January 1) as long as they feel the display site is adequate/large/safe. Make sure that the permit is for the exact street address where the display will occur. Also check how long the permit is good for and what are the contract terms if it rains on your wedding day. (It may be reasonable to pay a nominal fee for trucking the explosives/charges back and forth and setup/break down, but you shouldn't pay for the shells since they can use them for another event)! Have a blast on your wedding day!

♥ **SURPRISE EXPENSES.** Home weddings may entail several unexpected bills. At one home wedding we attended in Austin, Texas, the bride and groom hired a van service to shuttle guests back and forth because of limited parking—this cost an extra $900. You may also need extra insurance to cover liability at the event—call your homeowner's insurance provider to see what's covered.

CHURCH RECEPTIONS

The classic mid-America wedding typically has a low-cost reception that follows in a church fellowship hall. Yes, they are cheap, but fellowship halls can look more Spartan than fairy tale. A mother of the bride in a small Arkansas town came up with some thoughts on how to make this work: "Beg, borrow, use that church family! If people want to lend stuff and help, then let them! Give them a list! We borrowed almost all of the decorations from church friends whose daughters have married in the last three years. Latticework, columns, lights, artificial ivy, and flowers were used to cover up an ugly fellowship hall. We have friends who own a large restaurant and are letting us borrow silver serving pieces and 12 candelabras! We have other friends who are decorating the sanctuary and fellowship hall with tulle (very cheap yet a great bridal look), ivy, loose flowers, ferns, azaleas, etc. We have other friends who used to be caterers who are cooking all of the food at cost. We have another friend who is in food distribution who gave us free food for the reception. That's what friends are for!"

AND EVERYWHERE ELSE

Yes, you can have a wedding reception just about anywhere—theaters, ranches, private estates, chartered boats and yachts, bed and breakfast inns, and so on. Anything goes!

What's the message here? Don't think you must have your reception in a hotel or club just because all your friends did that. Every city has many romantic and beautiful settings for receptions—it may just take a little creative searching.

In fact, that's perhaps the biggest challenge to using a "non-traditional" site—finding one! (Perhaps the second biggest challenge is convincing parents and relatives that the site is better than the traditional options!) To find a non-traditional site, surf wedding message boards for ideas. Ask local caterers for suggestions. Often you must bring in your own caterer.

Now that you've found yourself a reception site, what to do about the food? Read on and you'll find tips on how to save on catering no matter where your reception is!

If you read just one chapter in this book, make it this one. That's because we give you 32 ways to cut your catering budget, the biggest expense area for any wedding. Wonder what to ask the caterer? Check out our 18 questions to ask, plus six pitfalls to avoid with wedding catering.

What Are You Buying?

Wedding catering varies dramatically across the country. When food is the topic, the United States of America is hardly united. And such variations make weddings in one part of the country much different than another. Sometimes the differences are also social in nature. For example, in the Northeast, nearly all receptions are sit-down dinners—folks there like to have their own space to enjoy the meal. While in the South and West, almost all weddings have buffets or hors d'oeuvre receptions—people there like to mingle, instead of being in one chair for the entire reception. No matter where you have your wedding, however, here are the four basic things you buy from a caterer:

♥ **Food.** Everything from hors d'oeuvres to dessert. The typical method of calculating the cost of wedding catering is based on a figure per guest. Costs can range from $15 per guest for a simple "cake, punch and mints" reception in North Dakota to over $300 per person for a full sit-down dinner with open bar at a posh hotel in New York City.

As you can see, food costs can vary dramatically from region to region. Yes, prices are less in the middle of the country and tend to be higher on the coasts and in major cities. In Oklahoma City, for example, a *simple* buffet dinner reception runs $25 per guest. In Seattle, that same meal is $70. But entry-level reception packages in catering halls in the Northeast can run at least $95 per guest.

In the mid range, a more elaborate meal (say a heavy hors d'oeuvre buffet or sit-down dinner of prime rib) is about $55 to $85 in a place like Houston, TX. On the coasts and major cities, you can see the tab soar to $90 to $175 for such a reception.

And what about the upper end? Once again, it depends on where you live. In Oklahoma, $75 per guest will buy you one fancy reception and open bar. Expect to shell out $125 to $180 for a top-end reception in Atlanta, up to $300 per guest in Boston and New York City.

In Chicago, a bride recently emailed us to say that she got proposals from six independent caterers for a meal consisting of six hors d'oeuvres per guest, salad, and a chicken entrée. The cost? Nearly $100 per guest. Rather amazing since that didn't include any dessert, wedding cake OR the alcohol. Most fancy downtown hotels in Chicago charge $150 to $200 per person just for food and beverage.

According to our research, the starting price for most weddings (whether seated dinner or buffet) in the Washington DC metro area is $100 per person. Fancy events from top caterers run $125 to $200 per guest. It's hard to find a venue in DC for less than $90 per guest, with prices over $200 per guest at four-star properties.

♥ **BEVERAGES.** Beverages can be priced one of several ways. A common method: the consumption bar. You pay for what your guests consume. This can be by the drink or by the bottle (or tenths of a bottle consumed). Some sites have a flat charge for soft drinks and juices. If your guests aren't big drinkers, a consumption bar might be the most affordable way to go—just be sure to place a cap on the bar tab and get in writing that you are to be asked before they exceed that amount.

Another alternative method of beverage charging: flat pricing. Some sites might offer all-you-can drink packages for a specified period of time (an hour or so). This is a common option at sites that offer cocktail hours before a seated dinner. If your guests are heavy drinkers, this might be the way to go. Ask the site to only charge you for *adult* guests. If you have 100 guests but 10 are children, be sure to get a flat pricing package that just covers the 90 adults.

Finally, you can sometimes bring in your own liquor at some sites—but quite a few facilities slap on a "corking fee" to chill and serve the booze. This can be $15 or more per bottle, plus a gratuity and (in some states) sales tax.

Whether your reception will just have punch and coffee or a full open bar with premium well brands, the cost of beverages can be a significant part of the catering budget. For one hors d'oeuvres reception at a four-star hotel with a full open bar serving premium liquor, the total bar tab for 300 guests came to $9200—almost half the $19,000 total cost of the evening!

Why are beverages so expensive? Sure, alcohol isn't cheap . . . but the real reason is price markups. This is where any caterer (or restaurant) makes the bulk of their profits. A caterer will take a $15 bottle of wine and charge you $65. A gallon of fruit punch at the grocery store costs $3—at a wedding, the price is $36. You get the idea.

Of course, the charge you'll end up paying for beverages at your wedding depends on what you serve and how the reception site accounts for this. An open bar of modest-grade beer, wine, sodas and champagne (for a toast) averages about $20 to $35 per guest, according to national averages. That's for the entire reception.

Costs can quickly soar above that for bars with mixed drinks and premium liquors—one bride in Chicago told us she priced a full open bar at a

REAL WEDDING TIP

Open vs. Cash Bars: Don't charge your guests for drinks.

One big controversy in the world of wedding etiquette is whether bars should be open or cash. In the latter case, guests pay for their drinks. Given typically high drink prices these days that means your guests could be paying $20 to $40 per person for a night of drinks. As you can imagine, open versus cash is a hot topic in the bridal world. Yes, we realize some couples simply don't have the funds to stock an open bar for several hours. Some couples compromise by having an open bar for an hour at the beginning of the reception and a cash bar for the rest of the evening. This also discourages guests from getting smashed toward the end of the evening when they might get behind the wheel. The liability issue is also forcing many couples (and reception sites) to rethink serving alcohol altogether. Yet, despite all the pros to limiting alcohol consumption, our advice is simple—skip the cash bar idea. If you can't afford even a simple beer/wine/champagne bar, don't charge guests for drinks. Go non-alcoholic with creative ideas like coffee drinks, exotic teas, etc. If you insist on going the cash bar route, the least you could do is warn your guests in advance (perhaps putting notice of this on a personal wedding web site where you discuss the reception details).

top reception hall at $14,000 for 200 guests for five hours. Yep, that's $70 per guest ... just for alcohol! Another bride told us she priced an open bar at a Hilton in Chicago at $17,000 for 175 people for four and a half hours. If you cut back to just beer, wine and two signature drinks (a martini and margarita), the price dropped to $11,000, which is still $63 a guest.

In Boston, an open bar runs $10 to $18 per guest *per hour*, depending on the site.

♥ **LABOR.** Hey, don't forget those folks who actually serve the food. Of course, most sites won't let you forget to pay the staff—they impose a mandatory gratuity of 15% to 20%. This applies to the food and sometimes the liquor served at the reception. If you serve a buffet that costs $8000, you may pay as much as $1600 extra for the servers, bus boys, etc.

Frankly, we think a percentage gratuity is deceptive—most sites don't pay their staff anywhere near the amount of money they collect for "service." They pocket the difference as revenue. For example, in the above case, let's assume the reception was for 150 guests. Using an industry rule of thumb of one server for 25 guests at a buffet reception, we would need six servers. Hence, each server would theoretically receive $165 for the evening. If the reception lasts four hours (plus another two for set-up and clean-up), do you really think the site is paying the servers a wage that totals nearly $30 per hour? In most cities, we wouldn't bet on it.

Perhaps a more equitable way of paying for service is a method adopted by some independent caterers. This involves paying a flat per hour fee per waiter at the event—say, $15 to $20 per hour per server. No matter what the total tab of your function, you pay only for the number of people actually serving your guests.

How many bartenders do you need? It depends on whether you plan a full bar or just beer, wine and soft drink service. The latter is much faster as you can imagine and requires less staff, say one bartender to 75 or 100 guests. A full bar might require a one-bartender-to-50-guest ratio.

♥ **RENTALS.** Certain reception sites may lack tables, chairs, silverware, china, glassware, table linens, etc. All these items must be rented separately and brought to the site. Some caterers have an in-house supply of rentals while others arrange the needed rentals through an outside company. Charges for this service vary greatly—sometimes the caterer will charge you what the rental company charges them. Other caterers may tack on an extra fee of 5% to 10% of the rental bill to cover the administrative expense of dealing with the rental company. Some caterers (who charge this fee) also absorb any charges for broken or missing rental items. However, in other cases, you may be responsible for any breakage.

REAL WEDDING TIP

Gratuities: Don't forget to budget!

A reader in New Jersey writes:

Your budget information is very helpful, however you left out one piece of information—GRATUITIES for all "labor" (photography, videography, drivers, florist, etc.). I understand that some contracts include gratuity, but I believe you should tip a small amount anyway. Although gratuities were included in our reception contract, we had to tip many other vendors, which totaled almost $1,100! (We had a 13-piece band!)

This is a perennial question—who do you tip? How much? First, understand that many wedding vendors (the caterer, limo, etc.) add a *mandatory* gratuity to the final tab. As a result, you don't have to tip anyone. However, if you believe an individual staffer has gone "above and beyond the call of duty," it may be nice if you slipped them an extra $20, $50 or more. A server who tracks down a missing special dietary meal for a relative, a limousine driver who makes a special return trip to your house to retrieve an errant bridesmaid, a catering manager who works miracles with a cake that's collapsed—these are examples of extraordinary service that you may want to reward with an extra tip. You may also give a tip to the band or disc jockey if they turn in a stellar performance.

We've noticed there are some regional differences when it comes to tipping. Brides in the Northeast (particularly Long Island, New York and northern New Jersey) tell us it's standard practice to "grease" all wedding vendors with a $50 or $100 tip on the day of the wedding. Some bridal vendors can be darn pushy about this; one Long Island bride told us she was informed by her photographer that he expected her to tip his assistant 10% of the bill. And the catering manager told her that even though a labor charge was built into her $70 per plate reception, an additional tip would be nice. Our take on that: it's rude for a vendor to demand a tip, either for themselves or their workers. We say ignore them.

If you really want to give a tip, give it directly to the worker(s). One waitress who works for a catering hall in Cleveland told us their staff never sees extra tips that are paid with the final tab. Apparently, the owner of the facility pockets these as extra profit. Hence, don't give that tip to the owner or maitre'd—hand it directly to the people you want to receive it. And there's no law that says you have to give cash: consider handing out gift certificates or a bottle of wine as a thank you to wedding vendors.

♥ COORDINATION OF THE RECEPTION. Many caterers now offer coordination of the entire reception as an extra service. This can range from simply referring names of good florists or entertainers to actually booking and negotiating with other services. Some caterers offer such coordination as a free customer service; others charge fees that are similar to that of a professional wedding consultant. The degree you will want your caterer to coordinate your reception will depend on how much you trust them.

♥ AVERAGE CATERING COSTS. So, what's the total tab? As we pointed out above, it highly depends on where the wedding reception will be. The exact menu (food and beverage) that costs $48 per person in Albuquerque could be $100 or more in Philadelphia. For example, one bride told us she had to move her reception from Dallas to Washington, DC. In Dallas, she priced her complete reception at $70 per person. A very similar menu at a comparable hotel in Washington, DC cost $160 per guest!

According to industry estimates, we peg the national average cost for wedding catering at $14,180 for 150 guests—about $94.50 per guest. This includes everything: food, beverages, gratuity/labor, rentals and any fees for the reception site. Of course, that "average" combines both lower-cost areas like the Midwest with expensive major metro areas. If you are planning a wedding in a big city, add 20% to 40% to those above prices.

Most caterers require a deposit that is as much as 50% of the total bill to hold a date. The balance is customarily due a week or two weeks *before* the date—some caterers will let you pay the final balance the day of the wedding. Get all payment policies in writing before you sign the contract.

Trends

♥ FOOD TRUCKS. Our favorite food town in the world is Austin, Texas. And a big part of the foodie scene in Austin is food trucks. Good news: you can now have these trucks cater your wedding. Think of them as large food stations on wheels. The Peached Tortilla, a delicious option in Austin, offers a minimum of two hours catering. At $11-$20 per person, it's darn affordable. One idea: some couples hire food trucks to show up later in the reception to provide snacks.

♥ MOLECULAR GASTRONOMY. This trend involves a bit of high school chemistry combined the mojo of a mad scientist. The result are foams, fizzes and dehydrated bursts of flavor, with the aim to up the ante on standard wedding fare. Expect these "special effects" to bump up your bill quite a bit.

♥ TRY FAMILY-STYLE MEALS. Everyone loves going out for Chinese with a bunch of friends, sharing various dishes on those lazy Susans. When transferred to a wedding, the concept of family-style dining encourages more table interaction among guests. Bonus: family-style catering saves on labor, as you need fewer waiters.

♥ **ARTISANAL FOODS.** Everything today seems to be artisanal. You know, cheeses made by small businesses with 20 Golden Gurnsey goats imported from a tiny island off Great Britain. Or a craft beer, like our local favorite, Crystal Springs Brewing Company's Summertime Ale. Of course, all this artisanal goodness isn't cheap—expect to pay a premium to include this trend in your wedding catering.

♥ **TASTING MENUS.** Just like the name implies, a tasting menu just offers your guests a "taste" or small plate in five to seven mini courses. An example from a New York caterer: winter caprese salad with beets, oysters three ways, beef tenderloin carpaccio, tandoori shrimp, lobster potatoes skins with New York strip, crème caramel. Cost: $125 per person. So not cheap, but not your traditional rubber chicken either.

♥ **EATING HEALTHY.** Heavy cream sauces are out, lighter entrees are in as more couples seek to include healthy options in wedding menus.

Types of Caterers

1 **In-house or on-premise caterers.** These are catering operations that exclusively provide the catering for a site. Examples are hotels and many country clubs. Unless they're really desperate, most of these sites won't allow outside or "off-premise" caterers. (The exception to this rule: the cake. Most sites let you bring in a wedding cake produced by an off-site baker).

2 **Off-premise caterers.** These caterers bring in food to an existing site. The caterer's services can be limited to just providing the food or include the coordination of the entire event. Here, caterers become more like party planners or wedding consultants—either providing or contracting out for services like decoration (table centerpieces, table skirting, for example) and entertainment (DJ's, musicians, etc.).

Sources to Find an Affordable Caterer

♥ **NACE.NET.** The National Association of Catering Executives (nace.net) has an excellent search function right on their home page: choose the type of caterer you are looking for (caterer: off-premise, for example), enter your zip code and voila! You get a list of possible caterers with contact info.

♥ **WORD OF MOUTH.** Finding a good, affordable caterer is by far the biggest challenge faced by engaged couples. The best caterers work strictly by word of mouth and hence, don't buy splashy banner ads on wedding web sites. Ask friends and co-workers for ideas; scan message boards online for other leads.

♥ **RECEPTION SITES THAT DON'T HAVE IN-HOUSE CATERERS.** Most will have a list of local caterers they recommend. This will be an invaluable time-saver. Ask them for their opinions as to which caterer offers the best service or most affordable prices. Another idea: photographers can often recommend good caterers (they usually sneak a taste during receptions!).

Getting Started: How Far in Advance?

Book your caterer as soon as you confirm your reception site. Many book up far in advance (as long as a year) for popular summer wedding weekends. Also, December is extremely busy for caterers, thanks to holiday parties.

Step-by-step Shopping Strategies

♥ **Step 1:** Using the sources above, set up appointments with at least three recommended caterers. When you call for an appointment, notice how promptly the caterer returns your call. Within the business day is good—if it takes them more than a day, that's a red flag. Prompt attention is your first clue to the caterer's commitment to service. Before your meeting, discuss with your fiancé your likes and dislikes for catering.

♥ **Step 2:** Ask to see photos of each caterer's previous work. Look for colorful and creative presentations of food. Are hors d'oeuvres artfully arranged with flowers and garnishes or just piled up on mirrored trays?

♥ **Step 3:** Ask for sample menus. These may list some popular hors d'oeuvre choices or sit-down options. Hopefully, prices will be listed to give you a better idea of costs. While most caterers customize menus for each reception, they should provide basic cost parameters for certain items.

♥ **Step 4:** Be honest about your budget. If you're not sure, give them a range of costs per guest that you feel comfortable with. What one caterer will offer you for $50 per person may be vastly different from what another may propose. Also, be specific about your menu likes and dislikes as well as any dietary restrictions.

♥ Step 5: Ask for a proposal that details possible menu options. Also, the proposal should clearly identify costs for liquor, rentals, and labor. Call the caterer back and ask them to clarify any part of the proposal that isn't clear. Don't assume the proposal includes extra items like glassware, china, linens, etc.—always confirm that detail. One bad sign: caterers who promise to send you a proposal and then fail to do so.

♥ Step 6: Confirm any "minimums." Some caterers require you to purchase a minimum amount of food (in dollars or meals). Hence, you may have to pay for 125 meals even if only 100 people show up to your wedding. While some of this is negotiable (depending on the date and time of your wedding), never book a caterer who has a minimum you don't think you'll be able to meet. Check to see if the wedding cake will count toward the minimum—sometimes that helps put the figure within reach. Also ask the caterer about the opposite case: when more guests show up than expected. Most caterers make 5% to 10% more food than is ordered, but confirm this to be sure.

♥ Step 7: Given the different proposals from each caterer, pick the one you most like and ask to visit one of their weddings during the set-up. Look for how organized they are and how the staff is dressed. Just observe.

♥ Step 8: Ask for a taste test of proposed menu items. You are most likely planning to spend several thousands of dollars on catering, so this is the least caterers can do. You may be able to combine the taste test with a visit to one of their weddings. Another suggestion: take pictures of the food at the tasting, in case the chef or catering manager changes before your wedding. That way you'll be able to show the new staffers what you expect.

♥ Step 9: Once you select a caterer, get everything in writing—down to the very last detail. Food, labor, beverages, and rentals (if necessary) should be clearly stated in a written contract. Make sure you understand any price escalation clauses (where the caterer has the right to up the price within a certain time period) and get any price guarantees in writing. Also get a drawing of the physical layout of the room (placement of the tables, dance floor, buffet tables, etc.).

♥ Step 10: Before you sign anything, take the contract home to read it. Pore over any fine print—note any refund policies and cancellation fees. Remember that just because the caterer's standard contract has certain boilerplate provisions doesn't mean such rules are set in stone and can't be changed—ask the caterer to alter or change any wording that makes you uncomfortable. Make sure any modifications or cancellations are made in writing.

Questions to Ask a Caterer

1 **Can we have a taste test of the foods on the menu?** You're spending thousands of dollars here— you should be able to sample the food.

2 **Can we see a wedding during set-up?** A truly organized and professional catering company should have no qualms about having you see this.

3 **Do you provide a written estimate and contract?** Verbal agreements are not wise. Make sure every last promise and detail is in black and white.

4 **Are you licensed?** Almost all municipalities (or counties) require caterers to be licensed. Local standards will stress clean and adequate facilities for food preparation and storage. Liability insurance on liquor and food may also be part of the requirements. Ask the caterer about insurance. Operating a catering business out of a residence is often illegal.

5 **Tell me about a wedding you did where something went wrong—how did you handle it?** Even the best caterers have things that go wrong—a crisis, accident or other unforeseen event that throws a wedding reception into chaos. How they handle the situation separates the professionals from the amateurs. We're always suspicious of caterers who say they "never" have problems with their weddings.

6 **Do you specialize in certain cuisines or types of menus?** Although they may claim to handle all types of weddings, caterers usually specialize in certain receptions (smaller versus larger, finger hors d'oeuvres versus full sit-down dinners). Some caterers may have chefs who specialize in certain cuisines (Mediterranean, Southwestern, Indian, etc.). What about vegetarians? Can you prepare a complete vegetarian menu (vegan, ovo-lacto, pesca-vegetarian, etc.)? A few veggie dishes? What about a Kosher meal? Are you certified?

7 **Where is the food prepared?** Will you need additional kitchen facilities at my site? Prevent any last-minute surprises by nailing down all the details. Example: if you are having a home wedding in a backyard, the caterer may need a separate, covered area for food preparation.

8 **When is the menu "set in stone?"** How close to the wedding can we get and still make changes to the menu? Trust us, there will be changes.

9 **How is your wait staff dressed?** The key here is professional attire. Don't assume the wait staff will be wearing tuxedos (the exception is hotels that always have uniformed servers).

10 **For cocktail or buffet receptions, how often will the food be replenished?** Will the servings per guest be limited? Who makes the decision on when to stop serving?

11 **Given the style of my reception, how many waiters do we need?** For seated receptions, one waiter per 16 to 20 guests is adequate. For buffet or cocktail receptions, one waiter per 25 guests is standard.

12 **How is the charge for labor figured?** Is the clean-up (dish-washing, etc.) extra?

13 **How much does a dessert table cost?** Is the wedding cake price included in the package? Dessert tables are popular in the Midwest and in parts of the Northeast. Be sure the cost of a dessert table is clearly identified.

14 **What are your cancellation/postponement policies?** Since catering is the biggest expense area, confirming this aspect would be prudent.

15 **Do you have a liquor license?** How is the cost of the beverages calculated? What brands of liquor will be served? Most caterers offer both "premium" (or "call") and generic or "house" brands. Can you taste the house brand of wine? If you plan to serve alcohol, you'll want the caterer to carefully explain what brands you are buying and how the cost is calculated.

16 **Are you familiar with my reception site?** If not, will you visit it with me? For off-premise caterers, don't assume they know your facility. Confirming details such as the kitchen facilities and the clean-up rules are very important if you want to get your security/damage/cleaning deposit back from the reception site. The site will hold you responsible for any damage or rule violations by your caterer.

17 **Do you receive any commissions from services you recommend?** Caterers may recommend bakers, florists or musicians but watch out! Some take "commissions" (we call them kick-backs) from the businesses they recommend. Don't just take their word—thoroughly check out any "recommended" services before contracting.

18 **Will you guarantee price estimates?** Many caterers raise their prices at the beginning of the year. Since we urge you to plan in advance, your reception may be several months away. Our advice: negotiate a price guarantee in writing (or at least a cap on future increases). Most caterers will be willing to do this to get your business. One couple we interviewed in Colorado learned this lesson the hard way—the site they booked raised their prices 15% just weeks before their event.

𝒯𝑜𝑝 𝑀𝑜𝑛𝑒𝑦-𝑠𝑎𝑣𝑖𝑛𝑔 𝒮𝑒𝑐𝑟𝑒𝑡𝑠

1 **Find a site where you can bring in an outside caterer.** Outside caterers are not only more affordable but many times offer higher-quality food and beverage service than caterers at hotels or other sites. The big savings for you is the caterer's lower overhead. Outside caterers may let you buy liquor at wholesale, provide rentals at cost and basically provide more food for the dollar. Best of all: outside caterers usually don't have lots of "nickel-and-dime" charges.

2 **Hold the reception in mid-afternoon.** A wedding reception at one or two in the afternoon will be much less expensive than evening affairs. Why? Guests will already have had lunch and won't be expecting a six-course, sit-down meal.

3 **Go ethnic.** Surprisingly, certain ethnic cuisines are affordable alternatives to traditional wedding fare. Chinese, Mexican, Italian and barbecue are crowd pleasers and, happily, 20% to 30% less than fancier, haute cuisine. Dress up an ethnic buffet with food stations (a design-your-own quesadilla bar or pasta station, for example) that lend some pizzazz to the meal. Instead of an open bar, tie in affordable alcohol alternatives (margaritas for a Mexican buffet, bottles of Chianti for an Italian meal) to save even more money.

4 **Consider a wedding brunch or luncheon.** Ever been to a restaurant and noticed the exact same menu is less money at lunch than dinner? The same rule often holds true for wedding receptions. Brunch or lunch is often less expensive because the food/beverage items are less pricey than what's served at dinner. Portions are also smaller too, as is alcohol consumption.

5 **Have a dessert reception.** Why not skip all those other boring courses and cut to the chase: have a dessert-only reception. A Chicago bride told us how she pulled that off: her late evening ceremony (9 pm) was followed by a reception for 200 guests that featured a lavish buffet of desserts. On the menu: a fondue of fresh fruits, torts, cheesecakes, an ice cream bar, and favorite dessert recipes from relatives, along with the traditional wedding cake. An espresso bar with flavored coffees provided refreshments. Sound expensive? Not really. Since there wasn't a full meal served, she saved $2500. (To avoid any confusion, it's appropriate to add on your invitation or reception card "Dessert Reception Following.") This tip might work best at a civic or independent site where you can bring in your own catering; facilities with large catering minimums (hotels, country clubs) may balk at this concept, especially during peak wedding months.

6 Avoid Saturdays, if you can. Some caterers have reduced rate-packages for Fridays and Sundays with 10% (or more) discounts. (The only bummer: some rental places may charge extra fees or overtime charges to deliver on Sundays.) Another way to save: some caterers have discounted rates for off-peak times of the year like April or November. One groom in New York City told us their reception site on Long Island had an off-peak rate that saved them $19 per guest for the very same menu. By moving their wedding date back one weekend, they were now in the "off-peak" season—and saved big. A tip: most sites don't advertise their "winter season discounts." You have to ask.

7 Negotiate. Yes, you can haggle with most caterers and reception facilities. Those written menus aren't cast in stone. If the caterer gives you a proposal for $58 per guest, ask what he or she can do for $50. If a competitor offers you a great freebie, ask if the facility will match the competition. Like all negotiations, you want to be reasonable and recognize that your leverage to get a good deal may depend on the date/time of year for your wedding.

Clever alternatives to an open bar

With the soaring cost of booze and worry over drunken driving, many couples are looking for alternatives to the standard-issue open bar at receptions. In San Diego, one of our readers had a wedding that featured an espresso bar with a selection of flavored coffees. Other couples are forsaking hard liquor for bars that serve a selection of micro-brewed beers, sparking waters, and other creative ideas. Go to any wedding in San Antonio, Texas and you'll probably see a frozen margarita machine humming away. All of these ideas are less expensive than the traditional open bar.

8 **Ask for the manager/owner.** The best way to negotiate a deal is to go to the top—ask to speak to the manager or owner of the facility. Yes, that smiling sales rep says she can get you the best deal . . . but it is often the manager or owner of the facility that makes the final decision.

9 **Avoid "budget-busting" menu items.** Certain food items are extremely expensive and can bust your budget. Two common examples are shrimp and beef tenderloin, while chicken is almost universally affordable. If you still want to have a "budget buster," get creative. Can't afford cocktail shrimp? Go for shrimp toast or a shrimp salad. Another tip: stay with fruits and vegetables that are in-season. Putting chocolate-dipped strawberries on the menu for a December reception will cost you a pretty penny.

10 **Choose items that aren't "labor intensive."** Certain hors d'oeuvres may be made of simple ingredients but require painstaking labor to assemble. For example, hors d'oeuvres like "Boursin cheese piped into Chinese pea pods" take a long time to prepare since the cheese has to be hand-piped into the pea pods. Caterers pass along that labor cost to you.

11 **Avoid the word "wedding."** As we mentioned in the reception site chapter, you can save money by *initially* telling a caterer that the event you're planning is a "family function" (reunion, anniversary, etc). That way, you get to see the "regular" menus, which (surprise) may be much less expensive than the "bridal packages."

12 **Forget bridal packages.** Most contain pricey items you don't need. One conference planner (who was also a bride-to-be) gave us this tip: it may be much more affordable to buy items like hors d'oeuvres a la carte. A good rule of thumb is eight to ten hors d'oeuvres per guest (less if your reception is outside standard meal times). If you've got 100 guests, then you need 800 to 1000 pieces of hors d'oeuvres. Our reader said she saved 25% by ordering a la carte (100 egg rolls, 200 beef skewers, etc.). Remember that what's considered an hors d'oeuvre can vary from region to region. In the Northeast, these may be tiny items (like cheese puffs) served during a cocktail hour before a sit-down dinner. In the South, they may be more substantial selections (referred to as "heavy hors d'oeuvres"; an example—Virginia ham on biscuits).

13 **For buffet and hors d'oeuvres receptions, have the caterer's staff serve the items instead of letting the guests serve themselves.** This will control the amount of food served (and hence, the cost). When guests serve themselves, the food always seems to go much quicker (wonder why)!

14 **Buy your own liquor, if possible.** While most hotels, catering halls and country clubs don't let you do this, other sites may permit you to buy your own liquor. The savings of buying liquor at or near wholesale prices will be tremendous (up to 50% to 70% off "retail" prices). Ask the caterer if they will refer you to a good wholesaler in your area. Or check out wholesale clubs like Sam's, Costco or BJ's—many sell beer, wine and spirits by the case at fantastic prices (see the box later in this chapter for more details). When you buy by the case, you can normally negotiate lower prices than retail. Some liquor suppliers may even let you return unopened bottles for full credit. (Check to see if they will allow the same return of unopened beer and wine bottles; some may not allow returns because of damage that might occur when beer or wine is chilled). One note of caution: most beverages must be chilled prior to the reception, so plan ahead.

Cheap vs. expensive wines?

Can average folks tell the difference between expensive and inexpensive wine? That question was recently answered in a study by the scholarly journal, *Proceedings of the National Academy of Sciences*. (We know, you read that all the time).

Researchers gave test subjects expensive and inexpensive wines and then measured their brain activity. Sure enough, the people who drank the expensive wine reported that it tasted better.

The only problem? It was the same wine!

Of course, all wine isn't the same—but even ardent wine drinkers are hard-pressed to tell the difference between so-called premium wine and the cheap stuff. A 2003 study by the Oenonomy Society discovered that "80% of wine drinkers could not distinguish between regular and reserve bottles of the identical wine." (*Wall Street Journal*, July 31, 2008). "The reserve offerings are made from the best grapes in a crop. So only one-fifth of the drinkers have palates sensitive enough to detect the reserve's superiority. Why, though, should the other 80% pay premium prices for a reserve bottle when they can't tell the difference?"

The take-home message: go for the most affordable wine on the reception site's list. Unless your friends and relatives are master sommeliers, your guests won't know the difference.

15 **Provide your own bar service.** In some cases, "free-lance" bartenders are cheaper than the caterers' own staff. If the caterer allows you to have your own bar service, do a cost comparison between the two options. On the other hand, some caterers may not allow freelance bartenders because of liability concerns. What about having a friend or relative tend bar? We don't recommend tapping Uncle Joe to do bar service. An amateur will waste more in booze than you'd save in bartender fees; skilled bartenders are more efficient at the task.

Deals at Wholesale Clubs and Gourmet Supermarkets

Liquor prices too much for your wedding budget to swallow? Full-service catering charges too high to stomach? Consider two alternatives that offer great deals: wholesale clubs and gourmet supermarkets.

Yes, you know wholesale clubs like Sam's, Costco and BJ's offer cut-rate prices on everything from electronics to groceries. Slightly less well known: most clubs fully stocked liquor departments where you can buy in case quantity at fantastic discounts. Costco has prices 15% to 30% below regular liquor stores. Name brands of wine, beer and spirits are available by the case at fantastic prices. If you're hiring a caterer who will let you purchase your own liquor, be sure to get a quote from a local wholesale club.

Another tip: in some states, you do not even have to be a member in order to buy liquor from a wholesale club. A reader in California pointed out that state law there forbids the charging of a membership fee to purchase liquor at such clubs. So, at a Costco or Sam's in California, all you need is an ID in order to get an "alcohol pass" to shop the store.

While many wholesale clubs have been adding liquor and groceries, supermarkets have remade themselves into "gourmet markets" with full-service catering departments. We've spoken to brides who have found affordable catering options for small at-home receptions at a local gourmet supermarket—and they found the quality to be excellent. Many markets also have pastry chefs on staff that can whip up a respectable wedding cake. With full-service floral departments as well, some markets offer an affordable one-stop shopping service. Prices for catering, cakes and flowers tend to be about 10% to 20% below retail.

16 **Don't move those hors d'oeuvres!** Having hors d'oeuvres passed on silver trays may look elegant but watch out! One Florida wedding planner told us about venues that charge exorbitant prices for "passed hors d'oeuvres." The more affordable alternative is to keep them stationary–scattered about the room at "stations" in chafing dishes. Of course, these exorbitant prices aren't the rule everywhere. A Wisconsin wedding planner told us there is no premium price for passed hors d'oeuvres in her area; as a result, she highly recommends them to keep guests from over-indulging at a buffet table. The bottom line: compare costs for these two options carefully to get the best deal.

17 **One word: chicken.** Yes, it sounds like a cliché, but chicken is almost always cheaper than any other wedding entrée–especially beef or seafood. Even when done in a fancy preparation, chicken is often HALF the cost of steak.

18 **Steer clear of course overkill.** For sit-down dinners, do you really need to serve both hors d'oeuvres and an appetizer? Or soup and salad? Some brides eliminate a dessert course and let the wedding cake suffice. Another money-saver: DON'T offer a choice of entrees at sit-down dinners. Some sites will charge a premium for this option.

19 **Slash the alcohol bill.** If you still want to have that traditional open bar, there are a couple ways to save money. First, use only house brands instead of pricey "call" brands for hard liquor. Here's another smart tip: if you're having a cocktail hour, serve affordable hors d'oeuvres to lower alcohol consumption (people drink less when they're munching egg rolls). Finally, close the bar early, say an hour or so before the reception ends. Have less expensive soft drinks or punch (or a coffee bar) available for the rest of the reception. Some couples only have an open bar during a cocktail hour; then wine is served with dinner and coffee/soft drinks are available thereafter. Another idea: some hotels and catering halls offer flat-rate packages for beverages. Instead of being billed per drink ordered, you pay a flat fee per guest. This might be a more affordable alternative.

20 **Hire a student.** Got a culinary school in town? See if you can hire a student(s) to cater your reception. A bride in Illinois called the Cooking Hospitality Institute of Chicago (888) 295-7222 (Web: chic.edu) and found graduate students will do her wedding for a fraction of what "professional" caterers charge. Sometimes these schools have their own restaurants, which might be another contact point. CookingSchools.com and Petersons.com/culinary are two web sites for finding a cooking school near you.

21 **Go for a keg.** A keg of beer is equal to about SEVEN cases of beer. The bottom line: you save about 50% on beer if you use a keg instead of bottles. Worried a keg will give your reception all the ambience of a college frat party? Don't worry. Most caterers can hide the keg behind the bar and use a carbon dioxide tapper system to draw the beer. Another caterer trick: boxed wine. Pour boxed wine into carafes and you'll save 50% over bottled wine. Avoid having multiple selections of wine available on tables; that adds dramatically to costs since much of it is wasted.

22 **Just do a champagne toast.** Even the cheapest champagne is very expensive—bubbly has a higher cost per portion than even a mixed drink using premium liquor. Offering champagne through-out the entire evening is a budget buster. A better alternative: just have a champagne toast (that is a single glass per guest at the appointed time). Or skip it altogether.

23 **Buy your champagne December 30th.** Reader Sara M. of Camanche, Iowa discovered this great way to save: she bought all of the champagne for her wedding right before New Year's Eve. She paid just $10 for a box of three bottles of champagne at Sam's Club. Stores often do champagne specials right before New Year's Eve at prices you won't find after January 1. Buy it in advance and save! FYI: if you follow this tip, store the champagne in a cool dark place around 55 degrees. It should not be refrigerated until just before the wedding.

24 **Cap it.** If you want an open bar but don't want to go bank-rupt because your guests drink like fish, consider capping the bar amount. That is, you have an open bar until you hit X dollars in spending (the bartender keeps a running tab), after which the bar is closed. You can serve soft drinks or coffee after that point in time.

25 **The signature drink.** Instead of a full open bar, just serve ONE signature drink that best matches the evening's menu. A mojito? An appletini? The signature drink is a clever way to put your personal stamp on a reception ... and save money at the same time. It's much cheaper to serve the signature drink (and perhaps a few non-alcohol alternatives) than a full open bar. One bride in Seattle told us she saved $1700 with this tip alone! Tip: match the drink color to the theme of your reception!

26 **Go magnum.** A magnum is a wine bottle that's twice the size of a regular bottle. If you are bringing in your own wine and paying a corking fee, go for a wine that's in these larger bottles. You'll save on corkage fees and the wine will be cheaper to boot (the price per ounce is less in magnums, as you might guess).

27 **Close the bar at dinnertime.** In many big cities, reception sites charge you for every hour a bar is open. But if you are planning a sit-down dinner, there is one sure way to save: close the bar during dinner (re-open it after the meal). One Chicago bride found she could save $3000 by shutting down the bar during dinner (wine was served with dinner). Most folks don't use the bar during dinner, so why pay for it?

28 **A bar count isn't your guest count.** Many facilities charge you per guest, per hour for alcohol. But remember there will be many guests who don't drink (guests under 21, pregnant or religious non-drinkers, etc). Hence the number of guests drinking alcohol (a BAR count) will be lower than the total number of guests (the GUEST count). Be as accurate with this count as possible, as you don't want to pay for alcohol for non-drinkers!

29 **Stay in season.** Choosing hors d'oeuvres and entrees with ingredients that are in season can shave 10% to 20% off food costs. Ditto for alcohol: a spiced, warm cider for a fall wedding fits the weather . . . and your budget if you forgo a full open bar.

30 **Save on alcohol; splurge on mixers.** Choosing a high quality margarita mix can mask the flavor of a lower-priced tequila. The same goes for other mixers such as juices, and syrups. Spend a bit more here and you can save by getting less-expensive grades of alcohol. Overall, you come out ahead.

31 **Instead of champagne, consider Italian and Spanish sparkling wines.** Prosecco from Italy, Espumante from Portugal and cava from Spain are sparkling wines that give you big bang for the buck. Most are under $15. You get the same look and feel as champagne at less than half the price.

How to feed 100 for $100

How much food do you need to feed 100 guests? 200 guests? You can find the information on line at lotsofinfo.tripod.com/wed-dinghelp.html. The page offers impressive tips on "feeding 100 for $100," as well as calculations for how much you need to serve at a buffet and how to figure beverage amounts.

Also recommended: "Secrets From a Caterer's Kitchen" by Nicole Aloni ($14; available at Amazon.com). Bon Appétit magazine called this book a winner, saying "the chapter called 'What Every Caterer Knows' and the detailed food-quantity and beverage-service charts make it invaluable!"

32 **Comfort foods.** Forget haute cuisine, which usually comes with an equally haute price tag. La Jolla, CA caterer Melissa Barrad (I Do . . . Weddings!; sdweddingplanner.com) points out that comfort foods are a great way to save: "It may seem silly, but mac n' cheese served in a martini glass with a beautiful garnish can be fun, inventive and reasonably priced."

Biggest Myths about Catering

MYTH #1 *"Maybe you can settle an argument I'm having with my mother. If I invite fewer guests, will my catering bill will go down dramatically?"*

Well, yes and no. Obviously, fewer mouths to feed will have an impact on your total bill. However, if you invite fewer guests, the price *per person* may go up. Why? That's because a large part of the per-per-

---

REAL WEDDING TIP

Affordable linens

Reader Virginia H. found a way to cut her rental bill for her reception linens by 40%:

"I checked with several party rental companies regarding rental of table linens, and I kept looking at a bill of about $600 to $800. I couldn't believe that companies in my area wanted at least $22 to rent a single tablecloth, or $2 to rent a napkin. I was certain I could buy them for the same or less.

"I finally found DeNormandie linens (denormandie.com; 773-731-8010). Boy, are they a find. It is a small company based in Chicago, operated by the same family for over 100 years. They custom made me new tablecloths for both my five-foot rounds and eight-foot rectangular tables for about the same price as I could have rented. Delivery took one week. Plus I had a huge choice of colors to choose from. The quality is nice, too . . . a non-wrinkling wash and wear fabric, but very nice to the touch. As for napkins, DeNormandie sold me 100 lightly used damask napkins in sage green for $1 each. I thought they would go nicely with the cloths, but DeNormandie told me that if I didn't like them together, just to ship them back for a refund. I ended up spending a total of about $450 on my table linens."

son price a caterer quotes you is "fixed." Fixed costs include the caterer's overhead, kitchen facilities, etc. No matter how many guests you invite, caterers still have to pay these administrative expenses. Hence, you're paying for more than just the food. Most caterers have an unwritten base price or minimum that engaged couples must pay—no matter how many guests they want to invite.

MYTH #2 *"Buffets are always less expensive than sit-down dinners. At least that's what several caterers keep telling me."*

This is one those great debates that has no right answer. The bottom line: the cost of a reception is often *what* you serve rather than how you serve it. A basic sit-down chicken dinner will be cheaper than a fancy buffet with shrimp, sliced beef tenderloin and other pricey dishes. Conversely, a five-course lobster sit-down dinner may cost several times more than a simple buffet with hors d'oeuvres like fruit, cheese and sandwiches.

We've noticed that caterers tend to steer couples toward the type of reception they do most often. Therefore, a caterer who frequently does buffet receptions will tell you (surprise) a sit-down dinner is too expensive. In the Northeast (where sit-downs dinners are most common),

---

REAL WEDDING TIP

Liquor price sticker shock

Recent bride Samantha D. of Canton, Michigan was amazed at the cost of liquor when she priced her reception:

"What is it with liquor prices? I almost fell out of my chair when I contacted a restaurant in Wyandotte, Michigan (just outside of Detroit). The reception costs were average for the area, however the bar costs almost made me want to elope.

"I was informed that their bar costs were done on a 'per bottle' basis and they would also pro-rate any bottles that weren't completely used. So far, it doesn't sound bad. However, then came the price per bottle—starting at $95 PER BOTTLE! My next question—how big are these bottles? The site said they were just average size bottles. Say what?! They wanted to charge me $95 for a bottle of alcohol, that I could buy in a store for anywhere for less than $20! That's outrageous!"

---

caterers will advise just the opposite.

Of course, you can combine both types of receptions if you prefer. A "seated buffet" is set up like a sit-down dinner, with tables and chairs for every guest. Waiters serve the salad or first course at the table, while the main dishes are served buffet style.

MYTH #3 *"Aren't plastic plates more affordable than glass?"*

Nope. In many cases, the cost of renting glass is actually almost as affordable as using plastic! Besides looking nicer, glass doesn't have the negative environmental impact caused by throwing away plastics. Ask your caterer to do a cost comparison between plastic and glass.

MYTH #4 *"Guests always drink and eat more at weddings than any other party."*

This myth is circulated by caterers to justify higher prices for weddings than other types of parties like corporate events, retirement parties and the like. We don't buy it. Why? Almost any host today (whether a bride or corporate party planner) buys catering packages based on consumption. That is, you buy 100 pieces of an hors d'oeuvre, 125 chicken dinners, etc. Most bars are also billed on consumption (per drink). Therefore, when a caterer says they charge more for weddings because guests are pigs, it rings hollow to us. Why is the same chicken dinner for a wedding 30% more than a corporate party? Do wedding guests really eat 30% more food?

Helpful Hints

1 **Make sure the catering representative who planned your reception will be there the night of the wedding.** Hotel catering staff are sometimes guilty of not showing up to make sure everything is right. If you contract with a smaller, off-premise caterer, make sure the owner is there. Obviously, the owner may not be able to be at your wedding reception every minute, but there should be a clear chain of command in case a problem arises.

2 **Have the caterer prepare you a going-away package.** Believe it or not, you probably won't get to taste any of the food at your reception. You'll be too busy shaking hands, giving hugs, posing for pictures, etc. Considering the amount of money you're spending, ask the caterer to prepare a going-away package with a sample of the evening's menu (don't forget to include the cake!). You and your fiancé will probably be starved when you leave the reception!

Green your wedding catering

"Going green" is a big trend in weddings and catering is no exception. But how do you green your wedding's reception?

Start by going local—ask your caterer to use locally sourced fruit and veggies that are in season. (Okay, this is easier said than done for certain locales—Maine in February doesn't have much locally grown fruit. But since most weddings are in the summer and fall, this is usually do-able).

Of course, anyone who's shopped at Whole Foods knows that organic foods can be pricey. But you can save by stressing to the caterer to use in-season items. A savvy caterer can hold down costs by working with local vendors to get the best deals.

Other ways of greening your wedding catering: avoid disposable plates or cups (instead, rent glass or china). Also: a green caterer should be dialed into recycling and composting any consumables at the wedding. And forget favors, those little trinkets that often get thrown away after the wedding. Instead, donate to your favorite environmental cause on behalf of your guests.

One reader pointed out that some cities and counties have laws that prohibit caterers from allowing you to take home leftovers. Rebecca, a bride from Minnesota, noted that it wasn't allowed in her state because the caterer could be held liable for any illness that results from the consumption of that food. Check with your caterer to determine the regulations in your area.

3 **Carefully budget food and liquor amounts.** No, guessing how much food or beverage you should budget for a reception is NOT an exact science. For hors d'oeuvres, one caterer suggested budgeting eight to ten hors d'oeuvres per guest for a one-hour cocktail reception. A Wisconsin wedding planner provided us with this rule of thumb to budget how many drinks guests will consume at an open bar: 2.5 drinks the first hour, 1.5 drinks the second hour and one drink per hour thereafter. Hence, for a four-hour reception, you should budget five drinks per guest. Wow! Do people really drink that much at wedding receptions? No, the caterer told us. Remember that you are charged for the number of drinks *ordered*, not consumed. "So, when Uncle Joe can't remember what he did with his nearly full drink, he figures it's 'free' and he just gets another one," the caterer said.

Pitfalls to Avoid

PITFALL #1 FROZEN FOOD.

"We went to a friend's reception last weekend at a hotel. I know the bride spent a lot of money, but the food was just so-so.

In our opinion, too many hotels have mediocre food. The culprit? Frozen food. Bought in bulk, frozen versions of mini-egg rolls and mini-quiche are mainstays on some reception site menus. Obviously, it is cheaper (and hence more profitable for the site) to buy these items frozen and quickly warm them in chafing dishes than to painstakingly make the same items from scratch. The problem? Besides obviously tasting "frozen," caterers who use frozen food often aren't any less expensive than those who hand-make food from scratch ingredients. If the food at your reception is one of your high priorities, shop carefully for a caterer who doesn't use shortcuts.

PITFALL #2 THE INFAMOUS CAKE-CUTTING FEE.

"Boy, am I steamed! The reception site I chose for my wedding said they would charge me $1 per person to cut my wedding cake. After spending thousands of dollars on food and liquor, I think they're trying to wring every last nickel from me!"

WE COULDN'T AGREE MORE! Boy, this is our number one pet peeve with caterers and reception sites. Some of these guys have the audacity to charge you a ridiculously high fee to cut your wedding cake. Ranging anywhere from $1 to $3 per guest, this "fee" supposedly covers the labor involved to cut the cake, as well as the plates, forks, etc. The real reason some reception sites charge this fee is to penalize you for bringing in a cake from an outside baker (instead of having the site bake it for you). Even more amazing are some sites that don't even bake wedding cakes themselves but still charge cake-cutting fees! Talk about abusive.

We say if you are spending thousands of dollars on food and liquor, the caterer or reception site should NOT tack on $100 to $400 more just for the privilege of cutting and serving the wedding cake! First of all, you are already paying a mandatory service gratuity to have staff present at the reception. Hence, the cake-cutting fee is double charging. Secondly, do you really think they pay the cake-cutter $100 to $400 for 30 minutes of work? We suggest you try to negotiate away this charge—don't forget that everything is always negotiable.

(Note: some caterers or sites try to sneak in the cost of serving coffee into the cake-cutting fee. We suggest you tell the caterer to forget the cake-cutting fee and just price the coffee out separately. If the site still insists on a cake-cutting fee, try to negotiate a flat fee, say $50 or $75, instead of a per guest charge.)

PITFALL #3 CORKING FEES AND THE LIQUOR THAT RUNNETH OVER.

"My friend had her reception at a country club that seemed to push liquor on the guests. Every five minutes, they went around to the guests and pitched more drinks. I also understand they charged the couple for every bottle that was opened! Isn't this a bit excessive?"

Not only excessive but also quite expensive. When couples are charged based on the number of $90 bottles of wine or champagne that are opened, one mad staffer with a corkscrew can inflict heavy financial damage. Such charges (called corking fees) are perhaps one of the biggest cost pitfalls of any wedding reception. That's because couples must pay for any opened bottles whether or not they were poured! Think you can just re-cork the bottles and bring them home? Think again—most sites prevent the removal of liquor from the premises.

In a different twist on the same problem, some sites push drinks on guests when the bar is "open" (that is, the engaged couple pays for each drink). Liquor is the biggest money-making area for sites like hotels and catering halls, and hence the temptation to push booze or open unneeded bottles is too great for some.

The solution to the corking fee pitfall is to give the caterer or reception site a LIMIT on the number of bottles they can open. Tell them to confer with you before they go beyond that limit. Get that detail in writing.

Another version of this scam surfaced in California. We spoke with a former employee of a catering company who admitted they brought *empty* bottles to receptions! Since the liquor charges were based on the number of empty bottles at the end of the evening, the caterer was able to pad the bill. Solution: if you are paying by the bottle, we recommend you count the bottles at the beginning of the evening and again at the end. If there are 100 full bottles at the start, there better not be 125 bottles (80 empty and 45 full) at the end.

Sites can also inflate the liquor tab by picking up half-full glasses, forcing guests who have just returned from the dance floor to go back to the bar to get something to drink. One wedding planner we spoke to suggested couples should explicitly tell catering managers to make sure the wait staff is not overzealous in clearing half-full glasses. Instead, instruct sites and caterers to only clear "complete" (empty) classes.

PITFALL #4 GRATUITOUS GRATUITIES AND SALES TAXES.

"When we saw the final bill for our reception, the facility charged us a 'gratuity fee' on everything including the room charge! Is this kosher?"

Many facilities look at the gratuity as "extra profit," not something that is paid to the staff. One bride in California called in the above story, where the facility was charging an 18% gratuity on the *room rental fee*, of all things (this worked out to an extra $300). In our opinion, the gratuity should only be charged on the food and beverage. (We should note in some states it is illegal to charge a mandatory gratuity on the liquor tab—as an alternative to the gratuity, facilities often charge bartender or bar set-up fees.) Placing a gratuity on other charges (like room rental, valet parking, coat check) is price gouging.

Another similar rip-off is the "double-charging" of labor. In Denver, for example, many caterers charge both a gratuity and a "labor fee." While the staff generally gets the gratuity, the owners usually pocket the labor charge. As a result of this double charging, couples are being socked with an effective 25% gratuity rate on receptions! (No, double charging for labor isn't illegal, but it still stinks).

What about sales tax? In some states, food and beverage is taxable. A few cities or counties even slap sales tax on labor charges like the gratuity and other services. Since the sales tax rate can be nearly 10% in some locales, this can add to the bill in a hurry. Be forewarned: some brides have told us that their sites have slapped sales tax on items like room rental that were clearly *not taxable*. Why? Maybe it's just sloppy bookkeeping. Or they may be pocketing the tax to pay for that Mercedes parked out front. If you have any questions on what's taxable and what's not, check with your local city or county government.

The state of California (always on the forefront of taxing everything that moves) has an inventive way of viewing this controversy. California law draws a distinction between a voluntary "tip or gratuity" and a mandatory "service charge." Basically, the state determines that voluntary tips are NOT subject to sales tax—but mandatory service charges (such as those 20% whoppers charged by California hotels) are. Adding insult to injury, the state also considers such items as corking fees and cake cutting charges as mandatory (and hence, taxable).

The best advice: watch out for all these sneaky charges and taxes. Be sure to question any item that looks strange.

Pitfall #5 Price rise surprise!

"I booked my reception site a year in advance and we agreed on a certain price per guest. One month before my wedding, the catering manager informed me of a 20% price increase and pointed to the fine print in their contract. Is this fair?"

Several readers tell us they've been stung by surprise price increases. Ironically, their own advance planning may trip up these couples—they booked their wedding site so far in advance that the facility wouldn't guarantee a price for food and liquor.

Instead, these couples received a written proposal and contract that included a "price escalation" clause. This enabled the site or caterer to raise the price with little or no notice. Obviously, that can be a painful lesson for brides and grooms who get socked with unexpected extra costs.

Certainly, the best course of action is to get a firm price guarantee. If that's not possible, try to negotiate a "reasonable" price increase cap in the contract—paying a small 5% increase isn't fun, but it's much better than being surprised with a 20% surcharge.

Never agree to a menu where the price for an item is "market price" at the time of the wedding. That leaves you exposed to a huge bill in

---

REAL WEDDING TIP

Liquor slight of hand

Lisa M. of Phoenix, Arizona wrote to us about a scam she encountered at her wedding: her caterer "forgot" about the paid-for bottles of wine the couple provided for guests and instead charged guests for drinks:

"We arranged with our caterer to buy 24 bottles of wine for our guests to enjoy at no charge to them. We followed your advice about counting the bottles before and after, and a good thing. The problem: our caterers hid the free-to-our guests bottles of wine below the bar shelf and sold people $5 glasses of boxed wine from clearly visible boxes! They obviously made more money from selling the wine by the glass instead pouring our bottles. So, only five bottles of our 24 were opened, but the caterer had an invoice for 24 bottles ready for us to pay at the end of the evening. Luckily, I had followed your advice, had a friend count the open bottles, and only paid for what we drank. HOWEVER, by charging our guests for their wine, they made us look cheap, as if we hadn't provided wine for our guests, and made more money for themselves. I guess in the future, brides should stipulate with the caterer that the wine provided by the bride and groom be clearly visible, and that other wine be hidden away, to be served only if the guests specifically request it."

Good point—never ASSUME that instructions like this will be followed at your wedding reception. Get it in writing!

case the item's price skyrockets for whatever reason.

Also look out for clauses that let the caterer substitute food items. Insist in the contract the caterer get your written approval *before* any changes to the menu are made by the facility. You want to be reasonable, of course. While a sudden frost in Florida might change your plans for Mimosas, you don't want your caterer or reception facility to start making wholesale substitutions to the menu without your approval.

PITFALL #6 DO-IT-YOURSELF NIGHTMARES.

"My family did all the catering for my sister's wedding. What a disaster! When we arrived at the reception site, the doors were locked so the food had to sit out in our hot cars. The potato salad spoiled and over 100 guests got sick from food poisoning."

Yep, that's a true story from a reader in Corpus Christi, Texas. While it's an extreme example of what can go wrong for those who want to go the do-it-yourself route, there are some important lessons—consider how BIG this task is before taking the plunge. Do you have time to prepare that much food? What about the delivery/set-up and refrigeration of the food before the reception?

If you want to do-it-yourself, you may want to compromise: have a restaurant cater the food. Or pick up prepared items from a grocery store or deli. Yes, this isn't as cheap as whipping up 400 canapés yourself . . . but it may be smarter in the end. Instead of serving the food from plastic trays or containers, dress up your buffet with some nice (rented) silver serving pieces.

Now that you've been inspired to slash the catering bill for your reception, what about photography? After the reception, the cost of photos is a big expense for most couples. In the next chapter, you'll learn how to preserve your memories without going bankrupt!

Ever hire a professional photographer? For most couples, the answer is no. And with over 27,000 wedding and portrait photographers out there, choosing the best one for you and your budget may seem daunting. From key questions to ask to important pitfalls to avoid, this chapter will give you a clear and concise guide to finding a great photographer at an affordable price.

What Are You Buying?

When you hire a professional wedding photographer, there are three main areas where your money goes:

1 Candids: These are the pictures taken at the wedding and reception that are assembled into an album for the bride and groom. Photographers often assemble candid packages for the parents (referred to as parent's albums) and gifts for attendants (usually two or four pictures in a gift folio). Note that parent's albums (usually 20 to 60 pictures) and gift folios are extra and are not included in our average photography tab.

2 Albums: Most photographers offer a wide selection of albums to hold the candids. Leather Craftsman (Leather Craftsmen.com) is but one example. Unfortunately, these albums are also expensive and are sold only by professional photographers. With Leather Craftsman albums, the pictures are mounted to the pages, which are permanently bound in the album. Some photographers skimp by using cheap, vinyl albums with plastic-covered pages. We'll explain later why these cheaper albums can damage your pictures.

The biggest trend in wedding albums: digital albums. Instead of printed photos inserted into album pages, digital albums print the photos right on the album page. See the nearby box for more details.

3 **Portraits:** Pictures taken prior to the wedding day fall into this category. A bridal portrait is a formal portrait of the bride in her wedding gown. Particularly popular in the Southern U.S., bridal portraits are taken in an indoor studio or on location, typically four to six weeks before the wedding. An engagement portrait is a more informal picture of you and your fiancé. This portrait is often used to announce your engagement.

Two expenses are involved with portraits: the sitting fee and the portrait print itself. Sitting fees are charges for the photographer's time and

Digital albums

Digital has made a big impact on photography; now digital has staked a claim on wedding albums. The result is a major sea change to how albums look and we're happy to report it's all for the better. In the past, if you looked at one wedding album, you looked at them all—sure you could change the color of the cover, but the album looked the same . . . printed photos slipped into page sleeves with little gold frames.

Digital has turned that world upside down. Now, you can combine photos, text and graphics on a single page. The result looks more like the pages of a glossy fashion magazine than a wedding album. More and more photographers are offering this option and the cost isn't much different  from old-style print albums. (Hint: see the money saving tips later in this chapter for advice on how to create an affordable digital album yourself).

range from $100 to several hundreds of dollars. The most popular print size is 16x20 and this can cost $500 to $2000, depending on the photographer and city.

Photography customs and traditions vary greatly across the U.S. and Canada. For example, in Sacramento, CA, many couples have a formal portrait taken *after* the reception at one of the area's many parks. In the South, a formal portrait of the bride taken a month before the wedding is often framed and displayed at the reception. In other areas, photographers bring studio-quality lighting systems to the wedding in order to do portraits of the bride and groom before the ceremony. A new trend for portraits: virtual backgrounds. Some photographers are using computer-generated backdrops to add sizzle to their portraits. The bride stands before a green background onto which a computer generated image is projected.

Average total costs: In most U.S. cities, the average tab for professional wedding photography—you might want to sit down—is $2260.

So what does that buy you? That figure just covers your album of candid coverage at your wedding and reception. Keep in mind if you add all sorts of extras (parent's albums, bridal portraits) or if you hire a "celebrity" photographer in a larger city, you could spend several times more than the average ($4000 and up). Couples in the DC area report that many wedding photographers charge $3000 to $6000 on average for their pictures.

No matter where you are, however, the process of selecting pictures is relatively the same. We should note that photographers don't usually talk in plain English, so here are three typical terms you will come across and their translations:

♥ EXPOSURES: Basically this is every time the camera goes click. At least 150 to 200 exposures are taken at the typical wedding and four-hour reception. Be careful of packages that limit the number of exposures below that level. FYI: This is more of an issue with photographers who still shoot on film instead of digital. Digital photographers don't worry about using up expensive film since there isn't any! Hence, they may be willing to take more images at your wedding. One wedding photographer told us he used to shoot 500 images in four hours with a film camera; with a digital camera, he now shoots 800 to 1200 shots in the same period of time.

♥ PROOFS: Digital photography has transformed the way proofs are handled today. In the past, film exposures were developed into proofs. The proofs were often 5x5 pictures from which you chose the final prints that would appear in your album. Unretouched, the proofs chronicled all the pictures that the photographer took at your wedding.

Digital photography has changed this in several ways. Some photographers give a couple a CD with proofs; others present the proofs via a slideshow in their studio. An increasingly popular method is online proofing: Pictage.com and EventPix.com are two of the biggest online proofing sites for weddings. Visit each site to get a feel for how this process works. EventPix.com, for example, has a helpful online demo.

Some photographers use a hybrid method for proofs—they take digital proofs and can create a "magazine proof" book. Here, a photographer prints 12 images on a 10"x15" page and bounds them into a book, creating a mini-magazine. That makes it easier to preview the larger number of images that most photographers take with digital cameras.

♥ **PRINTS:** The proofs are enlarged into final prints. For photographers who use medium format cameras (we'll explain this later), popular enlargement sizes are 5x7, 8x8, 8x10 and 10x10. The final prints are assembled into the album. (As a side note, some photographers offer to sell you the proofs, either individually or incorporated into the wedding

Are wedding photographers overpaid?

What are the ten most overpaid jobs in America? Sure, you could pick the obvious suspects—professional athletes, movie stars, Fortune 500 CEOs . . . but MarketWatch.com went one step further by identifying which *common* professions are over-compensated. And what was #10 on the list? Wedding photographers. (For the curious, others included airport skycaps, orthodontists, and real estate agents who sell high-end homes).

Here's how the site described wedding photographers:

"The overpaid ones are the many who admit they only do weddings for the income, while quietly complaining about the hassle of dealing with hysterical brides and drunken reception guests. They mope through the job with the attitude: 'I'm just doing this for the money until National Geographic calls.'

"Much of their work is mediocre as a result. How often have you really been wowed flipping the pages of a wedding album handed you by recent newlyweds? Annie Leibovitz and Richard Avedon they're not, but some charge fees as if they're in the same league. Photographers who long for the day they can say 'I don't do weddings' should leave the work to the dedicated ones who do."

album). As you'll read later, we recommend purchasing an album package that includes 60 to 80 prints to adequately tell the wedding story. Some of those pictures (say ten to 20) would be enlargements (8x10 or 10x10). The balance would be the smaller 5x5 or 5x7 prints. Exactly how many enlargements you want is a personal preference, but additional enlargements obviously tend to add to the final tab. As we discussed earlier, digital albums are changing the way photographers present their prints—see the box earlier in this chapter for details.

Can you just buy a disk of your wedding photos from the photographer and print them yourself? The answer is typically no. Nearly all photographers make their money selling your finished prints in a fancy album. Giving you a disk would eliminate most of that revenue.

Okay, so now you know the basics of what you are buying. But how do you find a competent, yet affordable, professional wedding photographer in the first place?

As you can imagine, wedding photographers were not thrilled at this. Several lit up message boards with posts, defending their profession's honor and compensation.

Their points? Wedding photography is hardly a one-day job—the prep work does take hours, including those pre-wedding meetings to go over logistics, etc. The actual wedding day is five to eight hours of work, standing on your feet, paying an assistant, etc. Then, thanks to digital technology, there is more post-production work than ever—processing images, designing an album, etc.

But MarketWatch.com has a point when it comes to arrogant photographers—yes, these folks are artists, but they are also providing a service to you, the CUSTOMER. For the big amount of money most photographers command, you should expect professionalism and respect, not attitude and sneers.

And, when it comes down to it, brides and grooms determine the market price for photographers. There is pressure to get the best, because you can't have a "do over" when it comes to the pictures. Even MarketWatch.com acknowledges this: "A lot of people are overpaid because there are certain things consumers just don't want screwed up," the site said. "You wouldn't want to board a plane flown by a second-rate pilot or hire a cheap wedding photographer to record an event you hope happens once in your lifetime."

Sources for Finding a Photographer

Photographers generally fall into two categories, commercial and portrait. While commercial photographers work for advertising agencies and other industrial clients, portrait photographers concentrate on weddings, special occasions, and (as you might guess) portraits. The best wedding photographers are those who specialize in just weddings and portraits, with several years of experience. They should do at least ten to 15 weddings per year. Here are three sources to find the very best wedding photographers:

♥ **RECENTLY-MARRIED COUPLES.** Yep, word-of-mouth referrals are key to finding the best photographers. Ask them how happy they were with the photographer and final prints. Was there anything they would change?

♥ **WEDDING COORDINATORS AT CEREMONY AND RECEPTION SITES.** These people have seen hundreds of wedding photographers come through their door. Ask them who they thought were the best. Of course, their impressions are limited to the photographer's behavior at their particular site. Site coordinators rarely see the final photo album. Nevertheless, their opinions are valuable.

♥ **BRIDAL SHOWS.** These shows (sponsored by local bridal shops and reception sites) often have several exhibits by local photographers. Be aware that these shows may feature young or new photographers who are looking to build their business. Unfortunately, bridal shows also tend to showcase large photography studios whose quality can vary greatly from associate to associate (we'll discuss these studios later). One tip: don't make a snap decision to book a photographer right there at a bridal show. Instead, visit with the photographer after the show at their studio and see more of their work.

Where not to look. Unfortunately, a Google search is *not* a good source for wedding photographers. And forget about local bridal web sites or magazines with ads for photographers. Many of the best wedding photographers do not invest heavily in this type of advertising. In fact, many don't advertise at all, working exclusively by word-of-mouth referral. Some photographers will also put an album of their work in local bridal shops. However, whose work is displayed has more to do with politics than merit.

Best Online Sources

While we don't recommend a generic Google search for wedding photographers in your area, the web can help in several ways. Target your search with the following sites. And then put your wedding pics on the web for guests to see them and order reprints. Here's more detail:

♥ To find a photographer, we suggest two sites: THE PROFESSIONAL PHOTOGRAPHERS OF AMERICA (ppa.com) and WEDDING PHOTOJOURNALIST ASSOCIATION (wpja.com). Each let you search for local photographers.

Readers report they've had success with CRAIGSLIST.ORG in finding affordable local photographers. Click on Services/Creative to read ads from available photographers; or post a query to Gigs/Creative for what you are looking for. Best of all, it's free (our favorite word). Hint: you can also use Craigslist to find more than just photographers; we've also seen hair/make-up artists listed here, as well as other wedding vendors!

♥ Getting your wedding pictures online is simpler than ever. Of course, most folks have two types of wedding photos—those snapped by guests and others taken by a professional photographer. Let's look at each type:

1 **Guest pictures.** Did your guests use their own cameras to help you fill out the candids from your wedding? If so, getting these pictures on the web is relatively easy.

For digital cameras, you can take the media card and upload the pictures to one of several free sties. Perhaps the best-known free photo sharing site is Flickr.com, but there is also PictureTrail (picturetrail.com) and Shutterfly (shutterfly.com). Most let you password-protect your photos so only your friends and relatives can view them.

2 **What about the professional pictures?** As with guest photos, you may want to post professional photos online for family and friends to view and order prints. Yes, this service is available, but in the case of professional photographers, your photographer has to set up the picture preview.

Professionals use several web sites including PhotoReflect.com, Pictage.com, EventPix.com, and Collages.net. See Figure 1 nearby for one example.

All of these services work much the same way. A photographer uploads the pictures to the site, which creates a password-protected web page for your wedding. You email guests with the site address and password. Guests can then view the pictures online and order reprints

FIGURE 1: PhotoReflect.com's main business is to sell wedding picture reprints—but you can also search for photographers.

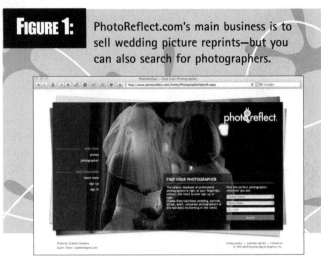

right from the site. Most of these sites are free to photographers; the sites make their money by taking a cut of the reprint revenue.

A few caveats: while some sites have interactive features like guest books, you can't print or email the pictures to others. If you try to save the image to your hard disk, a watermark that says "proof" appears on the image. And beware that some photographers mark-up the reprint prices to sell online. If you or your guests plan to purchase more than a single print online, you might consider contacting the photographer directly for a better price.

Understanding Wedding Photographers: Some Basics

As you shop for a good wedding photographer, there are three key areas that you must always keep in mind:

1 Equipment. Obviously, the quality of equipment the photographer uses is directly related to how good your wedding pictures will look. No matter how talented and personable the photographer is the resulting pictures will be a disappointment if he or she uses an inferior camera.

"I visited a wedding photography studio yesterday that said they use medium format cameras and shoot on film. They said this is better than digital cameras. Is this true?"

Well, that isn't necessarily true or false. To understand why, let's look at the three types of cameras mainly used for wedding photography: digital, medium format cameras and 35 millimeter.

♥ **DIGITAL CAMERAS.** Not more than a few years ago, most wedding photography was shot on film with a medium format camera. No longer—the majority of wedding photographers now shoot with digital cameras.

The digital revolution has radically changed the photography biz, in both big and small ways. An example: lighting. One of the first things photographers learn with digital cameras is that it is easier to work with an underexposed image than overexposed (it is the opposite with film). Why? Software can compensate for underexposed pictures and fix other glitches that previously required expensive manual re-touching.

Speaking of software, the biggest change for wedding photographers in the digital world is using image manipulation software like Adobe Photoshop, as well as electronically transferring the images to album makers for output.

As we discussed earlier, digital albums are opening up a wide range of design possibilities, combining text, graphics and photos in an infinite number of ways. The challenge: the photographer now has to be a graphic artist, using software to create those nifty album pages. Yes, many album companies offer templates and other shortcuts, but there is still a level of design skill required.

Finally, let's talk about the prints. While your album may be digital, you still may want printed photos to frame, give as gifts, etc. In the early days of digital photography and inkjet printers, there were many concerns about print quality and how long prints would last. Good news: in

$5,400 to be a "featured photographer"

When you surf the Knot to find local vendors, you probably realize that "featured" photographers pay to get that honor. But you might be surprised at how much that honor costs.

A photographer blog recently posted the Knot's prices—it costs $450 per month to get that coveted top-featured spot on the Knot's local vendor sections. Yes, that's $5400 a year.

For any wedding photographer, that's a hefty price to pay—and more than some small photographers probably spend on their entire marketing budget for the year. As a result, you probably won't see small photographers featured on the Knot. And those that are featured may have to charge prices to justify the Knot's hefty advertising fees.

the last few years, professional inkjet printers now produce prints that are of "archival quality"—in English, that means they will last for 100 years without fading. That may even outlast machine prints from film cameras, where the average life is 80 years.

♥ **MEDIUM-FORMAT FILM CAMERAS.** No, not all photographers have gone digital. Some are still more comfortable with film cameras—and the most popular type of film camera for weddings is medium format.

The main distinction between medium format cameras and 35mm is their negative size: a medium format's square negative is usually $2^1/_4$ by $2^1/_4$ inches. This provides much clearer photos when prints are enlarged. Medium-format cameras produce pictures that have richer depth, warmer colors and sharper contrasts than 35mm cameras. (To be technical, the warmth of a photograph is determined by the amount of flash light. However, medium-format cameras deliver pictures with more color saturation than 35mm. Color saturation relates to the richness of color in the print).

The Hasselblad is the Mercedes of medium format cameras. This camera (which was used by everyone from NASA to Ansel Adams) is still

Proofless Studios: How Some Photographers Use the 'Net to Speed the Delivery of Wedding Albums

In the ancient days of wedding photography (like before 2000), brides and grooms first had to look at dozens of printed "proofs" to assemble their albums. Trying to judge what a picture would look like cropped or enlarged was difficult—and the wait to get the proofs and the final album sometimes stretched into weeks. Or months.

New digital technologies have made this process quicker and easier, for both photographers and couples. Thanks to digital proofing and online ordering systems, final albums can be delivered to couples in a matter of days, instead of weeks or months.

Here's how it works: after the wedding, a photographer sends his film to a lab. The lab then scans the film negatives and creates digital pictures which are downloaded by the photographer off the 'net—all in a matter of days. (Of course, if your photographer shoots with a digital camera, he or she doesn't have to go through the above process.)

in use by wedding photographers. Bowing to pressure form digital photography, however, the company that makes the Hasselblad ceased production of the namesake film camera in 2013.

FYI: Another popular medium-format camera is the Bronica.

We should note in passing that there are also several larger-format cameras that produce even bigger negatives (and hence, greater color saturation) than standard medium-format. Cameras such as the Mamiya RB67 are considered the ultimate camera in this category. That camera takes a negative that is 6cm by 7cm.

One final tip about cameras: the best medium format cameras for weddings have a "leaf" shutter, instead of "focal plane." This enables flash-fill outside in the bright sun and prevents the bride's white dress from washing out. The leaf shutter allows a photographer to properly balance shadows. Most medium format camera makers sell both types of shutters, so it might be worth it to ask the photographer which type he uses.

♥ **35 MILLIMETER FILM CAMERAS:** This type of camera is being rapidly replaced by digital for wedding photography, but you still may find a

Next, the photographer uses a software program to create your album. Then, the pictures are shown to you. Most photographers will create a slide show with all your photos. Then you are presented with a suggested album layout (again on computer), complete with possible enlargements, mattes, crops and so on.

Many digital photographers use online proofing or give you a CD of the proofs or suggested album. As we mentioned earlier in this chapter, other photographers are using online reprint web sites to let your guests view and order pictures off the 'net. The days of passing around a proof book are numbered.

One caution to this "proofless" system: some photographers try to up-sell you by presenting a virtual album of, say, 100 pictures when your package just includes 75 shots. Photographers know showing you the possible album with all the enlargements and extra pictures convinces many consumers to pony up more money. If you want to stick with your budget, tell the photographer to construct the proposed album with the number of prints in your package—and no more.

few die-hard photojournalists using 35 mm film cameras. Why?

Photographers who are fans of 35mm point out that the quick action of the shutter on 35mm cameras lets them take more candid-style pictures (so-called photojournalism-style). They also say the equipment and film has improved dramatically in recent years, closing the quality gap with more expensive cameras.

The biggest rap on 35mm is the negative size—the smaller negative size means pictures blown up bigger than an 8x10 look grainy. Other photographers also say 35mm pictures look flat and the colors are not as vibrant compared to medium format.

This debate is becoming increasingly moot, however, as more photographers shift to digital.

For the curious, how do photographers who shoot on digital blow up their pictures to wall portrait size? Most use a PhotoShop plug-in called Perfect Resize by onOne software that enables digital photos to grow without losing resolution.

"Well, now I'm confused. Should I hire a photographer who uses a digital or medium format camera? Or 35mm?"

The key is to look at the pictures.

Also, consider the *style* of wedding photography you want. If you'd like a heavy emphasis on candid or spontaneous pictures, a photographer with a digital or 35mm camera might be a best bet. Traditionalists who like a more posed look should consider a photographer who shoots on medium-format. Since most formal bridal portraits are enlarged to 16x20 (or larger), these should always be shot with a medium-format camera.

Why do some wedding photographers use digital or 35mm cameras? One reason: money. These cameras cost several hundred dollars. Medium format cameras cost several *thousand* dollars—each. For example, a completely outfitted Hasselblad (camera, lenses, lights, flash) can cost from $10,000 to $15,000. Obviously, amateur photographers opt for the cheaper digital or 35mm cameras when they are starting out.

Of course, some professional photographers PREFER 35mm and digital cameras. Why? Because these cameras are smaller and less obtrusive. This enables the photographer to achieve that hip "photojournalist" style now the rage. One such photographer told us she uses a Leica RangeFinder, which is sort of like the Hasselblad of small-format cameras. "It looks like a toy but it costs a fortune ($3000 for a body and lens) because the lenses are so great. This makes it perfect for shooting during the ceremony, toasts or other quiet private moments. It is also great in low light because it can be handheld at slower shutter speeds." Her point is well taken: negative size and image sharpness is not everything. Capturing the moment as it happens may be more important and smaller format cameras provide that flexibility: "From my point of view, a big camera, a big flash, and an assistant or two to hold them just makes the photographer intrusive," she said.

Another key point: just as important as the camera is the lighting equipment. Lighting techniques often separate the amateurs from the pros. Amateurs will use only a flash mounted on the camera—the resulting pictures are flat and of poor quality. Professional wedding photographers will use a powerful flash placed about 45 degrees to the side of the subject. The resulting light provides shadows and depth. Some photographers will add one or more flashes aimed at the background. A California photographer told us he even puts light behind posed groups and dancing couples to give his pictures additional depth.

Who holds all these extra flashes? Usually it's an assistant. Many pros have one at their side the entire day. Not only does the assistant hold the additional flashes, but he or she also makes sure the photographer doesn't miss any detail. In Dallas, Texas, we found one expert photographer who brings *two* assistants to each and every wedding.

2 **Skill:** Equally as important as having a high-quality camera is knowing how to use it. Photographing a wedding takes a tremendous amount of skill. This is not something that can be taught in a classroom. Only by actually going out there and clicking the camera can anyone learn how to be a good wedding photographer.

Skill involves not only knowing where to stand to get the best shot of the couple as they are showered with birdseed, but also how to coax a reticent flower girl into that perfect pose. The best wedding photographers learn how to work around adverse lighting conditions and, perhaps, adverse relatives.

The only way to tell a wedding photographer's skill is by looking at many albums of his or her work. After seeing hundreds of wedding albums, we are convinced that you can tell the skilled pros from the unskilled amateurs. One key: posing. Does the photographer creatively pose his or her subjects or are they lined up against a blank wall (like police mug-shots)? And not every church looks like the Sistine Chapel— the best photographers mask ugly backgrounds with creative posing and lighting.

One last caution about skill: don't believe studios that tell you that every one of their associates is trained in the same style. This has to be the biggest exaggeration told by wedding photography studios. True, studios may have a professed quality standard that they strive for, but what matters most is the talent and skill of the individual photographer who will actually photograph your wedding. Despite the smooth sales pitch, quality can vary widely from associate to associate.

3 **Personality:** Besides professional equipment and the skill to use it, great wedding photographers also must have great people skills. This isn't nature photography where the photographer patiently sits out in a field for six hours waiting for that perfect photo of the yellow-finned butterfly. Wedding photography involves real people.

Obviously, this doesn't come as a surprise to you, but apparently this is news to some wedding photographers. Communication is key. Besides a sixth sense for good pictures, photographers must be persistent in getting the shots the engaged couple requests. Controlling large crowds of unruly bridesmaids and groomsmen for a group shot can be trying on even the best of nerves. Wedding photographers walk a fine line between being gentle conductors and absolute dictators. In the latter case, some fall victim to director's disease: barking orders at the bride and groom (or their guests) and turning the wedding and reception into a military exercise. (One good question to ask a photographer's references: how did he treat your guests? Was he polite and professional?).

Photographers must also work with other bridal professionals at the wedding, especially the videographer. Clashes between these two vendors have been legendary and sometimes nasty; we'll talk about this later in the chapter.

Remember that you will spend more time with your wedding photographer than any other merchant. For example, you won't see your florist or baker during or after the wedding. Not only do you meet with the photographer prior to the wedding, he or she will follow you around the entire wedding day. Then, you may spend several more hours with him viewing proofs and ordering prints. Make sure you like this person. We mean you need to *really* like this person. If anything makes you the slightest bit uncomfortable, consider hiring someone else.

Getting Started: How Far in Advance?

Unlike other wedding vendors such as florists and bakers, photographers can only be at one place at one time. This limited capacity leads to a spirited competition between brides to book the best photographers. Once you reserve the ceremony site (and therefore confirm your date), consider shopping for a photographer. While some photographers can be had on short notice (a few weeks to a couple of months), booking nine to 12 months in advance of your date is prudent. That way you won't have to settle on a third or fourth choice. During the wedding season in your town, prime dates will go quickly.

Step-by-step Shopping Strategies

♥ **Step 1:** Once you have booked your ceremony site, contact three to five wedding photographers you have identified by using the sources we listed earlier in this chapter. Make an appointment with each studio. Request to meet the actual photographer who will be available on your wedding day.

♥ **Step 2:** On your visit, view as many pictures as possible from the photographer's past work. Be sure that you are looking at the photographer's own work, not a compilation of the studio's greatest hits. Also, ask to see a proof book from a recent wedding. See complete albums, not just greatest hits collections.

♥ **Step 3:** While looking at the work, decide if the pictures strike an emotional chord with you. Is the posing natural or do the subjects look uncomfortable? Are the pictures in-focus and well framed? Check for any over or underexposed prints—a common problem among amateur photographers. Look to see details in the icing of a wedding cake and delicate lace in bridal gowns—if these subjects look washed out then the pictures are overexposed. Also check out the various poses a photographer uses. Are there any you'd like the photographer to mimic for your wedding?

♥ **Step 4:** Ask to see photos taken under low-light conditions, especially if you are planning to have a candle-lit ceremony. This is a good measure of the photographer's skill, since low-light photography is a technical challenge for even the most experienced.

♥ **Step 5**: Ask the photographer the questions we list later in this chapter. Get a good reading on the photographer's style and personality.

♥ **Step 6:** After visiting with several photographers, pick the one you think offers best quality for the most affordable price. Be sure to compare prices on an apples-to-apples basis, accounting for differences in package sizes and prices. Don't be pressured you into a quick decision.

♥ **Step 7:** Once you make your decision, get a written contract from the photographer. Before signing it, take it home and read it thoroughly. A good contract should specify:

The name of the actual photographer who will be at your wedding.
When the photographer will arrive and how long he or she will stay.

A minimum number of proofs to be provided.

The exact number of prints and the type of album.

The exact dates the proofs and the final album will be delivered.

Provisions in case the photographer gets sick or can't make the wedding.

A specific schedule with due dates for deposits/final balance payments.

Any additional charges for travel time, overtime costs, or other fees.

♥ **Step 8:** A few weeks before the wedding, set up another meeting with the photographer to go over details. Discuss your expectations of the photography and clearly state the types of pictures you want. Identify on a written list any special friends or relatives that you want photographed. The more explicit your instructions to the photographer, the better the odds your wedding photography will meet your high expectations. Frankly, you're paying big money to this person so the least they can do is take the pictures you want. Bring a copy of this list with you to the reception. After taking all the time to make this list, you want to be prepared in case the photographer forgets his or her copy.

A word on shot lists: you should make TWO lists. The first list is must-have shots. The second list is a B-list: shots of folks that aren't as critical. That way if you have an uncle who is a camera hog, you don't end up with 62 pictures of him.

♥ **Step 9:** In "Chapter 15: Last Minute Consumer Tips," we recommend you pick a trusted friend or relative to be a surrogate bad cop. This person ensures all the vendors are doing their jobs correctly, while letting you enjoy your wedding day. Introduce the photographer to this contact person early on the wedding day so the he or she knows whom to

What size album should we get?

Most photographers offer two sizes: a 5x5 album or a 10x10. The latter holds both small and large prints. If you have a choice, go for the larger album. Even if you don't purchase enlargements from the photographer, you may want to include a "memory" page at the front of the album with your wedding invitation and other mementos. These won't easily fit into a small album. What about all those guest candids you might get as well? It's probably best to put those in a different album, separate from the professional pictures. We'll discuss a online source for albums later in this chapter.

turn to for help when trying to take all your requested photos. Give your bad cop a copy of the list of requested photographs to make sure the shots are taken. (It would help if photographer liaison knew most of the key people at your wedding).

Questions to Ask a Photographer

1 Who exactly will be photographing my wedding? This is perhaps the most important question to ask. Don't settle for vague answers like "one of our expertly-trained associates will do your wedding." Avoid wasting time by making sure your appointment is with the actual photographer, not the studio's marketing representative or bridal consultant. Another good question to ask: does the photographer have an assistant who comes to weddings? This helps a photographer concentrate on the event instead of worrying about his equipment, tripod placement and so on.

2 Can I see a complete album from one wedding you photographed? By viewing a complete album from one wedding, you can see how the photographer tells a story from beginning to end. Even better: try to look at several complete albums.

3 Can I also see a proof book or disc from a recent wedding? This is the best way to see what you are buying. Proofs are an unedited and uncensored look at what you will receive after your wedding. Good wedding photographers probably have at least one proof book or disc that is waiting to be picked up—ask to see it. If the photographer does online proofing, ask to see a recent bride's pictures.

4 Describe to me your philosophy and approach to wedding photography. A simple but effective question. Sit back and listen to what they say. How active a role do they take in the direction of the day's events? Obviously, some photographers may have a canned speech for this question, but you can shake them up by asking good follow-up questions.

5 What is your shooting schedule during a wedding? When do you arrive and what is your general order of shots? How long does it take to do the traditional pictures after the ceremony? This is a real controversial area of wedding photography. See "The Great Before or After Controversy" discussion later in this chapter.

6 **Will you come to my rehearsal?** Some will do this; others don't. Photographers who do attend the rehearsal get a heads up on the different players for the wedding, meeting key relatives in advance.

7 **What is the balance between posed and candid shots?** Some photographers prefer to stage most pictures by formally posing the subjects. Ask the photographer's opinion about whether pictures should be posed or candid. Photographers who shoot in a photo-journalistic style will lean towards more candid shots, documenting the wedding as it happens without *any* formal posing.

8 **What tricks do you have to make the candids more creative?** "Creative" candids are a newer trend in wedding photography. Instead of merely shooting events as they happen, photographers set up a few creative shots (example: the groomsmen in identical sunglasses, walking down a street, in sync). Note, these aren't formal posed portraits, but the goal is to inject a bit of fun into the photography. To see some examples, check out the Wedding Photojournalist Association (wpja.com)—their contest gallery contains pics of award-winning candids.

9 **Is there a limit on your time at the wedding?** If shooting film, is there a limit on the number of exposures? Be careful of photographers who limit either one. Too many times we have seen weddings shift into fast-forward because the photographer's clock was running out. Limiting the number of exposures is also a problem since it restricts the possible choices for your album. About 150 to 200 exposures should be taken to provide enough choices for an album with 60 to 80 prints (our recommendation to adequately cover the day's events).

10 **Do you bring any backup equipment?** What will you do if you are sick and unable to shoot my wedding? Cameras (even expensive ones) are just machines. Sometimes they break. Good photographers should have backup cameras and lighting systems ready in case of a mechanical problem. Having an associate on call in case of emergencies is also prudent.

Another good question: how much equipment do you bring to a wedding? If your photographer is lugging six huge bags filled with cameras and lights, this can affect the flow of the day's events. It takes a while to move that equipment from place to place!

11 **Can I see the actual album that comes with my package?** A favorite sales tactic of some wedding photographers is to show you their past work lovingly bound into leather albums. Then they forget to mention that their packages come with cheaper vinyl albums with plastic-covered pages. And, oh yes, after the wedding, the photographer casually mentions that the leather albums are available at an extra fee. Besides the deceptive nature of this practice, some vinyl albums with plastic pages are also problematic since the chemicals in the plastic can damage the prints over time. (Some plastic is okay if it is of archival-quality; that is, free of damaging chemicals). Insist on seeing the actual album that is mentioned in the package before you sign the contract.

12 **Describe to me the most difficult wedding you ever photographed.** How did you handle it? We love this question. It can be fascinating to see what the photographer defines as difficult.

Another related question: how does the photographer deal with camera hogs? You know, the relative who just has to be in every shot. Think about giving the photographer a list of relatives who should be photographed in moderation.

13 **How long will you keep the original digital files or negatives? Can I buy them?** If money is tight, don't purchase a large number of prints right after your wedding. Instead, buy the minimum now and wait a year or two to finish out the album. Most photographers archive digital files or store negatives for a few years after the wedding and will be happy to do reprints later when you have more money. Yes, some photographers will even sell you the negatives/digital files for a small fee (granted, the majority do not sell them, but it doesn't hurt to ask!).

The photographer who shot our wedding called us five years later and offered to sell us the negatives for $1 each (an offer we accepted). You may want to ask how long the photographer will store negatives, whether you'll have an option to buy them and so on. Get it in writing. One caveat: while most photographers will keep your negatives/files on hand for a year or two, don't expect them to archive them for over five years. Most photographers have a limit on how long they'll keep them. (Hint: send the photographer updated email addresses or contact info, in case you move after the wedding; if they can't reach you, the photographer might eventually destroy the negatives/digital files).

14 **If you shoot with a digital camera, will the prints be of archival quality?** You can't just go down to Best Buy and purchase a $50 ink jet printer, expecting to get top-notch prints. Most professionals who shoot digital use expensive in-house printers or send their work to an outside lab. Ask the photographer how your pictures will be printed and make sure you are getting archival-quality photo prints.

_15_ **If you shoot with black and white film, do you do your own developing of the pictures?** A photographer who does his own in-house processing of black and white film is able to get the contrast just right. Many photographers we interviewed insist such in-house processing is the only way to insure black and white photographs are high quality. Interestingly enough, this doesn't seem to be a big deal with color film (most photographers send this out to a lab for processing). It is probably still best to use black and white film (which shows more subtle hues of gray) than to use tricks to turn a color negative into a black and white image. Of course, if your photographer uses a digital camera, this is less of an issue. Software programs can transform a color picture into black and white with appropriate contrast.

_16_ **How soon will my photographs be ready after I submit my order?** You might be surprised how slow photographers can be when it comes to delivering a final album—sometimes measured in MONTHS not weeks. Photographers who value customer satisfaction should always quickly process albums and reprints. Another measure of customer service: how quickly are your phone calls returned? Messages should be returned within one business day. Taking days to return a simple voice mail is a red flag.

_17_ **What rights do I have to the digital files?** Even with more wedding photographers going digital, don't assume you'll be able to get a disk with image files after the wedding. Most shooters want to keep the high-resolution master images in order to sell enlargements.

Who owns the digital files is a key question: smaller photographers may simply sell you the files as part of your agreement (you then arrange for reprints, build an album, etc). However, that's the exception: most photographers will retain ownership of the files.

Confirm the rights you will have to any digital files before you sign a contract.

_18_ **Can my relatives view the pictures online?** Most photographers use online proofing systems like pictage.com that let your relatives and guest view and order pictures online. But don't assume this is the case—some photographers are less web-savvy than others. Ask first.

Top Money-saving Secrets

1 Get married any time other than Saturday evening. Many photographers offer discounted packages for weddings held during Saturday afternoon or any other time of the week. Savings typically range from 10% to 20%. As a side note: some photographers charge extra to work on Sundays, although that is the rare exception. We find this kind of strange: some brides report that photographers tell them Sunday is "family time," but if you want them to work, they charge an extra fee. If Sunday really was family time, why work at all?

2 Hire a photographer who works out of his or her home. When you walk into a photography studio in a fancy office complex and see all that plush carpeting and furniture, who do you think pays for all that? That's right, you do. No one has ever explained to us how designer wallpaper translates into great wedding photography. Our advice: seek out a photographer who works out of his or her home or simple studio. Quite simply, the lower overhead of a home studio/office is often passed along in the form of more affordable prices. Believe it or not, after visiting with 200 wedding photographers, we found some of the best work was from home-based professionals. Savings here can range from 20% to 40% off our photography average.

3 Skip the extra frills. Forget about the extras that photographers will suggest you buy. Gift folios (pitched as the perfect gift for wedding party members) are fluff at $100 a pop. Bridal and engagement portraits are expensive extras. Instead, if you really want a portrait, take a candid from the reception and have it enlarged to a 16x20. You'll save the sitting fee (anywhere from $100 to $400) and the print is often less expensive too. Forget about ordering a frame from the photographer; this service is grossly overpriced. Instead, go to your favorite framing store.

4 Hire a professional for the ceremony only. Then let your guests capture the reception candids with their own cameras. Many engaged couples don't realize photographers offer a ceremony-only (two hours or less) package for small weddings. Of course, there is no law that says couples must have a small wedding to use this package. A no-frills ceremony-only package might run $1000 or less, depending on the photographer. One bride in Ohio told us she found a ceremony-only package there from a reputable studio for just $550— that was $1000 LESS than their five-hour plan. Obviously, prices will vary depending on the city you are in, but you can expect a savings of

photo

anywhere from 40% to 70%. (Note: beware of studios that might assign less-experienced photographers to shoot the ceremony-only packages.)

5 **Buy the album somewhere else.** Chances are you will get a photo album as a gift. If your budget is tight, forget the fancy leather album. If the photographer includes the cost of the album in the package, ask him or her what the discount would be for an album-less package. The retail price of an album from photography studios ranges from $150 to $400. Where can you find a great album for your wedding pictures without spending those kind of bucks? Check out the Real Wedding Tip below for a mail-order source. Another hot trend for wedding pics: scrap-booking. Many arts and crafts stores like Michaels (michaels.com) and Hobby Lobby (hobbylobby.com) have jumped on the scrap-booking bandwagon, offering a myriad of supplies, albums and ideas to the do-it-yourself crowd. Check their web sites for free projects and supply lists.

6 **Consolidate your orders to take advantage of quantity discounts.** Okay, you've decided which pictures you want but hold it! Now your parents want a few extra prints. And Aunt Bea wants an

---

REAL WEDDING TIP

Mail-order albums can cut costs

Our favorite site for photo albums is Exposures (800) 222-4947 (exposuresonline.com). They features albums, frames and accessories . . . and many are perfect for wedding photos. An example: the Felicity Memo photo albums hold 40 bound pages in a leather cover for $49, which includes personalized text on the cover.

Most Exposure albums use album pages made from archival quality Mylar that does not contain chemicals that damage pictures. Other albums are scrapbook-style, where you use old-fashioned photo corners to mount pictures to the acid-free pages, separated by protective tissue.

Scrapbook albums from Exposures cost $34 to $169—much less expensive than albums from professional photography studios. You can also add in invitations, newspaper clippings and other mementos from your wedding. Frames and other accessories are equally intriguing—great gifts for bridesmaids, friends and other relatives.

8x10 of you and your spouse exchanging vows. By consolidating several small orders into one large one, you may be able to take advantage of quantity discounts offered by your photographer. Also, you'll be able to avoid the service charges some photographers slap on orders after the bride and groom's album is delivered. One photographer we interviewed charges an extra 20% service fee on such reorders. In addition, we found several photographers who offer discounts if you turn in your order within a certain number of days after the wedding. Read the contract's fine print.

7 Buy the proofs at a discount. What do photographers do with all those nice 5x5 proofs of your wedding? Apparently, not much. That's why you can sometimes negotiate to buy ALL the proofs for one low price. One bride in Atlanta bought 100 proofs for just $350. She then used them to fill in spots in her albums and as gifts for friends.

8 Delay your purchase. Photographers will apply big pressure to purchase lots of prints NOW! Yet, if cash is tight, we say wait. Many photographers will keep negatives and digital files on hand from your wedding for a specified period of time (sometimes a year or more—be sure to confirm the exact details). You can buy your wedding prints when YOU (and your bank account) are ready. One bonus to this tip: after a few months, you might realize you don't really need all those extra shots of your bridesmaids whooping it up at the reception. Hence, you might order less than you would right after the wedding.

9 "You get the disk" packages. You just pay for the photographer's time; at the end of the evening, you get the memory storage card (or rolls of film) and handle the processing yourself. Obviously, these packages can be big money-savers—even if you pay a photographer $100 to $200 per hour for their time, the result is much less than what complete album packages run. But . . . there are some pitfalls to this strategy, which we'll discuss later in this chapter.

10 Hire a student. Call a local photography institute or college to see if they can recommend a student or recent graduate. Most will photograph your wedding at rates far below those of so-called "professionals." One reader said she hired a recent grad from a local photography school and saved $1000 over the going rate for wedding pictures in her city.

To help you with this tip, we've posted a list of photography schools (and web site links) on our site BridalBargainsBook.com (click on "Bonus Material.") Also: check local community colleges, as they may have a photography curriculum. Email or call the folks in charge of the photography program and tell them you are looking for a student to photograph your wedding. Some schools may be able to forward your email to interested students; other schools may ask you to post a flyer with the details.

Try to find a student who is at least in his or her second year (sophomore or later). Just like any other photographer, ask to see their portfolio. They may not have a sample wedding album, so ask to see other portraits and candids. Insist on a written agreement that covers all the basics outlined earlier in this chapter.

77 **Hire a newspaper photographer.** Call your local newspaper to find a photographer who might be able to moonlight at your wedding. Why is this a money saving tip? Such photographers are very experienced but aren't interested in selling you a fancy album or expensive reprints. Instead, you just get the pictures (probably digital files) and you go from there. The cost? We'd estimate this would be $500 to $1500, depending on the city and the photographer. Yes, more expensive than a student, but you'll get a more experienced photographer in the bargain. The downside? Most newspaper photographers aren't experienced in doing formal posed portraits, so your album will have more of a photojournalistic spin.

72 **Create your own digital album.** Like the look of digital albums . . . but not the price? Yes, this is a hot trend—but in some cities, the only photographers offering digital albums also happen to be the most expensive shooters. Our suggestion: do it yourself. The web site MyPublisher.com lets you create a digital album on the cheap, using software you download from their site. Albums run $30 to $60, depending on whether you want a linen or leather cover.

Biggest Myths About Photography

MYTH #1 *"A photographer I visited told me he has won several awards for his portraits. Should I be impressed?"*

Not necessarily. To understand why, lets look at how photographers win these contests. According to an article in a professional photography magazine, some photographers hire models to pose for these portraits and then take hundreds of exposures to get just the right pose. Then, an army of professional retouching and PhotoShop artists "enhances" the image into an award-winner. The final work presented before the judging panel bares little resemblance to the original print or negative, the article stated, adding that many award-winning photographers create exceptional prints specifically for competitions, while exerting little effort toward producing the same caliber of images for customers. That's why you need to see examples of actual wedding albums, not just the glossy prints produced to win competitions.

MYTH #2 "*I always see those photography specials advertised by big department stores. You know, the ones for $19.95 that include several dozen prints. Shouldn't wedding photographers be similar in price?*"

Sorry to say, but no. Stores that set up these portrait specials hire an amateur to shoot 35mm or digital pictures in a high-volume operation. Unfortunately, professional wedding photography ain't cheap. The time involved in shooting a wedding is one big factor. Weddings take hours of time, shooting on location with expensive professional equipment.

MYTH #3 "*The best bridal portraits are those that are mounted on canvas.*"

Yes and no. Studios like to pitch canvas-mounted portraits as top-of-the-line, but there is a catch. In fact, a bride in Alexandria, Virginia alerted us to this rip-off. She spoke with a professor of photography who does *not* recommend canvas-mounted portraits for a couple of reasons. First, in order to be mounted on the canvas, the print must be peeled. If not, the portrait may crack and reveal the canvas beneath. Second, canvas-mounted portraits must be oiled periodically to preserve the print. And guess who pockets these hefty re-oiling fees? You guessed it, the photographer. All in all, the extra expense of canvas may not be worth the hassle.

Helpful Hints

1 **Photographers pricing methods may be as easy to understand as the federal income tax code.** We are not quite sure why this is. One possible explanation is that photographers want to give you maximum flexibility in choosing prints, albums and portraits. The only problem is that every photographer approaches pricing with a different philosophy that ends up confusing you, the consumer.

Another, more Machiavellian explanation is that photographers want to make comparison-shopping more difficult. The lack of a pricing standard makes it very difficult to compare apples to apples. Instead you have one photographer who offers a complete package with an album of 50 8x10s for $1800 and another has an a la carte system. The only way for you to make sense of this is to try to equalize the prices, in the same way the grocery stores often display the price per ounce of certain products. We do this by asking ourselves "how much does the photographer charge for a four-hour package with 50 5x5s and 20 8x10s in an professional album?" This package provides adequate coverage for most weddings. You may have to take a photographer's package and add a

The Great Before or After Controversy

Ever attended a wedding where it seemed like the bride and groom took forever to make it to the reception? Where were they? Was their limo hijacked by an alien life force? More than likely the bride and groom were hijacked by a wedding photographer who took an amount of time equivalent to the Creation of Heaven and Earth to do the after-ceremony pictures.

So what exactly are the after-ceremony pictures? Basically, these are pictures of the bride and groom with the officiant at the altar, with the bridesmaids, with the groomsmen, with the whole bridal party, with their various relatives, etc. Also, since some churches restrict photography during the actual ceremony, several events from the ceremony (exchanging rings, lighting of the unity candle, the kiss, etc.) may be re-staged for posterity. All told, we are talking quite a few pictures here.

Photographers often mislead couples about how long this process takes. Sometimes photographers sound like a cartoonish version of Name that Tune. (Yes, Bob, I can take those after-ceremony pictures in 20 minutes. Well, Bob, I can do those same pictures in 15 minutes.) In reality, we have known several couples that took one to two *hours* to make it to their reception thanks to the after-ceremony photo session.

Of course, some bright person recently came up with a solution to this problem. Hey, why not do all those pictures before the ceremony? The only problem: this would require the bride and groom to see each other before the ceremony on the wedding day. "OH NO! How can you break such a sacred superstition?" they screeched.

Well, lets take a closer look at the prohibition of seeing each other before the ceremony. As far as we know, this started back in the year 1008 A.D. when all marriages were arranged and couples didn't see each other until the wedding day. Keeping them separate was intended to prevent Thor the Viking (the groom) from running away in case Freya the Bride was not the beautiful Viking goddess he was promised. Or vice versa.

Today, brides and grooms not only know each other before

few prints (from an a la carte pricing list) to come up with that above example.

the wedding, they also probably share the same tube of toothpaste. It seems a little silly that you wouldn't see your fiancé the day of the wedding when you were just sharing the same pint of Ben & Jerry's 24 hours earlier.

Furthermore, brides today are taught to believe that the groom stands at the end of the aisle and looks down toward his beautiful bride, all the while thinking, "Wow! Isn't she beautiful? Aren't I lucky?" In reality, most grooms are thinking, "Thank God she's here. Now we can get this over with."

We're not trying to take away from this special moment, but there are several advantages to doing the after-ceremony pictures before the wedding (i.e., seeing each other before the ceremony):

♥ Everything is perfect: Hair and makeup are fresh prior to the ceremony and hence those important pictures will capture you at your best. After the ceremony, all the hugging and crying can alter that perfect face, hairdo, etc.

♥ You can leave immediately after the ceremony for the reception: You will have more time seeing relatives and enjoying the party you spent so much effort (and money) planning.

Here's our recommendation: Get to the ceremony site two hours before the wedding. After everyone is dressed, clear out the church with just the groom at the head of the aisle. Then, with appropriate music playing, the bride emerges and walks down the aisle. After this initial meeting, all the formal group pictures are taken before the guests arrive.

Or here's another variation: in a private room at the ceremony site, have the bride and groom meet prior to the ceremony. Here, you and your fiancé can exchange gifts, marvel at each other's dapper appearance, gaze at the gown, etc. What's especially nice about this approach is that you actually get 15 minutes alone, just you and your fiancé. For the rest of the day, you'll be surrounded by friends, relatives, and that ever-present photographer. On a day that's supposed to celebrate your relationship, it is ironic that most brides and grooms have their first private moment in the car leaving the reception—after the whole shebang is over.

2 **Watch out for personality clashes.** One common problem: photographers and videographers who step on each other's toes. Since both are trying to document the wedding, there can be conflicts. One such clash occurred at a wedding in Wisconsin, where a photographer ordered a video company NOT to shoot any of the formal picture sessions. He claimed the formal poses of the bride and groom were his protected copyright images. Of course, that's nonsense. But . . . you may want to play it safe and tell the photographer you plan to have a videographer at your wedding—and find out how they can both work together without grabbing for each others throats.

3 **Consider going with a woman-owned photography studio.** Yes, men have dominated the profession of wedding photography for years. The only women at studios were secretaries or the wives of photographers who came along as assistants. Fortunately, today more and more women are actually behind the camera. While they may be harder to find, we suggest giving women photographers a look-see. Yes,

Should you feed the photographer?

A bride emailed us this question: should she provide a meal for the photographer? She asked because the photographer had not only required a meal in his contact, but requested a meal for his assistant as well. While that written demand is rather unusual, many brides and grooms wonder if they should feed the vendors at their wedding. We've seen this argued both ways. On one hand, you could argue that your boss doesn't pay for your lunch, so why should you do the same for a photographer? The other side is obvious—a well-fed vendor probably works better than a starving vendor. Photographers often work non-stop, five to eight-hour days for most of their weddings and may find it difficult to fit in a meal. Of course, if you do decide to feed the photographer, that does NOT mean you have to feed them the $95 per plate filet mignon dinner the guests are getting. First, ask your caterer if they would help—perhaps there would be no charge if the photographer (and videographer and DJ or band) eats after all the guests since the leftovers might be tossed anyway. There is always extra food at most buffets. Or perhaps the caterer can do a half-price vendor meal. Or the caterer whips up some sandwiches or alternative fare that doesn't cost $95 per person. That way you can make everyone happy—the vendors get fed and you don't get stuck with the bill.

we realize good wedding photography isn't dependent on the gender of the photographer . . . but we can't help but notice how many woman photographers seem better at capturing the *emotional* aspect of weddings on film. Perhaps this is because sometimes the guys are caught up in the technical end of photography, missing some of the emotion while focusing on f-stops. We know that might be an over-generalization, but don't overlook women photographers just because they are outnumbered 10 to 1 at local bridal shows.

4 **Have a photographer wrangler.** Designate a friend to round up the photographer, helping him or her find a wayward relative. Give this person your must-shoot and shoot-only-in-moderation lists. You enjoy your wedding, while your friend makes sure the photographer gets his job done.

Pitfalls to Avoid

PITFALL #1 BAIT AND SWITCH AT LARGE PHOTOGRAPHY STUDIOS AND CELEBRITY PHOTOGRAPHERS.

"My friend who recently got married contracted with a well-known, large studio to do her wedding. Everyone was shocked when the photographer arrived—the studio had sent out a person who had never shot a wedding before! The pictures were a disaster! How can I prevent this from happening to me?"

Bait and switch is probably the biggest consumer complaint with wedding photographers. Unfortunately, some large studios bait engaged couples with a great reputation only to switch them by delivering less-than-great wedding photography. How does this happen? Basically, some studios farm out their weddings to poorly trained associates or (even worse) stringers. Stringers are free-lance photographers who are often amateurs working on the weekend for a few extra bucks. The work of these photographers can be far inferior to professional wedding photographers.

"A famous photographer in our town has taken many pictures of celebrities. Since the studio also does weddings, I assume my fiancé and I will get the same high quality photography."

Don't bet on it. Here's how this pitfall works in this case: every city in the U.S. probably has at least one celebrity photographer who attracts engaged couples to her studio based on her famous name. But *who* would actually shoot your wedding? Instead of the famous photographer, weddings are often assigned to a no-name associate or a stringer. Hence, couples are baited into the studio by the famous photographer and then switched to a less-famous associate. While an associate may do good work, this is obviously deceptive since couples are duped into paying a hefty premium for celebrity photography.

Solution: You can prevent these problems by doing one simple thing: make sure the name of the actual photographer who will shoot your wedding is specified in writing in the contract. Most importantly, *before* you sign the contract, meet with the actual photographer who will do your wedding and view several albums of his or her work. Don't let the studio show you a few slick sample albums and feed you the line "all our associates are trained in the same great style." Remember your wedding pictures are dependent on who is behind that camera, not a fancy name that's embossed in gold on the studio's stationary.

PITFALL #2   HIDDEN CHARGES.

"I really liked my wedding photographer. Yet, when the final bill came in, we were charged an extra $200 for travel time at $3 a mile! When we protested this fee, the photographer pointed to the fine print in his price list. And if we didn't pay the extra $200, he said he wouldn't give us our pictures!"

Beware of fine print or hidden charges for travel time, over-time, special handling and other services. Sometimes, these fees are mentioned only in fine print on the price list, not your contract. One photographer charged an out-of-town bride a $500 penalty fee when she returned her proof book three days late, thanks to a delay at the post office.

This is why we recommend taking the photographer's contract home first and reading it thoroughly before signing. As we mentioned earlier in the catering chapter, you can request a change in the wording of any

---

The Package Game: Are you bronze, silver or gold?

Those cutesy names used by photographers to describe their packages aren't by accident. Many studios cleverly use psychological tactics to get couples to spend more. For example, some photographers use precious metals for package names: from bronze (the least expensive) to gold (top of the line). But what bride and groom just wants "bronze" wedding pics? Isn't daddy's little girl worth at least silver or gold?

Our advice: don't get caught up in all the clever marketing. Just pick a package that meets your needs and forget what the photographer calls it!

clause that makes you uncomfortable. Be wary of any requirements that may be unreasonable and ask for an adjustment to fit your needs.

PITFALL #3 SMALL PACKAGES AND HEAVY SALES PRESSURE.

"I contracted with a photographer for one of his small wedding packages that had 20 8x10s in an album. After the wedding, the studio tried to pressure me into buying more prints than the original package—at those high reprint prices! My only problem—I never realized how many more pictures I would want for my album! Help!"

Ah, this is a common deceptive practice. Here, the studio attracts wedding business with low package prices like "Just $795 for complete coverage and an album with 20 8x10s!" Sound like a great deal? No, it isn't. That's because most weddings generate dozens of great pictures—photographers often snap 40 to 50 pictures before the ceremony even begins!

The result is that most albums need at least 60 to 80 prints to adequately tell the story of an average wedding. Of course, photographers are well aware of this and realize couples will want to order many more pictures than those packages with just 20 prints. The result: the $800 package ends up costing $1200, $1500, or even $2000 by the time the total order is placed. We have talked to photographers who admit this deceptive practice is commonplace. Some studios even make matters worse by adding some heavy sales pressure after the wedding to increase the size of the order.

The most blatant example of this practice was one studio we visited that offered a package for $995 that included just 40 5x7s. The price list then went on to say that brides and grooms may purchase additional 5x7s or 8x10s to create a more complete story. Those additional prints cost $25 for a 5x7 and $45 for an 8x10. *Each.*

You can prevent this practice by selecting a package that offers the amount of coverage that will realistically tell the story of your wedding. For small weddings (under 100 guests with a short reception), this might be just 40 to 60 prints. Most will require 60 to 80 and some large weddings (with big bridal parties and long receptions) may require 100-plus prints.

In Milwaukee, a photographer was criminally charged with violating deceptive trade practice laws after several couples alleged he tried to pressure them to buy more wedding photos—if not, he refused to give them any pictures at all! The photographer's defense: he was an "artist" and the couples needed to buy "more pictures" ($1000 worth) because that was the only way to show their complete wedding story. While that guy was an obvious scam artist, it points up that even if you have a written contract for a reasonable number of pictures, you can still get heat from a photographer who thinks *his* artistry demands more of *your* money.

The bottom line: be prepared for at least some sales pressure when you select your wedding photos. But . . . don't get hooked by low-price packages that only give you a minuscule amount of actual pictures.

PITFALL #4 UNREASONABLE TIME LIMITS.

"I recently attended a wedding where it seemed like the reception moved at the speed of light. Apparently, the photographer was in quite a hurry."

We can't tell you how many weddings we've seen where the reception looked like a sped-up film because the photographer's clock was ticking. After researching this book we now know why: photographers often sell packages with unreasonable time limits.

For example, we interviewed one photographer whose main package had only two and half hour's coverage. Since most photographers start their coverage one hour before the ceremony and because the ceremony itself can take up to one hour (including those pesky after-ceremony pictures), this would leave just 30 minutes to cover all the reception activities! No wonder the bride and groom seemed in a frantic rush to cut the cake, throw the bouquet, toss the garter, and so on! Instead of enjoying the reception, the couple was racing to get everything on film before the photographer's clock expired.

You can prevent this from happening to you by selecting a package with reasonable time limits, or better yet, no time limits at all. In the latter case, the photographer stays at the reception until both of you leave. However, some photographers argue their time is precious and want to impose some time limit. In that case, select a package with at least four hours coverage for an average wedding. You'll need more coverage (perhaps five or six hours) if you have a long ceremony or a large wedding party (all those pictures take more time).

Of course, it shouldn't come as a surprise to you that those same photographers who have those unreasonable time limits also offer overtime at a pricey charge per hour!

We should note that a close kin to this pitfall are photographers who limit the number of exposures they take at a wedding. Ask the photographer about any such limits before you sign a contract.

PITFALL #5 GREATEST HITS ALBUMS.

"I visited a photographer who only showed me an album with pictures from several weddings in it. Shouldn't this person have shown me more work?"

Yes. This problem is what we call the Greatest Hits Album. Even lousy photographers can occasionally take good pictures. In order to convince you of their excellence, these photographers compile all those greatest hits into one album. Obviously, you are only getting a tiny glimpse of their work.

When you visit a potential photographer, try to see as much work as possible. The best photographers should have *complete* albums that chronicle a single wedding from beginning to end. This allows you to see how the photographer will tell the story of your wedding. Another helpful album to look at is a proof book. Unedited and uncensored, proof books will let you see what the photographer can (and can't) do.

PITFALL #6 FRIENDS AND RELATIVES.

"A friend of mine decided to let her uncle, who is a shutterbug, photograph her wedding. What a disaster! His flash didn't work for half the pictures and the other half weren't that exciting anyway."

As most brides and grooms realize, having friends and relatives do various part of your wedding can save you a tremendous amount of money. While you might have a talented aunt who can help alter your gown and a helpful friend who bakes great cakes, you may want to draw the line at the photographs.

Photography is typically high on everyone's priority list and its no wonder—the pictures are all you have left after the wedding. Investing the money in professional photography is a wise choice. Trying to save money by using an amateur is tempting but we say resist the urge—at least when it comes to your ceremony, the most important pictures of the day. Well-meaning friends and relatives who are amateur photographers often bite off more than they can chew when they shoot a wedding. Adverse lighting conditions and other technical challenges can vex even the most talented amateurs.

If you are on a tight budget and can't afford a professional photographer, consider some of the money-saving tips mentioned earlier. Specifically, hire a professional for the ceremony only and have friends and relatives cover the reception with their own cameras or single-use cameras you provide.

Also be aware that many photographers' contracts specify that they must be the only photographer at the ceremony or reception. They claim that friends who snap pictures of the bride and groom compete with their work and equipment (their flashes may prematurely set off the photographers' flash, for example). Ask your photographer about any such prohibitions.

PITFALL #7 YOU GET THE FILES/FILM PACKAGES.

"I met a photographer at a bridal show who told me that he could save me money by giving me all the digital files after the wedding. Then I go and get the pictures developed. Is this a good deal? What's the catch?"

The catch is that you have to get the pictures printed, order an album and assemble it. This was more complicated in the days of film cameras (and some photographers still shoot on film, usually medium format). Unlike 35mm film (which you dropped off at Target and then a day later—POOF! you had pictures!), medium format negatives must be developed by professional labs. These labs produce negatives that must be cropped and masked to make final prints. We won't go into more detail on cropping and masking, but we can say that we did this for some publicity pictures and it was quite challenging.

Once the lab develops the film, you need them to print out the pictures. As a consumer, you may not know the photo-speak that photographers use to communicate with the lab. For example, many labs offer two choices: less-expensive machine prints or custom prints, which include touch-ups and artwork. Furthermore, you have little leverage over the lab in case the developed pictures have quality problems, since you are a one-time customer.

Of course, these problems are lessened if your photographer shoots a "you get the film" package with a digital camera. It's pretty easy to design a digital album on your own. But if you want a traditional leather album, you probably want to deal with a professional lab to get your pictures developed. This involves time and expense—factor these costs into your budget if you go this route.

REAL WEDDING TIP

Spam! Spam! Spam!

Reader Pauline B. wrote to us with this warning about spam and wedding photographers:

"Last year I attended a friend's wedding in the Bay Area of California. The couple provided a web site where you could see and buy photos of the wedding. To access the photos, you had to provide an e-mail address. I provided a disposable address with the photographer's name in it, and guess what: after the wedding, I started to receive spam e-mail (having nothing to do with weddings) at this address. The photographer (or the picture web site) must have sold the guests' e-mail addresses to spammers within weeks of the wedding. Luckily I could disable this address so I wasn't bothered by more spam. I was annoyed, but if I were the bride I would be mortified if my guests' e-mail addresses were abused in this way."

PITFALL #8 HERE TODAY, GONE TOMORROW?

"My friend took some pictures of our wedding with his digital camera. We printed these out on an ink-jet printer and they looked great—UNTIL they started to fade just six months later! What happened?"

Here's a nasty surprise for those who like to be on the cutting edge of technology—digital prints that are here today and gone tomorrow. Cheap ink-jet printers produce prints that will start to fade after just six months. After a year, the image might be gone. Contrast this to conventional wedding photographs, which can last a generation or more when printed on special archival paper.

Fortunately, ink-jet printer manufacturers are working on a solution to the disappearing ink. Both HP (hp.com) and Epson (epson.com) have been rushing to roll out printers with longer-lasting ink. Printer manufacturers have been targeting professional photographers with new large-format printers that produce prints that can last 100 years when printed on special paper.

Sure, you can always output a digital photo again if the first print starts to fade out . . . but that's a hassle. If you decide to have a friend take digital pics (or hire a professional photographer who shoots with a digital camera), a word to the wise: confirm the subsequent prints will be of "archival quality." Find out what type of printer will be used to output the pictures and go to that manufacturer's web site to confirm how long the images will last.

PITFALL #9 PADDING THE BILL BY SPLITTING GROUPS.

"Our photographer insisted on NOT taking any big group pictures; instead all the relatives were shot in small groups. Was this done to increase his total bill?"

Yes, it was, in our opinion. One photographer admitted as much in a trade newsletter for professional wedding photographers: "By shooting the family in group shots, you are eliminating the possibility of extra sales. Taking (separate) groupings of relatives will produce as many as six portraits sold rather than the usual single group picture. It is almost forcing the parents to buy all of them rather than just the big group."

The same photographer also advised his fellow shooters that "grandparents are the real money makers." He makes sure to include the grandparents in many shots, knowing this increases sales. "God willing, all the grandparents are alive and still married," said the photographer since this adds to the profit dollars.

Trends

♥ **ODD ANGLES, BLURRY SHOTS, OFF-CENTER COMPOSITIONS.** That's how the *Wall Street Journal* described the hip trend of photo-journalistic wedding photographers. And they're right: these aren't your mother's wedding pictures. From celebrity photographers in Beverly Hills to the average wedding shooter in Des Moines, what's in is offbeat pics. What's out? Stiff, formal posed photographs. Instead, couples opt to make fun of their professions (a county prosecutor bride and her highway patrolman groom posed in handcuffs) and generally go for a lighter touch.

♥ **BLACK AND WHITE PHOTOGRAPHY:** Yes, its back. Some couples are rediscovering the contrast and beauty of black and white photography. We've seen several truly striking albums that mix black and white and color photography—à la *The Wizard of Oz.*

♥ **TRASH THE DRESS:** Sure, you've seen formal bridal portraits set in churches, formal halls and more. But how about in a pool? Or on railroad tracks? The goal is for a more relaxed, casual look—taking a formal white gown and putting it in a scene where you wouldn't expect it. (For obvious reasons, this picture takes places after the wedding!).

Special Touches to Make Your Photography Unique

1 **Add a memory page to your album.** This is a page at the front of the album with a copy of your invitation. We've seen couples add a few of the dried flowers from the bride's bouquet and some lace from the bridal gown to this page.

2 **Personalize your wedding photography.** Instead of an engagement portrait in a studio with a boring blue background, have the picture taken at a special location. Perhaps the place you first met or had your first date. Obviously, photographers will charge a little more to go on location, but it is a nice way to personalize the portrait.

3 **Chronicle your engagement with pictures.** With your own camera, document the wedding process (trying on gowns, tasting cakes, visiting various reception sites) from the proposal to the big day. Undoubtedly, you will receive a photography album as a gift, so here's a use for it. Add your honeymoon pictures in the back to complete the album.

Now that you've earned your black belt in wedding photography, it's time to talk about that companion in the memory department: video! That's what's up next.

Chapter 10

Cakes

It's the centerpiece of your reception—all eyes will be on your wedding cake. But how do you get one that tastes as good as it looks? We'll explore that issue, plus give you 19 money-saving tips to cut your cake costs. And what about that mysterious white icing you see on so many cakes? We'll explain the secret ingredient that bakers use to make white icing white, plus four other pitfalls to avoid.

What Are You Buying?

Wedding cakes have come a long way over the years. Once a dry, white tasteless confection with globs of sugary icing, wedding cakes have morphed into gourmet desserts. Across the country, we have found a dazzling array of gourmet flavors and high-style designs that turn the pedestrian wedding cake into a culinary work of art. No matter how fancy the design, however, there are four basic elements to a wedding cake:

♥ **THE CAKE, ITSELF.** Traditionally, wedding cakes were vanilla-flavored confections. However, today anything goes. Gourmet cakes are the rage, with options like you'd see from a four-star restaurant or top pastry chef. Cupcakes, cheesecakes, tortes, anything you can think of have been made into wedding cakes.

♥ **THE FILLING.** In addition to cake flavor possibilities, many bakers also offer a variety of fillings. Fillings used to be fruit jams or butter cream icing, but have expanded today to include liqueurs, fresh fruit, custards and mousses. The traditional wedding cake has two layers of cake with one layer of filling in each tier. Lately, we've seen more European torte-style cakes: confections with four or five layers of cake and filling. This torte-style cake tends to be richer than traditional wedding cake styles.

♥ **THE FROSTING AND DECORATIONS.** The options for wedding cake icing are numerous. Some bakers opt for the traditional butter cream icing (to which liqueurs are often added) while rolled fondant (a la "Cake Boss" or "Ace of Cakes") or marzipan is also popular. Whipped cream icings and meringue icings are yet more options. No longer are you limited to the typical white icing; many brides want their cakes tinted to match the bridal party colors or merely prefer the antique look of an off-white icing.

♥ **DELIVERY AND SET-UP.** Another element you are buying is the delivery and set-up of the cake. This means the actual engineering of the cake with its several layers. Most cakes today are stacked one on top of the other. Fresh flowers or delicate sugar decorations may have to be added at the reception site to avoid damage. Rental items like plates for separating tiers are another cost. Some bakers make a special stand for their cakes, which they rent to couples for the day.

Average total costs. What's our favorite scene from the Steve Martin remake of *Father of the Bride?* It has to be Martin's shock at cake prices. After Martin Short's wedding consultant says that $1200 is a reasonable price "for a cake of this magnitude," Martin rejoins: "Franc, a cake is made of flour and water! My first car didn't cost $1200!" To which, Short replies: "Welcome to the 90's!" Okay, it's an old movie, but the sticker shock is still realistic (and funny).

Yes, they are just made of flour and water, but the average wedding cake runs hundreds (if not thousands) of dollars. Cakes are typically priced per serving. We peg the average wedding cake at $545 for 150 guests—that's about $3.60 a slice. Of course, prices are usually less in smaller cities (the average in Louisville, KY, for example is about $3 per slice). But, as Steve Martin learned, cake prices can be much higher. We noticed Palm Beach, Florida bakers expect $5 a serving for their creations, while some wedding cakes in Boston fetch $8 per guest. Atlanta is about $6 per serving. And New York? Fuggetaboutit! A cake from renowned bakers like Weinstock *start* at $17 a slice and can run into the thousands.

The average deposit for a wedding cake can range from $50 to 50% of the total bill. The balance is due usually a week or so before the wedding.

Trends

What's new with wedding cakes? Here is a round up of the latest trends:

♥ SMOOTH FONDANT. Thanks to shows like Ace of Cakes and Cake Boss, smooth fondant cakes have increased in popularity. We'll discuss the pros and cons of fondant later in this chapter. Picture at right from sweettreetsbakery.com.

♥ CUTOUTS. A new, subtle design idea for fondant cakes: cutouts that reveal a contrasting color underneath the fondant top layer. Example at right.

♥ THEME CAKES. Again, blame the TV shows. You'll find everything from Viking raider cakes to Star Wars. Many of these unique designs are grooms cakes, but not all of them. And even a "traditional" stacked cake can be designed with amazing decorations that tie into a wedding theme. We saw one design from The Inspired Bride that was a Scrabble theme. Each layer was decorated with "tiles" that spelled out Love, Family, Laughter and Marriage. The topper was a larger tile with the couples' last initial on it (and the appropriate points too!).

♥ RUFFLES AND OMBRE. Ombre refers to gradually going from dark to light shades in the same color. So an ombre cake would start with dark blue on the bottom and rise to progressively lighter shades of blue on top (or the other way around). Where we see lots of ombre is on cakes that use a series of ruffles to decorate the sides. So the combination of ruffles and ombre is one big trend we see with wedding cakes.

Picture: The Cake Lady, Sioux Falls, SD (thecakeladysf.com).

♥ **IN A WORD: COLOR.** Forget the white! From pale celadon to bold Tiffany blue to a scrumptious chocolate brown, color is the trend for wedding cakes. Even white frosted cakes are decorated with boldly colored fresh flowers or bright sugar accents. Black as a color is creeping into wedding designs as well. Be careful not to overuse black, however. It might make the cake look inedible!

♥ **STACKED BUT DIFFERENT HEIGHTS.** No more tiered cakes with those fake columns between layers. We're just not seeing them anymore. And each tier is sized differently. So you might have a standard height layer for the middle and top but an extra tall tier in on the bottom.

♥ **MINI-CAKES.** When they first hit the scene a few years ago, we thought this was a "here and gone" fad. But we're still seeing mini cakes as an option to replace the traditional wedding cake. How does it work? Each guest gets an individual wedding cake instead of a slice of a larger cake. Since these are all the rage at celebrity weddings, you can be assured the price is high. In Boston, bakers sell elaborately decorated mini cakes for $15 a pop! In Manhattan, mini cakes can run $18 to $25 each. Why so expensive? We aren't talking about cupcakes here. Most are

hand decorated, and according to one baker, 100 can take a whole week to decorate.

Another take on this is small cakes (not as small as the mini cakes) placed as centerpieces at all the guest tables. This way, brides can decorate the table with dessert.

♥ **RIBBONS.** Ribbons are the hot accent for wedding cakes today. Most are laid flat against the layers like satin ribbons but you could drape them or use a ribbon bow as a cake topper. Ribbon accents may be made of fondant, white chocolate or real satin.

♥ **MATCHING THE INVITATION.** Use to be, wedding cakes were designed to match the bride's gown.

But with the advent of funky, unique wedding invitations (even stalwart Crane is selling colored paper invites) we're seeing brides and bakers gravitate toward the invitation as inspiration.

Some cakes now echo the invite's paper color, patterns or accents.

Sources to Find an Affordable Baker

There are three types of bakeries that do wedding cakes. Here's a breakdown:

1 **Cake factories/grocery stores.** Better known as commercial bakeries, these folks bake and deliver over ten cakes per Saturday. These businesses may be less personalized than the other two types of bakers. Grocery stores fall into this category, too.

2 **Reception sites and/or caterers.** Quality is sometimes great, sometimes not.

3 **Small bakers and pastry chefs**. These are the hardest to find, but often the best and most creative cake bakers. Some work out of their homes; others are pastry chefs that might also have a small cafe business.

Here are our sources for finding great bakeries:

♥ **FLORISTS.** Because they often work with bakers to help coordinate the floral decorations, florists may have great contacts.

♥ **PHOTOGRAPHERS.** Since they attend many receptions, photographers see the best and worst creations of local bakeries. They also often hear praise or criticism about cakes from guests.

♥ **RECEPTION SITES.** Besides helping set up the cake, as well as serving it, catering managers notice whether guests like the cake or not.

♥ **BRIDAL SHOWS.** Some bakeries offer samples of their cakes at bridal shows, so here's a great opportunity to taste without any pressure to buy.

Best Online Resources

♥ Not like it's a big secret, but **PINTEREST** is perhaps the greatest boon to brides on the Internet since Al Gore "invented" it. And there is no better category to research on Pinterest than cakes. You can search for certain themes (ombre, birds, pacman, Victorian), colors, shapes (square, petal shape) and style.

♥ **SUGARCRAFT.COM** has just about every supply for the do-it-yourselfer, including edible flowers made of gum paste or royal icing. "The prices are great," says a reader who emailed this tip.

♥ **WILTON** (wilton.com) is the undisputed leader in cake decorating supplies. Their crisply designed web site is fun to visit, complete with an online store and a "recipes and ideas" section. The latter featured a half dozen wedding cakes, complete with instructions, needed supplies and a picture of the final product.

♥ **ETSY.COM** is like the ultimate craft bizarre on steroids. Wedding categories include decorations, favors, lighting and candles and more. Cake toppers abound with monograms being the most numerous option. But not just any monograms: how about a rustic version made of rusted barbed wire? Or maybe you'd prefer hand made porcelain birds? A clever option we saw was a puzzle piece wedding topper ($38) with the words "meant" on one piece and "to be" on the other. So cute!

Getting Started: How Far in Advance?

Because bakeries can make more than one cake on a Saturday, brides may only need two to four months to plan. With some of the large commercial bakeries, you may even need less time (as little as a week's notice). Popular bakeries and popular dates may require more advance planning (between three and six months) and you may want to do this part early anyway to get it out of the way. If you're interested in sculpted wedding or groom's cakes, visit the baker early to discuss the design. Some bakeries will need time to engineer an unusual theme cake.

Step-by-step Shopping Strategies

♥ **Step 1:** Before visiting a baker, you will need to have an estimate of the number of guests invited. Final exact numbers won't be required until a week or two before the wedding date; this will allow you to get a basic price for a cake. Also, knowing your wedding colors will help guide the baker. How formal is the wedding? This will also influence the cake design.

♥ **Step 2:** Given the resources above, identify two to three bakers who have skill levels and style ideas to fit your needs. Make an appointment with them and ask if you can have a taste test. Time the appointment to make it easier for the baker to give you a sample (like Friday while they are decorating cakes for Saturday weddings).

♥ **Step 3:** At the baker's shop, be sure to look at *real* photos of their past cake designs. It's best to see their work rather than a cake design book.

♥ **Step 4:** Given the size of your reception, ask the baker for a proposal or estimate of the cost of a cake based on one or two of their styles. Also ask for suggestions on how much cake to buy. The amount of cake to order will depend on several factors: if you will be having a groom's cake or sweets table; how much other food you will be serving (sit-down dinner vs. hors d'oeuvres); the time of day; and the size of the slices (paper thin up to birthday cake size). Some bakers think a wedding cake slice should be four inches wide; others think just two inches.

♥ **Step 5:** Make sure you taste a sample of their cake. There is no substitute for having actually tasted it before buying. If a baker doesn't offer taste tests, you should be very cautious. You may have to buy a small six-inch cake from the baker in order to get a taste, but we prefer bakeries that offer free samples—these are usually the best.

♥ **Step 6:** Choose the baker and ask for a signed proposal detailing the design, flavors of both cake and filling, any rentals (like stands), delivery and set-up fees, and deposit information. Don't forget to have the date, place and delivery time clearly written on the proposal. If you are planning far in advance, you may have to adjust the number of servings you will need—find out the last possible moment when you can change numbers.

♥ **Step 7:** Confirm any last-minute details and pay the balance on the cake a week or two before the wedding.

Questions to Ask a Baker

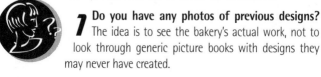

1 **Do you have any photos of previous designs?** The idea is to see the bakery's actual work, not to look through generic picture books with designs they may never have created.

2 **Can we have a taste test?** You may have to wait for a day when they are making cakes, but the best bakeries will offer free taste tests.

3 **Are there any extra charges?** Some bakeries have numerous extra charges. These items may include: fillings, complex decorations, silk or fresh flowers, delivery, set-up, cake plates and columns, and more. Find out exactly what these items will cost and get a written proposal.

4 **Who will decorate the cake with fresh or silk flowers?** If you prefer this type of decoration, find out how the flowers will be provided and who will decorate the cake. Some bakers can purchase the flowers and decorate it themselves. Others will get the flowers from your florist. In some cases, the florist is totally in charge. (Another tip for flowers intended for cake decoration: make sure you pick blooms that have not been sprayed with pesticides or preservatives).

5 **How far in advance is the cake prepared?** This may be a delicate question to ask, but you will want to know how fresh the cake is that you are buying. Almost all bakers must bake the cake a few days prior to the wedding, and then freeze it before applying the decoration. Of course, no one wants to have a cake that has been frozen for more than a week. Unfortunately, some high-volume bakeries may do just that.

Top Money-saving Secrets

1 **The cake "switcheroo" (rent a cake!).** Here's a clever way to cut costs. Instead of buying a huge wedding cake to feed your guests, get a small cake for photos. After the pictures, wheel that cake out of view. . . and have the caterer cut up sheet cakes in the kitchen. Out come slices of cake for the guests, who probably won't know the difference (a slice of cake looks like a slice of cake, right?).

But you'll notice the difference in your wallet. *Sheet cakes cost 75% less than wedding cakes (as little as 50¢ a serving).* Why? Much of a wedding cake's cost is the labor to decorate it, which sheet cakes omit. This trick gets you the best of both worlds—a nice wedding cake for photos and the ceremonial cake cutting, while giving your guests some cake as dessert at a price that doesn't break the bank.

Another twist to this tip: fake the cake. Buy or rent a styrofoam cake decorated to look like the real thing. The fake cake is used for pictures—and then shuttled back to the kitchen where the caterer cuts up affordable sheet cakes for dessert. Good news: there are now several places that rent or sell fake cakes. Fun Cakes Rental of Grandville, MI (cak-erental.com) charges $150 for a pre-designed cake or $250 for a custom design plus shipping. Fun Cakes builds in a secret compartment into the fake cake that you can put in a small slice of real cake (for photos of the cake cutting).

Another site that rents cakes is LCDsfakecakesandmore.com (western New York). FakeCakesByCatherine.com offers options from two to six tiers at prices from $110 to $220. Or you can buy them too for $150 to $300. She offers shipping anywhere in the US and requests a $50 damage deposit refunded when the cake is returned. If you buy a fake cake, you can resell it on eBay or Craigslist to recoup your investment, plus you avoid return shipping charges for a rental cake.

2 **Pass on your caterer's cake offer.** Many banquet halls, hotels and caterers will suggest you buy a wedding cake from them. Do they bake the cakes? Often, they just go to an outside bakery and order one of their cakes—and then mark it up to sell to you! Avoid the cake mark-up and contract directly with a baker. One caveat: some sites won't let you bring in an outside cake, so check first. Others slap brides with a "cake cutting fee" ($1 to $2 per guest) to discourage the use of outside bakers. We discussed this rip-off in our catering chapter; try to negotiate away this fee.

3 **Go simple and decorate with flowers.** All those fancy cake decorations (from sugar flowers to fondant icing) cost a fortune. Fondant can cost *twice* as much as buttercream icing. A better money-saving strategy is to get a plain, basic cake and decorate it with flowers. Blooms are more cost-effective than a baker slaving away for hours to create an icing masterpiece. Use the bridesmaids' bouquets to decorate the cake's base. And use our flowers-at-wholesale from the 'net tip from Chapter 5 to buy roses on the cheap to complete the look. You'll save 25% to 40% by going plain and dressing it up with flowers. And the cake will look just as beautiful for photos. One note: be sure to use flowers that haven't been sprayed with chemical preservatives or pesticides!

4 **Order less cake than the number of people.** If you have a sweets table or groom's cake, consider fewer servings than guests. Also if you will be eating a heavy sit-down meal or have a crowd that doesn't eat a lot of sweets, consider cutting back. Remember that some guests may leave the wedding before the cake cutting. Another idea: slice the cake thinner—a 2" inch slice is more than adequate for most guests. And that will make your cake go twice as far.

REAL WEDDING TIP

That's nuts!

Here's one way to save money with wedding cakes, from a reader in San Francisco:

"Since I have a favorite bakery that sells reasonably priced cakes, I assumed their wedding cakes would be too. Wrong! They were $6 a slice! Eek! But when I tried to cut costs, it was difficult. I made it clear that they didn't need to make frosting ribbons and roses, didn't need to have a balancing act with stacked tiers on little pillars, etc. But that made no difference in price. Why? Because, they explained, the majority of the labor to make a wedding cake is in getting the frosting smooth on the sides of the cake. Their wedding cakes are frosted, frozen, re-frosted to smooth, re-frozen, and so on. And the labor is most of the cost. So, we ended up buying our cakes with the sides rolled in nuts for $2.50 a slice. That way they don't have to have smoothly frosted sides, we don't have frostbitten cake, and we save a bundle! I just hope none of our guests have severe nut allergies..."

5 **Choose an independent or out-of-home baker.** This could mean as much as $1 to $2 difference in cost per serving. Out-of-home or small bakeries often have lower overhead, which they pass on to brides. Caution: Local health laws may prohibit bakers from operating out of their home. Each city is different, so you may want to check with your local health department.

6 **Skip the anniversary cake top** (see pitfalls later in this chapter for more details).

7 **Roll the sides in nuts.** One bride emailed us an interesting idea— she found a wedding cake from her favorite bakery was $4.50 a slice. But ... if she opted for a cake with sides rolled in nuts, the price was $1.50! So, she saved $3 per guest by going with that option! The complete story is in the Real Wedding Tip on the next page.

8 **Hire the teacher.** A bride in Iowa phoned in this tip. She called a local crafts store to see if they had cake-decorating classes. They did—and she hired the teacher to do her wedding cake. She estimated she saved about 30% off what a commercial bakery would have charged her for a similar cake.

9 **Consider offbeat places for cakes.** For example, Wal-Mart isn't exactly the first place brides think to look for wedding cakes. But one reader found the discounter to be a great deal: "My wedding cake was just $143! That's right—$143 for a 3-tier cake that feeds 125 people ($1.14 per slice)! The wedding cakes are beautiful and very affordable." And how do Wal-Mart cakes taste? Surprisingly good, say readers. And of course, no one would know you got your cake at Wal-Mart (unless you put one of those yellow rollback smiley faces on it!).

10 **Cake table centerpieces.** Instead of buying pricey floral table centerpieces, use cake centerpieces—small cakes on each table that serve both as dessert and decoration. See picture at right from a reader who said this tip saved her hundreds of dollars (thanks to Ann Arbor, Michigan photographer Nicole Blair, nicoleadonne.com for the photo).

11 **Cut out the groom's cake.** Instead, have a chocolate wedding cake. This eliminates the expense of a separate cake, yet gives your guests that chocolate fix.

12 **Deconstruct the cake.** A wedding cake is just several white cakes stacked together. But who says they have to be stacked? Katie, a reader in the San Francisco Bay Area, found she could save 50% off the price of a "wedding cake" by ordering three separate cakes (frosted white, of course) and displaying them on tiered cake stands. Where did she find the stands? eBay. And after the wedding, she sold the stands on eBay to another couple, recouping her $100 investment. Katie's total savings by using this trick: $200. Now that's clever!

13 **Skip the fancy cake stands/pillars. And topper.** Renting a cake stand can add another $50 to the cake bill—and who needs them anyway? Your baker should be able to cover the cake board with icing and wrap the edges with ribbon, Atlanta baker Karen Portaleo (HighlandBakery.com) advised us. That should be included in the price. "Most of the time, cake stands are bulky, flashy and detract from the cake," Karen said. And skip the cake topper as well. Why spend $30 to $100 for a topper when a few fresh flowers can do the trick for under $10?

14 **Consider your local supermarket.** Most national supermarket chains sell wedding cakes at prices that are a fraction of fancy bakers. Example: Safeway stores in Seattle have posted prices and pictures of their wedding cakes on WedNet.com/wedding-cakes/safeway.

Most cakes are about $2.60 a slice—that's about 30% to 50% less than what other bakers in Seattle charge for similar cakes. Other grocery stores charge as little as $1 per serving. And offer free delivery.

15 **Warehouse clubs.** Yes, Costco and Sam's have bakeries that do wedding cakes—and the savings can be 50% or more off traditional bakers (and even less than supermarket chains). Or simply buy a few four-layer cakes, place them on stands of varying heights and poof! Wedding cake at a fraction of the price. Example: Costco sells a two-layer chocolate cake for $17 that serves 50 guests (only 35¢ per serving).

16 **Stress your budget.** When you visit with a baker, talk budget first—and emphasize how you want this to be affordable. A standard flavor, filling and icing will always be less expensive than custom or specialty options. A big mistake: taking in a photo of an expensive or elaborate cake from a bridal magazine. That signals to the baker that you want to spend, not save. Most bakeries survive on volume—they'd rather sell you a simple, less ornate cake than none at all. (Thanks to baker Linda Fedewa, former owner of Michigan bakery A Piece O' Cake, for this advice).

17 **More height = more bucks.** The taller the cake, the more expensive it is. Why? It takes more labor to bake, frost and decorate the additional tiers. Hence, a three-tier cake costs less than a four tier cake—even if both cakes serve 200 guests.

Disappearing Deposits

Reader Julie H. e-mailed us this interesting story about a disappearing deposit—a good lesson for all brides. *"Our baker charged us a $75 deposit for the Lucite tiers used with our wedding cake—he told us we had one month to return them or we'd lose the deposit. Well, after the wedding, we had our maid of honor drop them off since we'd be on our honeymoon. Unfortunately, she forgot about the deposit and didn't ask for any money back. The bakery also wouldn't give her a receipt. Well, you can guess what happened next—we got back, asked the bakery for the money and they claimed they gave it to the maid of honor. It took three visits to the bakery before the manager agreed to refund our money."*

18 **Cut the cupcake.** It's all the rage in some bridal magazines and web sites: elaborately decorated cupcakes (pitched as "individual desserts") instead of a large wedding cake. But the labor to decorate 200 individual cupcakes can be more than a single cake that serves 200. If you have your heart set on cupcakes, keep it simple—a cupcake tree with fewer cupcakes than guests (not everyone will want one) is one approach.

19 **No cake.** What law says you MUST have a cake as dessert at your reception? A caterer in Redmond, WA told us couples there

---

REAL WEDDING TIP

Small versus large bakeries: an insider view

Recently, a bride who has worked in the bakery business wrote to us about our contention that "cake factories" (that is, large bakeries) don't make cake that tastes as good as smaller competitors. Her thoughts:

"Yes, many large bakeries do use mixes. Just like a cake mix that you would use at home. . . add water, oil, eggs, etc. Some bakeries have their own recipes converted into mixes. Although it is very cost effective, it's not something I personally approve of. I think that mixes often leave an aftertaste as opposed to a cake that is made from scratch.

But your readers should be aware that cakes made from scratch are more expensive. So they should consider which is most important: flavor (better from small bakers) or design (often technically superior at large bakeries). These are the two trade-offs with wedding cakes.

Finally, advise your readers to beware when using home bakers. Although many do know what they're doing, the potential for disaster is high. Putting together a stacked/tiered wedding cake requires knowledge. Making a cake that is structurally sound is a bit more complicated than making a small birthday cake. I've heard so many horror stories about home bakers who offered to do wedding cakes because they thought they could handle it. The heartache may not be worth the savings."

have done wedding pies, s'mores, and even chocolate sandwich cookies instead of the standard wedding cake. Usually these ideas cost far less than an elaborately decorated cake—and are more original as well!

Biggest Myth of Wedding Cakes

MYTH #1 *"At every wedding I've ever been to, the wedding cake was tasteless and dry. It's impossible to find a good-tasting cake."*

Wrong. This fallacy is based on all those tasteless white cakes with Crisco-based icings that wedding guests remember from years past. Today brides and grooms can have a cake that tastes as good as it looks.

Pitfalls to Avoid

PITFALL #1: THE REVENGE OF MARTHA: CAKES THAT TASTE LIKE SAND PAPER! AND COST THOUSANDS!
"I fell in love with a cake design from a famous baker's web site that featured rolled fondant icing. My baker warned me the cake would taste terrible! Not to mention cost 30% more. What's up with this?"

Martha sure makes pretty cakes, but look out—one of her faves (cake with rolled fondant icing) have some major drawbacks the diva of domesticity forgets to mention.

First problem, taste. Yes, fondant iced cakes have an ultra-hip smooth finish but don't ask how it tastes (some folks think fondant tastes too sweet or is like eating gum paste; some claim it's much better than it used to be). To understand why fondant lacks in the taste department, consider how it is made. Developed by British and Australian pastry chefs as a replacement for rock-hard royal icing, fondant is a mixture of sugar, gelatin and corn syrup. The result is a dough-like pastry. All the labor that goes into making and rolling out fondant onto cakes (not to mention hand-tinting) means higher prices—most bakers charge at least $1 to $2 *extra* per serving for fondant cakes. That's a 30% hike over average prices.

If you have your heart set on the fondant look, consider a couple of tips. Ask your baker to add a layer of butter cream frosting *under* the fondant to add flavor (guests can knock off the fondant icing and still have cake and icing below). Also, consider fondant look-alikes. One Texas baker we interviewed mixes butter cream and cream cheese to give a fondant look with better taste.

Another frosting option that is making a comeback: marzipan, which is basically almond paste. Unfortunately, marzipan doesn't come in white—instead, it is almond-colored or a darker hue.

PITFALL #2 ANNIVERSARY CAKE TOPS.

"The baker I visited told me that 'of course you will want to save the top tier of the cake for your first anniversary.' This sounds like a silly tradition!"

Yes, we agree. Saving the top of the wedding cake to eat on your first anniversary is a common tradition in many areas of the country. This entails having mom or someone else remember to take the top home, wrap it very carefully, and put it in your freezer. Even supposing you have room in your freezer, the taste of the cake after 12 months may leave much to be desired. In fact, if you serve the cake at your wedding instead, you may be able to save 10% to 20% off your bakery bill—a much better deal than a stale year-old cake! If you want to follow this tradition, we recommend calling up your baker in a year and buying a small, freshly made cake to celebrate with on your first anniversary.

PITFALL #3 MYSTERIOUS WHITE ICING.

"We attended a wedding last weekend that had a beautiful wedding cake. But, when we tasted the cake, there was this terrible, greasy aftertaste. Yuck! What causes this problem?"

The answer lies in what makes white icing *white*. Well, a key ingredient in icing is butter—which creates a problem for bakers. Most butter made in the US is yellow, which gives icing an off-white or ivory color. To get pure white icing, bakers must use expensive white butter (imported from Europe). Unfortunately, some bakers use a less expensive short cut to get white "butter cream" icing—they add white *shortening* like Crisco. Yuck! That's why some cake icing has a greasy aftertaste. If you want white icing, you might ask your baker how they make their icing white. For example, some bakeries offer a meringue icing (made from egg whites). Yet another trick: adding one drop of blue food coloring to the batch of icing, which turns off-white icing into a pure white hue. Each of these methods achieve a white look without the Crisco.

PITFALL #4 WELL-MEANING FRIENDS AND RELATIVES.

"My aunt has offered to bake my wedding cake. She's good at baking basic cakes but isn't a wedding cake much more complicated?"

That's right. Offers like this are made with the best possible intentions but, if accepted, can be disastrous. Baking a wedding cake is far more complex than baking a birthday cake from a Betty Crocker box mix.

You need engineering skills required to stack a cake and keep it from falling or leaning. Unless you have a friend or relative who is a professional baker or pastry chef, politely refuse their offer. Consider telling them you've already contracted with a baker to make your cake if you don't want to offend them.

PITFALL #5 EARLY DELIVERY AND COLLAPSING CAKES.

"My baker delivered my cake nearly five hours before my reception. In the interim, someone or something knocked the cake over and destroyed it! How could I have prevented this?"

This is a problem that often occurs when large bakeries deliver many wedding cakes on a single Saturday. The cake is dropped off (and set-up) hours before the reception and left unattended. As you can guess, Murphy's Law says that an unattended wedding cake is a collapsed wedding cake. No one at the reception site may admit to knocking it over but you can imagine how "things happen" during a wedding reception set-up. Prevent this problem by insisting the baker deliver the cake within two hours prior to the reception. You may want to coordinate with the catering staff to limit any scheduling snafus. Be sure someone (the catering manager, a maitre d', etc.) is there when the cake is delivered so they can keep an eye on it.

Now that we've covered dessert, let's talk about that important step in covering all the action at your reception—the wedding video. Up next, we'll go over tips and tricks to get your money's worth on this expensive purchase.

## Chapter 11

Lights! Camera! Money! Wedding video is a big part of any wedding budget. In this chapter, we cut through the technical mumbo-jumbo to give you a practical guide to finding an affordable yet talented videographer.

What Are You Buying?

Basically, there are two things you are buying when you hire a videographer: the cameraperson's time, and the video itself.

♥ THE CAMERAPERSON'S TIME. Many videographers will charge you for their time first and foremost. Most offer packages with a time limit of three or more hours. Overtime is charged on an hourly basis. Some videographers will charge a flat fee for the whole wedding and reception; others offer "multi-camera" shoots as an extra option.

Besides hiring a cameraperson for a certain amount of time, you are also buying his or her talent and personality. As with photographers, it is very important to find a videographer who is not only skilled at camera work but is also easy to work with. You will be working with him/her as much as with the photographer. And, of course, the videographer's investment in equipment is important too—we'll discuss this later.

♥ THE FINAL PRODUCT. The most important item you're buying is the video footage. There are several styles of wedding videography.

Here's an overview:

Raw footage. This video simply starts at the beginning of your ceremony and runs, uninterrupted, to the end of your reception. There is no editing or post-production graphics. Raw footage videos are the least expensive option, typically offered by amateur videographers. Professionals more likely will offer one of the next two options.

Post-edited. This category of wedding video is the most common—and the most expensive because the videographer spends the most time on it. Videographers "post-edit" footage after the wedding and reception. During this production, the videographer will take raw footage, cut out the boring parts, smooth the transitions, and add in titles and music. Some videographers add still photos (baby pictures, honeymoon photos) to give the video a truly personal feel. If you have multi-camera coverage, post-editing blends the footage from several cameras to make for a more interesting DVD. Many videographers charge an additional hourly fee for post-editing, while others may have packages that include editing and special effects.

Highlights. In addition to videos that cover the entire wedding and reception, some videographers offer brief highlight DVD's that condense the day's events into a short montage that is ten or 20 minutes long. Set to music and crisply edited, these videos are perfect when you don't want to torture your friends with the full-length version of your wedding video. A twist on the highlights reel is the wedding trailer, which we'll discuss later in this chapter in the trends section.

Copies. Most wedding video packages include one copy of the DVD. Extra copies often cost more; however some videographers have packages that include copies for parents.

Average total costs: The average wedding DVD costs about $1490, although prices are all over the board depending on what you get. In small towns, a one-camera, unedited video could cost as little as $750. The mid-range in most cities, $1000 to $2000 will buy you a one or two camera shoot, some editing, music and a few copies. Want to go whole hog? You could pay $3000 or even $5000 for a complete movie of your wedding, shot with multi-camera coverage and heavily edited with added music, titles and other special effects. In general, more money buys you more camera coverage and extra frills like special effects, highlight montages and artsy editing.

In recent years, videographers have started to get creative with selling all sorts of add-ons, like a "love story" (a five to 20 minute video that reenacts how you met, the proposal, etc.). The extras can start at $800 and go up from there, depending on how elaborate the production. Another option: the "retrospective" which is a post-wedding video where the bride and groom reminisce about the day (see the Trends section later in this chapter).

Most videographers require a deposit for one-third to one-half of the contract amount to book a date. Some require another one-third payment on the day of the wedding with the balance due when the completed video is picked up.

We should note one troubling trend with videographers and deposits: increasingly, we see video companies demanding complete payment UP FRONT, weeks before the wedding. That is troubling. When a videographer receives ALL their money before your wedding, there is no incentive for them to deliver the final product on time. We prefer a small balance that remains to be paid until the video is delivered—try to negotiate this point if a videographer demands total payment up front.

Sources to Find a Videographer

Wedding videography is a relative newcomer to the bridal market. Only in the last 15 years did the videotaping of weddings really take off. Despite its current popularity, finding a good videographer can still be a challenge. Here are some of the best sources:

♥ **PROFESSIONAL ASSOCIATIONS.** The Wedding and Event Videographers Association International (WEVA; 800-501-WEVA; weva.com) has 5000 members, both domestic and international. You can search for a local videographer from their web site.

♥ **TELEVISION STATIONS.** Many camerapersons at TV stations moonlight on weekends shooting weddings, using high-quality (broadcast) cameras. In Ft. Worth, Texas, for example, one of the most popular videographers for weddings is the chief videographer for the NBC affiliate. One tip we heard from a reader: when you call a TV station, bypass the receptionist and ask to speak directly to a cameraperson. Why? Some stations don't like their camera people moonlighting at weddings and instruct receptionists to tell callers that this service isn't available.

♥ **WEDDING PHOTOGRAPHERS.** This can be a good source. Photographers will be able to recommend good videographers they've seen at other weddings. Yes, some photographers and videographers have conflicts. You can avoid this by choosing two people who have worked together before. Don't, however, feel obliged to use a photographer's suggestion without checking out the videographer carefully to see if he or she fits your needs. Another caveat: some photographers have video divisions, so, of course, they will recommend *themselves* to do the video. Just because you hire the photographer doesn't mean you must go with their video package—check out other videographers before you make a final decision.

♥ **CEREMONY SITE COORDINATORS.** These folks often have first-hand knowledge about videographers since they are responsible for reciting the rules to camerapersons. Site coordinators can recommend people familiar with the site who are also easy to work with. And they may also hear back from brides about how good (or bad) the finished video is.

Understanding Video: Some Basics

When shopping for a professional wedding videographer, keep in mind these five elements:

1 **Lighting.** As with photography, lighting is key to a good video. Often, existing room light is not bright enough to get a good picture. In the past, videographers would need to flood a room with light in order to get good video, spoiling the ambiance of a candlelit reception hall.

Well, we have good news on this front. Advancements in technology have led to new professional video cameras that are sensitive enough for use with only available room light. If they do require any extra light, videographers can use smaller, low-wattage lights that are less distracting and still get good video.

2 **Sound.** Especially during your once-in-a-lifetime wedding ceremony, it is vital to get perfect sound on your video. Thanks to new technology, great video sound is possible without the use of giant boom microphones hanging over your head.

There are basically three ways to capture sound at the ceremony. The least effective is through a "boom" microphone. This is attached to the video camera and often picks up every sound in the room, including your vows. If you don't want to hear your seven-year-old nephew squirming around in his seat and fidgeting, the boom microphone is not for you.

The next option is the "hard-wired" microphone, connected to the camera via a cord. The other end, typically a small clip-on mic, is attached to the groom's lapel, the official, the podium or the kneeling bench. This may not be ideal for some weddings, especially if there is a lot of movement during the ceremony. The sound quality is usually average to good.

The final (and most common) option is a "wireless" microphone. This microphone sends sound to the camera via a radio transmitter (about the size of an iPod) attached to the groom's waist.

One caveat: wireless microphones that are "low band" may pick up interference from police radios or other radio equipment. "High band" microphones, on the other hand, can weed out most interference and produce a clean, clear "I do."

Remember that audio is as important as video. When looking at samples, listen for rough transitions or conversations that are cut off. Sloppy audio can keep you from following the sequence of events on the video. Another clue: check to see if the audio is in sync with the video.

3 Equipment. *"All this video camera stuff is so bewildering—I hear there are consumer camcorders, prosumer, broadcast. What should we look for?*

Here's the key point to remember: it doesn't matter so much the type of camera the videographer uses ... instead, focus on skill level and the final product.

Most videographers today shoot in high definition with digital video cameras. These cameras shoot either to digital video or flash memory. While there is a big difference between a $500 video camera you can buy at Best Buy and a broadcast-quality professional camera used by the local TV news, the ability of both cameras to shoot high definition video means the camera person's skills at shooting and editing matter more than the brand of camera he or she uses.

4 The DVD. *"Can I get my wedding video on a VHS instead of DVD for my grandma? What about a Blu-ray disk?*

Yes, while most videographers will provide a standard DVD, most should have no problem transferring it to VHS.

As for a high definition DVD, this is a bit trickier question. The most common high definition video format today is Sony's Blu-Ray. A key issue to remember: Blu-ray DVD's do NOT play in a standard DVD player. While most folks have a Blu-Ray player, this might be an issue if you are giving a DVD copy to a relative who only has a standard DVD player.

5 Camera Angle. *"Some sample videos I've viewed show the bride and groom only from the back or from strange angles in the church. Is there any way I can avoid such problems?"*

Some of the responsibility for these strange angles and shots belongs to your church or synagogue. Many don't allow the videographer to move once the bride begins her walk down the aisle. They may also assign the cameraperson to a particular part of the sanctuary (like the back balcony). This is why it is important to check the policies of your ceremony site. Also, you can ask the clergy if your videographer can get a better view (they might respond more to a bride and groom's request than that of the cameraperson).

It is crucial to have your videographer visit the ceremony site before the wedding (even attending the rehearsal) to see where he or she will be setting up. This advanced preparation may help avoid those camera angle problems. Be aware that some videographers will scout out the ceremony site for free—others charge a fee.

Many videographers today offer multi-camera shoots with two or even three cameras at the ceremony. So does that mean you have to pay three camera people to shoot your wedding? Not always. Some of these cameras may be remote-controlled from the back of the church. The different views are edited together on the final product to provide a much more interesting video than single-camera coverage.

6 Webcast your wedding. *"Can we live stream our wedding vows to out-of-town friends?"*

Why, yes, you can. Two companies, I Do Stream (IDoStream.com) and My Streaming Wedding (MyStreamingWedding.com) offer various services to webcast your wedding. Guests get a log in to a password-protected site, as well as an online guest book for folks to share their congratulations.

Do-it-yourself streaming packages run $200; My Streaming Wedding has packages that include a videographer who is trained in remote broadcasts for $800 to $3000. One tip: check the WiFi speeds at your ceremony location. Streaming services will try to trouble-shoot any video problems the day of the shoot, but most say they aren't responsible if the signal is too weak to broadcast the video.

As live streaming becomes more popular, we are also seeing more videographers offering this as an add-on service as well.

Getting Started: How Far in Advance?

As with photographers, good professional videographers can book months ahead of the date. Popular summer months are often spoken for by January or February in many major metropolitan areas. In New York City, videographers are commonly booked up to two years in advance! We recommend you hire your videographer six to nine months before the wedding (about the time you book a photographer).

Step-by-step Shopping Strategies

♥ Step 1: Using the sources discussed above, make appointments with two to three video companies. Ask to see a demo or a video of a recent wedding. If you contact a studio with several associates, make sure you will be meeting with the person who will shoot your wedding. As with photographers, each videographer's style is different, so meeting the actual cameraperson is key.

♥ Step 2: See the sample or demo video of each company. View more than just "highlight" reels—ask to see complete weddings. Even better, ask if they can show you any wedding videos shot at your ceremony site.

♥ Step 3: Check for sound quality and lighting—are there any awkward moments? Make sure you can hear the vows. This is the most important aspect of the video—isn't the exchange of vows the whole reason you are planning this wedding and reception anyway? If the lighting is extremely bright, guests may squint or turn away. You want everyone to feel comfortable so watch this aspect carefully.

♥ Step 4: If this is an edited video, ask yourself if the editing is smooth and professional. Does it have a home-movie feel or a raw-footage quality? Or is it seamlessly edited with a smooth flow? Is the video enjoyable or boring? Decide if the special effects (if any) add to or detract from the video.

♥ Step 5: Make sure the personality of the cameraperson is pleasant. If you don't feel comfortable, shop for another videographer.

♥ Step 6: Get references from previous customers. Ask these recent brides if they were satisfied with their videos. Did they meet their expectations? If they had to do it over again, would they choose that same company? How did the videographer deal with adverse conditions? Did they bark orders at guests or members of the wedding party?

♥ Step 7: Once you have decided on a videographer, get a signed contract. Specify the date, time, place, editing and other issues. Make sure they note any preferences too: will there be any interviews, for example.

♥ Step 8: Meet with your videographer again closer to the wedding date to discuss any special people you'd like on your video. It may even be a good idea to draw up a list of names. Also go over the sequence of events and talk about any changes or additions.

Questions to Ask a Videographer

1 **Are you familiar with my ceremony/reception site?** If not, will you visit the site before the wedding or attend my rehearsal? These are critical questions since the videographer must determine the best angle, lighting options and sound needs for each site. Many ceremony sites have specific rules about where the videographer can set up. Some sites may also present sound or lighting challenges—the more familiar he or she is with the site, the better. Of course, some videographers balk at attending the rehearsal or scoping out the site beforehand because of the extra time involved. They claim they'll figure out the camera angles when they get there. Whether you want the videographer to wing it or not is up to you.

2 **Exactly what will the final product look like?** Find out how long the video will be and what type of editing or graphics will be done. Often we've seen demos with music synced to the action, fancy script graphics and even dissolves or other effects. Then we've been

---

Wedding Videos: the good, the bad and the ugly

View a handful of wedding videos and you'll quickly realize this truth: quality can vary dramatically. Yes, there are some wedding videographers who do truly stunning work. And, there are others that should stick to taping high school choir performances. After viewing literally hundreds of wedding videos, here are some points that separate the good from the bad:

♥ **GOOD**: The best videos have a mix of close-ups and far-away shots. You'll see plenty of TV-style production tricks, including shots that "link" one scene to another. The best videographers also bring a small ladder to make sure their shots aren't blocked by the backs of guests' heads.

♥ **BAD**: Jerky movements and too-fast pans are signs that a videographer needs to go back to video school. We've also seen demos where the video and audio portions were not in sync (they looked like the dialogue in a bad Kung-Fu movie). Another bad wedding video sign: the cameras in a multi-camera shoot are all focused on the same image.

informed that all those options are extra, on top of the package price. Watch out for these tactics.

3 **Who exactly will be shooting my video?** Again, remember that some companies, especially in busy summer months, may send out unskilled amateurs (or stringers) to some of their weddings. Meet the actual videographer and see his or her work before booking. Unfortunately, some studios only assign their best camera people to the highest-priced packages.

4 **I've read that there is sometimes tension between photographers and videographers. How do you handle this?** True professionals realize they must work with photographers to document your wedding without stepping on each others' toes. You're not looking for a videographer to bad mouth area photographers, but instead provide some insight on how they smooth over any issues on wedding day.

5 **Explain your general wedding shooting schedule.** This way you can find out what they do before the ceremony, whether they do interviews or not and how they expect the evening to run.

6 **Will I get the master video (or digital file) and how many copies come with the package?** The master video is the original video or digital file. Some videographers keep this and give you copies just as photographers keep the negatives. If you want the master, shop for a videographer with a different policy. As for additional copies, they are usually extra. Plan ahead for this expense. The cost per copy could range from $20 to $100—or more.

7 **Do you have back-up equipment?** Do you edit your own work? Do you offer a guarantee? Back-up equipment is a critical issue—the best videographers have back-up equipment with them at your wedding, not in a van or office across town. Even if it takes just a few minutes to run out to a vehicle, you can miss important moments. Another point to ask about: what happens if the videographer gets sick? Do they have a substitute cameraperson who can cover the event?

8 **Will you take a little time to educate me about video production?** This is a trick question suggested by a New Jersey videographer. He told us you're not looking for a technical lecture but insights into the videographer's philosophy. The videographer should acknowledge that each wedding is different—and be honest about the shortcomings of his or her work. "Beware of the person who doesn't or can't explain things to you. Or one who thinks he's the greatest on earth. Deep down, he is probably insecure. Picking a down-to-earth 'realist' is often a better bet than a 'braggart.'"

9 **Tell me about a wedding where something went wrong. How did you handle it?** This is a great question for all wedding merchants, not just the videographer. The wrong answer: "nothing bad has ever happened on a wedding shoot." Come on—weddings are attended by human beings who make mistakes. Professionals roll with the punches and still produce an excellent product. One common area for problems: the photographer. See the box later in this chapter for more info on this perennial problem.

10 **When will my DVD be ready for pick-up?** Most professional videographers offer some kind of post-editing for their video packages. Even though digital cameras and editing software make this process go quicker, it still takes a LONG time to get your final video. The average is about eight to 12 weeks after your wedding! One videographer we interviewed takes six MONTHS to deliver the final product. Be sure to ask so you are not surprised.

Top Money-saving Secrets

1 **Use a professional to video the ceremony only.** Many professional videographers offer discounted "ceremony-only" packages costing anywhere from 40% to 60% less than complete packages. For the reception, consider asking friends and relatives to bring their cameras to shoot footage. Note: beware that some studios use their least-experienced videographer to shoot the "ceremony-only" packages. Confirm who will be your videographer and view his work before booking. (Other studios may refuse to do ceremony-only bookings unless it is the slow time of the year).

2 **Have a friend video your wedding.** Only as a last resort! If you choose to go this route, make sure your friend or relative has a tripod (to avoid those wobbly shots) and plenty of extra batteries. Frankly, this is not our first choice to saving money with wedding video. First, your "friend" will be stuck behind a camera for most of the day, missing out on all the fun. And while digital video cameras have improved the quality of homemade wedding videos in recent years, it still takes skill and effort to shoot a great video. Most amateurs simply don't have the camera skills.

3 **Use iMovie**. If you go the do-it-yourself route, you can use iMovie on a Mac or iPad to edit your wedding video. This free software that lets you whip up professional-looking videos (with special effects, editing, music and titles). Then you can burn a DVD of your wedding video with iDVD, also included on most Macs. Another idea: ask the videographer to just shoot raw footage (no editing). Then edit the video with iMovie yourself. FYI: this requires a significant amount of hard disk space, so you'll have some tech chops to accomplish this.

4 **Negotiate lower rates for less-popular wedding days/ months.** It never hurts to ask!

5 **Ask the videographer if they will do a scaled-back package for less money.** Fewer bells and whistles (post-editing, special effects) mean less time for the videographer. Ask them if they can work out a "special package" that meets your budget.

6 **Request a volume-discount for DVD copies.** If you need several copies, the video company should be able to offer you a volume discount off their normal prices.

7 **Use multi-camera coverage only at the ceremony.** While it's a nice luxury to have two or three cameras to cover the wedding ceremony, it may be overkill at the reception.

8 **Use your company's video or photo department.** Some large corporations have in-house photo or video departments. This can be a good money-saving strategy—some of these same experienced camera people free-lance on the weekends at much lower rates than you'd find in the bridal market.

9 **Check the next town over.** Not surprisingly, we found the most expensive videographers were the ones in big cities. By contrast, video companies in smaller towns or outlying suburbs often charge 20% to 40% less. And most videographers are willing to travel 50 to 100 miles one way to a wedding without an extra charge. So try to look at the next town over to save. The only trade-off: videographers in smaller towns usually offer fewer perks and choices for fancy video effects. But if that doesn't matter to you, go for the savings.

10 **Consider a weekend warrior.** About half of all wedding videographers are part-timers, so called "weekend warriors." Since wedding videos aren't their full-time job, they often charge less than their full-time competitors. Are these videographers any less professional? Nope, weekend warriors can produce just as professional a video as full-timers. Of course, check their references carefully and view several demos of actual weddings to make sure the part-timer is up to the job.

11 Don't mention what you're spending on still pictures. When negotiating with a videographer for a lower rate, there is one cardinal sin—*never* reveal what you are paying your still photographer. Many video companies have an inferiority complex when it comes to photographers, thinking they always get the short end of the bridal budget stick. And they're jealous of photographer's bigger paychecks. So whatever you are paying for wedding photography, keep it to yourself!

12 Hire a student or professor. A bride emailed us this smart tip—she found a local university had a "media studies" department, which is a great source for videographers. The bride hired a professor who shot her entire wedding and reception and edited the video all for $400!

Photographers versus Videographers

Sometimes videographers and photographers behave like guests on a Bravo reality show—and it usually is the consumer that suffers.

To understand why these so-called professionals sometimes act like toddlers, it is important to understand the roots of this feud. For years, the only person who documented a wedding was the photographer. This cushy role insured a steady stream of clients and profits. About 25 years ago, video came on the scene and things haven't been the same since.

Some photographers view video as a major threat to their livelihood. Despite the fact that most weddings today are both videoed and photographed, this feeling still dominates the photography profession. Photographer paranoia kicked into even higher gear in recent years when video went "digital" and videographers began talking about selling "digital stills" as prints to their customers. Most videographers and photographers realize the day is not far away when just one professional takes both digital video and still pictures. And that means "someone" is going to lose out on the lucrative

Biggest Myths About Videography

MYTH #1 *"We had a friend video our wedding. The video was just OK—there were several parts that are out of focus and shaky. Our friend said we could just get that fixed."*

Don't count on it. You can't just "fix" a bad video that's blurry or missing audio. The best you can do is cut out the bad sections and try to piece it together. We've heard quite a few horror stories from couples that had a well-meaning friend or relative video their wedding, only to end up with a video that needed extensive "fixing."

MYTH #2 *"I watched my friend's wedding video and found myself straining to hear the couple say their vows. We're writing our own vows and we really want to be able to hear what we say to one another on our video. Is it true that it's impossible to get clear sound on a video?"*

bridal "memories" market.

Hence, the bridal vendor version of Jerry Springer. Photographers complain that videographers interfere with their ability to capture the event on film—all the lights, mics and other video apparatus make photographers cringe. A typical battleground is the formal "posed" pictures that are taken of the bride and groom before the wedding. These are big moneymakers for the photographer and they jealously guard this turf.

Some photographers go as far as banning videographers from taking video of the formal posed picture sessions; they argue (somewhat unconvincingly) that their unique posings of the bridal party are their copyrighted images.

Videographers, for their part, claim that photographers try to sabotage their video by blocking shots and other sleazy tricks.

So, what's a bride and groom to do? First, make sure you tell the photographer you plan to have the wedding videoed. If they turn red and start spouting obscenities, then it might be time to find a different photographer. And be careful to look through a photographer's contract to make sure there are no restrictions on what the videographer can capture. Photographers should learn to co-exist with videographers, for the sake of everyone's sanity.

Sound quality depends heavily on the type of microphone. We recommend the use of a high-band wireless microphone attached to the groom's lapel. This type of microphone will overcome the disadvantages discussed earlier that come with boom microphones and hard-wired mics. If you can't find anyone with a wireless high-band microphone, listen carefully to the sound quality on demos and decide who offers the best sound.

Some videographers today use multiple microphones to capture audio at the ceremony. The best companies even mix the audio "live" at the site, adjusting the volume level during the ceremony to make sure the best possible video.

MYTH #3 *"I saw one sample demo that had interviews of the guests on it. I thought the interviews were kind of embarrassing and the guests seemed uncomfortable. Do I have to have interviews on my DVD?"*

The answer is an obvious "no." We've seen several videos where a good friend had too much to drink and related a sick joke. In another case, a guest suddenly had a microphone shoved into her face and made a few boring comments that didn't need to be saved for posterity.

Well this doesn't have to happen in your video. First, if you don't want any interviews, be specific with the videographer—especially if he or she has these segments on demos. But if you do want interviews, choose a package that will allow you to edit out any embarrassing comments made by your guests. And don't forget to specify what kind of interviews you want. One couple we talked to asked their videographer to only interview relatives. Another couple specified interviews of guests who really wanted to speak on the video.

Helpful Hints

1 Choose a package with enough time to cover the event. A four to six hour package should provide enough time to capture a typical wedding (allow more time for sit-down dinners or receiving lines). If you think your reception will go over, ask about overtime availability and charges. Some packages end when the cake is cut while others run to the reception's end. Ask when overtime kicks in—if the cake is cut an hour late? What if the bride gets to the church 45 minutes late? Confirming the exact conditions that lead to overtime charges is important.

2 Many uncontrollable factors can affect the quality of your video. For example, church P.A. systems can interfere with low-band wireless microphones. Another problem may be caused by your officiant or site coordinator. At one wedding we attended, the priest requested the videographer stand in a certain spot. The videographer thought she would have a good view of the couple's faces. However, the priest then decided to hold the entire ceremony with the couple facing the congregation. This left the videographer taping their backs for the entire wedding!

We feel its best to try to keep a sense of humor about these uncontrollable events. Having the videographer attend the rehearsal should also cut down on surprises.

Pitfalls to Avoid

PITFALL #1 DVD PROBLEMS

"I purchased a DVD copy of my wedding video, only to find it would NOT work in my DVD player! What went wrong?

Yes, you've just experienced the cutting edge of technology—incompatible DVD formats. While the technical discussion of why this happens is beyond the scope of this book, brides and grooms should realize that DVD technology is still evolving. As of yet, there is no one standard for recording DVD's, hence the possibility that the DVD your videographer whips out may not work on your DVD player. A word to the wise: get the videographer's promise in writing that his DVD will be something you can actually view!

PITFALL #2 "DIRECTOR'S DISEASE."

"I was a bridesmaid in a friend's wedding recently and I was very shocked at the behavior of the videographer. He kept ordering everyone around, telling us what to do. Is there a way to avoid this problem at my own wedding?"

Occasionally, we've run into an inexperienced wedding videographer who suffers from that strange malady known as "director's disease." These camera people tend to expect weddings and receptions to conform to some sort of script for an all-star movie production. Instead of simply capturing the day as it happens, they try to direct the actors (bride and groom) in a performance (the wedding).

In many ways, however, a wedding is a videographer's nightmare—unscripted and unrehearsed, things often happen spontaneously. Experienced videographers will have discovered this fact and (hopefully) will adapt to each fun, yet frantic event on your wedding day. If you check references carefully and ask former brides about this aspect, you can avoid a videographer infected with "director's disease."

PITFALL #3 MISSING KEY EVENTS.

"One of my friends complained that her wedding video was missing one of the events of the evening she thought was most important: her brother giving the toast. I don't want anything to be missed at my wedding. How can I prevent this?"

The bouquet toss, garter throw, toast and cake cutting among other things, are of paramount importance to most brides and grooms. Your videographer should at least be around for these events at your wedding. Amateurs and unseasoned professionals have been known to miss them—be sure to check with references.

To be fair, we should note a videographer does not typically video EVERY moment of your wedding and reception. Some videographers even leave before the event is over.

When you hire a professional, you should also meet with him or her prior to the wedding to discuss those things you want in your video. Be specific and have him write your preferences down. Any key events you want covered should be clearly detailed in writing. Also bring him a list of important people you want in your video. Have a copy of this list with you at the wedding.

Pitfall #4 Deceptive demo reel.

"We saw this video company at a bridal show. They were playing a demo reel that looked great. When we asked them where it was shot, however, they sheepishly told us it wasn't really their work. What gives?"

Some franchised video companies will give their new franchisees generic demo videos to help drum up business (since the fledgling company may not have examples of their own work yet). Confirm the video you are seeing is actually their work. While every new videographer has to start somewhere, we'd recommend he not learn the ropes at your wedding.

Pitfall #5 Nickel and dime charges.

"One video company in my area advertises a super-low price for wedding coverage. When I met with them, however, there were several 'additional charges' that inflated the package price."

We've heard this complaint from several of our readers. In Wisconsin, for example, we discovered a video company that charges extra for each microphone ($50 a pop). And, wouldn't you guess it, the videographer recommends *lots* of microphones. Other additional charges could include exorbitant fees for editing, music, graphics, special effects and copies. The best tip to avoid this is to get "apples to apples" bids from several companies. Don't be fooled by super-low prices that seem too good to be true.

Pitfall #6 Overtime surprise.

"At our wedding, slow caterers forced our videographer into 'overtime.' Unfortunately, he didn't inform us about this until 30 minutes into overtime—and then he said we couldn't get any of the footage after his time expired unless we coughed up another $200!"

Yes, overtime can be a thorny issue. While that four-hour package seems adequate, unforeseen events (a pokey photographer, a slow caterer) can make you run out of time in a hurry.

Our advice: find out what the overtime charges would be *in advance*. Get in writing that you will be notified 15 minutes BEFORE overtime will begin, so you can make a decision on whether to go forward or not. While we don't expect you to keep a constant eye on your watch during your wedding, it would be smart for a friend or relative to help make sure the photographer or videographer's clock isn't about to expire.

Some sleazy videographers (and photographers) make a bad situation worse by using hardball tactics to sell more overtime. Like in the above example, some will shoot for an extra 30, 40 or 50 minutes beyond the contracted period of time—and then refuse to give you the video (or pictures) for that time UNLESS you cough up the extra cash.

We say overtime issues are a two-way street. If the videographer has a strict policy on overtime, inform them the time they spend eating dinner (a meal you probably will pay for) is NOT on the clock. In fact, any significant time spent not shooting (such as the time it takes to drive from the ceremony to the reception) should not be counted toward your package limit.

A related issue to this scam: videographers (and other vendors) that charge your credit card for payments, overtime and other fees *without your permission*. We've heard an increased number of complaints about this. Couples say they give their credit card to the vendor to pay for a deposit. Then a payment or other fee is charged to the card without their permission. Make sure your agreement with the videographer (or any vendor) does *not* enable them to automatically charge your card when they (the vendor) think they are owed money. That is fraud. Require your signature on any credit card payment.

Trends

♥ **WEDDING TRAILERS.** Like a Hollywood movie trailer, this condensed version of your wedding video combines video, graphics, voice-overs and more. More than a highlights reel, the trailer is a teaser for the full wedding video.

♥ **VOICE-OVERS.** More videographers are adding "voice-overs" (a commentary track from the couple or parents) to give videos a new dimension. The narration gives background and emotional impact to certain video scenes. Instead of boring interview scenes (showing a father of the bride at the reception), more videographers are using this audio track over the processional, etc.

♥ **STREAMING VIDEO.** Did your grandmother miss the wedding? Today, some videographers can stream your wedding live on the 'net for distant relatives to enjoy. Yes, grandma needs a high-speed connection to make this work, but she's wired, right?

♥ **TIME SHIFTING.** There is no law that says your video must be edited in exactly the same sequence as the events happened. Some videographers are creatively shuffling various scenes to tell the day's story. Of course, this is tricky—a videographer needs skill to interweave wedding day events for maximum impact . . . and not confuse the viewer.

♥ **RETROSPECTIVE PACKAGES.** Here's a new twist: why not do a post-wedding interview where you reminisce about the wedding? Take that footage and cut-in "flashback" scenes of the wedding and you've got the "retrospective," a new video add-on that some videographers are selling. The price: $850 to $1500—that's *in addition* to the regular wedding video package. The retrospective interview is usually done the morning after the wedding (when memories are fresh) or after the honeymoon.

♥ **BETTER MICS.** New wireless mics have less interference problems and new "plug-on transmitters" can turn any mic into a wireless mic. These can be hidden in podiums to capture the ceremony vows or in the DJ equipment to capture the night's audio.

♥ **BONUS MATERIAL.** Wedding DVD's now rival the latest release from Hollywood—you get bonus material, commentary tracks and more. One videographer even divides up his DVD's into Bride and Groom areas, with specific content relevant to each.

♥ **SPLASHIER GRAPHICS.** These new and constantly improving techniques make videos less like home movies and more like Hollywood productions. Adding still photos of your childhood at the video's beginning and snapshots of your honeymoon at the end provides a complete video "album" feel. Of course, all these goodies tend to push up the price of wedding videos.

♥ **FOILING PIRATES.** In the last few years, videographers have started using new technology to prevent couples from copying their wedding DVD at home. How? Video companies can encrypt their DVD's with a signal that scrambles the video when you try to copy it.

We notice quite a bit of hypocrisy on this issue, however. Videographers who jealously guard their copyright are often the same folks who'll use pop songs as background music on their videos. And trust us, they are not paying a royalty to Maroon 5 or any other artist for their copy-written compositions. We've even seen videographers who brazenly use snippets of Disney animated movies on their wedding videos.

Now that you've received a doctoral degree in wedding video, let's talk music for your wedding and reception. That's what's up next.

Chapter 12

From harpists to dance bands to DJ's, choosing music for your wedding and reception can be challenging. In this chapter, you'll learn ingenious ways to find your city's best musicians. We'll also take an in-depth look at the rivalry between bands and disc jockeys as reception entertainment.

What Are You Buying?

♥ **CEREMONY MUSIC.** From royal weddings to Vegas nuptials, music has been an integral part of weddings for hundreds of years. However, the role music plays varies from ceremony to ceremony. The main issue for religious wedding ceremonies is the difference between liturgical and secular music. Basically, liturgical music features sacred words from the Bible, while secular music does not. Policies about what is and what is not appropriate will vary from site to site.

Nevertheless, most churches have a staff organist or music coordinator who will help you with selections. Organists charge a fee based on the amount of time needed to rehearse, learn new pieces, etc. Other musicians (such as soloists, pianists or harpists) may also be employed for the ceremony. Ceremony music can generally be broken down into three categories:

Entertainment

1 **The Prelude**. Typically 20 to 40 minutes prior to the ceremony, prelude music sets the mood. Even if you don't have specific pieces in mind for the prelude, you can tell the organist/musicians your preferences for happy, upbeat music or perhaps more somber, quiet pieces. Sometimes an eclectic mix of different tempos and musical styles is a nice compromise.

2 **Processional/Recessional.** Processional music heralds the arrival of the bridesmaids and, later, the bride to the wedding ceremony. At the end of the ceremony, recessional music is basically the music everyone walks out to. Typically, the slower processional has a slower, more majestic feel than the quicker-paced recessional music. Sometimes, different musical selections are played for the entrances of the bridesmaids and the bride. Or the same piece can be played at a different tempo as the bride enters the ceremony site.

3 **Music during the ceremony.** Soloists or the congregation's choir are often used during this part of the ceremony.

Average total costs: Most ceremony musicians charge $80 to $200 per musician per hour. Some may have two to three hour minimums. When you hire ceremony musicians, the only thing you may need to supply is sheet music for unfamiliar pieces. If you're having a string quartet, don't forget to provide chairs without arms so they can bow!

♥ Reception Music. Ah, now the party starts! Whether you plan to have only soft background music for listening or a raucous rockin' bash, there are several aspects to what you're buying. For listening music, a harpist, string quartet or guitarist may do double duty, playing at both your wedding and reception. If dancing is preferred, you have two basic choices, band or DJ:

1 **Bands.** When you hire a live band to play at your reception, you are contracting for a particular set of musicians to play a specified period of time. Most bands require periodic breaks throughout the evening and union rules may mandate break times. Bands provide everything (from instruments to the amplification system), but your reception site may need to provide a piano. Sometimes bands throw in a free hour of light cocktail music while guests dine. A specific repertoire of music is often implied in the contract—the best reception bands play a wide variety of music to please everyone's preferences.

So how much does a band cost? The price for four hours on a Saturday night can range from $1000 to $5000—the average is $3000. The key variables are the number of musicians and the popularity of the band. The majority of four-piece bands in major metropolitan cities charge $2000 to $4000 for a four-hour reception (the lower figure is for smaller metro areas; the bigger number for the largest cities). Want a seven-piece orchestra? Or a locally famous club band? Expect to shell out $4000 to $8000 . . . or more. Deposits for a band can range from 20% to 50% down.

2 **Disc Jockeys.** When you contract with a DJ, you basically get one DJ (plus, perhaps, an assistant), an entire sound system and a wide variety of music. Some DJs will add specialized lighting (colored spots that pulse to the music, for example) for an extra charge. Also extra may be rare or unusual song requests (such as ethnic music). A few pricey DJs may offer karaoke.

DJs are much less expensive than bands since, quite simply, DJs require less manpower. The average price for a professional DJ for four hours on a Saturday night in most cities is $235 per hour—about $940 for a typical four-hour reception (a deposit of $200 is often required to book a date).

Like most expenses, DJ costs vary depending on the size of the city. In smaller towns, you might be able to snag a DJ for $500 for s four-hour reception. In the big metro areas, however, a good DJ is $900 to $1200 . . . in New York City, a popular club DJ might even command $4000 for a night's performance.

What is the difference between a plain DJ and a "DJ entertainer"? The latter is more of a master of ceremonies, leading guests in special dances, hosting sing-alongs and more. As you can imagine, this costs about twice to three times the amount for a plain DJ—$1400 to $2000 is an approximate range.

Average total costs: Overall, couples spend about $1430 on the average for music at the ceremony and reception. If you live in a big metro area like New York or LA, you can double or triple that figure. What inflates entertainment costs in big cities are minimums. One Chicago bride told us bands there often have an eight-person minimum—that is, the bandleader insists on having eight musicians on stage. That inflates the cost. In Chicago, prices range from $4000 to $7000 for popular wedding bands.

Sources to Find a Good Entertainer

Every major metropolitan area has a plethora of good wedding entertainers. The only problem is finding them. Ceremony musicians, reception bands and DJs typically keep a very low profile, choosing to work by word-of-mouth referral. Many of the most successful bands don't advertise their services. So how can you find these people?

♥ **CEREMONY/RECEPTION SITE COORDINATORS.** For ceremony music, the wedding coordinator at your ceremony site may be able to suggest a few names of harpists, soloists, trumpeters, etc. Music directors are also another source since they have worked in close contact with local musicians. For reception music, the catering manager at your site will undoubtedly have heard a wide variety of bands and DJs. Ask who really kept the crowd hopping. See the pitfalls section later in this chapter for a disadvantage to using this source.

♥ **INDEPENDENT CATERERS.** If you are having your reception at a site where you are bringing in a caterer, you may ask that caterer for entertainment suggestions. They usually can provide a referral to several entertainers.

♥ **MUSIC SCHOOLS AT LOCAL UNIVERSITIES/COLLEGES.** Many students who are talented musicians pick up extra bucks by performing at weddings and receptions. A nice plus: most are more affordable than "professional" musicians. Be sure to get a contract from them, however. Also make sure the student will be dressed appropriately.

♥ **MUNICIPAL SYMPHONY ORGANIZATIONS.** Most symphony musicians moonlight by playing at weddings and receptions. Call your local symphony for any leads.

♥ **ASSOCIATIONS.** Looking for a DJ? Call the American Disc Jockey Association (301) 705-5150 (web: adja.org) for a local referral.

♥ **THE UNION DIRECTORY OF LOCAL MUSICIANS.** Most cities have musicians' guilds or unions that publish a directory of members. If you know a musician who is a member, this directory may be a good source. However, in some parts of the country (like California), musicians that specialize in weddings are not members of the local union.

♥ **PIANO STORES.** Looking for a great pianist? One reader recommended checking with the staff at local piano stores. Since employees have to be able to play the product to sell it, you can often find a talented pianist working at a piano store. Our reader found a jazz pianist with a degree from the Berklee School of Music for her wedding.

♥ **CRAIGSLIST.** Not only can you buy a wedding dress or a ring on Craigslist, local bands and DJs often take out ads on the site. You'll still want to make sure you see them perform before you book.

♥ **AGENTS.** Last but not least, many bands and some DJs are booked through agents. Big agents may book a wide variety of entertainers that specialize in weddings and receptions. In some cities dominated by unions, agents may be the only way to book a band. There are several advantages and disadvantages to using agents, which we will discuss later in this chapter.

Getting Started: How Far in Advance?

Don't leave the music for your wedding and reception to the last minute. For ceremony music, you must give the musicians time to learn and practice a special request. Meeting with ceremony musicians a month or two in advance will smooth the process.

For reception music, many of the best bands and DJs book up months in advance. In general, three to six months are enough time to book an entertainer in smaller towns and for "off-peak" wedding months. In the largest metropolitan areas, popular dates (the summer months and December) book up anywhere from six to twelve months ahead.

So what if you only have two months left to plan? Don't panic. You may get lucky and find a good band or DJ with an open date. It just may take a little more legwork.

music

FIGURE 1:

WeddingWire.com is a reputable source to find wedding DJ's and bands.

Step-by-step Shopping Strategies

Ceremony Music

♥ **Step 1:** Ask your ceremony site for any policies on wedding music. Houses of worship often have varying policies about what is considered "acceptable" wedding music. For example, music like the "Wedding March" is not allowed at some religious sites because it's deemed too secular.

♥ **Step 2:** Meet with the music director of your ceremony site several weeks before your wedding. If you need to bring in musicians, find three good candidates. Interview the musicians and discuss your ideas for the ceremony music.

♥ **Step 3:** Ask to hear samples of various selections. If you're getting married at a church, ask the music director if you can attend a wedding ceremony or rehearsal. Listen to how certain pieces sound on the organ or other instruments.

♥ **Step 4:** If you hire outside musicians, get a written contract specifying the date, time, place and selections of music. Find out if the musicians/organist will come to the rehearsal (and if there is any fee for this).

Reception Music

♥ **Step 1:** As soon as you have your wedding date confirmed, start your search for an entertainer. Decide what type of music fits your reception. Some important considerations include:

A. The time of day of your reception—For example, in the afternoon, few people feel like putting on their dancing shoes. Perhaps a good choice here would be a guitarist to play soft background music. But, hey, it's your reception so choose the music you want.

B. The ages of the guests—You can't please everyone but selecting a band/DJ that plays a wide variety of music will help keep everyone dancing.

C. The size of the reception—Typically, the "reception music axiom" says the larger the crowd, the bigger the band you need to keep the event hopping. In reality, a four or five-piece band can play a reception of 500 guests as easily as 200 guests. Do what your budget allows and don't get talked into a certain size band because you have X number of guests. For DJs, the size of the crowd may determine whether extra speakers/amplification are needed.

♥ **Step 2:** After deciding on the type of music you want, identify three good bands/DJs using our sources list. Call each of them on the phone and ask the questions we outline below. Ask to see them perform at an upcoming reception. Is it tacky to ask a band/DJ to visit them at someone else's wedding? We don't think so. See the nearby box for more on this topic.

♥ **Step 3:** When you visit the reception, don't go during dinnertime. Instead plan to stop in later in the evening around 10:30 when the

"The Tackiest Wedding Book I've Read So Far!"

That was a comment from a reader of this book posted in a review on Amazon (fortunately for our fragile egos, most of the rest of the reviews on Amazon are more positive than that). What was this person so upset about? Our suggestion that you ask the band or DJ to see them perform at another wedding before booking. "Think about it," the reader wrote, "How would you feel if a complete stranger showed up at your wedding reception to review the band/DJ you were paying to entertain you? As far as I'm concerned, the band/DJ can do their advertising on their own time!"

Well, let's take a look at this issue. First, we suggest the entertainer get *permission* from the bride and groom BEFORE a prospective client visits their reception. Second, if you visit someone else's wedding, use some common sense. Dress appropriately and stand in the back of the hall. No eating or drinking, of course. You are there to just observe the band or DJ for a short time.

And there is a quid pro quo here. If you visit a reception to check out a band, the same band might ask permission for another couple to do the same at your wedding—and we don't see any problem with that, of course. Yes, there are some bands and DJ's who refuse to let couples see them perform before booking. We think that is the bigger concern—what they are trying to hide?

dancing gets going full swing (ask the band or DJ for a suggested time to visit). Look for these key factors:

A. Is the band/DJ correctly reading the crowd? In other words, are they playing the right music for the guests at the wedding? Is anyone dancing? Are they ignoring one generation?

B. How much talking does the band leader/DJ do? Is this amount of chatter helping or hurting the reception? Do you like their announcing style?

C. Is the band/DJ professional? Are they dressed appropriately? Is the volume at a good level or a deafening roar? Is the entertainer varying the tempo, mixing fast and slow selections?

D. For live bands, is one instrument drowning out the others? Do all the members of the band sing or just one? How do their voices sound?

E. How creative are the arrangements—does every song sound like the last one? Are the musicians organized . . . or are they scrambling to get to the next song? Sets should be organized and tight.

♥ **Step 4:** After you preview as many entertainers as time allows, select the band/DJ you want. Get a written contract that includes the specific date, hours and place as well as the price and overtime charges. Also get the names of the exact musicians who will be there and the instruments they will be playing. If necessary, specify what dress you want the band members/DJ to wear. Finally, have specific sets of music written out such as your first song, special requests, etc. You may even want to attach a song list to the contract.

♥ **Step 5:** Remember that the better you specify the music, the more likely you'll get the music you want at your reception. Don't be ambiguous here by saying you want just "rock" or "dance music." Identify specific artists and songs and then star your favorites. For some artists, specifying a certain time period may be helpful. Don't forget to clearly mark the song you want for a first dance.

♥ **Step 6:** Meet with the bandleader or DJ a couple of weeks before the wedding to go over the evening's schedule and any last minute details. Meet them at the site if they're unfamiliar with it to gauge any needs or problems.

Questions to Ask an Entertainer

Ceremony Music

1 What is the ceremony site's policy on wedding music? Does the site have staff musicians or soloists? What is the fee? Don't assume anything is free.

2 Are there any restrictions on the music I can have at my ceremony? This is a particularly sticky area since some sites may have numerous restrictions on what is deemed "acceptable."

3 Do staff musicians require extra rehearsals if I bring in outside musicians too? Will there be an extra charge for rehearsals?

4 Who exactly will be performing at my ceremony? Especially when you hire outside musicians, confirm the exact performers who will be at your wedding.

5 How familiar are you with my ceremony site? Obviously this question is only for outside musicians. Inform them of any restrictions the site has on music. A pre-wedding meeting at the site might be a good idea in case there are any logistical questions (access to electricity, amplification, etc.).

Reception Entertainment:

1 Who exactly will be performing at my wedding? Be very careful here. The biggest pitfall couples encounter with bands/DJs is hiring one set of entertainers and getting another set at your wedding. See the Pitfalls section later in this chapter for strategies to overcome this problem.

2 For disc jockeys, do you have professional equipment? Novice DJs are most likely to use home stereo equipment from Radio Shack. While that's nice for a living room, it may not work in a large reception site. Experienced DJs have professional equipment (amplifiers, mixers and speakers like you'd see in a club) that produces crisp sound and has enough power to fill up the largest ballroom. Another question: do you have back-up equipment? Laptops can crash; speakers blow out—make sure the DJ has a plan to fix any problem.

3 **How do we choose the music?** A simple but critical question. How open is the band leader/DJ to letting you select the evening's music? Do they want you to submit a song/artist list? Some bands/DJs will interview you and your fiancé to find out your musical preferences. If the entertainer is evasive about this question or replies that they "have a standard set they always play," you may want to look elsewhere.

4 **Can we see you perform at a wedding or other event?** The best way to gauge whether a band/DJ is worth their asking price is to see them perform live. Most entertainers should let you attend an upcoming reception, with the permission of that bride and groom, of course. We've talked to some couples who feel uncomfortable attending a stranger's party. See the box earlier in this section for tips on this. If you can't see the band/DJ live, you might be able to view a video or listen to a demo tape (see the pitfalls section for drawbacks to this suggestion). Another smart idea is to call a few recently married couples for references. Ask the reference if there was anything they would have changed about the evening's entertainment.

5 **How many breaks will you take?** Will you provide recorded music to play during those times? Instead of having silence during a band's breaks, consider playing dance music to keep the reception hopping.

6 **Does the price include background music during dinner or cocktails?** Some bands and DJs throw in a free hour of background music during dinner. One bandleader we met said he always throws in a free hour of cocktail music. Besides being a nice freebie for the bride and groom, this gives the entertainer an opportunity to scope out the crowd. Then, when the dancing begins, the band is better attuned to the music guests want.

Top Money-saving Secrets

7 **The iPod wedding.** Simply mix together your favorite songs on an iPod playlist and poof! Instant party.

A couple of tips here: be sure to find a place to plug the iPod in. Yes, the battery lasts for up to 12 hours, but you don't want to have the battery die in mid-party.

What about the sound system? Yes, you can now RENT audio equipment (speakers, amplifier, iPod connection) from most party rental companies for just $75 to $150 for an evening. Some DJs are now even renting basic audio equipment for couples to do their own iPod event.

Of course, we realize DJs are probably having a fit right about now. Memo to DJs: relax. iPods are not going to replace DJs at all weddings. DJ's argue (and we agree) that mixing the music for a wedding does take some effort . . . and sometimes you have to *adjust* the mix of tunes depending on the crowd, evening's events and so on.

That said, we recommend the iPod wedding for couples who want the ultimate control over their reception music. For smaller weddings or for folks on a very tight budget, an iPod wedding may be the alternative to not having any music at all.

2 **Get married any other night than Saturday.** As we've discussed in other chapters, you can score discounts on many items for a wedding that is NOT on Saturday night . . . and that includes the music as well. Most bands and DJ's will cut their fees 10% to 20% for a Friday or Sunday event.

3 **Get married during the "non-peak" wedding season.** This varies from region to region, but generally entertainers offer discounts for particularly slow months like November and January. Entertainers that would normally sit idle during these slow times might be willing to knock 5% to 15% off their regular rates. Ask and ye shall receive.

4 **Don't get married in December.** This is an absolute no-no. Corporate and private holiday/New Year's Eve parties push up the demand for entertainers and (surprise!) up go the prices. One popular band we interviewed regularly charges $1900 for a typical reception. However, dates in December go for $2950 and (are you sitting down?) New Year's Eve goes for a whopping $6000.

5 **Hire a DJ instead of a band.** DJs charge an average of 60% less than most live bands. If your parents can't stand the thought of recorded music at your wedding, a possible compromise could involve incorporating live music at the ceremony and then a DJ at the reception. We'll examine the pros and cons of bands and DJs later in this chapter.

6 **Select a band with fewer musicians.** Prices for bands are often scaled to the number of musicians. Fortunately, today's technology enables a four-piece band to sound like an orchestra (or at least a larger band). That's because synthesizers and drum machines can add a string section to a ballad, a horn section to a swing tune or even Latin percussion to a salsa dance track. We met one pianist who uses a computer and keyboard to simulate a several piece band for receptions. Another band we interviewed augments a live drummer with a drum machine to add a complex percussion track to current dance songs. Fortunately, couples today don't have to pay for an extra percussionist or horn section to get the same sound.

7 **If the DJ doesn't have the ethnic music you want, borrow it from the public library.** Many public libraries have an extensive collection of music (from polkas to Santana) all available to the public on loan. This is a cost-effective way of getting the music you want at a price you can afford.

8 **Use a band member to play cocktail music.** As we mentioned earlier in this chapter, some bands throw this in as a freebie. Or they may offer you a cut-rate since they are already there.

9 **Consider hiring student musicians from a local university or college.** As we discussed earlier in this chapter, many students charge 20% to 30% less than so-called professional musicians. If you go this route, be careful to audition the musicians before signing a contract. For more on how to do this, check out the Real Wedding Tip on the previous page. Another reader recommended approaching bands you see at clubs. She noted that a new band that she found was willing to play at her wedding for only $400 for four hours.

10 **Think about the acoustics.** Does the reception site have large expanses of windows? Or hardwood floors? Good news: such sites will let you get away with a SMALLER band, as the acoustics will compensate for fewer musicians.

Biggest Myths About Entertainers

MYTH #1 *"I'd never consider having a DJ at my daughter's wedding. All DJ's are unprofessional, dress sloppily and play techno music."*

We often hear this refrain from parents, who fear the DJ the bride and groom want to hire will turn out to be MTV's Pauly D of Jersey Shore fame. The good news is that most wedding DJs are professionals with sophisticated equipment and a broad music repertoire. They've become a credible alternative to live bands. We'll discuss the pros and cons of DJs in "Canned vs. Fresh: Should you have a DJ or a band at your reception?" later in this chapter.

Real Wedding Tip

The Smart Way to Hire Student Musicians

Reader Melissa M. had a unique perspective to share on how to hire student musicians—she works for the music department at Rice University in Houston, Texas. Here are her thoughts: *"I get at least eight to ten calls per month from brides looking for cheap entertainment. It's amazing how abusive some people can be when I say that I can't help them. I am not a booking agent, and I can't make a student take a job offer. I can only pass on information as I receive it. And some people try to take advantage of student labor. One person offered $25 for a six-piece jazz combo to play for a four-hour reception! That's total, not per musician!"*

"Our jazz instructor is a professional musician whose talents are well known in Texas. Occasionally I will pass on names and numbers to him to handle, since he knows better than anyone which students can handle a job. Sometimes he offers his own services. Once again, I will get calls asking why I referred them to him, because he is too expensive, or he doesn't play the right kind of music, or he wanted a contract . . . "

Here's Melissa's advice for brides-to-be: *"The couples who have had the best results in my experience have been the ones who come in person to the music or band department with a printed notice of what they are looking for, with all pertinent information also listed, and a number to contact or a time/location for auditions. Students see these on bulletin boards or on job postings, take them down and photocopy them, and follow through far more frequently than on phone messages."*

MYTH #2 *"For our reception, we've decided to hire a great band that plays in several local clubs here. Is this a good choice?"*

Be careful. A great club band does not necessarily make a great wedding reception band. The main reason is variety. Playing a wedding reception requires musicians to be "jacks of all trades." Not only must they play Justin Timberlake for the bride and groom but they must also satisfy Mom and Dad's request for Stones and Grandma's request for Glenn Miller. Switching between the Rolling Stones and Benny

Goodman can be vexing for even the best bands.

While good club bands may feature competent musicians, they often play to a narrow audience. For example at one wedding, we saw one great club band that did excellent covers of 60's standards. While the bride and groom and their friends loved this music, the parents and grandparents stood in the back of the room for most of the evening.

Of course, you can't please everyone all the time. However, bands should play music for all the generations present at a wedding. Before you hire that great club band, make sure they have a wide repertoire encompassing many musical eras.

Helpful Hints

1 For ceremony music, remember that sheet music is often written for instruments other than a church organ. Hence, give the organist plenty of time to transpose and rehearse the piece so it's perfect by the wedding day.

2 Should you feed the band/DJ? Obviously, this is up to you. You may not want to provide a meal to each band member at a $90 per plate sit-down dinner. However, at least try to arrange with the caterer to provide them with some snacks or sandwiches. Remember that bands/DJs have to be at the reception a long time, and a well-fed entertainer performs better than one with an empty stomach (the same goes for the photographer and videographer). Of course, the flip side of this argument is that entertainers can often figure out how to pay for their own meals the other six days of the week, so why do you have to feed them at your wedding? Whatever your decision, inform the band leader/DJ about food arrangements before the wedding.

3 Tracking down obscure ethnic music. You may want to provide a DJ with mp3 files of specific ethnic songs, since finding some of this music may be difficult.

SPOTLIGHT: BANDS VS DJ'S

Canned vs. Fresh:
Should you have a DJ or a band at your reception?

DJs are often the Rodney Dangerfield of wedding reception music—they just don't get any respect. For years, bridal experts dismissed DJs as an inferior choice for reception music.

Yet, the popularity of DJs at weddings continues to grow. According to our research into reception music for weddings in the top seven biggest metro areas, DJs hold a commanding 83% market share.

Yes, money is a big reason—the average $3000+ tab for a band towers over a DJs fee, typically in the $900 to $1000 range. Battling soaring wedding costs, couples are obviously opting for the more affordable alternative to reception music.

Beyond cost, there is a another more subtle reason for why DJs are so popular: the state of pop music today, such that it is. Almost all the dance music you hear today is a complex mix of programmed keyboards and drum machines. There is little chance a live band can reproduce both Lady GaGa and classic Michael Jackson tracks.

Weddings typically include several generations of guests—and the most professional DJs can make everyone happy.

Another plus for DJs: they never take breaks. Most DJs play music continuously, unlike bands that need to take breaks every hour. Just when the crowd gets into a particular groove, the band shuts down for five to ten minutes. Obviously, this can kill the mood. With a DJ, the beat never stops until the party ends.

Yes, we know, a live band is, well, live. Watching a live band crank out "Louie, Louie" is more visually interesting than seeing a DJ play the same song via an laptop. Yet for most couples, a professional DJ more than fits the bill, both budget and music-wise.

Pitfalls to Avoid

PITFALL #1 BAIT AND SWITCH WITH BANDS AND DJ'S.
"My fiancé and I saw this great band perform at a friend's wedding so we hired them for ours. At our reception, different musicians showed up and it just didn't sound the same."

This is perhaps the #1 problem brides and grooms have with their reception entertainment. We've known some agents and bandleaders who play "musical chairs" with backing musicians—sometimes known as "pick-up bands." Here a group of musicians are thrown together at the last moment . . . and the lack of rehearsal shows. You might hire a certain "name brand" band but then the bandleader substitutes some different (and possibly inferior) musicians at your reception. Bottom line: you don't get what you paid for, that is quality entertainment. Large DJ companies with several crews are also guilty of this tactic. You can prevent this deceptive practice by specifying in a written contract the exact musicians/DJ you want at your wedding. Stay away from agents, bandleaders or DJ companies who won't guarantee the entertainers who will be at your reception.

PITFALL #2 CHATTERBOX BAND LEADERS AND DJs.

"We recently attended a wedding where the band leader incessantly talked to the crowd. No one found this constant chatter amusing and it detracted from the elegance of the reception."

Band leaders and DJs often have their own "shtick"—a certain routine they do at a wedding. How "energetic" you want the band to be is your call since, of course, it's your money. Don't be surprised by a chatty band/DJ. See them perform at another reception or event before you sign that contract. If you have any doubts, ask them about the amount of talking and tell them what you believe is appropriate for your reception.

PITFALL #3 DECEPTIVE DEMO REELS.

"We heard a demo track from a band that sounded great. But later we saw the same band live and boy was it disappointing! What happened?"

Auto-Tune isn't just for the latest pop diva who can't sing—some wedding bands use it to air brush their demo reels posted online. Add some computer wizardry and even the cheesiest band can sound amazing.

Our advice: listen for style, not production quality. Beware the slick demo track and try to see the band perform in person before booking.

PITFALL #4 KICKBACKS AND "REFERRED" LISTS.

"My wedding site recommended a musician who turned out to be lousy! Meanwhile, several great musicians in my town are nowhere to be found on their 'recommended list.' What's going on here?"

Kickbacks are a problem with some wedding site coordinators (as well as catering managers at reception sites). Believe it or not, some of these coordinators take fees from entertainers to be placed on the site's "recommended list." A harpist in Northern California told us this unscrupulous practice is rampant in her area. Ask the coordinator if they take fees from recommended musicians. If you don't get a straight answer, be careful.

Pitfall #5 Disco may be hazardous to your health.

"I went to a wedding last weekend where the DJ had a fog machine. That was cool, except it left a slippery residue on the dance floor—several folks lost their footing!"

Special effects (fog, strobes, pulsating lights) might be fun in a nightclub, but sometimes they can be hazardous at a wedding reception. Example: fog machines that leave a slick film on the dance floor. Excessive use of strobe lights can cause seizures among elderly guests. And watch out for that bubble machine—the soap solution that's used for bubbles can stain the delicate fabric of your wedding dress. (If you use wedding bubbles as a send-off substitute for rice, make sure the solution is non-staining).

Trends in Wedding & Reception Music

♥ **iPod weddings.** See our money saving tip earlier in this chapter for this latest trend.

♥ **DJs are replacing bands at many receptions.** Perhaps it's the cost. Or better technology. Whatever the reason, bands are losing the wedding market to DJs in most towns.

♥ **At the ceremony, the "Wedding March" is being replaced by a wider variety of classical and modern music.** This is partly due to some churches forbidding this song on religious grounds. To others, the song has become too clichéd.

Special Touches to Make Your Wedding/Reception Music Unique

1 **Personalize the wedding and reception music with your favorite songs.** Incorporating special songs that have personal meaning for you and your fiancé is a great way to make your celebration unique. Before the wedding, give the band leader/DJ a list of special requests.

2 **Instead of standard organ music, consider different musical instruments.** The combinations here are endless—harp and flute, a single trumpeter, classical guitar, violin and more.

3 **Use ethnic music to celebrate family heritage.** Several weeks before the wedding, talk over the possibilities with your band/DJ. Some songs may take a band time to rehearse or a DJ time to track down.

4 **If you're unsure about classical music for your ceremony, consider checking out a local library.** Many have extensive music selections (including wedding music) you can borrow to see what might work for your wedding.

SPOTLIGHT: AGENTS

Booking a Band with an Agent

So, what exactly is an entertainment agent? Agents function as middlemen between bands or DJs and consumers. An agent's primary activity is booking bands and DJs at various engagements—in return they receive a commission. The standard commission is 15% of the band's regular performing fee. Now, the power of agents varies from city to city. In cities with strong musicians' unions, agents tend to proliferate. In general, we've found agents more likely to dominate older cities such as New York and Chicago rather than Sun Belt towns like Atlanta and Dallas.

Agents cite several reasons for their existence. First, they can more effectively market the bands to engaged couples by pooling their resources. Also, many bandleaders (who have other daytime jobs) hate the paperwork associated with deposits, contracts, etc. Agents do all the legwork and remove the administrative hassles.

Fine, you say, but what can an agent do for me as a consumer? Well, agents provide "one-stop shopping," enabling you to make one call and get information on a wide range of bands and DJs. If you are in a hurry or just aren't aware of the entertainment options in your area, an agent can certainly help. Agents don't charge you a fee for their services; instead they collect a commission from the bands.

As you might imagine, some entertainers are less than enthusiastic about giving agents a 15% cut of their salary. Many of the entertainers we interviewed for this book held unanimously negative opinions about agents. And, frankly, we've met some agents who were in desperate need of a personality transplant. Other agents make used car salesmen look like Mother Teresa.

The main gripe we have with agents is their lack of "product knowledge." Too many just book a band or DJ without giving thought to whether their music is appropriate. Other agents deny brides and grooms the right to preview the band/DJ at a wedding before booking— a cardinal sin in our view.

Another major factor in this controversy: many bands say off the record they will give brides and grooms discounts off their regular rates if they book them directly. For example, one band told us they would knock off 15% (which, of course, is equal to the agent's commission) from their $2000 normal reception rate if you book them directly—that's a savings of $300, no small potatoes.

Agents respond to our criticism by claiming they can save brides and grooms money. One agency told us they can "get a lower price because they do a volume of business with a band, whereas a band leader contacted directly can get very greedy." Furthermore, agents claim that legitimate, professional bandleaders will keep their prices the same—whether the booking comes directly from the couple or through an agent.

Well, we've "mystery shopped" dozens of bands and DJs and have yet to find any entertainer quoting a fee over their "regular rates." Agents gave us no special discount deals and we often found many professional bandleaders who offered a quiet discount when approached directly.

So what should you do? Try to book a band/DJ directly if you have found them from one of our sources listed earlier. If you need help, call an agent. Be careful to check out any band/DJ the agent recommends before you sign that contract. You might even contact a local Better Business Bureau to check on the agent. Most importantly, meet the band to talk over the music, scheduling, and other reception details.

Now that the music is settled, what about the rest of the details for your wedding? In the next chapter, we'll tackle a host of small details— from the wedding rings to the honeymoon and more.

Chapter 13

Etcetera

How do you get the best deal on a limo? What the heck is wedding insurance? Do you really need a wedding consultant? This chapter gives advice on these and more bridal topics. Plus, we'll examine online gift registries, wedding rings, and honeymoon bargains.

Limousines: Getting to the Church on Time

What is it about limos? Sure, a limo is a special treat for most folks—but many brides find a limo ride is the road to hell. The complaints? Late limo. No limo. Stinky limo. You name it, we've heard it.

And it's not just limo companies that target the bridal market—we've heard plenty of complaints about all sorts of limos from other consumer advocates. The industry seems rife with sleazy operators and questionable tactics. Here's our advice on how to book a limo without getting taken for ride:

What Are You Buying?

♥ **THE LIMOUSINE.** A stretch limousine has several basic amenities such as an extra long body, plush carpeting, top-of-the-line stereo, possibly a TV, sunroof and a privacy window. More luxurious models have been known to contain even a hot tub or other interesting amenities.

When limo companies give you a quote on a stretch limo, ask how many people the limo will hold. Why? Let's say you choose a limo for six adults. This passenger limit assumes that each person weighs an average of 150 lbs. But if you have two or three big men in your wedding party, you can see that you'll be packed in pretty snugly (and that doesn't include the train of your gown). So if you have a large party, ask for a bigger limo (like an SUV limo) or consider renting more than one.

Of course, there is no law saying brides and grooms must be driven to their reception in a limo. Non-traditional forms of transportation include horse-drawn carriages, antique and classic cars and even buses or trolleys.

♥ **THE DRIVER.** Yep, that limo doesn't drive itself. The driver should be dressed appropriately, either in a dark suit and chauffeur's cap or a black tuxedo.

Average Cost: Limousines will cost approximately $150 to $250 per hour. Usually, they have a three-hour minimum rental time, with the total cost for the car is $700 per car per evening. The driver is paid with an additional mandatory gratuity of about 15% to 20%. The price you pay for a limo depends on the type of car—basic stretch limousines are less than Rolls Royce or Excalibur packages. For non-traditional transportation, the cost usually starts at $100 an hour and goes up depending on the vehicle you rent.

Sources to Find Transportation

By all means, ask a recently married friend for recommendations and look for information about transportation companies at bridal shows. Another creative idea: Google classic or antique car clubs in your area. These non-profit groups of car buffs may have members who'll rent out their vehicles by the day.

Best Online Resources

♥ Jeff & Nancy Ostroff are a couple that have put together a web page (**BRIDALTIPS.COM**) with their hard-won consumer knowledge of all things bridal. Their section on hiring a limo is a great example of their clear, concise advice. From there, you can explore other topics, from gowns to gift registries.

♥ The **NATIONAL LIMOUSINE ASSOCIATION** (nlaride.com) has a great site to help brides find a limo. Just input the kind of vehicle you're looking for and your city and state. They'll locate companies in your area. The information will include web site (if available), phone numbers, and types of vehicles available. You can even ask them to submit a price request to the company. No legwork for you!

Getting Started: How Far in Advance?

For most limousine companies, you may not need to start looking until a month or two before your wedding date. If limos are popular in your area and you have a wedding date in the busy summer months, consider planning three months in advance. For carriage companies and classic or antique car rentals, you may also have to plan farther in advance because the demand is greater and the supply limited.

Step-by-step Shopping Strategies

♥ **Step 1:** Using the sources mentioned above, identify two or three companies that offer the transportation you need.

♥ **Step 2:** Find out what type of vehicle you will be hiring. See if you can visit the company and see the cars or carriages. Get details on available options, minimum required hours and the cost per hour.

♥ **Step 3:** Visit the company and check out the vehicles. See how clean the cars are and what amenities they have. Find out who will be driving and what they will be wearing. Don't just rely on a phone call to book a limo—seeing is believing.

♥ **Step 4:** Consider contacting the National Limousine Association (800-NLA-7007; web: nlaride.com), to find out if the company you want to hire has adequate insurance and is licensed. These folks can give you that information or advise you of how to find it for yourself.

♥ **Step 5:** Choose the company you like the best and get a contract detailing the exact vehicle, date, pick-up times and any special requests. As you get closer to your wedding day (say a week before the event), call to remind them of your date and time. Clearly identify arrival times and other special requests IN WRITING. Another smart tip: get the vehicle license number for the car you are reserving IN WRITING. That helps prevent a last-minute substitution of a substandard vehicle.

Questions to Ask with Limos

1 **Will we be able to bring champagne?** Will you provide us with ice and glasses? Some companies will allow you to bring alcohol while others will even supply it.

limo

However, in some areas, it is illegal for the limo company to provide the alcohol, but they will bring ice and glasses for BYOB. As a side note, don't expect the limo company to provide good champagne—it usually is the cheapest stuff they can find.

2 **Who will be the driver?** How much is the gratuity for the driver? Typically, you aren't given a choice about how much the gratuity will be. Gratuities range from company to company, so check around before you book.

3 **Do you have any discounts available?** Many companies will discount their service for weeknights. Other discounts may be available if you hire more than one vehicle or if you hire them for longer time periods.

4 **Do you specialize in weddings?** Those companies that do may have special bridal packages or other freebies. Confirm the basic amenities of the car.

5 **How many vehicles do you own?** Small companies may only have a handful of limos. If things get busy, they might contract out cars and drivers from other companies—that's a red flag. If you go with a smaller limo company, make sure you get IN WRITING a promised car the service actually owns and the driver you expect. Even better: get the owner to agree to do the driving.

6 **How many people do your vehicles carry?** Limos come in several sizes. Traditional sedans can carry up to five guests, stretch limos up to 12 and super stretch up to 24. Not all limo companies offer the super stretch option. Luxury vans are another option (seven to 15 passengers), as are buses (up to 80 passengers).

7 **How much is overtime?** Even the best-laid plans can go awry. Make sure you know what overtime rates will be and get that in writing. That way the driver won't just make up a high overtime charge on the fly.

8 **Do you have a back up in case the car breaks down?** It's always possible that a car will break down or get a flat on your wedding day. Find out what the limo company will do for you so you can make it to your wedding on time.

Top Money-saving Tips

1 Call a funeral home. Yes, you read right—call a funeral home for a great deal on a limo rental for your wedding! Now, we should say right off the bat that this sounds nutty, but it does work. And we are not talking about renting a hearse from the funeral home but a limo they normally use to shuttle relatives back and forth. We heard about this bargain from recent bride Stephanie Kampes in Drexel Hill, PA. She priced regular limo companies at $400 for three hours, plus a 15% gratuity. "Then I called a reputable funeral home and was surprised with the price!" Apparently, this funeral home rents out its standard stretch limos during down times (Saturday night must not be a big time for funerals). The cost? $150 for the evening. "This may sound rather morbid, but it works!" she said. "While they don't have hot tubs or TV's, funeral homes have lovely limos!" While not every funeral home rents out limos for weddings, it's worth a try.

2 Find a transportation company with a short minimum time requirement. Most companies require you to hire them for a minimum of three hours. You may be able to find someone who requires only an hour or two-hour minimum, thus saving 30% to 60%.

3 Rent a trolley! A bride in Trenton, NJ called in this great idea—she found a company that rents a 30-seat trolley for four hours for $715. We found trolley companies in other cities that had even lower rates (look online under "Wedding Services," "Limousine Rental" or "Buses-Charter/Rental"). If you're having a large wedding party and don't want to rent a fleet of limos, this might be a smart idea.

4 Consider a "pick-up/drop-off" service. Instead of having the limo driver wait outside the church during the ceremony, simply hire a limo to pick you up after the ceremony and go to the reception. Often this will cost you much less than hiring someone for three hours.

5 Have your wedding on an off night. Some companies offer deals for brides having weddings during the week.

6 Rent a luxury car. Many car rental companies rent Cadillacs and Volvos, even large SUV's for as little as $75 to $125 per day. While you'll need to find a driver (perhaps a friend or relative), this is a big savings over a limo. A bride in Turnersville, NJ rented a white Corvette for $179 for her wedding transportation. And that fee is for 24 hours, not per hour!

7 **Consider hiring a "regular limo."** These are regular luxury cars—not the stretch variety. Many limo companies offer these cars at reduced rates. Another tip: ask if the limo company has discounts for slightly less fancy limos (like those without window tint). Compare a regular luxury sedan at $150 for three hours to a stretch hummer for $900 for three hours.

8 **Hire a corporate limo company.** Companies that specialize in limos for executives and business travelers sometimes have better deals than limo companies that target the bridal market. Why? Corporate limo companies can get really lonely on the weekend and hence discount their rates. One bride told us she saved 35% by going this route.

9 **Don't say the word "wedding."** Bridal packages at limo companies always seem to be more than corporate rates. You might want to leave the word "wedding" out of your discussion with a limo company at first just to make sure you see ALL their rates. Negotiate for a better rate if the bridal package is more expensive.

Pitfalls to Avoid

PITFALL #1 COMPANIES THAT DON'T SHOW UP.

This is one of the biggest problems with limousine companies. We recommend you check with the Better Business Bureau in your area to verify the limo company's track record. Checking with the city agency that licenses limousines will also determine whether the company you are considering meets local requirements.

PITFALL #2 WE DON'T OWN THE CAR!

Some limo companies advertise they carry exclusive brands like Rolls Royce. The problem—they don't actually own the car, they just contract for it from another company. As you can imagine, this is a major cause for limo headaches (such as cars not showing up) since the company doesn't have control over the vehicle. Bottom line: if the company doesn't own the car you want, don't book them.

PITFALL #3 SMALL LIMO COMPANIES MAY NOT HAVE ENOUGH CARS.

If you've decided one limo is not enough for the entire bridal party, you may be in the market for two or more limos. In that case, your limo company will often contract out with another limo operator for additional cars. Ask if this is the case before you sign a contract. And if your limo operator will be contracting out, ask to meet and interview the company who will supply the additional cars.

The problem here: the other company may not be as professional as the original. If you have any doubts, look for another limo operator.

Wedding Rings

The good news about wedding rings is you can buy a beautiful band in just about any budget range. Unlike other goods and services you're purchasing for the wedding, there is a plentiful supply of jewelry stores and other sources to find rings. For example, in our town of 100,000 people, we have no bridal dress shops, but over 30 jewelry sources (from chain stores in the mall to independent shops and custom jewelry makers). The plentiful supply means you'll probably find something to fit your budget and style. And online sources like BlueNile.com offer even more choice.

What Are You Buying?

What does a set of rings cost? Couples spend on average $900 to $6000 for wedding bands. Yes, that's a thousand dollars per ring or more. Prices range from as little as $80 for a plain 10K gold ring to $2500 or more for a heavy, solid platinum ring.

What does 14-karat mean? That number refers to the purity of gold in the ring—and that's just one factor that influences a ring's value. Here are the five key aspects to keep in mind when ring shopping:

♥ **GOLD PURITY.** The "karat" is a term that refers to the purity of the gold. 24-karat (24K) gold is pure, 100% gold. Most wedding rings, however, are 18K, 14K and even 10K gold. 18K has 75% gold (25% other metals), 14K is 58.5% gold and 10K has a mere 41.6% gold. Which is best? There are trade-offs to each karat class. While 18K has a higher gold content, it's also softer (and perhaps more susceptible to damage). By contrast, 14K is harder and wears better—and it's less expensive.

♥ **OTHER METALS.** Don't limit your thinking to gold and platinum when it comes to wedding bands. Consider metals like titanium, tungsten carbide, zirconium (and black zirconium), stainless steel and even ceramic.

Why go for one of these other metals? Price for one thing. For example, an $1000 platinum men's band would retail for $215 in white gold. In tungsten, titanium or steel, it would run you only $60. Brides, on the other hand are still matching the metal in their band to the metal used in their engagement ring (gold, white gold or platinum). Hence some couples will have rings of two different metals—platinum for the bride and gold (or another alternative) for the groom.

If you're still set on having platinum rings, consider this tip: ask the jeweler if the platinum ring is pure platinum. Since platinum rings are so pricey (yet so popular), many mall jewelers have begun offering water-downed rings with just 65% to 75% platinum (the balance are other metals) to sell at a lower price point. Rings should be stamped with their purity; 95% pure platinum rings are considered top of the line.

Can't make up your mind between platinum and gold? Now you don't have to—many stores now carry two-metal weddings bands. These are available in combinations of 18K gold and platinum or 14K yellow and white gold (a 50% savings over the platinum/gold combos).

♥ **STYLE.** Consider color. While pure gold comes only in one color (yellow, as you might guess), gold can be combined with other metals to form different colors. A 14K white gold ring is a mix of gold (58.5%) plus copper, nickel and zinc. In order to cover over any yellow tint, white gold rings are often coated with rhodium, a metal that's a member of the platinum family. In addition to color, the style of the ring also refers to its shape. Rings can be either flat or half-round—a dome-like or curved appearance. Rose gold, now a popular trend in jewelry is gold that has been tinted with the addition of copper. Total gold content in a rose gold band is equivalent to regular white or yellow gold.

♥ **WIDTH.** Ring width is measured in millimeters (mm). Most women's wedding bands are 2 to 5mm, while men's are 4 to 7mm. Of course, the wider the ring, the more expensive it is. Other widths are also available.

♥ **FINISH.** Just like the icing on a wedding cake, a ring's finish can range from simple to ornate. Like the shiny look? Then choose a high polish ring, instead of a matte finish. Rings can have monograms, diamond cut patterns and other finishes. A milgrain edge is perennially popular—that's an ornamental border on the edge of the ring that resembles a string of tiny beads. Want diamonds in your wedding ring? You can have stones that encircle the band or just on top.

Top Money-saving Tips

1 **One word: palladium.** Are platinum wedding rings out of your budget? Then consider palladium, a white metal that is part of the platinum family. But here's the good news: while palladium looks much like platinum, it costs 30% less. Hence, if a platinum ring runs $1600, you can find the same ring for $500 in palladium. Palladium isn't quite as dense as platinum, but wears just as well and still has that silvery-white luster.

A couple of cautionary notes on palladium: the metal will become brittle over time if heated and dipped in water repeatedly (something that is done when jewelry is repaired). Therefore, palladium might be better in a band but is more risky for rings with prongs that hold stones.

Palladium will also react with sulfuric acid, which means palladium rings aren't the best choice for someone who works around such chemicals.

2 **Tungsten.** What metal is as dense as gold, won't scratch and never needs polishing? Tungsten has become a popular wedding ring alternative and price is a big reason: most tungsten rings are under $100. The only disadvantage: tungsten rings are more of a darker grey color compared to metals like platinum and palladium.

3 **For gold, consider 14K.** Yes, it has less gold in it than 18K or 24K rings, but this is also an advantage. As we mentioned above, 14K gold is harder and wears better than higher-karat rings. And, best of all, it's much less expensive. While a 10-karat ring would be even less expensive, these rings can actually snap when sized. We recommended staying away from the 10-karat option.

4 **Check out pawn shops.** Divorces and other financial mishaps often lead folks to pawn their wedding rings. As a result, pawnshops have an incredible selection of jewelry at very good prices. One of our readers found an antique engagement ring at a Denver pawnshop for only $400. She had it appraised for $3400. Another good bet: estate sales often feature rings and other jewelry.

5 **Comparison shop.** Which place has the best deals on wedding rings—mall stores or independent jewelers? Well, there is no one answer. Sales, special deals and other events may make one jeweler temporarily less expensive than another. Make sure you're comparing "apples to apples" with rings (same width, metal purity, etc.).

6 **Don't forget about antique stores.** One bride called us with this incredible bargain: she found a platinum wedding band from the 1920's at an antique store. The ring, which had a half-carat diamond and sapphires, cost her $700. She had it appraised at $1400.

7 **Go online.** See the Spotlight: Best Buy below for a discount source for wedding rings.

8 **Consider synthetics.** If you have your heart set on a diamond wedding ring but your wallet can't handle diamond prices, consider new synthetic alternatives. One option: Moissanite (moissanite.com), a diamond look-alike that is made by Charles & Covard (a lab that fabricates man-made gemstones). A one carat Moissanite ring runs $600 in white gold; a similar-size and quality diamond would run you $5500.

The only bummer: Moissanite is only available at certain jewelers (check their web site for a dealer near you); some states only have a small number of Moissanite dealers.

9 **Check out warehouse clubs like Costco.** Yes, Costco sells engagement and wedding rings at huge discounts. Quality and selection varies by store, but you can special order a certain size. One recent reader sang the praises of Costco's special order service: "The telephone operators are helpful and friendly and will fax GIA certificates of any diamond you are interested in within minutes. Their employees are not on commission and it shows because there is no pressure to buy. They then ship the ring to the closest store to your home and if after seeing it you decide you don't want it there is no obligation."

Costco's web site's posts diamond certifications from IGI and GIA, which indicate retail value for the stones. Example: for 1.02 ctw cushion-cut H color diamond in platinum ring that Costco sells for $3000, the IGI appraisal is $7015.

Not to be outdone, Wal-Mart also offers great deals on bands and you don't have to be a member (of course). A reader said she got her diamond band there for a mere $250. We checked on line and found prices start at $280 for a diamond and 10K gold band. And of course, no one has to know you got it from Wal-Mart.

10 **Recycle, reuse.** Consider reusing a family heirloom. You can reset the ring with different stones and with most rings you can resize them to fit. Or recycle some broken gold jewelry by taking it to a local jewelry store. Couples are surprised at how much they can get for gold today (gold sold for over $1000 an ounce at the time of this writing). Then they can take the cash and buy the rings they want.

Helpful Hints

1 **Independently confirm the ring's quality.** If you're buying a ring online or from a self-described "discounter," find an independent appraiser to check out the ring after you buy it. Make sure that the price you paid is what the ring is worth.

2 **Confirm return policies.** Be certain to check with each retailer for return policy. Some only give you 30 days or less to return a ring. Have the ring appraised with enough time to return it if the ring's quality and value is questionable.

3 **If you're spending a lot of money for a ring, buy a loose stone.** The ring's setting may hide flaws in the stone. As one bride noted, her diamond had an inclusion (defect) that was easily seen in the loose stone, but was hidden completely by the setting. She got a great price on it because of the defect, but no one could see it once it was set. While she knew of the problem and was fine with it, you might never know about it with a pre-set diamond until you want to reset it or appraise it. Then you may find out you spent too much and got less than you expected.

4 **Before you order or buy a ring, check to see if is a cast band.** A cast band is made to a specific size and cannot be sized down to fit. One bride contacted us about just such a problem. In trying to downsize a cast ring, the jewelry store dented the band. Ultimately, the bride put her foot down and they reordered her band in the correct size.

5 **Titanium caveats.** Yes, titanium wedding bands have increased in popularity in recent years. But consider these tips: first, titanium rings are DARKER than platinum or gold. Although they are marketed as scratch-resistant, a titanium ring WILL show scratches (good news: the rings can be polished to remove scratches). Finally, titanium rings are nearly impossible to re-size. It is very difficult to make a titanium ring larger or smaller.

That said, we should note that titanium rings are very durable while at the same time, very lightweight. That makes a titanium ring perfect for the guy who doesn't like wearing rings—or works in a hands-on job like construction.

Best Online Resources

As with every aspect of today's wedding, you can buy your wedding bands (and even engagement ring) online. Web based jewelers make up about $9.8 billion of the $150 billion jewelry industry—and that share is increasing at a rapid clip. Even Amazon.com has joined the many online options with their own fine jewelry store.

So what's the big attraction? Price. The typical retail jeweler marks up items as much as 60% to 100%. But online retailers limit their markup to about 15%. By bypassing convoluted supply lines and cutting out middlemen, online jewelers can sell diamonds and other wedding jewelry for 40% less than retail jewelers.

Is there a big risk to buying online? No, nearly all online jewelers offer 30-day money back guarantees—so you can take your items to a gemologist for an appraisal.

Spotlight: Best Buy

WEDDING RING HOTLINE
(800) 985-7464 or (732) 972-7777; weddingringhotline.com

Tired of the high prices of mall jewelry stores? Like the prices but not the styles of discount stores? Well, we found a great alternative: The Wedding Ring Hotline of Englishtown, New Jersey.

Owner Mitch Slachman has been in the business since 1983 and has developed a loyal clientele in New York and New Jersey. The Wedding Ring Hotline not only carries Mitch's custom designs, but also the styles of leading designers' lines as well.

And talk about good deals—The Wedding Ring Hotline's prices are 25% to 33% below retail on most designs. Or Mitch can custom-design a ring for even bigger savings. Wedding Ring Hotline's retail showroom (under the name Bride & Groom's West) in Englishtown, New Jersey has over 1000+ styles on display. (It's best to call for an appointment).

If you don't live in that part of the country, you can surf their extensive web site. We saw an impressive number of styles, from monogrammed rings to diamond-studded bands. A simple 4mm plain woman's band in 14K white or yellow gold starts at $176. A simple

FIGURE 1: Why pay retail for your rings? Sites like the WeddingRingHotline offer discounts up to 70% off mall jeweler prices.

men's style in white gold is about $260. Want platinum? A man's solid platinum 5mm ring sells for $905 (the same style in palladium is $245).

Another cool part to the Wedding Ring Hotline: they also sell designer brands like Christian Bauer (among others) at attractive prices. So if you see a ring advertised in a bridal magazine, call them first to get a price quote before you pay a hefty mark-up at a retail store.

Mitch noted that recently he's selling more men's rings in metals like tungsten. For $100 or less, you can get a stylish ring that is also much stronger than typical metals like gold and white gold. Mitch tells us tungsten is also actually scratch proof, doesn't tarnish and doesn't wear.

The Wedding Ring Hotline takes all major credit cards and has a 30-day 100% money-back guarantee if you're not happy. There's also no sales tax if you live outside New Jersey, a big money-savings as well and free ground shipping for items over $100.

More web sites for diamond rings:

♥ **BLUE NILE** (bluenile.com) is one of the most popular sites online to find affordable wedding and engagement rings. They offer an education section as well as "Expert Live Help" when selecting a ring. There is also a customizing option if you don't see the design you want. We liked playing with the "Build Your Own Ring" options.

♥ **DIAMOND CUTTERS** (diamondcutters.com) has an excellent tutorial on buying a diamond. Check out their "Education" section to learn what rip-offs to avoid when diamond shopping. Diamond Cutters offers an option similar to Blue Nile to create your own ring. They offer to show you different shapes of diamonds in different settings—and you can choose settings by price—pretty cool.

♥ **DIAMOND** (diamond.com) also offers brides an opportunity to customize their own engagement rings along with name brand options. Check out their clearance section for some bargains.

♥ **ICE** (ice.com) Ice's sells everything from engagement and wedding rings to gifts for the wedding party and even men's cuff links.

♥ **AMAZON** (amazon.com) lets you shop by price using their sort feature. You can also choose to browse by setting type, material and brand.

♥ **TRADE SHOP** (tradeshop.com) offers custom wedding rings you can help design yourself. And they post pictures of your ring as it "takes shape" while they're making it.

♥ **DIAMOND.CA** (diamond.ca) This Canadian company (part of Canadian

Diamond Exchange) sells only diamonds from Canada—so you can avoid buying a "conflict diamond" that may be funding some despotic regime

Royal Prestige: Cookware pitch exposed

Royal Prestige pitches engaged couples to come to their seminars to learn about their cookware and win a free honeymoon. Many of our readers, however, think the cookware is a joke and the sales tactics are heavy handed at best. The following letter, from a reader who has extensive experience in the cookware and china biz, summed it up best:

"After attending a local bridal show at which I registered, I was called by Royal Prestige and invited to a 'marketing presentation' at a local hotel with dinner included. Even though I was skeptical, I didn't have any plans that evening, so I dragged my fiancé out for what I thought would be a fun presentation.

"When I got there, surprise, surprise, it was a sales pitch! The centerpiece of the sales pitch was their waterless cookware and china. Rather than focusing on exactly what you would be getting for your hard-earned money, the salesperson pitched the substantial savings to be gained by using less energy to cook the food, and using no oil! He also spelled out the benefits of healthy cooking and the easy payment plan. The 'dinner' was a small piece of cooked chicken, and a few carrots and pieces of broccoli, followed by a glass of water! Some dinner—and it was a long presentation, at dinnertime.

"I was amazed at how they distorted the facts. For example, they showed off their four ugly china patterns, and told us that the patterns have never been discontinued, and never will be. Lenox china, however, discontinues 50% of their china patterns every four years, he told the appalled group of brides- and grooms-to-be. All that hard-earned money spent on Lenox china, and after four years, there was a 50% chance that the pattern wouldn't be around! What he failed to accurately mention is that the majority of patterns sold by Lenox are in their Top 25 line, which does not get discontinued. Any bridal consultant can easily obtain that information and educate prospective customers. His other point was that if a piece or two gets broken, then Lenox makes you buy the entire place setting, not just a dinner plate! Helloooo, ever heard of open stock? You have to ASK someone at the store, and it usually requires a special order, but it is not difficult to just buy one piece of china!

"His talk about the cookware was also full of inaccuracies,

or terrorist organization. A side benefit: they also claim their diamonds are 30% to 50% cheaper than comparable diamonds on the market.

but one in particular stands out. While talking about their lifetime guarantee, he referred to one of the best cookware brands on the market—Calphalon. At that point, he whipped out a Calphalon box, and showed it to all the amazed attendees. The warranty on the Calphalon box was only for ten years! All that money, and such a small warranty period! The nerve of Calphalon to do such a thing! He neglected to explain to everyone that the box he was holding was part of Calphalon's "Pots & Pans" line, which is its low-end cookware. You don't spend a lot of money to get that set! All their other lines do come with a lifetime warranty, but he never mentioned that.

"By this point, everyone was ready to thank this guy for doing them such a favor. And he was ready for the kill. There were reps available now to discuss the payment plans with you. If you made the purchase today, then you would get a 40% discount, in the form of a gift. Will wonders never cease? For free, you would get a service for four of any china, crystal AND flatware pattern that they carry. Hmmm, don't most people buy a service for eight or 12? Could this be yet another ploy to con people into spending more money?? I wonder. . . . .

"Everybody had to speak to a rep to get his or her "free" voucher at Divi resorts. I had already checked into it, and found out they had timeshares, so I put two and two together. Still, I wanted the voucher, just to check it out. I was not one of the first people called, so I had to wait. Fortunately, another couple who my fiancé knew happened to be there as well, and they were up first. While she had bought into the scam, she wasn't ready to put up $2,000 for the 17-piece cookware set, which, by the way, contains only five or six pots—another issue they failed to mention. She left the rep, and started talking to me, where I started educating her on the scam that she had just witnessed. Other confused brides started coming up to me, to hear what I had to say. Lo and behold, I was immediately called as being next! It took me about two seconds to inform the rep with really bad breath that I already had everything I needed. He looked scared, handed me a voucher, and I walked out.

"I don't plan on wasting another weekend at Divi Resorts. However, my fiancé was interested in the benefits of waterless cookware, and wanted to look into it. I bet him I could find it on the Internet for at least half the price they were selling it at. Guess what? I bought a complete set on eBay for about $70!"

rings

Further reading. This section mainly addresses wedding bands. We assume you already have a diamond engagement ring. Yet, if you're more interested in learning how to purchase diamonds and colored stones, there are three excellent books to read (all are available on Amazon or in bookstores):

♥ DIAMOND RING BUYING GUIDE: HOW TO EVALUATE, IDENTIFY, AND SELECT DIAMONDS & DIAMOND JEWELRY (pictured) by Renee Newman ($18.95, International Jewelry Publications).

♥ ENGAGEMENT & WEDDING RINGS: THE DEFINITIVE BUYING GUIDE FOR PEOPLE IN LOVE by Matlins, Bonanno, Crystal (18.95, Gemstone Press 800-962-4544).

♥ PRICE SCOPE (pricescope.com) has an excellent tutorial on buying a diamond. You can also use the site to search for the perfect loose diamond for your ring.

Dubious Items: Wedding Insurance, Name Change Kits

What's the silliest bridal accessory we've discovered? Would you believe lucky pennies for $5 each? Yes, that's what a company in Texas was selling—a penny wrapped in tulle and tied with a ribbon. If that wasn't enough, we found another catalog selling "lucky six-pence" for $12. Last time we checked exchange rates, a six-pence was worth, say, 12 pennies. $12 for 12 cents. What a deal, eh? Here are some more dubious items:

♥ WEDDING INSURANCE. Do you need wedding insurance? R.V. Nuccio (800-ENGAGED, web: rvnuccio.com) offers a policy (Wedsure) that protects you in case of cancellation of the wedding, lost photos, damaged bridal attire, lost gifts and personal liability for bodily injury or property damage at your wedding and reception. Premiums start at $95.

So, should you buy? Well, *Money Magazine* picked wedding insurance as a great example of insurance you really don't need, pointing out that the skimpy coverage doesn't justify the hefty premiums. We have mixed feelings about this insurance—if your reception site requires you to purchase liability insurance, this might be an affordable alternative. If your spouse is in the military and you worry a surprise overseas deployment may scuttle the wedding plans, this insurance may also help. Of course, read the policy carefully to catch all the fine print. Wedsafe.com is another wedding insurance vendor with premiums starting at $175.

So what's covered by wedding insurance? Accidents that occur at the wedding or while guests are on their way home as well as vendors who don't show up, cancellation by the site, damage or destruction of wedding attire, theft of gifts or jewelry, illness among key members of the wedding party, site fees and loss of rental property among other items. Weather is also covered but only if it is disaster level (Florida hurricanes anyone?) that keep guests from attending. Military deployment is covered as well, but only if it was totally unexpected at the time you bought the policy. Those in the military reserve may not be covered.

♥ **WATCH OUT FOR NAME CHANGE RIP-OFFS.** Don't fall victim to "name change scams" where companies promise they'll handle your name change for a fee. Authorities have been cracking down on such rip-offs and recently arrested a Las Vegas couple that tricked thousands of women into paying them for services the Social Security Administration offers for free. The couple ran a business that mailed out letters to "help" brides change their names on their Social Security cards for a fee of $15. Yet forms for that purpose are available to the public *free of charge* from local Social Security offices (check the web at ssa.gov for locations).

Bridal Shows: Fun Afternoon or Highway to Bridal Hell?

If you need a good laugh, attend a local bridal show in your town. If you aren't convinced that the wedding "industry" is a joke, this is the place to give your cynical side a booster shot.

Basically, most bridal shows attempt to stage a fashion show (we use the word "fashion" here very loosely) and a trade fair. The latter consists of various booths with displays from merchants with names like "Brides 'R' Us" and "Fred's Professional Wedding Photography."

The fashion show is what entices brides to visit these shows. During this fashion show, you will actually see live and in person a selection of bridal and bridesmaids gowns from tasteful to tacky. You probably didn't realize how unattractive some dresses can be! After hearing the announcer say for the twentieth time, "Here's a lovely off-the-shoulder taffeta design" you'll probably be able to actually feel your teeth grind.

After the show and the non-stop commercial plug-a-thon (yes, Bob, we'd love to thank Burt's Wedding Chair Rental for providing the chairs you're sitting in today! Aren't they just lovely! And they're just $13.95 plus deposit!), you have time to walk around the booths and chat with local merchants. Photographers, bakeries, tux shops and more will encourage brides to sample their goods and services at a bridal show.

Perhaps the best known bridal show operator is The Great Bridal Expo, based in that state known for bridal bliss, New Jersey. Bridal Expo mounts this massive multi-media show that admittedly is much more polished than the typical dog-and-pony show put on by locals. Slickly choreographed, Bridal Expos are thick with plugs for the Official Sponsors.

Bottom line—is it worth it take one of your valuable Saturdays and visit a bridal show? Our biggest beef with these shows is the requirement that you give out personal information. They tempt you with so-called door prizes. As you enter, most bridal shows will ask you to register for A FREE EXCITING HONEYMOON TRIP TO SLOVENIA. Of course, besides your name and address, the "registration card" will ask for your phone number, email, fiancé's name, yearly income, birth place, blood type, and so on. Then you'll get all the junk mail, phone calls and emails from bridal show participants like that photographer or bakery.

Bridal merchants pay hundreds of dollars to do these shows and THE

REAL WEDDING TIP

Welcome to the jungle!

Heather K. of Southgate, MI discussed her recent experience at a bridal show: *I have read your book, and I just wanted to write to thank you for all the great tips and advice. Unfortunately I didn't get to the part about bridal shows until after I went to one. It was at a local hotel and it was just a zoo. I wanted to go with my mom thinking it would be fun to just get a look at some stuff. My mom wanted to bring some extra money just in case, but I told her only to bring enough for the entry fee and that I just wanted to get some ideas. We got there, paid our fee and were handed a checklist. We were told that if we got all the vendors to check off the list when we went to their booth, we would get a free "bridal gift".*

For a while we shuffled along behind the other brides to be and got our little lists checked and took information and (oops) filled out the little "drawing slips". After a while I had so much information that my cheap little plastic bag broke and I was just checking the list off myself as I passed booths that didn't interest me. (I did get some really great info for the most part though and MANY of the vendors were really nice.) Only a few of the booths wanted me to book that day and I said, "Thanks, but no," and moved on. My "bridal gift" at the end? A tube of waxy chapstick with the hotel's name on it and they didn't even look at my list! We were so tired by that point that my mom and I decided to skip the "fashion show" and go get some lunch. After I read the bridal show section of your book I am glad we did.

BIG REASON is that list of brides, all neatly alphabetized with their home phone numbers, email addresses, wedding date, bank account numbers, and more. Many brides are alarmed to find after attending a bridal show that they must buy extra storage for their email account, thanks to the volume of spam.

The lesson? If you've got an afternoon to kill and would like to overdose on sugar from 67 cake samples, then a bridal show may be for you. But, if you value your privacy, be careful out there. Nothing says you have to give these shows or merchants your real address, email or phone number.

Wedding Consultants

Wedding planners have been satirized in movies, glamourized by bridal magazines—and generally ignored by brides. Once a fixture of weddings in the 1950's, wedding consultants were hunted to near extinction in the 1970's when weddings were less formal affairs usually held on a beach.

As weddings have become more complex and formal events, professional wedding consultants have made an impressive comeback. We should note, however, that there are several types of wedding consultants. Many people who work at bridal shops or retail florists call themselves "wedding consultants." In addition to helping the bride with their own specialty, these folks pass along referrals of other bridal professionals. While they may be helpful, these are not the wedding consultants we are referring to in this section.

We define a "professional wedding consultant" as an independent businessperson who, for a fee, helps plan and coordinate the entire wedding. They don't actually bake the cake or sew the gown—this is done by outside suppliers. In a sense, a wedding consultant is like a personal shopper.

So How Much Do Wedding Consultants Cost?

Most charge an hourly fee or a percentage of the wedding budget. For example, one consultant we met charges a 15% fee on wedding expenditures. So, if you spend $20,000 on a wedding and reception, you then write out a check for $3000 to the consultant. Other party planners we met charge a flat hourly fee ($100 per hour, for example) no matter what your budget. Many consultants offer different levels of help—coordinating just the rehearsal and wedding ceremony costs a small fee, while planning the whole affair from the ground up will run you much more.

Sources to Find a Consultant

♥ **CALL A PROFESSIONAL ASSOCIATION.** June Wedding (702-474-9558 junewedding.com) will give you a referral to a local bridal consultant (their membership is mostly in the Western US). Another group is the Association of Bridal Consultants (bridalassn.com). Unfortunately, they ask you to fill out a form before they'll send you a list of consultants in your area. And, no surprise, they ask you for your wedding budget. Why do they ask this? So consultants can cherry pick those brides with the biggest budgets. Don't enter your budget on the form—wait for the opportunity to speak to the consultants in person.

♥ **ASK YOUR FRIENDS.** The best planners work by word-of-mouth referrals.

Questions to Ask a Consultant

1 **Exactly how do you get paid?** Do you accept commissions or finder's fees from other bridal merchants? See the Pitfall section below for more information on this practice. Ask the consultant to clearly explain his/her fee schedule.

2 **How will you incorporate my tastes into the wedding?** If the consultant will be doing the majority of the legwork, ask them how they will personalize your wedding. Will they get your approval at various stages in the planning process?

3 **How long have you been a consultant?** How many weddings have you planned? This is a key question. Many "consultants" we've met in the course of researching this book were far too inexperienced to entrust with the planning of a $20,000 wedding. Some have been in business for less than a year or so. We recommend you trust your wedding only to a seasoned professional with at least three years minimum experience. Sure, consultants with less experience can still plan and coordinate a beautiful wedding—but be careful. You don't want someone "learning the ropes" on your big day. Other related questions: How many weddings do you do in a year? On a typical weekend?

4 **Are you certified?** If the bridal consultant belongs to a professional organization, that's nice . . . but it's even better if they've been certified or accredited. Check out the organization that certified the planner to insure they are in good standing—and ask how they certify consultants (education, experience, license requirements).

5 **Do you have five vendor referrals?** Yes, you want to check with past clients of the consultants. But then go one step further: ask for referrals from five wedding *vendors* they work with all the time (photographers, florists, etc.). You'll get an idea of the caliber of the consultant's contacts by the names they provide.

6 **Will you provide regular written updates?** Communication is key—you should be updated on the planning at regular intervals.

7 **Can you work within our budget?** Yes, that's the $64,000 question. Sure, you may not have a firm grasp on what the budget should be, but a good consultant should be able to estimate what the wedding you want will cost. If the consultant can't work within that budget, ask if you can hire them on a "per meeting" basis. Many planners offer this "limited service" option, which enables couples to tap the planner's expertise without paying full price.

Pitfalls to Avoid with Wedding Planners

PITFALL #1 KICKBACKS AND VENDOR REFERRAL FEES.

"I visited a wedding planner who recommended I buy my wedding gown from a particular bridal shop. Later, I learned the shop paid her a commission for recommending me. Is this legitimate?"

Well, it certainly isn't ethical. This points up a central problem we have with some less-than-professional consultants. In a clear conflict of interest, some consultants collect "finder's fees" or "commissions" from other bridal merchants on the products and services they recommend to brides. So who are they representing—the bride or the merchants? We don't believe a consultant can negotiate effectively for the bride when they receive a kickback from bridal merchants. If you use a consultant, make sure the consultant clearly identifies how he or she gets paid.

PITFALL #2 PERCENTAGE–BASED FEES MAY ENCOURAGE GREED.

"One bridal consultant told me she could save me hundreds of dollars. However, her fee is based on a percentage of the money I spend. Where is her real incentive to save me money?"

Of course, a professional consultant relies on word-of-mouth referral for new clients. If they don't deliver what they promise, word will spread quickly. However, we do agree that a conflict exists here: when their income is based on how much money you spend, less-than-ethical consultants may feel the temptation to encourage lavish spending. Or at least, the incentive to save you money comes in conflict with their bottom line. Realize that all consultants do not charge a percentage-based fee—others charge flat fees or hourly rates. This might be a better alternative.

Pitfall #3 Counterfeit consultants.

"I called a so-called 'wedding consultant' from a web site. Instead of offering a consulting service, she pitched me on her wedding chapel and reception site."

Yes, many "all-in-one" wedding companies deceptively advertise themselves as wedding consultants. Don't be fooled—these businesses aren't interested in consulting on your wedding. They just want you to book their wedding and reception site, photography and so on.

Pitfall #4 Lack of regulation.

"I contacted a wedding consultant to talk about my wedding. Boy was I surprised! This person knew nothing about weddings. Aren't these guys supposed to be licensed?"

Unfortunately, very few laws regulate wedding consultants. When you think about it, wedding consultants are quasi-financial planners—they advise people on how to spend money. Big money. Unlike other financial planners, however, there is very little regulation. Anyone can call himself or herself a wedding consultant—and sometimes it seems like everyone is. Some cities do require wedding consultants or party planners to be licensed. In most areas, however, the industry is left to police itself. Consider hiring a consultant who is a member of a professional association. Many require their members to subscribe to a basic ethics pledge. Other groups offer on-going training through seminars and workshops.

Advantages of Consultants

♥ **Bridal consultants can save you time.** If you and your fiancé are working too many hours to plan your wedding, you may find a wedding consultant to be worth the expense. Frankly, planning a wedding is very time-intensive (it takes about 100 hours to plan a typical wedding). Realistically evaluate your schedules and time commitments to decide if you can handle it alone. Brides planning large and expensive weddings may find consultants a necessity.

♥ **Long-distance weddings may require such help.** Planning a wedding in another city is quite challenging. Having a local bridal consultant to coordinate the details may be prudent.

♥ **SEASONED EXPERTS MAY BE ABLE TO NEGOTIATE MORE EFFECTIVELY, GETTING YOU A BETTER DEAL.** Now we aren't talking about novices here but wedding consultants with years of experience. These people are on a first-name basis with catering managers and other bridal professionals. Some consultants are tough negotiators who can make sure you get the best price. Other consultants claim that other bridal professionals have a vested interest in doing their very best work for their clients—if they don't, they may lose future business. We are not sure to what extent these claims are true but we do believe one thing: a talented, experienced consultant may be worth the extra expense.

Disadvantages of Consultants

♥ **THE "PROFESSIONAL ORGANIZATIONS" FOR BRIDAL CONSULTANTS AREN'T THAT PROFESSIONAL.** Unlike other fields, most bridal consultant associations don't have rigid standards for membership. Printed up business cards that say you're a wedding consultant? Have a pulse? That's enough for some wedding planner associations to add you as a member. Their main business is selling "home study" courses that are of dubious value.

Other groups are better—June Wedding (junewedding.com) is probably the best-run professional organization of the bunch. Director Robbi Ernst teaches on-going training courses for both new and experienced wedding planners. And June Wedding takes a strong position on the kickback issue; they advise members to NEVER take vendor referral fees.

So what does this mean for you? While it's a good sign if the bridal consultant you've discovered is a member of one of these groups, don't assume they are all-knowing "experts." Check references and ask some tough questions to weed out the amateurs.

Gift Registries

Bridal gift registries have been around in various forms for over 50 years and it's no wonder: they offer convenience for both the guest and bride. Last year, the wedding gift industry racked up $19 billion in sales of china, salt and pepper shakers, toasters and a gazillion other items.

Yet, for all the promise, registries are among the bigger complaint areas for brides and grooms. Just about everything that CAN go wrong has happened with these so-called "convenience" services—items that are out of stock for what seems like a decade, surly clerks, technical snafus and more. We'll discuss all of the sordid details in Pitfalls to Avoid later in this section.

For years, the bridal registry biz was dominated by big department stores. These stores offered gift registries for a limited selection of china, crystal, flatware and so on. Fortunately, this all began to change in recent years when discount stores and specialty chains added gift registries, giving couples more choices.

Yet, the biggest news of all in recent years is the advent of the online gift registry. The marriage of the gift registry (essentially a database, of course) with the web (open 24/7) promised to give both couples and their guests more convenience. Now, you can register for gifts at 3am in your pajamas, see what items your guests are buying and even change the registry as your wedding draws near. Like many tech promises, however, the reality of today's bridal registries falls short of the ideal world.

On the plus side, there are more competitors than ever in the gift registry biz. Dot-coms are battling with established department stores for the online gift registry market and the biggest winner so far is the consumer. We'll review the best sites to register online next.

Best Online Resources

Looking for a simple, free registry? One reader recommended **FindGift** (findgift.com). "FindGift.com features gift ideas from nearly 30 stores. And it provides guests with a web link to purchase the gift online."

MyRegistry (myregistry.com) is a universal site that allows users to add gifts to their registry lists from any web site. You can instruct the

FIGURE 2: FindGift.com lets you browse gift ideas from 30+ stores.

site to email you whenever anyone makes a purchase. **The Things I Want** (thethingsiwant.com) also lets you add gifts from any web site.

Pitfalls to Avoid with Gift Registries

PITFALL #1: OUT OF STOCK!

"We registered for a china pattern, but when guests made their purchases, we found the items were out of stock! And we'd have to wait three MONTHS for delivery."

Yes, stores are famous for letting you register for items that have long been out of stock. Then when you go to pick up the items, you get the bad news—thanks to a back-order, you can come back in several WEEKS or MONTHS to get the gifts! A word to the wise: BEFORE you register, check the stock status of items you want. If the store doesn't stock many of the items, it could be a recipe for frustration.

PITFALL #2: SEASONS CHANGE.

"We thought we'd be smart if we registered six months in advance of our wedding, only to learn that by the time the wedding rolled around, some of the items we wanted were long gone!"

Sometimes, it DOESN'T pay to plan ahead. Registering too early can be a problem—items change, get discontinued, go on back-order or worse as time rolls by. Our advice: wait until two or three months before your wedding to register for gifts. Sure, you can do shopping before that, but don't actually create the registry until closer to the wedding. Guests don't start buying gifts until right before the bridal shower, so you aren't making anyone's life difficult by waiting. Another tip: don't register for seasonal merchandise. Such items typically go out of stock or are heavily discounted, making returns or exchanges difficult.

PITFALL #3: SIXTEEN SALT AND PEPPER SHAKERS.

"Hey! I thought the gift registry was supposed to stop duplicate gifts! We registered and STILL got three toasters, four blenders and other duplicates!"

Theoretically, when your guests buy a gift from a registry, a computer sitting in a climate-controlled server room somewhere in Delaware is supposed to SUBTRACT that item from your list. That way, your Aunt Mabel doesn't buy you that sixteenth salt and pepper shaker. Yet, note we used the word "theoretically" in that first sentence. The reality: sometimes clerks still have to hand-enter gift items into a computer . . . and those clerks forget. Or the registry fails to get updated for a myriad of reasons only a computer tech knows. The take-home message: expect glitches and deal with a store that has good customer service to handle such problems.

Money Saving Tips with Gift Registries

1 **Price shop BEFORE you register.** Don't assume one store has the lowest prices just because they offer a "low price" guarantee. That usually means they will refund you the difference if you find a better price. Before you register, visit at least three different stores to get an idea about prices, policies on returns and other details. Be aware that "sale prices" at one store may be higher than the "everyday low price" at another.

2 **Consider lower-price alternatives.** No, you don't have to just register at a department store. Off-price retailers have moved into the bridal registry biz in recent years and offer a great alternative. Remember that not ALL of your guests can buy $250 gift items at department stores; giving them a wide option of items at different price points in several stores is smart.

3 **Get sale guarantees in writing.** Department stores are famous for running numerous sales throughout the year. Unfortunately, some "forget" to give your guests the discounted price when purchasing a gift. Double check the registry's promises regarding sale prices and verify purchases to make sure you get the best price.

4 **Use a discounter to fill in purchases.** Get seven of eight place settings you wanted? Want to fill in the final items? Consider buying china and tableware from a discounter. Ross Simons (ross-simons.com) offers popular patterns at discounts of up to 30%, with additional coupon deals and clearance items (especially flatware). Ross Simons has been around since 1952 and has excellent customer service.

5 **And don't forget to consider registering for your honeymoon!** This is a particularly attractive idea for couples that already have all the dishes, coffee pots, etc. they could ever use. You can set up a honeymoon registry with most full service travel agencies.

6 **How can you turn unwanted wedding gifts into cash?** Use an in-store credit card. If you want to return a gift (say you got three salt and pepper shakers but two are plenty), many couples will have the returned gift credited to their in-store charge account. Now what's the big deal with this? Well, federal law requires that the store refund any positive balance to the cardholder if they request it. So you get cash back! Needless to say, retailers are not happy about folks discovering this loophole (particularly those like Target with incredibly strict refund policies). In fact, some stores now will not credit back items to your credit card—they only issue a store credit voucher. Check with the stores you are registering with to see if they will allow returns to be charged back to in-store credit cards. Macy's, for example, allows these types of returns. And other stores like Crate & Barrel are willing to refund cash for any exchange. Check with your registry.

Honeymoons

What are the best honeymoon deals? How can you hurricane-proof your honeymoon? Where do you go online to save? We'll explore these and other tips in this section.

What are you buying?

The average honeymoon costs $4500 and lasts eight days, according to a recent bridal magazine survey. Honeymoons can be found in almost any price range. On the dirt-cheap end, close-to-home get-aways can be had for under $1000. Conversely, a week's stay on a posh Caribbean island can be double or triple the "average" honeymoon budget.

Remember the golden rule of honeymoon shopping: NEVER PAY RETAIL. Honeymoons are a $9 billion business. But we'd guess 90% or more of honeymoons are sold at prices that are discounted off the "brochure price," "rack rate" or other stated rate.

What are the most popular sites to honeymoon? Travel agents say Mexico, Las Vegas, Bahamas, Orlando, Jamaica, Italy, US Virgin Islands, Aruba, Hawaii, and Fiji are the top honeymoon destinations. Cruises are also at the top of the list.

Sources to find honeymoon info

♥ TRAVEL AGENTS. A few do still exist and if you can find a good one, they can be invaluable. Savvy agents know which hotels have the most romantic views and which tour operators are most reliable. Sadly, it is hard to find a decent agent these days, much less one that is a "honeymoon expert." Ask friends and co-workers if they know good agents.

♥ **THE WEB.** If there is one thing the web is great for, it's travel. From discount airfare sites to official tourism bureaus for far-flung locales, the web can't be beat. We'll go over some of our favorite 'net spots for deals later in this chapter.

Money Saving Tips with Honeymoons

1 Go "off-season." Discounts of up to 40% can be had on lodging and airfares when you travel in the so-called off-season. But just when is the off-season? It depends on the location. See the chart on the next page for details.

2 Try the shoulder seasons. If you don't want to go to a tropical island in the heat of summer, consider the "shoulder seasons." These are times in between the peak and off-peak seasons. For example, in the Caribbean, packages in the weeks after Easter before the summer rush and between Thanksgiving and Christmas can be great deals. Search hotel sites directly for shoulder season discounts, like stay for six nights, get the seventh night free.

3 One word: Orlando. There are so many deals to Orlando and so much to do there (it's more than just Disney) that you can't go wrong. Many airlines offer packages for around $600 (per person) for a week in Orlando—that includes airfare and hotel. One airline that offers such great deals is Southwest Airlines. Which brings us to tip number #4:

4 Two words: Southwest Airlines. This low-cost airline has expanded in recent years and now serves such honeymoon friendly destinations as Orlando, Denver (think ski vacation) and Ft. Lauderdale (a great jumping off point for a cruise). In the past year, Southwest has expanded to Puerto Rico, another cruise hub.

5 Alternative airports. Low-fare airlines like Spirit and Allegiant tend to fly out of smaller airports that enable them to avoid congested hubs. Hence you'll find lower fares out of Midway in Chicago compared to O'Hare. Want a cheap fare to the Caribbean? Fort Lauderdale is often a more affordable gateway than Miami. Always consider an alternative (usually smaller) airport when trying to save.

6 Plan in advance. The cheapest seats and hotel rooms tend to go first; booking several months ahead of time will ensure you won't have to pay premium prices for peak season dates.

7 **Don't plan in advance.** Okay, we know that contradicts #6, but think about it. There are many last-minute honeymoon options that can be steals. For example, later in this chapter we'll review a web site that offers cut-rate deals for cruises booked at the last moment.

8 **Take an e-fare honeymoon.** Speaking of not planning in advance, many airlines now post super-low airfares for travel the following weekend. You leave on a Saturday and must return on a Monday or Tuesday—and you won't know where you are going until Wednesday before the honeymoon (that's when the airfares are posted).

9 **For destination weddings, see if the airline has a "bridal discount."** If you plan to take ten of your closet friends and/or relatives on a destination wedding, ask about discounts. American and other airlines offer a 5% to 10% discount on the lowest fare for wedding parties of ten or more.

WHEN IS THE OFF SEASON?

You can save big when you take a honeymoon in the off-season. Here's a list of what's off when:

DESTINATION	OFF-SEASON
CALIFORNIA WINE COUNTRY	FALL MONTHS (SEPTEMBER AND OCTOBER)
ROCKY MOUNTAINS	SUMMER HAS GREAT DEALS AT SKI RESORTS; FROM EASTER UNTIL THANKSGIVING.
EUROPE	NOVEMBER THROUGH MARCH.
CARIBBEAN	MID APRIL TO MID DECEMBER. (BUT WATCH OUT FOR HURRICANE SEASON).
ORLANDO	AFTER EASTER TO EARLY JUNE. SEPTEMBER TO BEFORE THANKSGIVING AND THE MONTH OF DECEMBER UP UNTIL CHRISTMAS; JANUARY AFTER NEW YEAR'S DAY.
HAWAII/SOUTH PACIFIC	PRICES CAN BE SLIGHTLY HIGHER IN WINTER (ESPECIALLY THE CHRISTMAS HOLIDAY) BUT THEY DON'T CHANGE MUCH YEAR-ROUND. FALL (LABOR DAY TO MID DECEMBER) USUALLY BRINGS FARE SALES AND HOTEL DEALS.

honeymoon

10 **Book early for peak times.** Be careful if your honeymoon corresponds with any peak travel times, like Europe in the summer, the Caribbean over the holidays, spring break in Orlando and so on. In those cases, booking early to get the best deals is prudent.

11 **Travel on off-days.** The slowest days for air travel (Saturday, Tuesday, Wednesday) often see the lowest fares. In contrast, fares tend to be higher on busy travel days like Monday, Thursday, Friday and Sunday.

12 **Follow the disaster.** A hurricane just hit a Caribbean island? A heat wave bakes a region in Europe? Such events usually create tremendous bargains, as other travelers cancel their plans. Go against the flow for good deals.

13 **Bid on a bargain.** Many couples have found deals on Priceline.com and other travel auction sites. But beware: Priceline tickets often require bizarre schedules (6am departure, anyone?) and connections that leave you open for delays. Hint: check web sites like BiddingForTravel.com to see what current winning bids are on Priceline.

14 **Consider a consolidator.** The cheapest way to fly internationally is to check out travel consolidators, who buy blocks of tickets from airlines to re-sell at good prices. A good example: onetravel.com.

Island hopping

For tropical getaways, the Caribbean and Hawaii offers plenty of options. But what is best for different interests? Here are some thoughts:

Best Scuba: Cozumel and Bonaire.
Best Snorkel: Cozumel, St. Croix and Virgin Gorda.
Best Shopping: Bermuda.
Best Music: Jamaica.
Best Beaches: Aruba, Antigua and Barbados.
Best for food: Martinique, Guadeloupe, Curacao.
Best for Eco Trips: St. John, US Virgins.
Best Upscale: St. Maarten, St. Bart's, Nevis and Anguilla.
Best Volcanoes: Big Island Hawaii.

15 **Tour companies.** Vacation package companies like Apple Vacations (applevacations.com) book affordable vacations with charter airlines and decent hotels. These combined deals can be great steals—$825 per person for a week in the US Virgin Islands, including airfare and hotel, for example.

One cautionary note: we have heard occasional complaints about tour companies. If the hotel you are expecting to stay in is full, they will move you to another, not necessarily comparable hotel. In fact, one reader noted that this happened to her in Cancun: "When we got there, we were told that there wasn't a room available. We had to stay at another hotel down the road (which ended up being much smaller and not nearly as nice as the original hotel). We were never refunded the difference in price between the hotels, and no apologies were offered."

The take-home message: only use tour companies as a last resort. Double check policies on hotel placements and other guarantees.

Pitfall to Avoid

PITFALL #1 THE FREE HONEYMOON SCAM.

"I was contacted recently by a travel agency who offered me a free vacation in the Bahamas. They said all I'd have to pay is the taxes on the package, but I have to put down a deposit immediately to qualify. Is this really a good deal?"

If it sounds too good to be true . . . well, you know. This is a common scam perpetrated by a few unscrupulous travel companies. In the instance above, the "taxes and fees" came to $320. In searching the Internet, we discovered you could get a similar package at the same hotel for $310, including all taxes. The lesson here? If you can't wait a day or two to think about and research a deal, it's no deal.

Another twist to this scam: you are contacted by a company that is offering a free honeymoon . . . all you have to do is buy airfare through the travel agency. Great deal, right? Wrong. The airfare will be grossly inflated (several times what you could book yourself) and often, the "free hotel stay" turns out to be a stay in a cheap time-share hotel. And you are required to attend a high-pressure sales presentation as part of your freebie.

Best Online Resources

Sure, you know about Expedia and Travelocity. But what are some offbeat sites that can help you save on a honeymoon? Here are our picks:

♥ **FARE COMPARE** (farecompare.com) gives you a snapshot of what the average fare is from your home city to any destination worldwide. The site lists current best deals as well as historical averages for fares so you know whether the price you're being quoted is a bargain or not. See the next page for a graphic.

♥ **BING** web: bing.com. Bing, Microsoft's travel search engine predicts whether airfares will rise, fall or remain steady in the near future. With airfares sometimes changing by the minute, this site lets you know if you are getting a bargain . . . or a raw deal.

Hurricane proof your honeymoon

Most weddings (and therefore, honeymoons) are in the summer. And since many couples opt for a beach getaway, the temptation to hit the Caribbean is high. Unfortunately, so is the risk for hurricanes. While the hurricane season peaks in September, you can encounter a vacation-destroying tempest anytime from June to November.

So, what can you do to hurricane proof your honeymoon? Remember your ABC's. Not all Caribbean islands are in the high-risk zone for hurricanes—the "ABC" islands of the Dutch Antilles are a good example. Aruba, Bonaire and Curacao each have a 2% or less chance of getting whacked by a hurricane annually. And here's another bonus: the summer "low season" produces some great deals to these tropical getaways.

If you like diving, Bonaire is your island. For a more European feel, try Curacao. Aruba has more of a party atmosphere, with casinos, great beaches and decent restaurants.

Other destinations with very low hurricane risk include Panama, and Tobago.

Finally, consider booking a honeymoon vacation with a company or resort that offers a refund guarantee. For example, Club Med offers guests a future travel certificate if a hurricane impacts the resort at any time during the vacation. Sandal's/Beaches resorts offered a free replacement vacation (land only) at any one of their resorts should a hurricane directly hit the resort you're staying on. The catch? The replacement is subject to "certain blackout dates," which unfortunately, the company doesn't define.

Many airlines and web sites offer low-cost travel insurance the covers hurricanes—this might be a worthwhile if you plan a Caribbean honeymoon during the peak of hurricane season.

♥ **TRIP ADVISOR** (tripadvisor.com) has extensive user reviews of hotels, restaurants and more.

Helpful Hints

1 **Don't assume you are booking a single bed!** When you book your honeymoon accommodations, be sure to at least book a double if not a queen size bed. This includes cruises.

2 **Go for at least one special treat.** On other vacations in your life you can cut corners, but this is your one honeymoon. So go for the room upgrade. Book the helicopter flight around Kauai. Go for the day spa package.

3 **Don't be afraid to tell people you're on your honeymoon.** When the flight attendants on our British Airways flight to London found out we were honeymooners, we got a free upgrade to business class—a plus on that long flight.

Creating your own Wedding Web Site

Want a personal wedding web site with details for your guests? With over 20 options out there, here are our tips on getting the best deal:

♥ **SURF USER REVIEWS.** WeddingWebsites.com has a comparison chart for 16 make-your-own wedding web sites, including cost comparisons, page limits and more. The site also has dozens of user reviews.

♥ **FREE OR PAID?** Free sites often restrict what you can post (for example, only allowing one picture per page) while you have more design freedom on the paid sites. Prices range from $25 to $400 for a year.

♥ **HOW SECURE ARE THE SITES?** Password-protected areas are a must.

♥ **MAKE SURE THE SITE IS EASY TO NAVIGATE.** Remember, a wedding attracts relatives and friends of all ages and computer experience. An easy-to-navigate site is a must!

♥ **DETAILS CAN MAKE THE SITE.** The best wedding web sites have more than just pictures and wedding details. Sites like eWedding.com offer online polls/quizzes, RSVP management, event calendars and even mailing list management.

web sites

Notes

## Chapter 14

Canada

Canadian brides face some of the same challenges as their US counterparts—soaring costs for weddings is making getting married just as expensive north as south of the border. We'll discuss the ways to cut the costs of a Canadian wedding in this section.

Bridal gowns

The average bridal gown in Canada sells for $1847 Canadian—that's about 60% more than the price of an average wedding dress in the U.S.

How does that compare to total wedding expenses? In Canada, the average wedding is $21,489 so the bridal gown is as much as 8.5% of total expenses. The average Canadian couple invites about 140 guests to the wedding—that's less than the 175 guests invited to US weddings.

In other ways, the Canadian bridal market is similar to the US. The average engagement is 18.5 months and over half of the couples are paying for their wedding themselves. The average age of Canadian brides and grooms could have something to do with that statistic: the bride is typically 29, the groom 30.

AVERAGE WEDDING COSTS IN CANADA

(all figures in Canadian dollars)

BRIDAL GOWN	$1847
WEDDING BANDS	2470
FLOWERS	1343
CAKE	584
RECEPTION	9255
PHOTOGRAPHY	2206
VIDEOGRAPHY	1400
INVITATIONS	384
MUSIC	1247
TRANSPORTATION	753
TOTAL	**$21,489**

SOURCE: WeddingBells.ca

Of course, there are important differences. The number of weddings in Canada each year is about 150,000. That contrasts to the US, with two million weddings annually. As a result, Canada's bridal "industry" is not as developed as the US —and that's both good and bad news. On the upside, the less-lucrative nature of the Canadian market means scam artists are more likely to concentrate their efforts in the US. However, the smaller number of brides translates into a smaller number of wedding merchants. And less competition usually means higher prices and less selection.

Top Money-saving Tips

Yes, the average bridal gown in Canada costs $1847. Is that too much for you? Here are five tips to save money:

1 **Order online.** Many of the gown discounters we review in Chapter 2 will ship to Canada; unfortunately, they usually don't note this on their web sites. So call or email in advance. You can save up to 40% by ordering online.

2 **Watch out for "designer dumps."** What happens when bridal designers have too many gowns and not enough customers? It's sale time! Yet, American designers don't want to sully their fancy, full-price image in the United States. So, they load up the truck and head north. The designers rent a hotel ballroom, take out ads that scream "MONSTER BRIDAL DRESS SALE! ONE DAY ONLY" and let the bargains rip. While there is no schedule to these sales, you might want to keep an eye on the papers to see if one comes to your town.

3 **Check out David's.** As we mentioned earlier in this book, David's is an off-the-rack operation that has dozens of outlets in the US. One is in Blasdell, NY (outside Buffalo). The store told us they see quite a few brides who make the short trip from Toronto. David's periodically has $99 gown sales, but even their regular dresses ($500 to $700 US) are pretty good deals. (Since David's is growing rapidly, you may be able to find a store closer to you; davidsbridal.com). Of course, cross-border shopping has its own drawbacks—call your local Revenue Canada office for duty information. On the plus side, the recent surge in the Canadian dollar makes that cross-border shopping a better deal.

4 **Go for one of our "best buy" designers.** Affordable gown makers like Mon Cheri, Eden and Mori Lee are all available in Canada. See the designer's web sites for Canadian stores.

5 **Dicker the price.** Off the record, Canadian bridal manufacturers tell us it is a buyer's market for wedding dresses in Canada. The plain fact: there are too many gowns chasing too few brides. As a result, shops are hungry for business and may make you a deal. While that doesn't mean they'll knock 40% off that dream dress, you might be able to negotiate a small discount . . . it can't hurt to ask!

Canadian Bridal Designers

As a Canadian bride, you basically have two choices when it comes to selecting a bridal gown: imported or domestic. Many US importers have Canadian distribution (most notably Mori Lee and Demetrios/ Sposabella). Therefore, you can use the US designer chart earlier in this book to gauge various styles and price options.

Of course, you can go domestic. Canada has a dozen or so manufacturers of bridal gowns and their reputation for quality is earning fans on both sides of the border.

Invitations

Many of the mail order invitations catalogs we review earlier in this book ship to Canada. A prime example is Dawn, which markets extensively to Canada. Dawn's web site is www.InvitationsbyDawn.ca. Here are other choices:

Canada Invitations Outlet

CanadianInvitationsOutlet.CarlsonCraft.com

Based in Mississauga, Ontario, Canada Invitations Outlet features a wide variety of invites, from photo to layered, seal 'n send and more. Prices start at around $40 per 100 invites. Turnaround for most items is 24-48 hours. Overall, this site offers an excellent selection of affordable invites.

Empire Invites

Empireinvites.ca

Clever, non-traditional invites are the focus of Winnipeg-based Empire Invites. How clever? How about a wedding invitation disguised as a lottery scratch-off card? Or a boarding pass? Or a lift ticket? Prices run $2 to $4 per invite, depending on the level of customization (zip tie or no zip tie for your lift ticket invite?). We were impressed with the many customization options and premium matte 110 bl. stock.

Brides in Cyberspace: What's on the Web?

Wedding Bells

Web: www.weddingbells.ca

What it is: Canada's coolest wedding web site.

What's cool: Trying to find a photographer in Edmonton? A florist in Winnipeg? Then, you need to check out this massive web site, run by Wedding Bells, a Canadian bridal magazine. Our search for photographers in Toronto, for example, yielded 71 possibilities. For reception sites, each listing provides contact info and a descriptive paragraph that provided basic facts (capacity, special features, etc.). Besides local wedding merchant info, other sections of the web site featured fashion news, Canadian bridal trends and traditions, etiquette issues and an email monthly newsletter with "fresh new ideas" that aren't on the web site.

Needs work: Since the site is so huge, it can be daunting to navigate. While the site recently grouped its content into channels, it is still a bit hard to find your way around. We would also liked to see more links to vendor home pages in the local resources section.

Other web sites to consider: we love the **Frugal Bride** (frugalbride.com), which has some great money-saving tips and advice, all with a Canadian focus. The only bummer: the site is rather heavy on ads. And Frugal Bride lets vendors "opt out" of being discussed on their message boards. That's right, you can't discuss a few vendors that have threatened the site with legal action because of negative reviews on the message boards. While we aren't experts on Canadian libel law, we think this policy fails to serve brides and protect consumers.

Looking for a message board that focuses on Canada weddings? Both FrugalBride.com and WeddingBells.ca have active boards.

Cakes. The traditional Canadian wedding cake—the fruit cake—is out of favor as brides opt for more gourmet options. A baker in Mississauga told the *Toronto Star* recently that the only exception are Jamaican dark rum cakes, which are sometimes cut up in souvenir pieces for guests to take home. Otherwise, Canadian brides are going for mousse, fresh fruit fillings or cheesecakes. Prices for a wedding cake in Ontario start $5 to $8 per serving.

Entertainment DJs must have their businesses registered with the Audio Video Licensing Agency, Inc. (AVLA.ca) to legally play pre-recorded music in Canada. A good question to ask a DJ before you hire him.

Our local message boards for Canadians. Yes, we have special message boards on our web site (BridalBargainsBook.com) that lets local brides swap tips and advice. No, we haven't forgotten about Canada! You will see specific boards for the provinces, plus special boards for Canada's largest cities. Need a florist in Vancouver? A photographer in Montreal? Wonder who is the best wedding cake baker in Toronto? Log in to chat with other Canadian brides. Best of all, the boards are ad-free and spam-free.

Notes

What can you do to deal with these last-minute wedding crises? Here's our answers to a Bridal 911.

Okay, let's assume you're the perfect consumer. Instead of using cash or a check, you've put all the deposits on a credit card. All the agreements with each service are in writing. You've dotted all your "i's" and crossed all your "t's." But what if your wedding day arrives and, for example, the florist delivers dead flowers? Or the photographer sends a last-minute "stand-in"? Or the wrong wedding cake is delivered? Here are some thoughts on how to deal with such crises.

Meet the Surrogate Bad Cop

No matter how careful you are, things can still happen at your wedding and reception that are not according to plan. That's why you need a Surrogate Bad Cop as an "enforcer" to fix last minute problems and correct wayward merchants.

Who can be a surrogate bad cop? Anyone you believe is trustworthy and reliable. This can be your best friend, your mother or a close relative. Of course, if you were hiring a professional wedding planner, they would play this role typically.

What does the surrogate bad cop actually do? *Their job is to make sure you enjoy your wedding.* While you're greeting guests and having fun, it's the surrogate bad cop's role to tell the florist to fix the flowers. Or track down the photographer. Or find out why the wrong wedding cake was delivered and see if it can be fixed.

In addition to major problems, the surrogate cop also handles any minor situations. One bride told us she was upset with the band she hired when the musicians launched into an unscheduled set of heavy metal favorites. While she was posing for pictures, the bride had her surrogate bad cop (her sister) talk to the bandleader. She informed him of the band's mistake and said the bride had requested they change the tempo. And the band complied.

The Surrogate Bad Cop's Bag of Tricks

Any good enforcer needs the right tools at their disposal to do their job effectively. Here's a look into their "bag of tricks," a special folder/notebook that you give to them on the wedding day:

1 Phone numbers of every contracted vendor (cell, business, home). Okay, it's Saturday night, the wedding is in one hour and the florist is nowhere to be found. You call the shop and, of course, it's closed. Now what? That's why you also need a home number for the key contact at every service. Even better: get cell numbers as well. These numbers will be crucial if your surrogate needs to track down an errant florist, photographer, DJ, etc.

2 Copies of each contract and proposal. Let's say the florist has shown up, but she's missing several arrangements. Or a special orchid corsage for your grandmother. However, the florist claims you never ordered that. What can you do? Well, if you're smart, you'll put copies of every contract and proposal into your surrogate cop's bag of tricks. That way she can whip out the florist's proposal and tactfully point out that, yes, there is supposed to be an orchid corsage. Usually, florists carry a few extra flowers with them (or they can perhaps pop back to their shop and pick up the missing pieces). One hopes that you won't have to resort to producing written contracts to correct problems, but it's a nice back-up just in case. Also, it helps the surrogate bad cop figure out just what you ordered.

3 Authority to act on your behalf. This "invisible" tool is important. You must tell each service (photographer, florist, caterer, DJ, band, etc.) that this special person will be acting on your behalf during the wedding and reception. If your surrogate comes to the merchant with a request, they should know it is your wishes.

The Final Check-Up

A week or so before your wedding, you should schedule a "final check-up" with each merchant and service. Whether it is an in-person meeting or by telephone, you should discuss the following:

♥ CONFIRM ALL DATES, DAYS, TIMES AND LOCATIONS. You need arrival or drop-off times from such services as the florist and baker. Be careful if you're not getting married on a Saturday—make sure the merchant knows your wedding is a Friday or Sunday. We've heard stories of "no-show merchants" who assumed all weddings are on Saturday. Don't forget to call the officiant—you can't get married without him or her.

♥ GET ALL THE PHONE NUMBERS WE MENTIONED ABOVE.

♥ TELL THEM THE IDENTITY OF YOUR "SURROGATE BAD COP.? While you may not use those words exactly, let the companies know that this one special person will be helping you that day. They should treat any request from this person as your direction.

♥ CONFIRM THE ORDER. Now is the time to make sure that the florist can do bird of paradise flowers in your bouquet. Or that the wedding cake will be a certain flavor. Go over the menu with the caterer and fix any problems. Make sure they have your special requests in writing in their files.

♥ PAY THE BALANCE. Many services and merchants will require the payment of the balance due at this time. Try to pay by credit card.

Strategies for Dealing with Wedding Day Crises

Bridal 911 problems fall into one of three categories:

1 **Improper deliveries.** What can you do if the wrong cake is delivered or the caterer serves the wrong main course? While you (or your surrogate cop) may be able to contact the company before the start of the ceremony, there may not be enough time to fix the problem. Solution: ask the company to make an "adjustment" in your final bill. This doesn't mean you get the item for free—but a discount or partial refund may be in order.

2 **No shows/Late arrivals.** If the photographer is late, use the contact numbers to track him/her down. Solution: anyone who charges by the hour should make an adjustment in their bill if they run late. Or they may be able to make up the time by staying later.

3 **Inferior quality.** You were promised big, beautiful roses, but the florist has delivered half-dead, miniature roses. The DJ said he had an extensive collection of country music, but it turns out that it's just one Garth Brooks CD. Honestly, there isn't much you can do on the day of the wedding if a company has deceived you about the quality of their products or services. However, after the wedding, you may want to dispute the charge on your credit card. If you paid by check or cash, you may have to take the merchant to small claims court to recover your money. Document the problem with pictures or video. Also, complain to the Better Business Bureau and your city/county's consumer affairs office.

Many so-called wedding "disasters" are due to the lack of written agreements or ambiguous contracts. You can stop this problem by simply getting everything in writing.

Another source of problems are "early deliveries." One bride in Texas told us about a wedding cake that was delivered six hours before her reception. As the hotel was setting up the ballroom, someone with a ladder whacked the cake. The lesson: don't have the flowers, cake or other items delivered too early. There's just too much of an opportunity for problems.

Finally, some goofs are due to a lack of organization on the businesses' part. Whether the mix-up is an honest mistake or an intentional fraud, it doesn't matter. As a professional, the vendor should act to correct the mistake or give you a refund. Sadly, not all wedding merchants are professionals and you must take steps to protect yourself as a consumer.

The Bottom Line

While there's no such thing as a perfect wedding, there is such a thing as a consumer-savvy bride and groom. With credit cards, complete written agreements and a well-armed surrogate bad cop, you can get the quality that you're paying the big bucks for at your wedding and reception.

## Chapter 16

Parting Advice

After reading through all the tips and advice in this book, your first thought may be "Let's elope!" And, if you didn't question your sanity in this process at least once, we would be worried about you.

Of course, it's easy for us to sit here in our Author Chair and tell you that you need to keep your "perspective" while wedding planning. In truth, perhaps many married couples take perverse joy in seeing engaged couples go through the anguish of planning a wedding. It's almost like a boot camp for marriage: if you can survive this, then you are fit to join the rest of us on the other side of the fence of marital bliss.

Even if weddings are some sinister plot to initiate the single into the married world, this doesn't excuse the fact that the entire US wedding industry, your friends and relatives are trying to convince you that YOUR WEDDING DAY IS THE SINGLE MOST IMPORTANT DAY OF YOUR LIFE. And, of course, unless you get everything perfect, the wrath of the WEDDING GODS will be on your head.

We hope this book is useful as you plan your trip down the aisle. We sincerely appreciate your purchase of this book and we want to help you any way we can. If you have any questions about this book or just want to chat, see the "How to reach us" page at the end of this book.

In the face of all this, our message to you is quite simple: have a good time. Don't take this bridal stuff too seriously. Remember that you are planning a party to celebrate you and your fiancé's relationship. And, theoretically, people are supposed to have fun at parties. Even the guests of honor.

the end

The first step in setting the budget is to prioritize your needs—and consider your larger financial goals. Next, you will set the overall budget you want to spend. Finally, we will show you how to budget money according to your priorities.

A financial check-up

As you plan your wedding, now is a great time to talk about the one subject most folks like to avoid: money. Planning your finances while you plan your nuptials has one major benefit: it can keep you from getting divorced. Since arguments over money are the number one reason couples split, now is a great time to give yourselves a financial check-up.

Some basic tips: both partners should be involved with family finances (paying bills, etc.). Decide whether you will have joint accounts—and joint goals toward money management and other financial issues. Talk about debts, credit cards and retirement planning. While many of these issues are beyond the scope of this book, it's important to consider all angles.

Prioritizing Your Needs

We suggest that both you and your fiancé (and your parents if they will be contributing to this event) sit down together with separate sheets of paper and make a list like one on the next page.

Once everyone has drawn up a "priority worksheet," rank each category in order of importance from one (most important) to nine (least important). Be sure not to confer on your choices until everyone is finished.

In order to understand exactly what each

SPENDING CATEGORY	PRIORITY
APPAREL	_____
FLOWERS	_____
CAKE	_____
RECEPTION/CATERING	_____
PHOTOGRAPHY	_____
VIDEOGRAPHY	_____
INVITATIONS	_____
MUSIC	_____
MISCELLANEOUS	_____

category entails, the following is a brief explanation, including average costs.

1 Apparel. This includes the bride's gown, veil, shoes, accessories, undergarments, and alterations. It may also include a separate going-away outfit. The groom's formal wear is also part of this category. The average cost for apparel is $1935 (gown plus accessories, alterations, etc.). The groom's tux is typically free (when you get four or five additional tux rentals, which most folks do). Yet, as you read earlier in this book, if you get carried away with accessories, the bride's tab alone could top $3000. Or $4000.

Note: For parents who are paying for the wedding, include the price of your gown and/or tux in this section. Also, some couples or their parents may pay for siblings' formal wear. Include such extra apparel expenditures in this category if necessary.

2 Flowers. This category includes "personal" flowers (bouquets, boutonnieres, corsages) as well as flowers for the ceremony and reception sites. Most weddings average about $1800 but elaborate floral decorations can cost $2300 to $3000 or more.

3 Wedding Cake. A groom's cake or a dessert table may also be included. For 150 guests, the average cake costs about $545.

4 Reception/Catering. Basically, this category includes all food (except the cake), beverages, labor and rental items. Charges to rent the reception facility are included here, when applicable. For a basic sit-down dinner or hors d'oeuvre buffet, we've budgeted about $95 per person—that includes beverages and gratuities. That's the national average.

5 Photography. The bride and groom usually only need to budget for their album and possibly a bridal portrait. The average couple spends about $2260 for professional wedding photography—but the photo tab in larger metro areas is more like $4000 to $5000. Parents should include a separate album in their budget as well as any additional photos they will want.

6 **Videography.** A rough estimate for a professionally-shot video is about $1490. However, prices can range from $800 up to $5000.

7 **Invitations.** First, you buy the invitations and/or announcements. Add on any extras like reception or response cards and other enclosures. Don't forget napkins, programs, and favors if you want them. You'll need informals (a.k.a. thank you notes) for all those gifts, and you may want to add in calligraphy. Don't forget to account for postage too. When you add in all these extras, the average expenditure here is about $428.

8 **Music.** Ceremony music may consist of as little as a church organist or as much as a string quartet and a soloist. As for the reception entertainment, choices range from a pianist to a professional DJ or band. Music costs average $1430 for entertainment at both the ceremony and reception if you have a DJ; plan for $3000 and up for a band.

9 **Miscellaneous.** This isn't actually a fair category because it covers many things, but we mention it anyway. Some areas to think about are ceremony fees, blood tests and/or marriage license fees, accessories like guests books, beauty make-overs, transportation, or even lodging for members of the wedding party. Another cost area: gratuities for wedding vendors ($50 or $100 per vendor can up quickly). A fair average for this category is about $2100—that figure can also cover cost overruns in one of the other categories if necessary. Two other items not included in our calculations are the engagement and wedding rings. For the curious, the average engagement ring costs about $5350 and wedding rings now average $1725 for the pair.

Now compare worksheets. Are everyone's priorities the same? Probably not! In fact, by using the priority worksheet, you may be able to spot possible conflicts before you get started.

For example, Mom may think that flowers are extremely important to make a wedding festive; the bride may be more concerned about her dress, while the groom's priority is the reception music. Now is the time to discuss differing opinions before they cause major problems with your wedding planning.

The Overall Budget

As you read in the introduction, the average wedding in the U.S. today costs about $35,232! And averages are deceiving—brides and grooms in expensive metro areas like New York can easily shell out two or three times that average.

Our message: you can spend HALF as much and still have a wonderful wedding. The cost involved is dependent on several items: how far in advance you can plan, what time of day and day of week you want your wedding, where (in the U.S.) you get married, what time of year you choose, and what your priorities are.

♥ **HOW FAR IN ADVANCE.** When you have little or no time to plan in advance, you may have to accept what is available regardless of quality or price. Bridal gowns are a good example. Many of our bargain sources require more advance planning than buying at retail.

♥ **TIME OF DAY AND DAY OF THE WEEK.** Yes, the most popular day of the week to have a wedding is Saturday. If you choose a Saturday to get married, you will have to compete with many more brides than if you choose a Friday evening or a Sunday. Weekdays will be even more open. Some bridal businesses offer discounts for non-traditional days.

Time of day is also an important factor with your budget. If your budget is very tight, consider having your wedding in the morning or the afternoon instead of the evening. Food is the largest expense for most wedding receptions and dinner is the most expensive meal to serve. A late morning brunch or afternoon tea reception may save considerable money. These options and even a cake and punch reception are perfectly acceptable alternatives to the high expense of evening receptions.

♥ **TIME OF THE YEAR.** If you plan on having a holiday reception (such as Christmas or New Years), you should also plan on higher expenses. For example, flowers are more costly during December because of high demand and limited availability. Caterers are also busy with corporate parties at this time of year, as are bands and DJ's. As a result, prices are higher than at other times of the year. Other holidays such as Memorial Day, Valentine's Day, Labor Day, and Thanksgiving weekend may be similarly more expensive.

♥ **NUMBER OF PEOPLE INVITED.** Since we noted above that food is your highest expense, it makes sense that cutting down on your guest list will save money. Enough said.

♥ **YOUR PRIORITIES.** When you look at your priority list, remember that you want to spend a larger part of your budget on the highest priorities. For example, if the reception catering is a high priority, this could be as much as two-thirds of your total budget. Even more if you are serious about food.

And that leads us to our next section: allotting money. First, before we do that, you need to come up with a total figure you want to spend on your wedding. We do not recommend that you go into debt to have the kind of wedding you want. In fact, there is no reason you should have to. There is also no magic formula for determining an overall amount. Look at what you *can* afford and determine the total from there.

Allotting Money

Again, take up your illustrious priority worksheet. At the top write in your total budget figure. Begin to allot your money to correspond with your priorities. Spend money where you think it is important. The following is a sample priority worksheet with a budget.

TOTAL BUDGET: $10,000

	Priority	Your Budget
Apparel	1	$1,000
Flowers	5	600
Cake	6	350
Reception/Catering	3	4,500
Photography	2	1,000
Videography	7	500
Invitations	8	300
Music	4	900
Miscellaneous	9	850
Total		**$10,000**

With this sample, the reception, the photography and the dress are the highest priorities, therefore we are going to spend $6500 or 65% of our budget on these three items. You mayecide you don't want to spend this much on the dress for example, and you will order a gown through a discounter. Instead you may want to spend more money on the flowers because you want a bright garden-like wedding. And so on. The choices are up to you! That's what makes planning a wedding both exciting and challenging.

Here's another good tip: open up a new checking account for wedding expenses. By separating out funds from your personal monies, you'll be able to get a better grip on the budget and expenditures.

REAL WEDDING TIP

Wedding day survival kit

What else can go wrong on your wedding day? Let us count the ways! Let's see— your bridesmaid who lost the back to her earring. Or you forgot to bring your panty hose. What would you do if a flower girl's dress hem came undone? Enter the Bridal Emergency Kit ($48 from ClassyBride.com and other etailers). The kit, in a cool hangeable tote, includes items like deodorant, earing backs, super glue, double sided tape and 26 other items you might need for those last minute wedding disasters. While you can make up your own kit, this might be a cool gift for the bride-to-be at a shower.

Tradition vs. Reality

Traditionally, the bride's family paid for nearly the entire wedding and the groom's family paid for the rehearsal dinner. Of course, that was in 1955. Today, couples are writing their own rules. In some cases, families split the expenses 50/50. Other wedding budgets are split three ways among the families and the couple. Still other couples pay for the *entire* wedding themselves. Obviously, this is a personal decision.

One more thing we'd like to add: We believe that it is too easy to get caught up in the planning and paying for a wedding. Even with our own wedding, we found ourselves having to step back from the event and remember why we were getting married in the first place. In fact, it's good to keep in mind that all you really need to get married is a license, a bride, a groom and an official. All the rest is fluff. If you keep this in mind and remember that the wedding is the beginning of your lives together, instead of a huge social event used to impress your friends and family, it will be easier to keep calm and cool!

Planning a wedding these days may seem to involve the same logistics as, say, the Normandy Invasion. But, no, things don't have to be that nutty—check out our Mother of All Wedding Checklists. Guaranteed to maintain sanity or your money back.

The Mother of All Wedding Checklists

Nine months and earlier

❏ Choose your date.

❏ Announce your engagement to family and friends. If desired, you can send a photo and engagement notice to your hometown newspapers at this time.

❏ Decide what type of wedding you want. Formal? Informal? Religious or civil ceremony? Afternoon or evening reception?

❏ Set your budget. See Appendix A for advice. Find out what financial contributions your families might be making to the wedding.

❏ Prepare your Bridal Master File: one place where you can organize copies of contracts, receipts, sketches and swatches. A master calendar of special events like showers would also be helpful.

❏ Organize your guest list. Request that other family members develop their guest lists as well and forward them to you as quickly as possible. Typically, these lists include the bride's friends, groom's friends (and/or both), bride's family, and groom's family. Will your wedding be an "adults only" affair? See the box about children and weddings.

❏ Choose your ceremony site.

❏ Make an appointment with your officiant and reserve the date with him/her.

❏ Choose your reception site.

❏ Select your colors and/or theme.

❏ Start shopping for your wedding gown. If you are special ordering the gown, place your order within this time frame as well. There are other options that can unite you with a gown without such a long lead-time if you prefer.

❏ Shop around for a photographer. The best book up early so don't delay.

❏ Start thinking about your honeymoon. Planning in advance can help you get better prices on airfare and hotels. Also, if you'll be choosing a foreign destination, you'll need to order a passport (or visa if necessary) now to make sure you get it in time.

❏ Once you've reserved your ceremony and reception site, consider sending guests "save the date" postcards or a wedding newsletter to give everyone the heads up. More on this later in Chapter 16, Invitations.

❏ Check into requirements for a marriage license at the location of your wedding ceremony. Some localities may require a birth certificate, blood test or other documents to obtain a license.

Six to nine months

❏ Draw up a list of attendants: maid of honor, bridesmaids, best man, groomsmen/ushers and child attendants like flower girl and ring bearer. When you ask each person, be prepared to explain what their responsibilities will be should they choose to accept.

❏ Choose bridesmaids' gowns and accessories. Collect sizing information from each bridesmaid as well as deposits and place the order. Now is also the time to order the bride's accessories such as the veil, shoes, undergarments, etc.

❏ Shop for and hire your caterer (if necessary).

❏ Select the ceremony and reception music and hire musicians.

❏ Determine your florist.

❏ Choose a videographer.

❏ If you need ceremony or reception rentals, shop for your rental provider now.

❏ Research accommodations for out of town guests comparing rates and availability. Don't forget to look for a wedding night bridal suite for yourselves as well. While you typically don't have to book these accommodations this far out (we list this as an action item in the 4-6 month below), you may consider reserving earlier if it is a busy holiday weekend.

Four to six months

❏ Select an invitation style and order invitations and any inserts (maps, RSVP cards, etc). Also order any other stationary items such as Thank You notes, menus, napkins and programs.

❏ Shop for men's formal wear. Start badgering the best man and ushers to get their measurements sent in so you can order their formal wear. Give them a drop-dead date for these measurements and threaten them with exclusion from the bachelor party if they don't take care of it.

❏ Determine the type of transportation you'll be using the day of your wedding. If you plan to hire a limousine company or other transportation specialist, now is the time to reserve this. If you plan on renting cars or vans, begin price shopping as well.

❏ Plan your rehearsal dinner.

❏ Choose your reception menu and confirm other details with the reception site and/or caterer.

❏ Start registering at gift registries.

❏ Book accommodations for out of town guests. Begin planning any wedding weekend activities (besides the wedding itself) you might want to recommend to your guests. If you'll be giving hostess bags to out of towners, begin to collect maps and information they can use during their stay.

❏ Shop for wedding rings.

❏ Now is the time to consider what to buy for each other as wedding gifts. Memo to grooms: floor wax does not make for a good wedding gift. Save it for the first anniversary.

Two to four months

❏ Finalize your invitation guest list. Here's your chance to argue with your in-laws over their last minute additions—the beginning of a beautiful relationship.

❏ Shop for and select your wedding cake baker.

❏ Confirm the details of your wedding flowers and decorations for both the ceremony and reception.

❏ Confirm you have the necessary documentation you'll need to get married: license, blood tests, etc. Check on any waiting periods your state or county may require. Other legal documents like name changes, prenuptial agreements and wills should be addressed now as well.

❏ If you're having a bridal portrait, you'll need to make an appointment to sit for it. Also, finalize the wedding day plan with your photographer and videographer. Confirm they will be at the rehearsal.

❏ Address invitations and take a sample (with all the inserts) to the post office to be weighed. This way you'll be sure to include enough postage. See next section for mailing guidelines.

❏ If you plan on giving favors to your guests, now is the time to purchase them or buy supplies to make them yourself.

Six to eight weeks

❑ Mail out of town invitations eight weeks from your wedding date. Locally addressed invites can go out six weeks in advance.

❑ Begin writing thank you notes as soon as gifts begin arriving. Don't let it get away from you. Record your gifts as you receive them.

❑ Meet with your hairstylist to discuss bridal hairstyle and makeup. Schedule any appointments you'll need right before or on your wedding day.

❑ Contact your local newspaper for wedding announcement information.

Two to six weeks

❑ Organize the reception seating and fill out place cards if you're using them.

❑ Be sure you have all the accessories you'll need or want for your wedding day. These may include the garter, toasting glasses, cake knife, ring pillow, special candles, etc.

❑ Confirm with the musicians what music you'd like them to play. If a band or ceremony musician is learning new music, be sure they have the sheet music at least six weeks before the event so they can rehearse.

❑ Plan and hold a bridesmaids' party as well as bachelor and/or bachelorette parties.

❑ Schedule final fittings for both bridal gown and bridesmaids' dresses.

❑ Take delivery of wedding rings—and make sure they fit.

❑ Call all wedding vendors to confirm times/schedules. If necessary, give them a copy of the day's schedule. You may want to meet with certain key vendors (like the photographer) one final time.

❑ Two weeks from your wedding, begin calling any guests who have not responded to confirm their attendance.

❑ Organize the seating of guests at the ceremony. Instruct ushers where to seat special guests and, if necessary, which side of the aisle is for which side of the family.

One week

❑ Confirm you have your marriage documents (license, etc.).

❑ Visit with the transportation company regarding the schedule of events. Provide them with the times and locations for pick up and drop off.

❑ Time to pick up all the wedding attire. Confirm it all fits including tuxes and dresses.

❑ Finalize the guest count to give to your caterer/reception site.

❑ Confirm the details of your honeymoon. Call airlines and hotel to reconfirm bookings.

❑ Pack for your honeymoon. Don't forget the bikini!

❑ Stop the mail and newspapers while you're away on your honeymoon.

Day before your wedding (rehearsal day)

❑ Prepare a bridal emergency kit (nail glue, sewing kit, hair spray, mouthwash, masking tape, etc).

❑ Confirm your attendants have all the appropriate accessories and makeup for the wedding.

❑ If you're having someone at the wedding help you distribute payments and gratuities for vendors, now is the time to give them those envelopes and instructions.

❑ Assign someone trustworthy the task of bringing all the accessories you need including guest book and pen, ring bearer's pillow, etc.

❑ Pass out schedules of the wedding day to members of the wedding party.

checklists

❑ Meet with ushers to discuss seating again.

❑ Go to rehearsal!

❑ Go to rehearsal dinner! Practice smiling till your mouth hurts.

Day of your wedding

❑ Give your wedding rings to the appropriate attendant (groom's ring to maid of honor, bride's rings to best man).

❑ Don't forget to bring the wedding license. It ain't official till the officiant signs on the bottom line.

❑ Eat something during the day before your wedding. You don't want pass out during the ceremony from lack of food. Also, try to get some food at the reception or at least have the caterer pack you a to-go box.

❑ Take a deep breath and say goodbye to the single life. Remember, the goal here is to have fun today!

After your wedding

❑ Arrange for someone to return any rental items the first Monday after the wedding.

❑ Assign someone to have your wedding gown cleaned and boxed for storage.

❑ If you're changing your name, complete appropriate paper work with the Social Security Administration, your banks, place of work and any other necessary institution.

❑ When you get back from your honeymoon, send out change of address cards if necessary.

Bridal Gown Shops Compared

When visiting traditional bridal shops, it helps to compare apples to apples when you're ready to make a decision. In the following worksheet you'll be able to make notes about all the policies and procedures at each shop. You'll also be able to compare price ranges for dresses. Copy this sheet if you need to compare more than two shops.

	SHOP #1	SHOP #2
Shop Name		
Location		
Contact Person/Number		
Hours Open		
Bridal Designers Carried		
Price Range for Bridal Gowns		
Average Delivery Time Bridal Gown		
Bridesmaids Designers Carried		
Price Range for Bridesmaids Dresses		
Average Time for Maids Dresses		
Headpiece Price Range		
Shoe Dyeing	❏ yes ❏ no	❏ yes ❏ no
Rentals Available *Slips* *Other*	❏ yes ❏ no ❏ yes ❏ no	❏ yes ❏ no ❏ yes ❏ no
Payment Policy: *Deposit Required* *Final Payment Due:*	Amount: Date:	Amount: Date:
Alterations *Available On Site?*	❏ yes ❏ no	❏ yes ❏ no
Authorized Dealer?	❏ yes ❏ no	❏ yes ❏ no

checklists

Bridal Gowns Compared

Finding the right gown can be as easy as falling in love with the first gown you try on, or as difficult as falling in love with all of them. . . or none of them. This chart will help you compare and contrast your top three favorite gowns so you can make the best choice for you.

	DRESS #1	DRESS #2
Store Name and Contact Info		
Describe the dress: Lace Fabric Neckline Length Train Special Features		
Manufacturer		
Color		
Size		
Cost		
Veil Style Color Cost		
Undergarments Bra Slip Cost		
Shoes Sizes Color Style Price		
Fittings/Alterations Cost (estimate)		

Bridesmaids Gowns Compared

It just may be a bit harder to choose the bridesmaids' dresses than your own wedding dress. Why? Because you're trying to please all your friends. In the end, you'll have to make a decision and live with the fact that somebody will be unhappy. Use this chart to compare your choices and help make that tough decision.

	DRESS #1	DRESS #2
Store Name / Contact Info		
Describe the dress: *Fabric* *Neckline* *Length* *Special Features*		
Designer		
Color		
Size		
Cost		
Undergarments (cost) *Bra* *Slip* *Other*		
Shoes (price) *Sizes* *Color* *Style*		
Fittings/Alterations Cost (estimate)		

checklists

Florists Compared

	FLORIST #1	FLORIST #2
Shop Name		
Location		
Contact		
Hours Open		
Photographs of work	☐ yes ☐ no	☐ yes ☐ no
Type of arrangements available	☐ fresh ☐ silk ☐ dried	☐ fresh ☐ silk ☐ dried
How many weddings each Saturday?		
Familiar with my ceremony/reception sites Consultation on site? Additional cost	☐ yes ☐ no ☐ yes ☐ no	☐ yes ☐ no ☐ yes ☐ no
Delivery/set up fee		
Arrival time for: ceremony set up reception set up		
Rental items available Cost?	☐ yes ☐ no	☐ yes ☐ no
Bridal Bouquet	$	$
Maid's Bouquet	$	$
Average Ceremony Altar Arrangement	$	$
Credit Cards?	☐ yes ☐ no	☐ yes ☐ no
Payment Policy: Deposit Required Final Payment Due:	Amount: Date:	Amount: Date:
Comments on Design		
Comments on Service		

Reception Sites Compared

	SITE #1	SITE #2
Name		
Location/Web address		
Contact		
Capacity (seated/standing)		
Hours available?		
In-house Caterer?		
Approved Caterer List?	❑ yes ❑ no	❑ yes ❑ no
Restrictions on Caterers?		
Restrictions on Alcohol?		
Restrictions on Noise?		
Amenities: Piano Dance Floor Sound System		
Union rules?	❑ yes ❑ no	❑ yes ❑ no
Insurance Required?		
Surcharges On Outside Caterers?		
Photos?	❑ yes ❑ no	❑ yes ❑ no
Comments on set up		
Extras Offered		
Can I see a wedding reception set up? When?	❑ yes ❑ no	❑ yes ❑ no

checklists

Invitations Sources Compared

	INVITE SOURCE #1	INVITE SOURCE #2
Shop Name		
Location/Web address		
Contact Person/Number		
Hours Open		
Brands Carried		
Given my wedding details, what is your opinion of		
Samples? Comments	☐ yes ☐ no	☐ yes ☐ no
Proof Available? Cost:	☐ yes ☐ no $	☐ yes ☐ no $
Discounts?		
Rental items available Cost?	☐ yes ☐ no $	☐ yes ☐ no $
Calligraphy Computerized addressing	☐ yes ☐ no ☐ yes ☐ no $	☐ yes ☐ no ☐ yes ☐ no $
Comments		

Caterers Compared

	CATERER #1	CATERER #2
Name		
Location/Web		
Contact		
Are you licensed?	❏ yes ❏ no	❏ yes ❏ no
Taste test?	❏ yes ❏ no	❏ yes ❏ no
Sample menus?	❏ yes ❏ no	❏ yes ❏ no
Photos of past events?	❏ yes ❏ no	❏ yes ❏ no
Specialties		
Where is food prepared?		
Wait staff *How many needed* *Dress* *Cost estimate*		
Wedding cake included? Cost?	❏ yes ❏ no	❏ yes ❏ no
Liquor license?	❏ yes ❏ no	❏ yes ❏ no
When is balance due?		
Average cost per guest		
Last date for guest count		
Comments		

checklists

Bakeries Compared

	BAKER #1	BAKER #2
Name		
Location/Web		
Contact Person/Number		
Hours open		
Photos of Past Cakes Comments	☐ yes ☐ no	☐ yes ☐ no
Taste test?	☐ yes ☐ no	☐ yes ☐ no
Will you decorate the cake with flowers?	☐ yes ☐ no	☐ yes ☐ no
Price range (per slice)		
Extra Charges: Cake plate/stands: Premium flavors: Special decorations:		
How far in advance is the cake made?		
Comments		

Photographers Compared

	PHOTOG #1	PHOTOG #2
Name		
Location/Web address		
Contact		
Sample albums: Complete wedding? Greatest hits?		
Camera—film or digital?		
Assistant?	☐ yes ☐ no	☐ yes ☐ no
Package price that best fits my wedding		
Number of finished prints in package		
Time limit of package		
Proofs: average number? Format of proofs?	☐ digital ☐ paper	☐ digital ☐ paper
Album type Album brands?	☐ digital ☐ paper	☐ digital ☐ paper
Deposit required Balance due/when?		
Bridal Portraits: Sitting fee Price/size		
Parents albums (size/cost)		
Comments		

checklists

Videographers Compared

	VIDEOGRAPHER #1	VIDEOGRAPHER #2
Name		
Location/Web address		
Contact Person/Number		
Format of video?		
Camera format: HD? Standard?		
Assistant?	☐ yes ☐ no	☐ yes ☐ no
Package price that best fits my wedding		
Time limit of package		
Editing Comments:		
Camera coverage (1,2,3)		
Other services		
Deposit required Balance due/when?		
Comments		

Music Options Compared

Ceremony musicians

	MUSICIAN #1	MUSICIAN #2
Name		
Contact Person/Number		
# of Hours to Play		
Cost		
# of Musicians		
Music Style		
Comments		

Bands Compared

	BAND #1	BAND #2
Name		
Contact Person/Number		
# of Hours/Breaks?		
Cost		
# of Musicians? Backup equipment?		
Comments		

checklists

Disc Jockeys Compared

	DJ #1	DJ #2
Name		
Contact Person/Number		
# of Hours to Play		
Cost		
Assistant?	☐ yes ☐ no	☐ yes ☐ no
Backup equipment?		
Comments		

Limo Companies Compared

	COMPANY #1	COMPANY #2
Name		
Contact		
Type of vehicles available		
Cost per hour/ Overtime fee?		
Gratuity included? Amount?	☐ yes ☐ no	☐ yes ☐ no
Comments (is driver uniformed?)		

Bride's Wedding Day Checklist

Here's a list of what NOT to forget on your wedding day. Not everything on this list is required for your particular wedding. And we've left plenty of blank spaces at the bottom for you to add to it. You never know, you may need to bring a doggy water dish for your canine flower girl. Hey, weddings are definitely individual affairs!

- ❏ Wedding gown
- ❏ Headpiece and veil
- ❏ Undergarments
  - ❏ Bra
  - ❏ Panties
  - ❏ Hose (at least two pairs)
  - ❏ Slip
- ❏ Shoes
- ❏ Jewelry
- ❏ Gloves
- ❏ Nail polish
- ❏ Perfume
- ❏ Make-up
- ❏ Curlers
- ❏ Curling iron
- ❏ Brush/comb
- ❏ Hairspray
- ❏ Bobby pins
- ❏ Mirror

- ❏ Toothbrush and toothpaste
- ❏ Iron/steamer
- ❏ Items to carry
  - ❏ Bible
  - ❏ Handkerchief
  - ❏ Written vows
- ❏ Garter
- ❏ Lucky penny or sixpence
- ❏ Something blue
- ❏ Ring pillow
- ❏ Flower basket
- ❏ Bridal emergency kit
- ❏ Going away clothes
  - ❏ Outfit
  - ❏ Shoes
  - ❏ Undergarments
- ❏ Clothing for overnight hotel stay
- ❏ Suitcases for honeymoon

checklists

Groom's Wedding Day Checklist

❑ Tuxedo or suit

❑ Shirt

❑ Tie

❑ Cummerbund, suspenders or belt

❑ Cufflinks and studs

❑ Undergarments

❑ Shoes

❑ Socks

❑ Handkerchief

❑ Hat

❑ Gloves

❑ Toiletries

❑ Money/credit cards

❑ Going away clothes

    ❑ Outfit

    ❑ Shoes

    ❑ Socks

    ❑ Accessories

❑ Clothing for overnight hotel stay

❑ Suitcases for honeymoon

❑ Honeymoon tickets and information

Bridal Emergency Kit

Once again, it's time to repeat that Boy Scout Motto: Be Prepared. In this case, put together a Bridal Emergency Kit in a box or backpack that you take to the ceremony and reception. Here's a list of items to include.

❑ Extra hose in a neutral color (2 to 3 pairs)

❑ Nail glue

❑ Needle and thread (black, white and the color of the bridesmaids dresses)

❑ Double stick tape for hem repairs

❑ Masking tape

❑ Stapler

❑ Extra bobby pins

❑ Hair spray

❑ Safety pins (several sizes)

❑ Buttons (white, black)

❑ Scissors

❑ Static cling spray

❑ Sanitary pads or tampons

❑ Mouthwash

checklists

PHONE/WEB DIRECTORY

Wonder where these contact names appear in the book? Check the index for a page number. **Remember that many of these contacts do not sell to the public directly; the phone numbers are so you can find a dealer/store near you.** Refer to the chapter in which they are mentioned to see which companies offer a consumer catalog, sell to the public, etc. For space reasons, we omitted the "www." prefix in front of the web site addresses.

Contact Name	Toll-Free	Phone	Web Site
Introduction			
Alan & Denise Fields (authors)		(303) 442-8792	bridalgown.com
Apparel for the Bride			
The Wedding Channel			weddingchannel.com
The Knot			theknot.com
White House, Black Market			WhiteAndBlack.com
Romantic Headlines			romanticheadlines.com
Veils A La Mode			veilsalamode.com
August Moon Designs			bridalstuff.com
Aloha Originals			custombridalheadpieces.com
Discount Dyeables			discountdyeables.com
Dyeable Shoes Online			dyeableshoesonline.com
Shoe Buy			shoebuy.com
Bridal Gloves			bridalgloves.com
Trousseaux			trousseaux.com
Federal Trade Commission		(202) 326-2222	ftc.gov
JCPenney's bridal catalog	(800) 527-8345		jcpenney.com
Barenecessities.com			barenecessities.com
Bridesmart			bridesmart.com
eBay			ebay.com
The Perfect Gowns			theperfectgowns.com
Alfred Angelo stores			alfredangelostores.com
Fabric sources			
Hyman Hendler		(212) 840-8393	hymanhendler.com
Dulken & Derrick		(212) 929-3614	dulkenandderrick.com
Greenburg & Hammer	(800) 955-5135		greenburg-hammer.com
David's Textiles	(800) 548-1818		
The Fabric Mart	(800) 242-3695		fabricmartfabrics.com
Fabric Depot	(800) 392-3376		fabricdepot.com
McGowen's		(908) 965-2298	
Milliners Supply			milliners.com
Vogue Fabrics		(847) 864-1270	
Sense & Sensibility Patterns			sensibility.com
RomanticThreads.com			RomanticThreads.com
Flowers in the City			flowersinthecity.com
Bead Shop			beadshop.com
J Crew			jcrew.com
DaVinci Bridal			davincibridal.com
Consignment Shop Search			consignmentshopsearch.com
Nearly New Bridal			nearlynewbridal.com

PreownedWeddingDresses.com		PreownedWeddingDresses.com
Bridal Couture (book)	(800) 258-0929	
Academy of Fashion	(888) 493-3261	
Making Memories	(503) 252-3955	makingmemories.org
Just Once (rental)	(212) 465-0960	
An Alternative (rental)	(888) 761-8686	(816) 761-8686
Filene's Basement sale	(617) 542-2011	filenesbasement.com
Nat'l Assoc. of Resale & Thrift Stores		narts.org
Nearly new Bridal		nearlynewbridal.com
VeilShop		veilshop.com
BridesAndProm.com		BridesAndProm.com
ShoeBuy.com		ShoeBuy.com

Gown manufacturers

Alex Hanson	(800) 817-0767	alexhanson.com
Aleya Bridal	(888) 797-4023	
aleya.com		
Alfred Angelo	(800) 531-1125(561) 241-7755	alfredangelo.com
Alfred Sung	(800) 295-7308	
alfredsungbridals.com		
Ann Barge	(404) 873-8070	annbarge.com
Alvina Valenta	(212) 354-6798	alvinavalenta.com
Amsale	(800) 765-0170 (212) 971-0170	amsale.com
Barbra Allin	(416) 469-1098	barbraallinbridal.com
Birnbaum & Bullock	(212) 242-2914	
birnbaumandbullock.com		
Bonny	(800) 528-0030(714) 961-8884	bonny.com
Casablanca	(714) 758-8888	
Chris Kole	(718) 786-3319	
Christos	(212) 921-0025	christosbridal.com
Cupid	(314) 726-0416	
Demetrios/Ilissa	(212) 967-5222	demetriosbride.com
Diamond Collection	(212) 302-0210	diamondbridal.com
Eden	(800) 828-8831 (626) 358-9281	edenbridals.com
Emme	(888) 745-7560 (281) 634-9225	emmebridal.com
Eve of Milady	(212) 302-0050	
Exlcusives by A.C.E.	(901) 385-1400	
Forever Yours	(800) USA-Bride	foreverbridals.com
Group USA		groupusa.com
Helen Morley	(212) 594-6404	helenmorley.com
Impression	(800) BRIDAL-1(281)634-9200	impressionbridal.com
Jacquelin	(941) 277-7099	jacquelinbridals.com
Janell Berte	(717) 291-9894	berte.com
Jasmine	(800) 634-0224(630) 295-5880	jasminebridal.com
Jessica McClintock	(800) 333-5301(415)495-3030	jessicamcclintock.com
Jim Hjelm	(800) 924-6475(212) 764-6960	jlmcouture.com
Judd Waddell	(212) 354-5402	
Justine	(800) 866-4696	
L'Amour	(800) 664-5683	lamourbridals.com
Lady Roi	(888) 802-8588	ladyroibridals.com
Lazaro	(212) 764-5781	lazarobridal.com
Maggie Sottero	(801) 255-3870	maggiesotterobridal.com
Marisa	(212) 944-0022	marisabridals.com
Mary's	(281) 933-9678	marysbridal.com
Mon Cheri	(609) 530-1900	mcbridals.com
Monique L'Huillier	(310) 659-9888	moniquelhuillier.com
Moonlight	(800) 447-0405(847)884-7199	moonlightbridal.com
Mori Lee/Regency	(212) 840-5070	morileeinc.com
Paloma Blanca	(416) 235-0585	palomablanca.com
Priscilla of Boston	(617) 242-2677	priscillaofboston.com

phone/web

Private Label by G/Ginza	(800) 858-3338(562) 531-1116	privatelabelbyg.com
Pronovias	(516) 371-0877	pronovias.com
Reem Acra	(212) 431-9232	
Robert Legere	(212) 631-0606	
Scaasi/Forsyth	(804) 971-3853	
St. Pucchi	(214) 631-4039	stpucchi.com
Stephen Yearick	(212) 221-8188	
Sweetheart	(800) 223-6061(212) 947-7171	gowns.com
Tomasina	(412) 563-7788	tomasinabridal.com
US/Little Angels	(213) 624-4477	usangels.com
Venus	(800) 648-3687 (626) 285-5796	
Vera Wang	(800) 839-8372 (212) 575-6400	verawang.com
Vicortia's	(714) 847-2550	victoriascollection.com
Chinese Gown Sellers		
BlueCatalog.com		BlueCatalog.com
China-Ekt		1koo.com
JuliusBridal.com		JuliusBridal.com
Bridal Marketplace		bridalmarketplace.com
Dori Anne Veil		DoriAnneVeils.com
GownsOnline	(408) 985-5594	gownsonline.com
NetBride		netbride.com
Pearl's Place	(504) 885-9213	pearlsplace.com
Priceless Bridal	(818) 340-6514	b a r g a i n w e d d i n g -
gowns.com		
RK Bridal	(800) 929-9512	rkbridal.com
Wedding Expressions	(319) 753-5217	
weddingexpressions.com		
PlusSizeBridals		plussizebridals.com
Angeri		angeri.com
Stump's Party		stumpsbridal.com
David's	(800) 399-2743	davidsbridal.com
Bridal Garden		bridalgarden.org
Jessica McClintock Company Stores		jessicamcclintock.com
South San Francisco	(415) 553-8390	
Mont Clair, CA	(909) 982-1866	
Huntington Beach, CA	(714) 841-7124	
El Paso, TX	(915) 771-9550	
BridePower		bridepower.com
House of Brides		houseofbrides.com
Bridal World Outlet	(619) 426-2100	
Alfred Angelo Company Store	(954)846-9198	alfredangelostores.com
JcPenney outlets	(800) 222-6161	
Affordable Bridal Warehouse		(602) 279-4933
1Koo.com		1koo.com
Julius Bridal		juliusbridal.com
Bridal Cod Outlet		bridalco.com
Vows Bridal Outlet		bridapower.com
Container Store	(800) 733-3532	containerstore.com
I Do Veils book	(800) 295-0586	(440) 333-3143

Apparel for the Wedding Party

BestBridesmaid.com		bestbridesmaid.com
Formals Etc	(318) 640-3766	formalsetc.com
ShopShop.com		shopshop.com
Jessica London		jessicalondon.com
Dillards		dillards.com
Bloomingdales by Mail	(800) 777-0000	bloomindales.com
Spiegel catalog	(800) 345-4500	

Talbot's catalog	(800) 882-5268	talbots.com
Chadwicks of Boston	(800) 525-6650	chadwicks.com
One Hanes Place	(800) 300-2600	onehanesplace.com
Ann Taylor		anntaylor.com
Outlet Bound		outletbound.com
Alexia	(800) 235-0681	
Cybernet Plaza		cybernetplaza.com
Roamans		roamans.com

Bridesmaid Manufacturers

After Six	(800) 444-8304	(212) 354-5808	aftersix.com
Alyce Designs		(847) 966-9200	alycedesigns.com
Bari Jay		(212) 391-1555	
Belsoie	(800) 634-0224	(630) 295-5880	belsoie.com
B'Gezell		(972) 239-8447	bgezell.com
Bill Levkoff	(800) LEV-KOFF		billlevkoff.com
Champagne		(212) 302-9162	
champagneformals.com			
Dessy Creations	(800) 52-DESSY	(212) 354-5808	dessy.com
Jordan		(212) 921-5560	jordanfashions.com
Loralie		(817) 605-9004	loralie.com
Marlene	(800) 826-2563	(412) 243-7560	marlenesbridal.com
New Image	(800) 421-4624		newimagebridesmaids.com
Watters and Watters		(972) 960-9884	watters.com
Moa Kid's			moakids.com
Britches & Bows			britchesAndBowe.com.
Dapperlads.com			dapperlads.com
Tux Express		(480) 991-6655	tux-xpress.com
Gingiss			gingiss.com
Etuxedo.com			etuxedo.com
Cheap Tux			cheaptux.com
Men's Wearhouse			menswearhouse.com
Jim's Formalwear			jimsformalwear.com
Tuxedos.com			tuxedos.com
FCGI			fabiancouture.com
Santana Apparel			santanaapparel.com

Ceremony Sites

USA CityLink		usacitylink.com
Places (book)	(212) 737-7536	
Nat'l Assoc. of Wedding Officiants (NAWOON)		nawoononline.com

Flowers

About Flowers		aboutflowers.com
California Flower Commission		ccfc.org
Flint Hill Flower Farm	(301) 607-4554	
Flowersales.com		flowersales.com
International Floral Picture Database		flowerweb.com
C. O. D. Wholesale		codwholesale.com
Favor Frenzy		favorfrenzy.com
Idea Ribbon		idearibbon.com
Bliss' Floral Chart		www.blissezine.com/weddingfloral/
Romantic Flowers		romanticflowers.com
Obie's Floral		obiesfloral.com
Save-On-Crafts		save-on-crafts.com
Hanaya Floral		hanayafloral.com
Annie & Co		AnnieAndCompany.Homestead.com
Dried Flowers R Us		driedflowersrus.com
Dried Flowers Direct		driedflowersdirect.com
LA Flower District		LAFlowerDistrict.com

phone/web

Elegant Cheesecakes	(650) 728-2248	
elegantcheesecakes.com		
Love Message Florist		lovemessageflorist.com
Nancy Liu Chin		nancyliuchin.com
West Lake Village Florist		westlakevillageflorist.com
Petals By Alice		petalsbyalice.com
Iluminations catalog	(800) CANDLES	illuminations.com
Linen & Lace	(800) 332-5223	linen-lace.com
Butterfly Celebration	(800) 548-3284	butterflycelebration.com
Butterfly Chateau		butterflychateau.com
Amazing Butterflies.com		amazingbutterflies.com
WireStore (floral supplies)		wirestore.com
2G Roses	(800) 880-0735	freshroses.com
Fresh Petals		FreshRosePetals.com
Sommer Flowers		sommerflowers.com
TheFlowerExchange.com		TheFlowerExchange.com
BridesNBlooms.com		BridesNBlooms.com
FiftyFlowers.com		FiftyFlowers.com
Oriental Tradiing		orientaltrading.com
Wax Wizard (candle discounter)		waxwizard.net
BridalShopStore.com (candle discounter)		bridalshopstore.com
GenWax (candle discounter)		genwax.com
Get Fresh		getfreshwithme.com
eFlowerWholesale		eflowerwholesale.com
RibbonTrade		ribbontrade.com
EZ Bowz		ezcraft.com
Michaels Arts & Crafts	(800) 642-4235	michaels.com
Hobby Lobby	(405) 745-1100	hobbylobby.com
MJDesigns	(817) 329-3196	mjdesigns.com
Little Cindy Candles		littlecindycandles.com
Candle Comfort Zone		candlecomfortzone.com
Printed Candle		printedcandle.com
Rosewood Candle and Craft		rosewoodcandleandcraft.com

Invitations

WedNet	wednet.com
Einvite	einvite.com
Evite	evite.com
Invitations4Sale	invitations4sale.com
Wedding Invitations 411	weddinginvitations411.com
Custom Shots (photo invites)	customshots.com
Absolute Invitations	absoluteinvitations.com
SandScripts	sandscripts.com
Invitation by Karina	invitationsbykarina.come
Catalog Orders Headquarters	catalog.orders.com
Fine Stationery	finestationer.com
Indian Wedding Card	indianweddingcard.com
Costco	costco.com
ED-iT Software	ed-it.com
Mountain Cow	mountaincow.com
Wedding Control	weddingcontrol.com
Wedding Maps	weddingmap.com
Wedding Mapper	weddingmapper.com
Ocean of Roses	oceanofroses.com
My Party Pal (napkins)	mypartypal.com
Little Cindy Candles	littlecindycandles.com
Candle Comfort Zone	candlecomfortzone.com
Printed Candle	printedcandle.com
Rosewood Candle and Craft	rosewoodcandleandcraft.com
Send-N-Seal	send-n-seal.com

Invitation Printers/Manufacturers

Birchcraft		birchcraft.com
Carlson Craft	(800) 328-1782	carlsoncraft.com
Chase Paper	(508) 478-9220	consortiuminvitations.com
Checkerboard Invitations	(508) 835-2475	checkernet.com
Crane	(800) 472-7263	crane.com
Elite	(800) 354-8321	consortiuminvitations.com
Embossed Graphics	(800) 362-6773 (630) 236-4001	embossed.com
Encore	(800) 526-0497	encorestudios.com
Jenner	(502) 222-0191	jennerco.com
NuArt	(800) 653-5361	nuartinvitations.com
William Arthur	(800) 985-6581(207) 985-6581	williamarthur.com

Mail order catalogs

American Wedding Album	(800) 428-0379	theamericanwedding.com
Ann's Wedding Stationery	(800) 821-7011	annswedding.com
Creations by Elaine	(800) 452-4593	creationsbyelaine.com
Dawn	(800) 332-3296	invitationsbydawn.com
Heart Thoughts	(800) 648-5781	heart-thoughts.com
Now & Forever	(800) 521-0584	now-and-forever.com
Precious Collection	(800) 537-5222	preciouscollection.com
Reaves Engraving	(910) 610-4499	reavesengraving.com
Rexcraft	(800) 635-3898	rexcraft.com
Willow Tree Lane	(800) 219-1022	willowtreelane.com

Clover Creek invitations	(800) 769-9676	(802) 425-5549
Invitesite		invitesite.com
Fine Paper Co	(626) 584-9804	
Dreamland Designs		dreamland-designs.com
Designer Paper		designerpaper.com
Wedding Invit. CD-ROM	(888) 727-3772	easytoprintpapers.com
Invitation Hotline	(800) 800-4355(732)536-9115	invitationhotline.com
Invitations 4 Sale		invitations4sale.com
YoureTheBride.com		
Elegant Brides Invitations		ElegantBrides.Invitations.com
Paper Direct	(800) 272-7377	paperdirect.com
Paper Showcase	(800) 287-8163	papershowcase.com
Art Paper		artpaper.com
First Base		first-base.com
Geographics		geographics.com
Grafcom		grafcomm-inc.com
LCI Paper		lcipaper.com
Marco's		marcopaper.com
Paper & More		paperandmore.com
Paper Studio		paperstudio.com
Paper Zone		paperzone.com
Southworth		southworth.com
Nashville Wraps		nashvillewraps.com
Fairy Tale Brownies		brownies.com
Hercules Candies	(800) 924-4339(315) 463-4339	herculescandy.com
Moon Favors		moonfavors.com
Tender Seed Co		tenderseedcompany.com
Moosie Wrappers		moosiewrapper.com
Friends & Family Cookbooks		friendsAndFamilyCookBooks.com

Reception Sites

UniqueVenues.com		UniqueVenues.com
Minnesota Zoo	(612) 431-9215	
CitySearch		citysearch.com
FieldTrip		fieldtrip.com
Here Comes the Guide (CA)		herecomestheguide.com

phone/web

ChairCovers.com	chaircovers.com
Wedding Mapper	weddingmapper.com
Planagaza.com	planagaza.com
FieldTrip.com	fieldtrip.com
BBJ Linen	BBJlinen.com
Unique Venues	uniquevenues.com

Catering

WeddingChat	weddingchat.com
National Association of Catering Executives	nace.net
About.com	weddings.about.com
Food Network	foodtv.com
Cooking Schools	cookingschools.com
Petersons.com/culinary	Petersons.com/culinary
Sam's Club	samsclub.com
BJ's Wholesale Club	bjswholesale.com
Melissa Barrad, I Do . . . Weddings	sdweddingplanner.com
How to Feed 100 for $100	angelfire.com/bc/hobbyhorse/
Cooking Hospitality Institute (Chicago)	(312) 944-0882
Wizard Publications	Wizardpub.com
DeNormandie linens	denormanie.com

Photography

Waterhouse Albums	(860) 526-1296 waterhousebook.com
Professional Photographers of America	ppa.com
Wedding and Portrait Photographers	eventphotographers.com
Wedding Photojournalists Association	wpja.com
Photoworks.com	photoworks.com
Our Album	our-album.net
Collages.net	collages.net
Club Photo	event.clubphoto.com
ShotsOnline	shotsonline.com
Pictage	pictage.com
Event Pix	eventpix.com
PhotoReflect	photoreflect.com
Proshots	proshots.com
The Wedding Photographers Network	theknot.com
Kodak Wedding Party Pak	(800) 242-2424
Exposures catalog	(800) 222-4947 exposuresonline.com
Art Leather albums	(718) 699-6300 artleather.com
Leather Craftsman	leathercraftsman.com
Capri	caprialbums.com
C&G Disposable Cameras	cngdisposablecamera.com
Albums & Frames	albumsandframes.com
Professional Photographers of America	ppa.com
Wedding & Portrait Photographers	wppionline.com
Flickr.com	flickr.com
PictureTrail	picturetrail.com
Shutterfly	shutterfly.com
You've Got Pictures	pictures.aol.com
Kodak's Easy Share Gallery	kodakgallery.com
Photoworks	photoworkds.com
PhotoReflect	photoreflect.com
Collages	collages.net
Genuine Fractals	lizardtech.com
My Publisher	mypublisher.com

Cakes

SugarCraft supplies	sugarcraft.com
International Cake Exploration Societe	ices.org
Wilton	wilton.com
Toppers With Glitz	topperswithglitz.com

DesignerdDisplayCakes.com		DesignerdDsplayCakes.com
Ayr Hill Events		ayrhillevents.com
Cake Rental		cakerental.com
Rent the Cake of Your Dreams		rentthecakeofyourdreams.com
Atlanta Cake Rental		atlantacakerental.com
Food Attitude		weddingcakeonline.com
Highland Bakery		highlandbakery.com

Videos

WEVA	(800) 501-9381 (941) 923-5334	weva.com

Entertainment

DiscJockey Online		discjockeyonline.com
New Wedding Traditions		new-wedding-traditions.com

Etcetera

Limo consumer tips		bridaltips.com
National Limo Assoc.	(800) NLA-7007	nlaride.com
Blue Nile		bluenile.com
Moissanite		moissanite.com
Diamond Nexus Labs		diamondnexuslabs.com
Russian Brilliants		russianbrilliants.com
Wedding Ring Hotline	(800) 985-7464(732)972-7777	weddingringhotline.com
Engagement Rings book	(800) 962-4544	(802) 457-4000
Diamond Cutters		diamondcutters.com
Diamond.com		diamond.com
Ice		ice.com
Trade Shop		tradshop.com
Diamonds.ca		diamonds.ca
Diamond Ring		ring.com
Price Scope		pricescope.com
Diamond Grading		diamondgrading.com
Wedding insurance	(800) 364-2433	rvnuccio.com
WedSafe		wedsafe.com
June Wedding (assoc.)	(702) 474-9558	junewedding.com
Felicite (registry)		felicite.com
Find Gift		findgift.com
Just Give		justgive.com
The Things I Want		thethingsiwant.com
Michael Round	(800) 4 MROUND	mround.com
Ross-Simons		ross-simons.com

Honeymoons

SunTrips		suntrips.com
Expedia		Expedia.com
Fare Compare		farecompare.com
Bidding For Travel		biddingfortravel.com
One Travel		onetravel.com
Fare Compare		farecompare.com
FareCast		cast.live.com
Trip Advisor		tripadvisor.com
eWedding.com		ewedding.com
theWeddingTracker.com		theweddingtracker.com
WeddingWebsites.com		weddingwebsites.com

Canada

Wedding Bells		weddingbells.ca
Wedding Canada		weddingcanada.com
Frugal Bride		frugalbride.com
Discount Invitations	(888) 969-9394	discount-invitations.com

INDEX

index

index

index

index

index

Index

index

index

Notes

Notes

Notes

How to Reach us

We want to hear from you! Tell us what you think about this book . . . or give us a suggestion for the next edition.

♥ Email:
authors@BridalBargainsBook.com

♥ Phone: 303.442.8792

If you like the book, you'll love the web site . . .

www.BridalBargainsBook.com

♥ Message boards—chat with other readers about great local sources!

♥ Blog and free e-newsletter with updates, advice and new bargains!

♥ Corrections/updates to the book!

♥ And more! Read about our other books, order copies of our books as gifts and more!

www.BridalBargainsBook.com

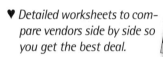

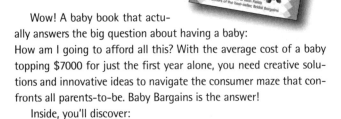

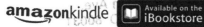

Westminster Public Library
3705 W. 112th Ave.
Westminster, CO 80031
www.westminsterlibrary.org